Searching 2.0

Michael P. Sauers

Neal-Schuman Publishers, Inc.
New York   London

LINKS

The Web page containing any errata for this book is located at:
www.travelinlibrarian.info/writing/searching2.0/
Links to all the resources referenced in this book, and more, can be found at:
http://delicious.com/travelinlibrarian/searching2.0

Published by Neal-Schuman Publishers, Inc.
100 William St., Suite 2004
New York, NY 10038

Printed and bound in the United States of America.

The paper used in this publication meets the minimum requirements of American National Standard for Information Sciences—Permanence of Paper for Printed Library Materials, ANSI Z39.48-1992.

Library of Congress Cataloging-in-Publication Data

Sauers, Michael P.
　　Searching 2.0 / Michael P. Sauers.
　　　　p. cm.
　　Includes bibliographical references and index.
　　ISBN 978-1-55570-607-4 (alk. paper)
　　1. Internet in library reference services. 2. Internet searching. 3. Web search engines. 4. Web 2.0.
I. Title.

Z711.47.S28 2009
025.5′24—dc22

2008050854

Dedication

For Mary, Diana, and Sara

Contents

Foreword

Searching 2.0 by Michael Sauers came to me for review just when I was trying to make sense of all of the white knowledge[1] concerning Web 2.0 that I've been collecting for the past couple of years. The Web 2.0 concept is fascinating, entertaining, and time-consuming. What I needed to decide is why it should be important to me and other librarians.

Truly, this is one of the most useful books I've read this year. The discussion of Web 2.0 communication and organization tools is accessible for Web 2.0 beginners. For those of us who have been swimming in Web 2.0 for awhile, the depth and scope of the discussions provide the patterns and key pieces of information needed for more experienced users to become more efficient and proficient. In addition, throughout the text, Sauers uses "mental exercises" to demonstrate what he is trying to explain. These are both very effective and enjoyable. I will be stealing this idea for my own teaching in the future.

The first chapter is clear discussion of Web 2.0 knowledge management basics. Sauers's discussion of folksonomies versus taxonomies clarifies the issues in a way that readers can use in their own teaching and research. The Web 2.0 information snarl is neatly managed in Sauers's identification of the interrelated information convergence, remixability, and participation aspects of Web 2.0 knowledge management. These concepts, taken together, are convincing justifications for using Web 2.0 tools in providing library services. Most other justifications I've encountered emphasize only participation. Although participation in Web 2.0 communications is a good way to market library services and to network with colleagues and library users, participation alone is not enough to justify the extensive professional time and labor spent on these tools.

Convergence alludes to the fact that print (ink and paper and electronic), audio, video, and other sources of information have been brought together on the Web. Multiple forms of information are made accessible via technical mechanisms, such as RSS (really simple syndication), central databases such as Google (Books, Scholar, etc.), and Amazon.com's book search, and are globally searchable. This gives us a central knowledge base that allows us to take advantage of the "remixability" of the data. We can pull the information from the converged sources and organize it into usable forms, such as e-libraries, knowledge bases, research guides, etc. Participation in Web 2.0 communications tools lets us share this content—this organized knowledge—with our colleagues and library users.

Organizing the information we acquire from the Web has been a challenge since the first days. Many solutions have come and gone. Creating Web sites with organized content—e-libraries, research guides, or knowledge bases—is a generally successful but labor-intensive solution. In the interim, since creating e-library pages is time-consuming, Sauers recommends using Web 2.0 knowledge management tools such as Delicious as a kind of first draft. His discussion and ideas for setting it up and integrating it into reference work convinced me to try using it again. The book discusses the different sources of information, search tools, and databases available in Web 2.0 and when to use them. The book also offers advice on how to think critically about these resources. I will be quoting his overview of Wikipedia in my own work.

I wholeheartedly recommend this book for every librarian. It will be worth your time and energy to read it, take many notes, and ultimately put into practice the many ideas for efficient and practical use of the Web 2.0 information sources in library services.

Diane K. Kovacs
Kovacs Consulting
www.kovacs.com

NOTE

1. *White knowledge* can be defined as "information acquired without conscious effort." *Double-Tongued Dictionary,* s.v. "white knowledge," www.doubletongued.org/index.php/dictionary/white_knowledge/ (accessed October 7, 2008). Also, *The Official Dictionary of Unofficial English,* Grant Barrett (New York: McGraw-Hill Professional, 2006, p. 394), s.v. "white knowledge."

Preface

Here's a simple list of technologies and resources that searchers, including reference librarians, should know today that did not even exist in the year 2000:

- Tagging and folksonomies
- Delicious
- Web 2.0
- Wikis
- Flickr
- Podcasting
- Video search
- Local search
- Online searching of print content
- Desktop search
- Visual search engines

Ask yourself how many of these terms and concepts you're familiar with. If the answer is few to none, then *Searching 2.0* is the book for you. If you're familiar with some to most of them, I'm sure you'll still pick up some pointers as you're reading this book. If you're familiar with all of these topics, I still encourage you to read the book and use it as a blueprint for passing your knowledge along to others.

While basic search strategies haven't changed much in those nine years, the sheer number of tools and online resources that exist today that weren't even dreamed of then mean searching skills and applications of basic search strategies need to be upgraded. I designed this book to provide this upgrade.

HOW TO USE THIS BOOK

Searching 2.0 was written to be read in chapter order, but due to the nature of the material I'm covering here, this book's design allows flexibility. I do recommend that you read Chapters 1 and 2 first to give you the basis for what I discuss in the later chapters. The later chapters can be read in any order.

Chapter 1, "What Is Web 2.0?," takes a look at the underlying changes that have happened to the Web in the past several years. These changes are collectively referred to as "Web 2.0." Topics such as tagging, the "read/write Web," and social software are discussed here to lay a foundation for the rest of the book.

Chapter 2, "Getting Organized Using Delicious," is the most related to my previous book for reference librarians, *Using the Internet as a Reference Tool: A How-To-Do-It Manual for Librarians* (Neal-Schuman, 2001). In this chapter I explicitly update some of the recommendations that I made previously to take into account newer services that will allow you, and your patrons, to have better access to your online resources. Importantly, and one of the reasons I recommend everyone read Chapters 1 and 2 first, this chapter also introduces the concepts of tagging and folksonomies, which are woven throughout the rest of the book.

Chapter 3, "Popular Search Engines," takes a look at the status of the major search engines today. Many of the popular search engines of 2000 (AltaVista, Excite, Lycos) are still around but are rarely used by librarians. Today just three dominate the Web-search arena: Google, Live Search, and Yahoo!

Search. Chapter 3 examines these three and describes their major features.

Chapter 4, "Wikipedia," discusses, you guessed it, Wikipedia. In this chapter, I explain the basic concepts of wikis using this free, online, editable-by-anyone encyclopedia. I also discuss whether Wikipedia should be considered a resource reliable enough for reference desk use.

Chapter 5, "Searching for Media," explores the world of finding multimedia content online. With the ever-increasing speed of connectivity, more and more information is being stored in graphical, video, and audio formats. This chapter shows you several resources to assist you in finding such information.

Chapter 6, "Local Search," brings searching to the local level. Local searching allows you to find online not only phone numbers but also directions, reviews, maps, and, in some cases, satellite images of the building you're looking for and bird's-eye views of just how to get there.

Chapter 7, "Print Search," blends the search capabilities of the Internet with the content of the print material in your library. Services such as Amazon.com's Search Inside the Book and Google's Book Search allow you, in ever-increasing cases, to search for keywords within the books on your shelves. I also look at the major points of both sides of the issues involved in print searching and copyright.

Chapter 8, "Google Cache, the Wayback Machine, and Wikipedia," looks at the current tools for finding information that was available previously but may not be technically "available" now. For example, you may still be able to find an online newspaper article even though it is no longer officially available on the newspaper's Web site. This chapter will also show you ways to look back into the Web's past, to see what pages used to look like.

Chapter 9, "Searching There without Being There," delves into the world of tools to assist you and your patrons with searching online resources without having to go to the resources first. Known as OpenSearch plug-ins, these allow you to embed the ability to search almost any resource directly into your browser.

Chapter 10, "Desktop Search," looks at desktop search tools that give you the ability to search the content of your computer and, in some cases, integrate the results of searching your hard drive with your Web search results, thus blurring the line between online and offline resources.

The final chapter, Chapter 11, "Data Visualization," discusses some of the cutting-edge search engines and the possible future of search. The key difference between these search engines and the others covered in this book lies not necessarily in how they're searched but in how they present their results. In these cases the results are presented graphically, instead of as a text-based list, and they show the relationship between the results, rather than being purely based on relevance. This graphical method is known as data visualization.

THE COMPANION WEB SITE

Knowing that as you're reading you'll want to look at the sites I mention and try them out, I direct you to Delicious (which I cover extensively in Chapter 2) to find links to all of the resources referenced in this book. Those links can be found at http://delicious.com/travelinlibrarian/searching2.0. Additionally, any errata can be found on my Web site, www.travelinlibrarian.info/writing/searching2.0/.

A NOTE ON THE TITLE

Some of you may be wondering about the genesis of the title *Searching 2.0*. This title is the result of two factors: first, a lot of talk in the library world today concerns Web 2.0 and Library 2.0. Both of these topics have an impact on searching, which I address in this book. Second, as I discussed at the beginning of this preface, we're now dealing with the second generation of search strategies, and this is my second book on Internet searching for librarians. Thus, the title just seemed to fall into place. I hope the skills and resources covered in this book will help you become a Searcher 2.0, able to dazzle your library's users and your coworkers with your new skills.

Acknowledgments

As usual there are many people I need to thank:

Christa Burns, Devra Dragos, Gwynneth Gunnels, Susan Knisley, Steve Lawson (See Also…), Allana Novotny, Jeanette Powell, Laura Prakel-George, Kelli Staley (Lansing Public Library), Rod Wagner, Shannon White, and the staff of the P Street Starbucks here in Lincoln, NE

And a special thanks once again to Louise Alcorn for another sexiest index ever.

This book was written in the following locations:

The Bibliographical Center for Research (Aurora, CO), Smoky Hill Library (Arapahoe Library District, Centennial, CO), my former home (Aurora, CO), Panera Bread (Omaha, NE), Holiday Inn (Council Bluffs, IA), our new home (Lincoln, NE), Laundryland (Lincoln, NE), Starbucks (Lincoln, NE)

Chapter 1

What Is Web 2.0?

INTRODUCTION

What do all of the following items and events have in common?

- The current browsers are Netscape 4.7,[1] Internet Explorer 5.5,[2] and Opera 4.[3]
- Windows 2000, Windows Me,[4] and Mac OS9[5] are released.
- Google releases the Google Toolbar,[6] but Google News and Gmail are yet to exist.[7]
- The Bill and Melinda Gates Foundation finishes its initial round of providing computers for public libraries,[8] resulting in more than 95 percent of public libraries having Internet access.[9]
- Less than half of public libraries have broadband connections to the Internet.[10]
- AltaVista, Excite, Web Crawler, and Lycos are popular search engines.
- Yahoo! is a directory.
- There are only about 10 million registered domain names.[11]
- There are only about 9.5 million Web sites.[12]
- Napster is the way to download music online, but lawsuits have been filed.[13]
- XHTML 1.0 is approved as a standard by the W3C (World Wide Web Consortium).[14]
- The first 1GHz chips are released from Intel and AMD (Advanced Micro Devices).[15]
- The "I Love You" virus is released.[16]
- President Clinton says, "[I] won't send e-mail to Chelsea because I don't think it's secure."[17]
- The dot-com bubble bursts.[18]
- Neal-Schuman Publishers Inc. publishes my first book for librarians, *Using the Internet as a Reference Tool: A How-To-Do-It Manual for Librarians.*

All of these were the state of libraries and the Internet in the year 2000.

Many changes have happened to the Web in the past nine years. The rise of broadband connections to the home, the increased number of people not just connected to the Internet but contributing content, and the increased sophistication of the technologies supporting the Internet have all led to an online paradigm shift commonly labeled Web 2.0. In this chapter, we take a look at just what Web 2.0 is, its main features, and how it has led us to the search utilities and new types of content that we can search today.

DEFINING WEB 2.0

Web 2.0 as a concept was first labeled and defined by publisher Tim O'Reilly in an article titled "What Is Web 2.0" published in September 2005.[19] In this article, he doesn't so much define Web 2.0 as he describes what he thinks are its seven central components: (1) the Web as platform, (2) harnessing collective intelligence, (3) data as the next Intel Inside, (4) the end of the software release cycle, (5) lightweight programming models, (6) software above the level of a single device, and (7) rich user experiences. (Some of those are a bit technical, I'll admit. Don't worry about it right now; it'll all make sense by the end, I promise.)

For a more narrative definition, we can look to Wikipedia (a Web 2.0 resource):

Web 2.0 generally refers to a second generation of services available on the World Wide Web that lets people collaborate and share information online. In contrast to the first generation, Web 2.0 gives users an experience closer to desktop applications than the traditional static Web pages.[20]

If you're not clear on the differences between a desktop application and a Web page, perform this quick mental exercise: Picture what you could do with the first Web page you ever saw compared with what you could do with any Microsoft Office product at the same time. You could do much more with Word than you could with a Web page. Today, Web pages are more like Word—in fact, if you're familiar with services like Google Docs, some Web pages are even attempting to directly compete with desktop applications.

For a visual representation of this concept, take a look at Figure 1-1. Even with these explanations of the concept of Web 2.0, many people are still confused as to what it means and its implications. I attempt to clarify this in the following section by focusing on how Web 2.0 affects search and reference from a librarian's perspective.

WEB 2.0'S CORE CONCEPTS AND IMPLICATIONS

How Web 2.0 affects librarians involves three important considerations: convergence, remixability, and participation (all represented in Figure 1-1). Let's look at these one at a time.

Convergence

The use of convergence in this context implies that disparate sources are integrating into one single source. Think about the first cell phone you ever used

Figure 1-1   Web 2.0 visualization

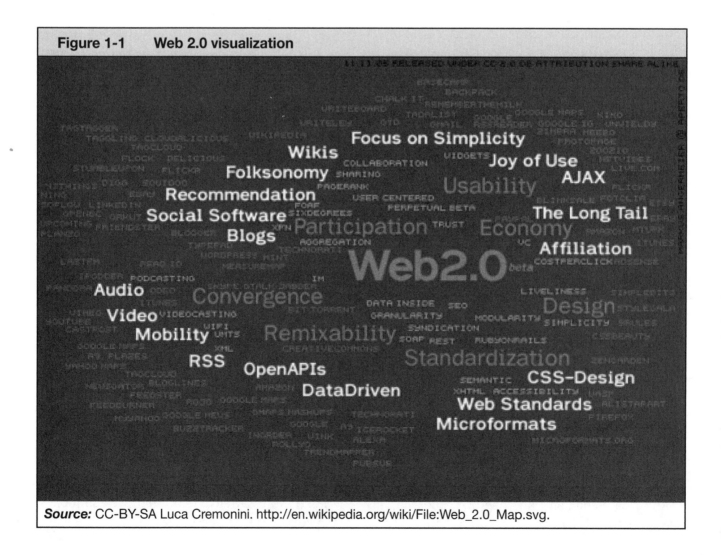

Source: CC-BY-SA Luca Cremonini. http://en.wikipedia.org/wiki/File:Web_2.0_Map.svg.

verses today's iPhone, which can do almost anything a desktop computer can do. This is an example of convergence.

With the increased availability of broadband Internet connections to the home, more people have the ability to not only take advantage of Internet-based audio and video but also combine them with each other and with text. With the increased use of these more bandwidth-intensive services, more of the information we librarians will be seeking may no longer be text-based. Especially with the advent of RSS (really simple syndication), a code used to allow readers to subscribe to online content, and the resulting distribution of audio and video (in the form of podcasts), the answer we seek may not be found using Google or Yahoo!. We're going to need another way to search for that information. This topic is covered in Chapter 5, "Searching for Media."

Convergence can also be as simple as Google Print Search or Amazon.com's Search Inside the Book feature. In both of these cases the content of the more traditional print medium is converging with the online environment, giving us the possibility of moving beyond the library catalog to online services that allow us to search the content of the books on our shelves, not just titles, authors, and subject headings.

Remixability

The next important Web 2.0 concept for librarians and searchers is remixability. Due to the more technical aspects of Web 2.0—open APIs (application programming interfaces/Web services[21] and AJAX (asynchronous JavaScript and XML)[22] most specifically—it is becoming relatively easy to take the data from one source, add it to the data of a second (or third or fourth) source, and create a new resource independent of the originating sources. For example, Feed Digest (www.feeddigest.com/) allows a user to pull in the content from several RSS feeds, perform a search of the content, and output a new feed and/or Web page containing only the content that matches the search criteria. The common term used for such a result is a mashup, the result of combining two or more disparate data sources to create a single result.

For example, the use of online mapping services is a case of searching services based on remixability. Results of a Google Local search (covered in Chapter 6) will bring data from many different sources, such as mapping data, satellite images, Web site indexing data, consumer reviews, and photos taken by regular people. Performing a single search in Google Local will present us integrated results from these many different sources. This is how we take advantage of the benefits of remixability.

Participation

If I had to pick a single factor of Web 2.0 as being the most important it would have to be participation. Participation is so important to Web 2.0 that the concept itself has also been labeled "the read/write Web" by some, including Tim Berners-Lee, the inventor of the World Wide Web.[23]

Blogs represent the single largest implementation of the participatory factor in Web 2.0. Blogs are an easy way for Internet users to contribute content, not just absorb content, thus leading to a more participatory experience. Wikis are another form of participation in the Web 2.0 environment. With wikis, anyone can contribute and change any of the content within the wiki. If that isn't participation, nothing is. We'll be looking at the most familiar example, Wikipedia, in Chapter 4.

Participation, however, is more than just contributing content. Take Flickr (http://www.flickr.com/), for example. Flickr is an online service that allows users to not only upload their photographs to the service but also create "photo pools" in which many users may contribute their photographs on a common topic. Flickr also supports the ability to create contacts or friends, allowing you to easily track what others are contributing to the system.

Other social networking services, such as MySpace (http://www.myspace.com/) and Facebook (http://www.facebook.com/), take the "friends" concept further, allowing you to automatically cross-reference your content with the content of others. This kind of participation has led to the advent of "social software" and "social services."

Delicious (covered in detail in Chapter 2) is a "social bookmarking service." Users of Delicious, instead of storing their bookmarks in their browser, send them to their Delicious account. Delicious will then automatically track every user that bookmarks the same site and give you access to those users' public bookmark collections. This way, you can easily discover the bookmarks of other users who have bookmarks that overlap yours.

These types of contributions make participation a central concept of Web 2.0. One type of participation in particular has a large impact on searching: the concept of tagging, also known as "folksonomy."

TAGGING AND FOLKSONOMIES

Most librarians, especially catalogers, are familiar with the concept of taxonomy. The standard definition for taxonomy is "the science of finding, describing, classifying, and naming organisms."[24] However, over time the concept of taxonomy has come to include categorizing not just "organisms" but anything that can be categorized, leading to the second definition of "the classification in a hierarchical system."[25] For example, both Library of Congress Subject Headings (LCSH) and the National Library of Medicine's Medical Subject Headings (MESH) are considered taxonomies. Most important, taxonomies are generally created by "experts" in the field to which the resulting taxonomy is being applied.

What has happened online, with new social services such as Flickr and Delicious, is that the creators of those services wanted (needed in some cases) to give users the ability to add to their submissions additional keywords for which other users could search. For example, when a photograph is uploaded to Flickr, the person submitting the photo has the ability to add keywords, or tags, to the photo, making it potentially easier to find by using a keyword search. Looking at Figure 1-2, you can see that the tags for this photo are *library, sign, libs&libs, libraries andlibrarians, bsu,* etc. In the case of Flickr, only photo titles and descriptions are indexed by default.

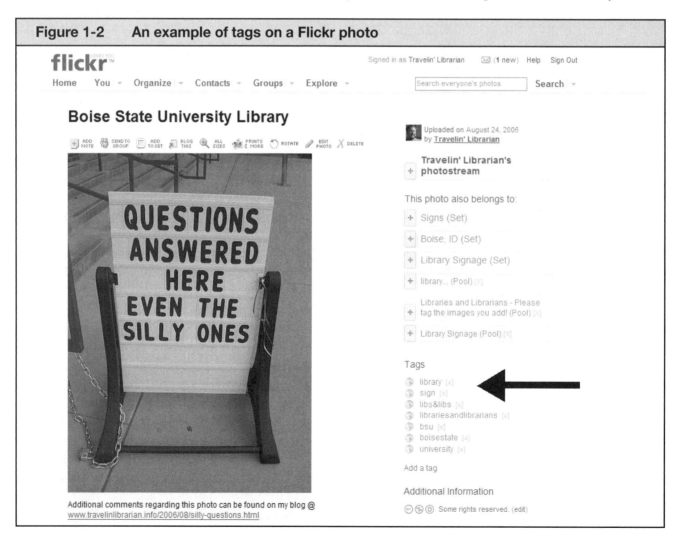

Figure 1-2   An example of tags on a Flickr photo

Figure 1-3   An example of tags on a Delicious bookmark

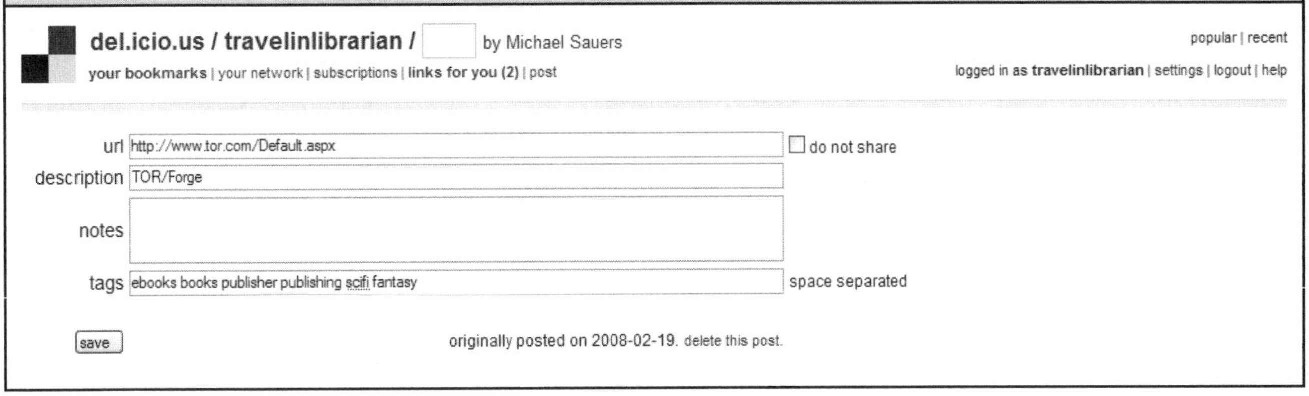

del.icio.us / travelinlibrarian /   by Michael Sauers   popular | recent

your bookmarks | your network | subscriptions | **links for you (2)** | post   logged in as **travelinlibrarian** | settings | logout | help

url http://www.tor.com/Default.aspx   ☐ do not share

description TOR/Forge

notes

tags ebooks books publisher publishing scifi fantasy   space separated

[save]   originally posted on 2008-02-19. delete this post.

By adding tags to a photo, all of those keywords will also be indexed, and users can simply click on a tag to see other photos (either in your collection or from throughout Flickr) labeled with the same tag.

Delicious also supports tagging when it comes to adding bookmarks to the service. In this case, content is still searchable based on the title of the bookmark and any narrative text the user might add, but adding tags to an entry makes additional points of access available to a user searching for a topic. Figure 1-3 shows a Delicious bookmark with the tags *ebooks, books, publisher, publishing*, etc.

The term "folksonomy" was applied to this concept of indexing user-generated tags as a way to describe a taxonomy generated by common people (just plain folks) instead of a small group of experts. A more fully formed definition of folksonomy, courtesy of Wikipedia, would be "a collaboratively generated, open-ended labeling system that enables Internet users to categorize content such as Web pages, online photographs, and Web links."[26]

The Benefits of a Folksonomy

The Wikipedia definition of folksonomy also notes that "the freely chosen labels—called tags—help to improve a search engine's effectiveness because content is categorized using a familiar, accessible, and shared vocabulary."[27]

Let's think about Flickr again. Although image-based search engines are available today, most of them work only moderately well since they're searching for your keywords against the file name of the image and the surrounding text. So, for example,

you may be searching for a picture of a rose, but if the file name is flower.jpg, chances are you won't be presented with that image as a result.

When I upload an image to my Flickr account, I am not only able to give the image a descriptive title but I am also able to add tags that describe the location of the photograph (*boisestate* and *bsu*), the content of the photograph (*sign*), and details about the particular content of the photograph (*library*). Now, whenever a user searches with any of those keywords, my photographs will be in the results list.

These systems also allow for easy cross-referencing and the linking of like items. Once viewing this particular photo, a user can then click on one of the tags (*bsu*, for example) and see all of my other photos with that tag. They can even search further and see every photograph in the system that has the *bsu* tag associated with it.

All of this works because most people tend to use the same words to describe similar things. Photographs taken at the Boise State University tend to get the tag *bsu* assigned to them as it's the shorthand for the campus. In other cases, groups of people who get together will devise a tag for the group to use for a certain type of photograph. For example, Figure 1-4 shows the results for searching Flickr for the tag *CIL2007*, which was used by everyone submitting photographs of the Computers in Libraries 2007 conference. For a more humorous example, try searching Flickr for the tag *librarianwithgiantcalculators*.

Where Folksonomies Can Fail

I apologize for repeating myself, but I feel I need to

Figure 1-4   Results for the Flickr tag CIL2007

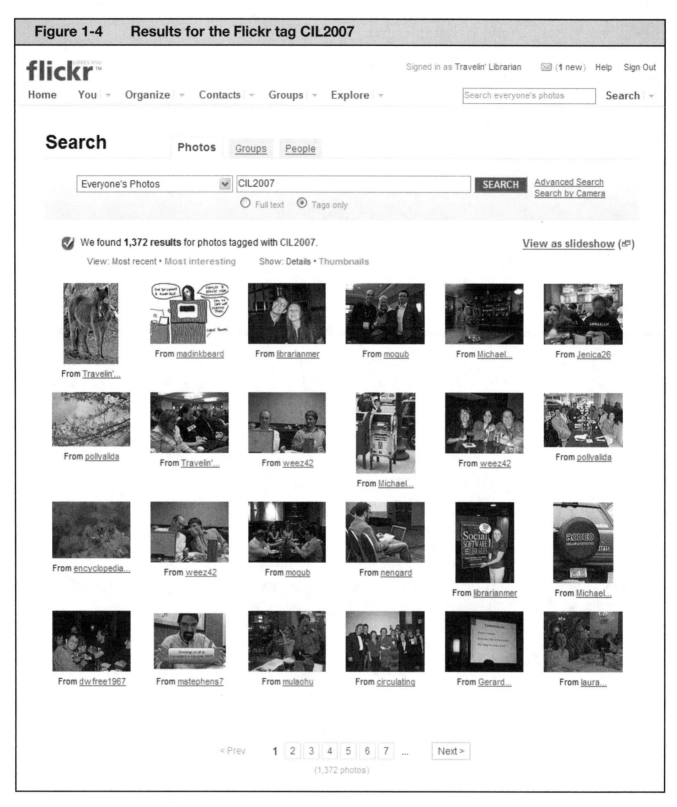

say this again: All of this works because most people tend to use the same words to describe similar things. This is the central reason why those who aren't happy with the concept of a folksonomy have the feelings they do.

Taxonomies are created by experts to make sure an organization scheme is done "correctly" and followed consistently. Granted, even the best of taxonomies must change over time, but those changes occur infrequently and after much deliberation by those same experts. A folksonomy, on the other hand, is a constantly evolving set of descriptors generated by people who may have no idea what they're talking about beyond their own particular examples.

Here's a simple example that I notice all the time: the use of plurals when it comes to tagging images. If you have a picture of one book, do you tag it as *book* or *books*? If you have a picture of a stack of books, do you tag it *book* or *books*? If your picture is of a single book but other books are in the background, do you tag it *book* or *books*? The decision is up to you. Maybe you'll use both tags on all three images just to cover the possibility that someone may search on either term. These are the problems with a folksonomy. In my opinion, any additional points of entry attached to what I'm searching for increases my chances of finding what I seek.

CONCLUSION

The concept of Web 2.0 is often bogged down in a lot of technology-related gobbledygook, but when it comes to its relationship to librarians and searching, keep three main points in mind. The first is convergence: the idea that disparate resources and platforms are being combined into single resources and objects. The second is remixability: the idea that a user can take multiple types of data and mix them up into a new single output. The third is participation: the idea that sources are no longer created by a set group of self-appointed experts but by everyone. Last, out of this comes the concept of a folksonomy, based on the tagging of resources by the group as a whole. Through tagging, new methods of both indexing digital objects and finding those digital objects are available to us as both librarians and searchers.

Now that you have a basic understanding of how Web 2.0 relates to search and also of tagging, in Chapter 2, we'll examine one more underlying issue before moving on to searching proper: keeping and organizing what you find so that you can get back to it easily in the future.

NOTES

1. Brian Wilson, "Netscape Navigator," www.blooberry.com/indexdot/history/netscape.htm.
2. Brian Wilson, "Internet Explorer (Windows)," www.blooberry.com/indexdot/history/ie.htm.
3. Brian Wilson, "Opera," www.blooberry.com/indexdot/history/opera.htm.
4. The History of Computing Project, "Microsoft Company 15 September 1975," February 13, 2008, www.thocp.net/companies/microsoft/microsoft_company_part2.htm.
5. *Wikipedia, the Free Encyclopedia,* s.v. "Operating Systems Timeline," May 30, 2006, http://en.wikipedia.org/w/index.php?title=Operating_systems_timeline&oldid=55911904 (accessed June 5, 2006).
6. Google, "Corporate Information: Google Milestones," www.google.com/intl/en/corporate/history.html.
7. Ibid.
8. Bill & Melinda Gates Foundation, "Libraries," www.gatesfoundation.org/topics/Pages/libraries.aspx.
9. John Carlo Bertot and Charles R. McClure, "Public Libraries and the Internet 2000: Summary Findings and Data Tables," September 7, 2000, http://www.nclis.gov/statsurv/2000plo.pdf.
10. Ibid.
11. Jeremy M. Norman, From Gutenberg to the Internet: A Sourcebook on the History of Information Technology," August 12, 2008, www.historyofscience.com/G2I/docs/timeline/timeline_2000_2002.shtml.
12. Ibid.
13. *M/Cyclopedia of New Media,* s.v. "Filesharing—Napster—History," October 28, 2005, http://wiki.media-culture.org.au/index.php/Napster.
14. Brian Wilson, "HTML Overview," www.blooberry.com/indexdot/history/html.htm.
15. *Wikipedia, the Free Encyclopedia,* s.v. "Timeline of Computing 1990–Forward," June 1, 2006, http://en.wikipedia.org/w/index.php?title=Timeline_of_computing_1990-forward&oldid=56265240 (accessed June 5, 2006).
16. Wikipedia, the Free Encyclopedia, s.v. "Timeline of Notable Computer Viruses and Worms." May 31, 2006, http://en.wikipedia.org/w/index.php?title=Timeline_of_notable_computer_ viruses_and_worms&oldid=56160507 (accessed June 5, 2006).
17. Marc Lacey, "Clinton Calls for Stronger Measures to Protect the Privacy of Computer Users," *New York Times,* March 4, 2000, http://partners.nytimes.com/library/tech/00/03/biztech/articles/04bill.html.
18. *Wikipedia, the Free Encyclopedia,* s.v. "History of the Internet,". June 5, 2006, http://en.wikipedia.org/w/index.php?title=History_of_the_Internet&oldid=57012712 (accessed June 5, 2006).
19. Tim O'Reilly, "What is Web 2.0: Design Patterns and Business Models for the Next Generation of Software," September 30, 2005, www.oreillynet.com/pub/a/oreilly/tim/news/2005/09/30/what-is-web-20.html.
20. *Wikipedia, the Free Encyclopedia,* s.v. "Web 2.0," June 5, 2006, http://en.wikipedia.org/w/index.php?title=Web_2.0&oldid=56995039 (accessed June 5, 2006).
21. *Wikipedia, the Free Encyclopedia,* "Web Service," June 5,

2006,http://en.wikipedia.org/w/index.php?title= Web_service&oldid=57021954 (accessed June 5, 2006).

22. *Wikipedia, the Free Encyclopedia,* s.v. "Ajax (Programming)," June 5, 2006, http://en.wikipedia.org/w/index.php?title=Ajax_%28programming%29&oldid=57022829 (accessed June 5, 2006).

23. Mark Lawson, "Berners-Lee on the Read/Write Web," BBC News, August 9, 2005, http://news.bbc.co.uk/1/hi/technology/4132752.stm.

24. *Wiktionary,* s.v. "Taxonomy," June 3, 2006, http://en.wiktionary.org/w/index.php?title=taxonomy&oldid=1110609 (accessed June 5, 2006).

25. Ibid.

26. *Wikipedia, the Free Encyclopedia,* s.v. "Folksonomy," June 3, 2006, http://en.wikipedia.org/w/index.php?title=Folksonomy&oldid=56663437 (accessed June 5, 2006).

27. Ibid.

Chapter 2

Getting Organized Using Delicious

INTRODUCTION

Reference librarians, as with most other Internet users, are constantly going back to sites that they've visited before. One could argue that reference librarians may do this even more than most. In fact, some sites are continually accessed to answer those most common questions—local statistics, value of a used car, what time zone a certain country is in, etc. Even the first Web browsers offered ways to mark a site in order to return to it easily. That method was, and still is, known as bookmarking. However, as the Web becomes more and more complex and the needs of users also become increasingly complex, bookmarks as we've known them may no longer be the solution. Then again, the "better" solution I offered in the past may also no longer be up to the task. In this chapter, I'll walk you through the online world of bookmarks, through static "resource Web pages," to the solution I offer today, the online social bookmarking service known as Delicious.

Bookmarks

One of the first things we learn to do in a browser, beyond using the back button, is how to set a bookmark. Bookmarks give us the ability to return quickly to an online resource without having to remember an often long and cryptic URL. In my previous book, *Using the Internet as a Reference Tool* (Neal-Schuman, 2001), I discussed the following problems with using bookmarks to store previously found resources for use at the reference desk:

- *Bookmarks are rarely well organized.* Whenever I've asked a room full of librarians how many of them have taken the time to organize their bookmarks (usually hundreds of them) into logical folders, generally less than 20 percent of those in the room raise their hands. The rest of us have just one long list of bookmarks without any convenient way to find any specific one.[1]

- *Bookmarks were restricted to one computer.* If you have multiple computers at your reference desk, the bookmarks on one might not be on another, thus making it inconvenient to find the information you're looking for if the bookmark you need is on a computer being used by another librarian.

- *Bookmarks were restricted to the staff computers.* Unless a staff member took the time to copy the bookmark files from the staff computers and place them on the patron computers, the patrons in the building were forced to speak to someone at the desk to be able to take advantage of the librarian-created bookmarks.

- *Bookmarks placed on library computers are not available to remote-access patrons.* In this age of continuing mobility of information access, libraries need to make the information they provide accessible outside of the physical boundaries of the library building.

Web Pages

In *Using the Internet as a Reference Tool*, I offered a solution to all of these problems: the library should create a Web page (or group of pages, depending on the number of resource links needed) to provide access to those links. This solution, at the time, solved all of the previously mentioned problems in the following ways:

- Web pages were generally well organized in a logical manner whether alphabetically or by subject.
- Web pages are available to all devices containing a Web browser. So, regardless of which computer someone is using (public, staff, a patron's laptop) or even if using another device such as a smartphone, the links are available in any location, at any time.

I continued in the book with several excellent examples of libraries implementing this exact solution. Most libraries of at least a moderate size had or have since created such Web pages. However, even though this solution at the time was a good one, it still had one major problem: you needed to learn some markup—HTML (hypertext markup language) or XHTML (extensible hypertext markup language)—to implement it. Though I think everyone should still learn at least some basic Web page creation skills, today an even better solution not only solves this last nagging problem but also provides additional features that no Web page I described back in 2000 could ever have provided. That solution is Delicious.

DELICIOUS

Delicious (http://www.delicious.com/) is a "social bookmarking" service that "allows users to tag, save, manage and share web pages from a centralized source. With emphasis on the power of the community, Delicious greatly improves how people discover, remember and share on the Internet."[2]

At its most basic level, Delicious (currently owned by Yahoo!) stores your bookmarks for you on its Web site, allowing anyone to access those bookmarks from any Web-accessible device *without any markup knowledge required*. Beyond this benefit, Delicious offers several additional features, such as the following, that allow it to be a more flexible solution than a static Web page:

- Delicious bookmarks can be added to your account with just a few mouse clicks.

- A Delicious account can be shared by multiple users, thus allowing you to have a single account for the entire library staff, at the branch or system level.
- Bookmarks in one Delicious account are automatically cross-referenced with all other Delicious user accounts, creating connections among all of its users.
- Anyone can subscribe to RSS (really simple syndication) feeds from Delicious and receive automatic notification of new bookmarks.
- Delicious bookmarks are easily searchable, allowing for less structure and more free-form organization through the use of tags.

Let's take a look at each one of these in a little more detail. Even if you had extensive HTML knowledge, updating a Web page takes at least a few minutes to accomplish. You need to enter the username and password for the server, log in, find the correct file, open it, make your changes, save the changes, and log out. This process assumes that you have the correct level of access on your server. If you don't, you may face the situation of needing to submit your change to the appropriate person in the IT (information technology) department and then wait a few days before your change appears. With Delicious, as I'll show later in this chapter, all you need to do to add a new bookmark is click on an icon, wait for the "add item" window to appear, and click "OK." This is a much simpler and faster procedure than updating a Web page.

As with Web pages, Delicious accounts can be shared among staff members by giving them the appropriate username and password. However, since this service is hosted by a third party, there's no need to get your IT department involved, especially if you have one that is loathe to give out server usernames and passwords to nontechnical staff.

Delicious stores all of the links submitted by their users in a large database. The benefit to this method is that Delicious is then able to track which users have added which links. With this information, Delicious is able, not only to tell you that 368 other users have also added the same link that you've added, but also to link you to those other users' accounts. This is the "social" aspect of the service: users who add the same

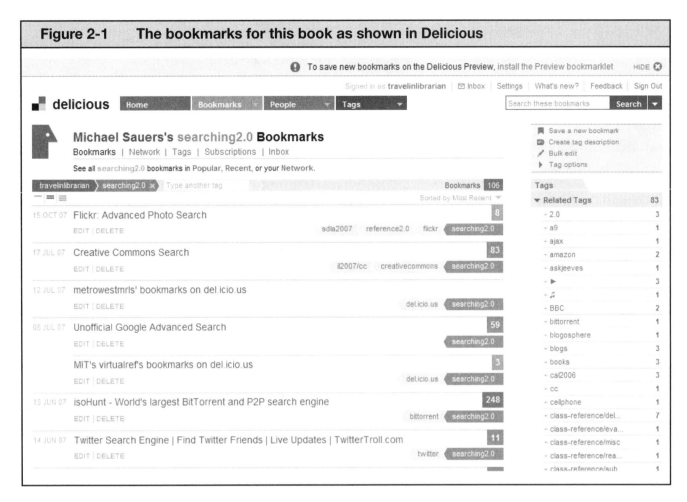

Figure 2-1   The bookmarks for this book as shown in Delicious

bookmarks are interested in the same topics. This function allows a user to "browse" related resources, closely mirroring the serendipity that people once associated with card catalogs and now bemoan the loss of in modern-day online catalogs.

Through the use of RSS, patrons can subscribe to your library's Delicious account and receive near-automatic notification of new bookmarks added to your account. Through the use of "tags" (discussed next) patrons can also use RSS feeds to receive notification of new bookmarks on particular topics of interest.

When you add a new bookmark to your Delicious account, the link title and URL fields are automatically populated. You are also offered two additional fields: notes and tags. The notes field allows you to enter a narrative description of the page you're bookmarking. The tags field allows you to add additional keywords that you wish to have associated with this bookmark. Figure 2-1 shows my Delicious account with items tagged *searching2.0*. (All of the

links presented in this book have been tagged with this keyword.) Let's go ahead and walk you through the creation of a Delicious account and the basic workings of what the service has to offer.

Creating a Delicious Account

The first step to using Delicious is to create a user account. To do so, open Delicious's homepage (www.delicious.com; see my Delicious homepage in Figure 2-2) and click on the link in the upper right corner labeled "Join now." Choose a username and password, enter your e-mail address, and click "register." (Feel free to create your own personal account for practice. Eventually you'll want to create an account for your library with an appropriate username, such as the name of the library.) Once logged in, you'll be on the "install bookmarking tools" page.

Adding Bookmarks

There are four main ways for adding bookmarks to your account: via importing, via "Save a new book-

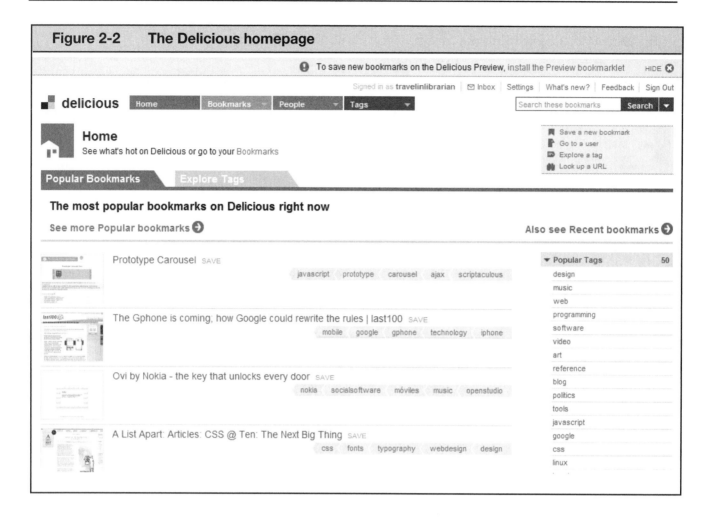

Figure 2-2   The Delicious homepage

mark," via the browser buttons, and via the Delicious bookmark. Although importing is something you're likely to do only once, let's cover this first since it's the best way to get numerous resources into your account to play with.

Importing

The current step on your "install bookmarking tools" page should be "add bookmarking buttons." Skip this step and go to step 3, "import existing bookmarks." Your page should look similar to the Web page in Figure 2-3.

Importing allows you to add an existing list of bookmarks, generally from your browser, into your Delicious account. Assuming that the browser at your desk already has a great number of bookmarks, this is an excellent starting point. This process occurs in two steps. The Web site (https://secure.delicious.com/register/import) offers instructions for Internet Explorer 7 users. A link is offered for users of differ-

ent browsers, such as Internet Explorer 6, Firefox, Safari, and Opera. First, you'll need to export your bookmarks (step A). If you're an Internet Explorer 7 user, choose "File" from the menu bar, then select "Import and Export." Once the Import/Export Wizard starts, click "Next," select "Export Favorites," and click "Next" again. Select "Favorites" to export everything, or select a particular folder to export and then click "Next." Browse for an appropriate location to export your file (I suggest your desktop) and click "Next." Click "Finish" to start the export process. After just a few moments you should be told that the export was complete. Click "OK" to close this window.

If you're a Firefox user, select "Bookmarks" then "Organize Bookmarks" from the menu bar. Once the Bookmarks Manager has opened, select "File" then "Export." Choose a location for your exported file (again, I recommend the desktop) and click the "Save" button. Once you return to the Bookmarks

Figure 2-3   Importing interface

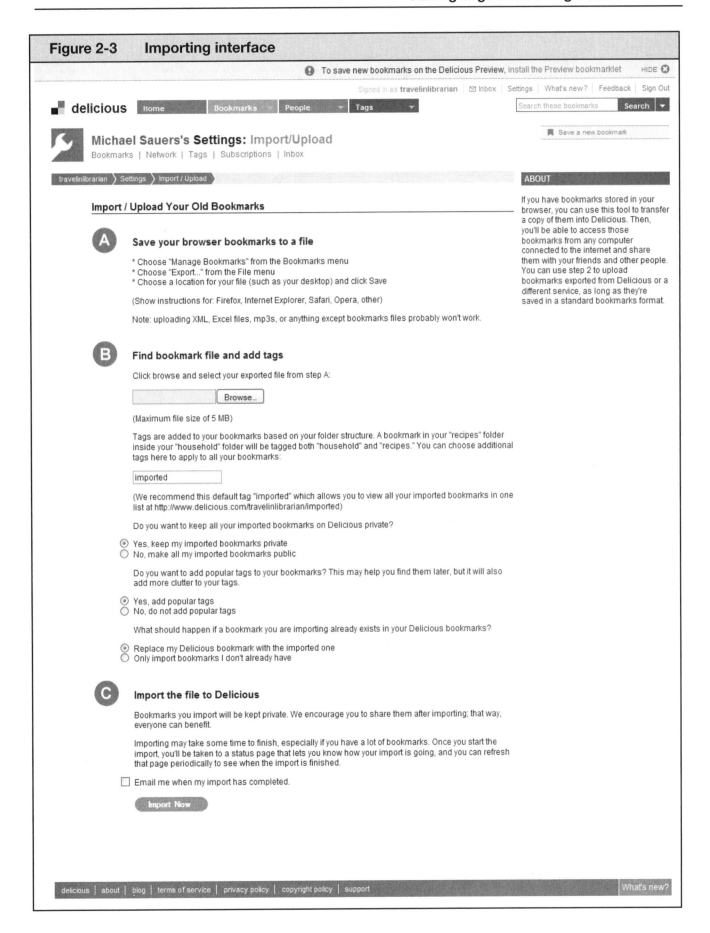

Manager you can close it to return to your browser. For those of you using other browsers, the directions should be similar to those for Internet Explorer and Firefox. Check your browser's help file if you can't find the correct menu item.

This completes the first step in the importing process. In the second step (step B) you need to click "Browse" to locate and select your exported file. You then need to answer a few questions and (maybe) provide some tags. You are provided with a form field that contains the word "imported." This means that all of the bookmarks you import through this process will have the tag "imported." You can remove this tag if you wish. You can also add additional tags by creating a space-delimited list in this field. In many cases, my students can think of no one keyword (other than "imported") that would apply to all of the bookmarks they're about to add to their account. However, one possible situation may be, for example, a library creating a single account for all staff to use, with many staff wishing to contribute their own bookmarks. You could import individual staff bookmark lists and tag each list with the name of the staff person who contributed it. It's not perfect, but it's an example.

The next three questions are, at this point, much more important.

- *Do you want to keep all your imported bookmarks on Delicious private?* In the past all imported bookmarks were automatically labeled as private—only you could see them unless you made them public. The purpose of this was to keep people from accidentally importing a single bookmark out of thousands that they didn't necessarily want other people to know they had. Although this was nice from a privacy perspective, it caused problems for some. (When the Nebraska Library Commission imported 4,500 bookmarks into our account, someone had to go through every one and make them public, one at a time.) With this new version of Delicious, you have the ability to make all of your imported bookmarks public or private. Choose wisely. If you do choose public, be sure you want them all to be public. If you choose private, remember that it'll take some work to make them all public later should you change your mind.

- *Do you want to add popular tags to your bookmarks?* This is the handiest of the three questions. Choosing yes here will instruct Delicious to automatically compare your bookmarks to the bookmarks already in the system and add tags to those already used often enough by others to be considered popular. Again, if you're importing thousands, or even just a hundred bookmarks, this will simplify your life by saving you from having to individually tag most of your resources. Please keep in mind that this system isn't perfect. For example, if you're the only person with that resource, it won't be assigned any tags. If just a few people have previously added the resource to Delicious but it doesn't have any commonly used tags, again, your bookmarks won't be assigned automatic tags during the import process. Also, if you've devised some unique tagging scheme, this will need to be implemented manually. If the bookmarks you exported were organized into folders, the name of the folder containing the bookmarks will be added as a tag when imported into Delicious.

- *What should happen if a bookmark you are importing already exists in your Delicious bookmarks?* If you're importing bookmarks as a way to populate your account that currently has no bookmarks, this option will not be relevant. However, if your account already includes a number of bookmarks and you're now importing more, this option requires your close attention. If you choose "Replace," any imported bookmark that matches an existing bookmark (by URL) will replace the original bookmark. Choosing "only import bookmarks I don't already have" will cause the import to ignore any duplicated bookmarks.

Before the import is completed, you're offered the option to be e-mailed when the process is completed. Unless you've got just a few bookmarks, this process tends to take a bit of time, hours for some, so you may want to take advantage of this option. Just check the box and enter your e-mail address in the provided field.

All that's left to do is to click the "Import Now" button to start the process. As previously mentioned, it will most likely take at least a minute or two for the first bookmarks to show up in your account and perhaps hours for all of them to appear depending on the number you're importing. Be patient; they will all appear eventually.

"Save a New Bookmark"

When viewing any page in Delicious, you will see a "Save a new bookmark" link in a box near the upper right corner of the page. (This link was previously known as "Post" and located in a bar near the top left of the page.) Clicking on this link will open the "Save a new bookmark" page, as shown in Figure 2-4.

Enter the URL of the page you would like to bookmark into the URL field. The easiest way to do this is to open the page you wish to bookmark in another browser window or tab, copy the URL from the address bar, and paste it into this field. Once you've entered the URL, click the "Next" button to continue. You'll then be presented with the full interface for entering a new bookmark into your Delicious account, as shown in Figure 2-5.

This page has four fields—URL, title, notes, and tags—and an option—"do not share"—that you can edit:

- **URL:**
  This field should contain the URL that you entered on the previous screen. Should you need to edit it, you may do so here. This is a required field.
- **TITLE:**
  This field should contain the title of the Web page

located at the URL given, as set by that page's author. In many cases, this title may contain too little or too much information. Feel free to edit it to fit your needs. (In Figure 2-5, I edited the title by removing the supplied "Providing a Safer and Faster Internet" tagline.) This is a required field.

- **NOTES:**
  Here you may enter up to 1,000 characters of descriptive content. In some cases, I copy and paste some text from the site itself, as I've done in Figure 2-5. This information will be displayed in your bookmarks list and will also be completely searchable.[3]
- **TAGS:**
  Unlike your browser, Delicious does not rely on folders to keep your bookmarks organized. Instead it relies on user-supplied tags, as I discussed in Chapter 1. Here you need to enter whichever tags you might use to find this bookmark again as a space-delimited list. You may enter as many tags as you think are appropriate. If you're not sure which tags to use or you're just interested in seeing what tags others have used for this bookmark, scroll down the page to the "Tags" tab. Here you'll find up to three sections: "Recommended," "Popular," and "All my tags." Each one may be opened or closed by clicking on the triangle to the left of the section header. Any of the tags in these sections may be clicked and automatically added to your list of tags. (At first, the "All my tags" section

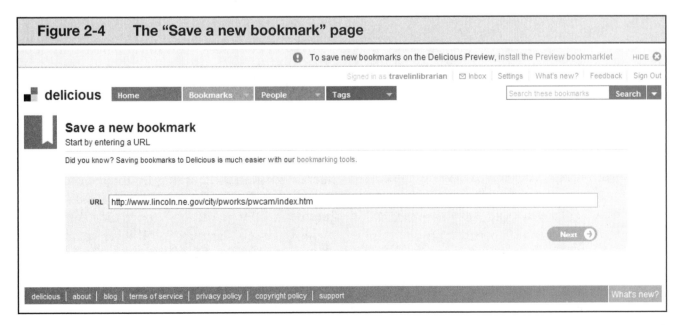

Figure 2-4   The "Save a new bookmark" page

Figure 2-5   Add tags and notes

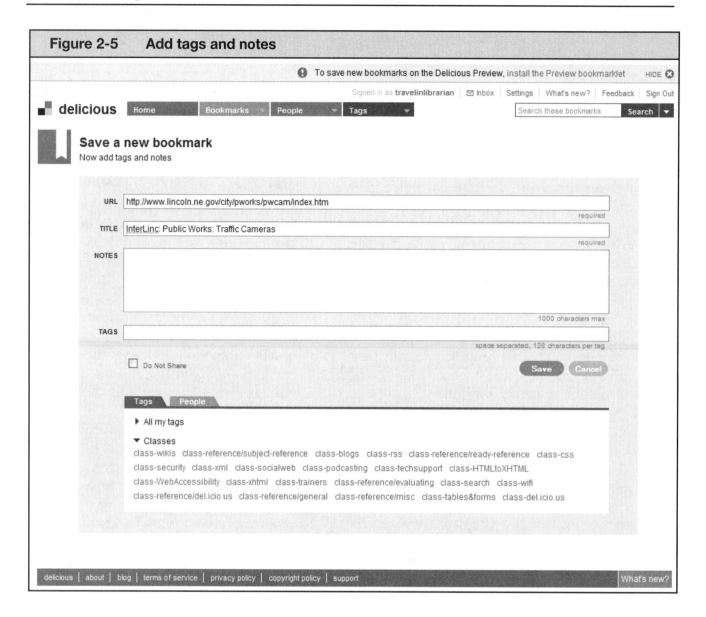

will be sparse, but as you use your account, the list will grow.) There is also a "People" tab, which is discussed later in this chapter.

- **Do Not Share:**
  Checking this option keeps this bookmark private. This means that only you will be able to see it when you're logged into your account. The fact that you have bookmarked it will still be counted in Delicious's statistics (discussed later), but others will not see that you have done so. Figure 2-6 shows the results of my filling in this form.

All that's left to do is to click the "Save" button to add the bookmark to your account. You'll be sent to your bookmarks page, where it should appear at the top of your bookmarks list. You also have the option of clicking the "Cancel" button if you decide you do not wish to save this bookmark to your account.

Browser Buttons

The browser buttons were made available for you to install as part of the account creation process or for later installation by choosing "Help" and then either "Quick tour for Firefox Add-on" or "Quick tour for Internet Explorer Add-on" under the "Learn more about Delicious" heading. Whichever you pick, the results will be the same.[4] At the bottom of the page is a link to install the add-on. Click on this link, click on "add button," and then confirm to your browser that you wish these buttons to be installed.

Figure 2-6	The completed "Save a new bookmark" form

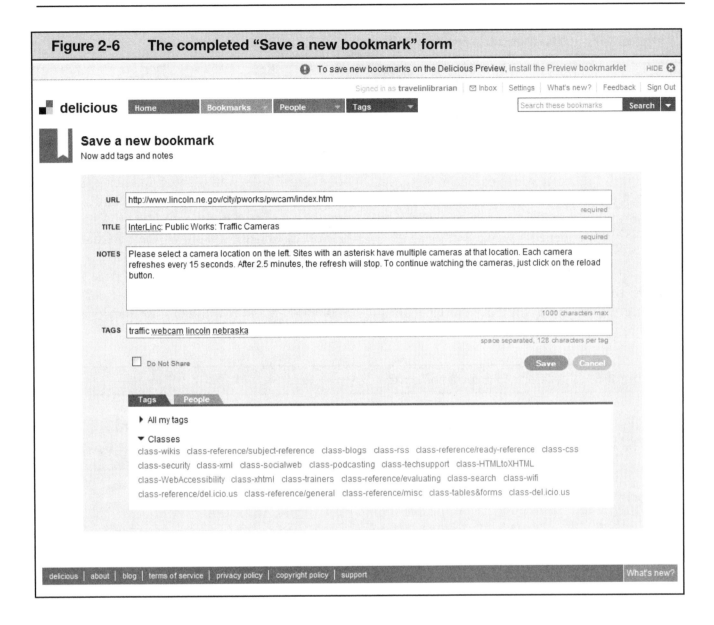

Soon you'll find an additional two buttons in your browser's button bar, as shown in Figure 2-7.

The first button is of the Delicious logo, which when clicked will retrieve your bookmarks page. (If you are not already logged into your account, you will be asked to do so.) This allows simple one-click access to all of your resources. The second button looks like a small old-style price tag and is labeled "Tag." This button saves you from all of the copying and pasting from multiple browser windows or tabs described in the previous section. Once you're on a page that you wish to add to your account, just click on the "Tag" button and a window will appear giving you access to the "Save a bookmark" form, as shown in Figure 2-8. The URL and title of the page

will automatically appear in the appropriate fields. If you had selected any text on the page, it will appear, subject to the 1,000 character limit, automatically in the notes field. All you need to do now is add tags (by typing or choosing from the provided suggestions), make any other edits, and click the "Save" button. The window will disappear and your new bookmark will have been added to your account. This is how I add the majority of my bookmarks to my account.

Bookmarklet

Should you find yourself in the position of not being able to install buttons into your browser, another way to accomplish the button-like adding of bookmarks to your account is the Delicious bookmarklet. You

Figure 2-7   The Delicious browser buttons

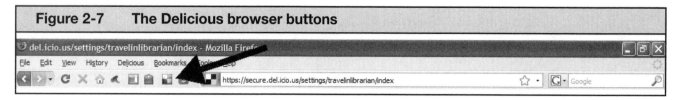

can add a bookmarklet to your browser just as you would add any traditional bookmark, but bookmarklets, instead of pointing you to particular Web pages, are actually little scripts that perform an action. In this case, the action is to open the same window that the "Tag" button opened.

Next, choose the version that works with your browser and follow the directions. This involves dragging the appropriate link (www.delicious.com/save, accessed by clicking the "Save a new bookmark" link) onto your browser's bookmarks toolbar, or right

clicking on the page and selecting "Bookmark This Page" or "Add to Favorites" or whichever choice accomplishes this in your browser. In Internet Explorer, the bookmarklet will appear in the "Links" toolbar when you save the page to the "Links" folder under "Favorites." Figure 2-9 shows the bookmarklet installed on my browser bookmarks toolbar. From this point forward, whenever you're on a page you wish to add to your Delicious account, just click on the bookmarklet and it will work the same way as the browser button.

Figure 2-8   Adding via a browser button

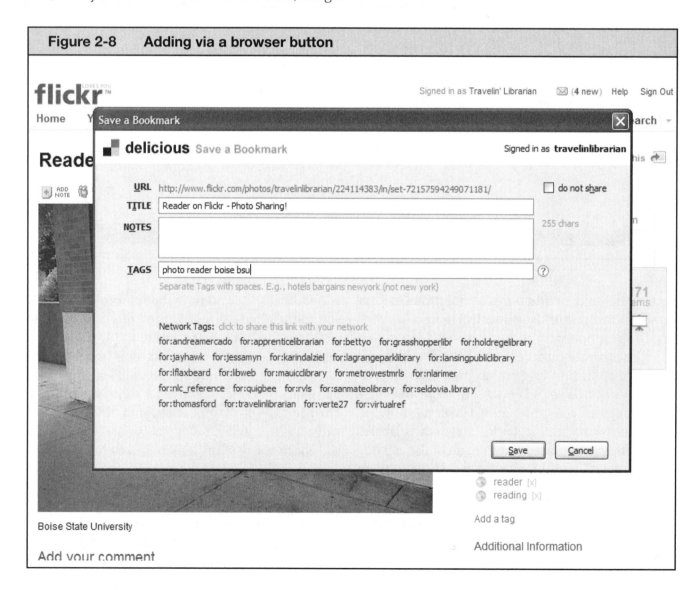

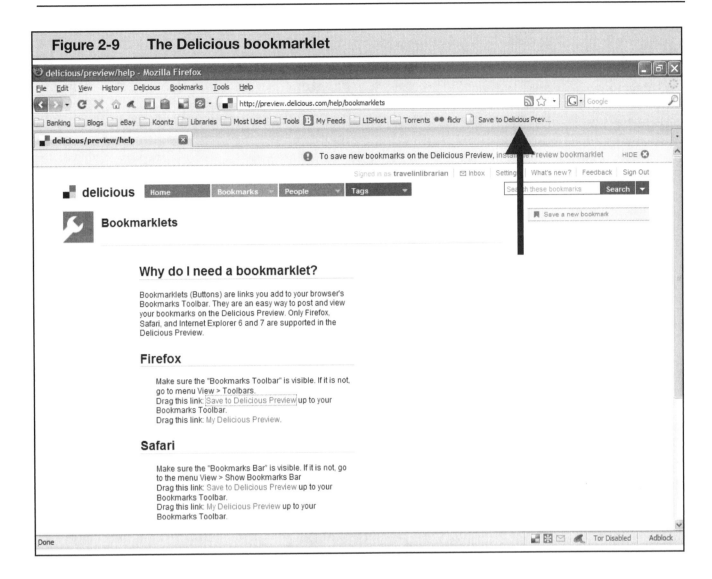

Figure 2-9   The Delicious bookmarklet

My Bookmarks

Now that you have an account and know how to add bookmarks, let's look at the main interface for Delicious, your bookmarks page. As you can quickly see from Figure 2-10, a lot of different features appear on this screen. Let's begin with an overview of the major features of this screen and then examine some of the specifics. I won't go into extensive detail about every single feature but will provide more than enough information for you to become familiar with navigating Delicious.

Across the top of the page are links for your account profile (in Figure 2-11, mine says "Signed in as travelinlibrarian"), such as "Inbox," "Settings," and "Sign Out" (always useful when you're on a public computer). Also included is a link for information about Delicious services labeled "What's New?" As

you can see in Figure 2-11, a link for feedback was once offered, but no longer.

Below these, to the left, are buttons for "Home," "Bookmarks," "People," and "Tags." The "Home" tab takes you back to the Delicious homepage, which is what you saw when you first came to the site but hadn't logged in yet. "Bookmarks" offers subchoices of "My Bookmarks," "Popular," "Recent," and "Look up a URL." "People" offers subchoices of "My Network" and "Go to a User." "Tags" offers subchoices of "My Tags," My Subscriptions," and "Explore." You can see these tabs in Figure 2-12.

Below this, the main body of the page tells you the name of the account for the bookmarks you're currently displaying and, assuming you're logged into your account, shows links for your "Network," "Tags," "Subscriptions," and "Inbox" (see Figure

Figure 2-10   The default "My Bookmarks" view

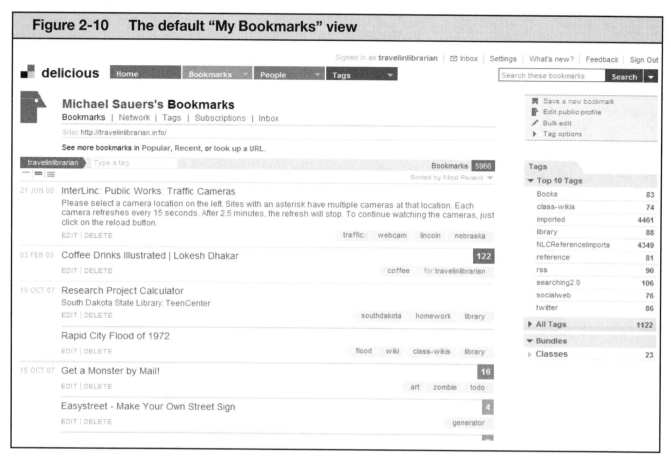

Figure 2-11   Links about Delicious

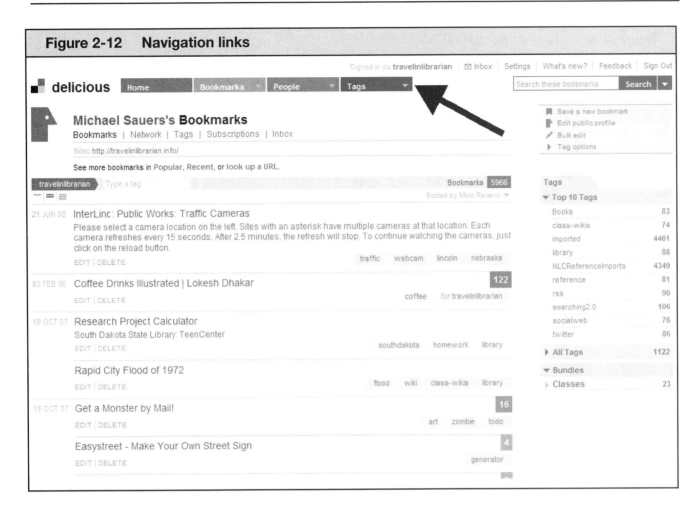

Figure 2-12   Navigation links

2-13). You'll also find a link to the user's homepage, if provided in the user's public profile, as well as links to more bookmarks in "Popular," "Recent," or "Look up a URL."

Now you'll see the name of the account you're currently viewing ("travelinlibrarian" in Figure 2-13), along with a "Type a tag" field. Off to the right, you'll see the number of bookmarks currently listed in this account and that they are "Sorted by Most Recent." Clicking on the "Sorted by" link will give you the ability to re-sort your bookmarks alphabetically or by popularity, or you can reverse the current order. Below this, if sorted by most recent, you'll see the ten most recent bookmarks added to your account in the "Regular view." Two other views are available: "Title view" and "Full view." Figures 2-14 and 2-15 show these different views of the current screen. For the rest of the chapter, I'll be staying in the "Regular view."

Figure 2-16 highlights a single bookmark for us to examine. To the left is the date the bookmark

was added to the account, followed by the title of the bookmark, which is also the hyperlink to that page. Beneath this will be displayed any text that was entered into the bookmark's notes field. Below this are links that allow you to "EDIT" or "DELETE" this particular bookmark. To the right you'll find the number of other account holders who have also bookmarked the page and the tags that are assigned to that bookmark.

Clicking on the number of other users for a bookmark will take you to the "People" page for that bookmark. This page, as shown in Figure 2-17, shows you the names of the users who have publicly bookmarked the page and the tags and notes they added to that page. Links to those users' public pages and all of the tags are hyperlinked to their appropriate Delicious pages. Clicking on a tag associated with one of your bookmarks will take you to a page listing the bookmarks in your account that have that tag. Figure 2-18 shows the page for my "generator" tag.

Figure 2-13   Account links

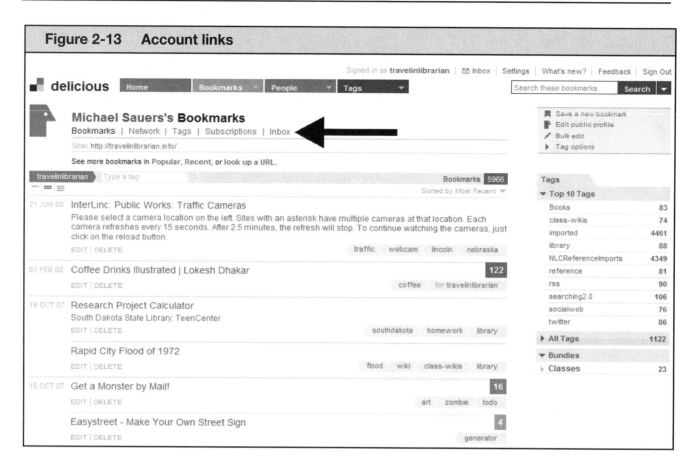

Figure 2-14   Title view

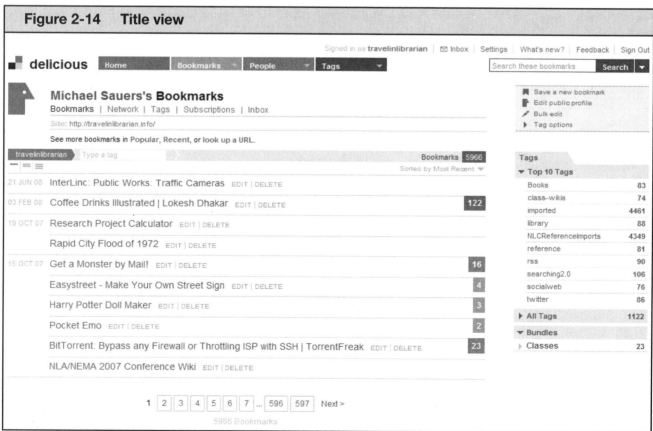

Figure 2-15   Full view

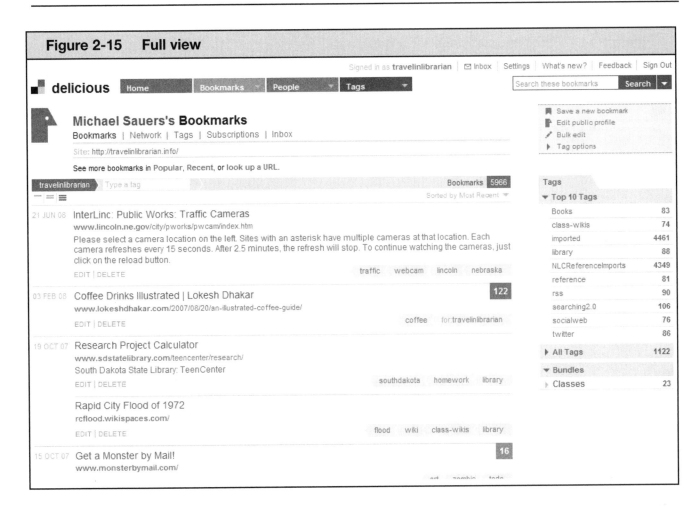

Another way to see all of the bookmarks for a particular tag in your account is to type it into the "Type a tag" field at the top of your bookmarks list. If I were to type "generator" into that field and then press Enter I would end up at the same page shown in Figure 2-19. At the bottom of this page is the link for the RSS feed for what you're looking at (in this case, all of the bookmarks for this account) and the link to change the number of bookmarks shown per page: 10, 25, 50, or 100 (see arrows in Figure 2-19). At the very bottom of the page are all of the "about" and "legal" links for Delicious as a company (see Figure 2-20).

Back on your bookmarks page, if you scroll back up to the top of the page and look to the top right of the screen, you'll see a light blue box containing three links: "Save a new bookmark" (covered in previous section), "Edit public profile," and "Tag options."

- **Edit public profile:**
  Clicking this link takes you to the edit screen of your account's public profile. Figure 2-21 shows the edit screen, and Figure 2-22 shows the public version of my profile. Here you can enter such information as your real name, e-mail address, and Web site. Fill in as little or as much information as you feel comfortable providing.

Figure 2-16   Details of a bookmark

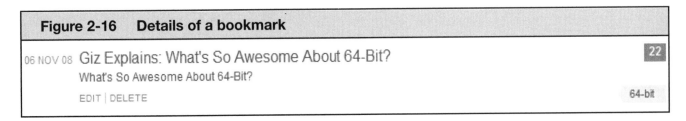

Figure 2-17   The "People" page for a bookmark

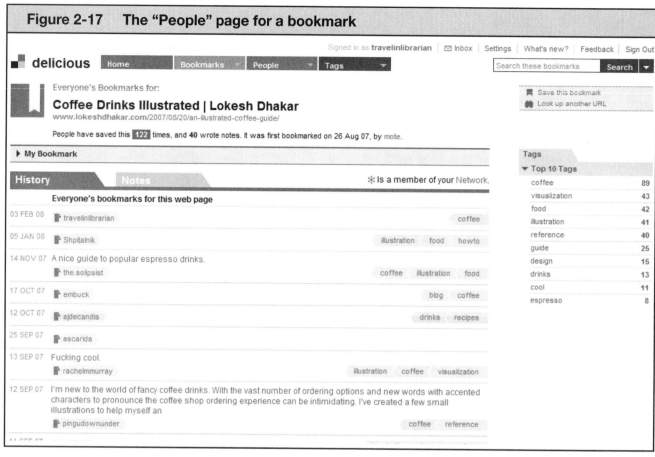

Figure 2-18   My "generator" tag page

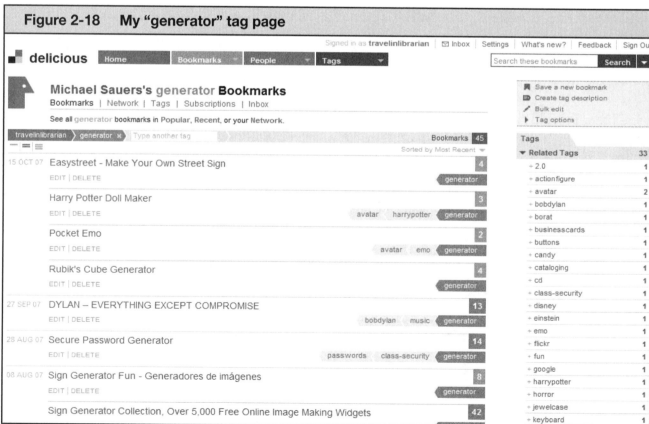

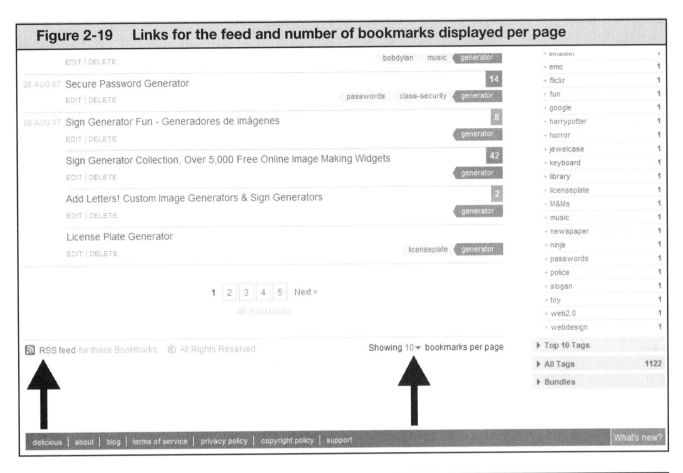

Figure 2-19   Links for the feed and number of bookmarks displayed per page

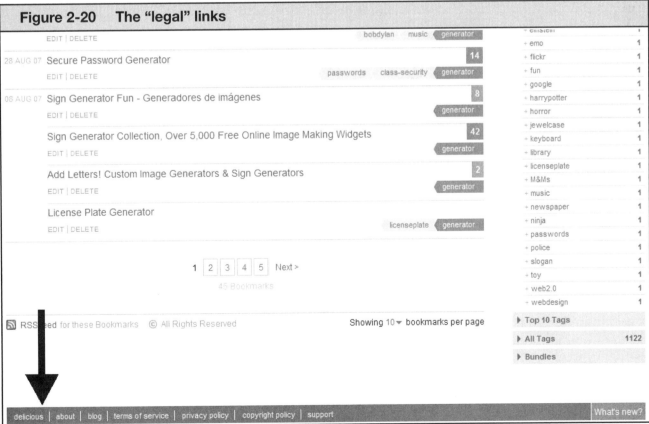

Figure 2-20   The "legal" links

Figure 2-21   Edit public profile

Figure 2-22   My public profile

- **Tag options:**

    Clicking this link will show some additional options for how you wish your tags list to be displayed (see Figure 2-23). Here you can choose to display your tags as a cloud or a list; sort alphabetically or by frequency; limit the displayed tags to ones that are used only one, two, or five times; rename or delete tags; and manage tag bundles. Since most of these options won't make much sense until I cover the tags list itself, I'll come back to these options later.

Finally we come to the tags list itself. By default, it doesn't look like much, but much of the sorting power of your bookmarks lies here. Figure 2-24 shows my tags list, but all you can see is the "Top 10 Tags." Clicking on any of these will take me to the page for that tag. At the bottom of the list is a link for "All Tags," which, when clicked, will show me a complete list of every tag I've ever used in alphabetical order. Since I've used more than 1,100 tags, Figure 2-25 shows just an abbreviated version of this

list. As with the "Top 10 Tags" list, clicking on any of these tags will take me to the page for that tag.

Tag Options

Now that you have a basic grasp of the tag list, Figures 2-26 through 2-30 show you some of the different ways you can view this list based on the available tag options previously mentioned.

As you can see, you can use these options to view your tag list in many different ways. Of course, different views will seem more or less usable to different people, so don't feel too discouraged if you think that one of my examples doesn't seem very helpful. Chances are, someone else will find others not as useful as you do. Let's now take a look at the other tag options: rename, delete, and manage tag bundles.

RENAMING TAGS

When you click the rename link under tag options, you'll be presented with the "Rename Tags" interface as shown in Figure 2-31. Here you are asked to

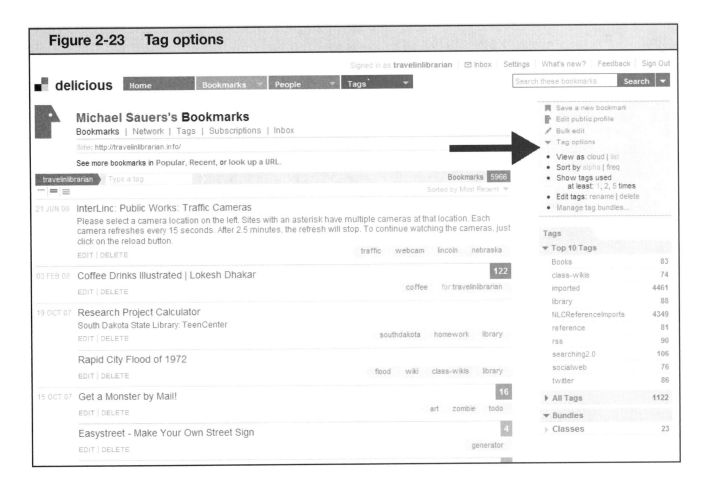

Figure 2-23   Tag options

Figure 2-24   My "Top 10 Tags"

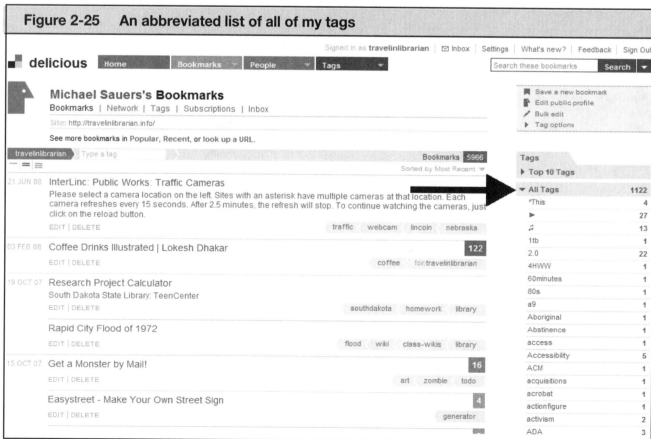

Figure 2-25   An abbreviated list of all of my tags

Figure 2-26 Tags viewed by frequency as a list	
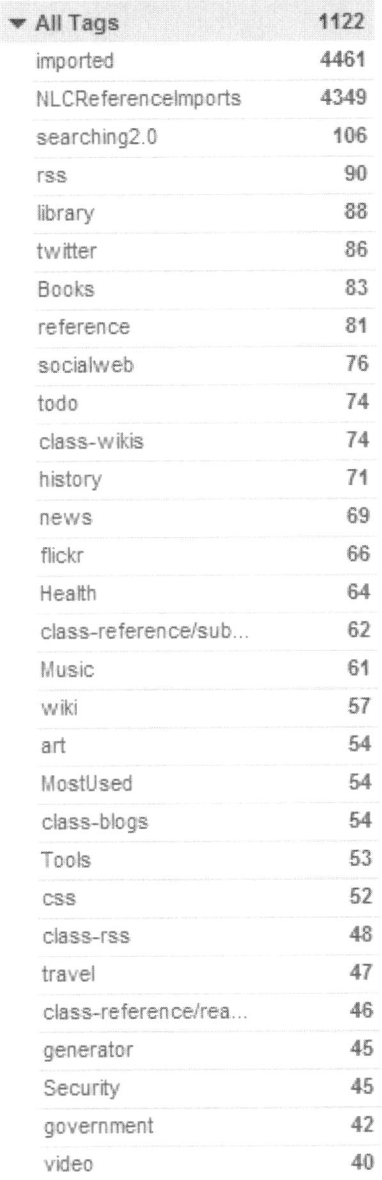 ▼ All Tags	1122
imported	4461
NLCReferenceImports	4349
searching2.0	106
rss	90
library	88
twitter	86
Books	83
reference	81
socialweb	76
todo	74
class-wikis	74
history	71
news	69
flickr	66
Health	64
class-reference/sub...	62
Music	61
wiki	57
art	54
MostUsed	54
class-blogs	54
Tools	53
css	52
class-rss	48
travel	47
class-reference/rea...	46
generator	45
Security	45
government	42
video	40

Figure 2-27 Tags viewed by frequency as a cloud

▼ All Tags   1122

imported NLCReferenceImports
searching2.0 rss library twitter
Books reference socialweb todo
class-wikis history news flickr
Health class-reference/sub... Music
wiki art MostUsed class-blogs
Tools css class-rss travel class-
reference/rea... generator Security
government video class-css
webdesign il2006/flickr search
cil2007/rss sdla2007 science
il2006/rss usb firefox movies
politics statistics blogs photography
copyright library2.0 law maps
software wikipedia shopping
microsoft google class-security
recipes cil2006 Food education
nebraska ▶ business web2.0
genealogy windows libraries
class-xml class-socialweb BCR
il2006 tv fridayvideo unvocab vista
2.0 class-podcasting class-
techsupport ebooks email del.icio.us
edublogging SecondLife xhtml
datavisualization searchengine
SPORTS architecture class-
WebAccessibility class-xhtml
Dictionary class-HTMLtoXHTML
reference2.0 finance tool blog
converter wikis internet jobs
photos writing weather environment
research SCKLS2006 amazon
bittorrent ♫ class-trainers ICPL2006
NLC gaming mashup fun book
tagging lincoln F3/Library2.0 html
religion grants ipod economics
psychology passwords design

choose an existing tag from your tag list in the first field and then enter a replacement tag in the second field. When you click the "Save" button any instance of the tag in the first field will be replaced with the tag in the second field.

Here are two examples of how this could be used. First, let's say you're looking through your tag list and notice that you've accidentally used the tag *historu* when you really meant *history* more than once. To correct this spelling error, just select *historu*

in the first field, enter *history* in the second, and click "Save." Another example was given to me by one of my students. In her case, she used tags based on teacher names to group resources related to the classes of particular teachers in her school. During one year she had bookmarks tagged *MsSmith*. When Ms. Smith moved away and was replaced by Mr. Stevens, the student was easily able to retag all of her *MsSmith* bookmarks with *MrStevens* using this interface.

Figure 2-28   Tags viewed alphabetically as a cloud

▼ All Tags   1122

*This ▶ ♫ 1tb 2.0 4HWW 60minutes
80s a9 Aboriginal Abstinence access
Accessibility ACM acquisitions acrobat
actionfigure activism ADA adobe
advertising aggregator aging agriculture
aids aim aircraft airfare airline airlines
airports ajax alltel alumni amazon
Amazon.com Anatomy Animal animals
animation anime anniversary anonym.OS
anonymous Antarctica antiques AntiSpam
antivirus APA apple application
architecture archives art ARTHRITIS
artists asia askjeeves asl associations
astronomy auction audio AUP author
authors auto automation autopsy avatar
avi aviation awards azureus baby
backup badge badges bag bags band
bank banking baseball battlestargalactica
BBC bbq BCR beads bermuda Bible
bibliography bicycle bigfinish bills
bioinformatics biology birds birthdays
bittorrent blog blogger blogging
bloglines blogosphere blogs bobdylan
boingboing book bookbinding bookmarklet
Books booksellers boot borat borders
braille brain breastfeeding broadband
broadway browser browsers bsg
buddhism building business
businesscards butterflies buttons cable
cal2006 calculator calculators calculus
calendar camping canada cancer candy
capture car cards Career carnival cars
cartoon cartoons castles cataloging
catholic cats cbs cc cd cdl cellphone
censorship Census cfp cgi charity
charlotte charts chat chemistry ChickLit
chinese christian Christianity cil2006
cil2007 cil2007/rss cingular cities

Figure 2-29   Tags viewed alphabetically as a list with a use threshold of five

▼ All Tags › 5	1122
▶	27
♫	13
2.0	22
Accessibility	5
ajax	8
amazon	13
antiques	8
antivirus	5
architecture	18
art	54
astronomy	7
audio	7
awards	6
baseball	8
BBC	7
BCR	24
biology	5
bittorrent	13
blog	16
blogger	6
blogs	32
book	12
Books	83
browsers	5
business	26
cal2006	9
calendar	7
canada	6
Career	10
cars	8

DELETING TAGS

The "Delete Tags" screen, as shown in Figure 2-32, allows you to remove every instance of a particular tag. Just select the tag from the list and click the "Delete" button. Be aware that this does not remove any of the associated bookmarks, just the tag.

MANAGING TAG BUNDLES

Tag bundles do not seem to be useful to many people at first, but when you start adding a lot of bookmarks

to your account and in turn have many tags in your account, they can help you more easily find the tag you're seeking. You can even think of bundles as a sort of folder system for tags. Let's take a look at why I use tag bundles.

As you have seen in previous screenshots, I currently have over 1,100 different tags associated with my bookmarks. Even when they're presented as an alphabetical list, this list is almost prohibitively long when trying to find a particular tag. Additionally, one

Figure 2-30 Tags viewed by frequency as a cloud with a use threshold of five

▼ All Tags › 5   1122

imported NLCReferenceImports
searching2.0 rss library twitter
Books reference socialweb todo
class-wikis history news flickr
Health class-reference/sub... Music
wiki art MostUsed class-blogs
Tools css class-rss travel class-
reference/rea... generator Security
government video class-css
webdesign il2006/flickr search
cil2007/rss sdla2007 science
il2006/rss usb firefox movies
politics statistics blogs photography
copyright library2.0 law maps
software wikipedia shopping
microsoft google class-security
recipes cil2006 Food education
nebraska ► business web2.0
genealogy windows libraries
class-xml class-socialweb BCR
il2006 tv fridayvideo unvocab vista
2.0 class-podcasting class-
techsupport ebooks email del.icio.us
edublogging SecondLife xhtml
datavisualization searchengine
SPORTS architecture class-
WebAccessibility class-xhtml
Dictionary class-HTMLtoXHTML
reference2.0 finance tool blog
converter wikis internet jobs
photos writing weather environment
research SCKLS2006 amazon
bittorrent ♫ class-trainers ICPL2006
NLC gaming mashup fun book
tagging lincoln F3/Library2.0 html
religion grants ipod economics
psychology passwords design

of the ways in which I've used tagging is to create a tag specific to each of the classes I teach so as to easily point my students to a particular page for all of the online resources related to the class's topic. Each of these tags starts with *class-*. So, I have tags such as *class-socialweb*, *class-xhtml*, and *class-wikis*, just to name a few. Granted, alphabetically, all of these tags will group together, but I need to scroll down several screens just to find them. This is where tag bundles can help.

Figure 2-33 shows the "Manage Tag Bundles" screen when you first get to it, having not previously created any bundles. Clicking on the "Create" button will bring you to the screen shown in Figure 2-34. Here I name the bundle and then either type in the tags I want to include in this bundle or, more easily, choose them from the supplied list of my tags by clicking on the ones I wish to include. As I enter/choose tags, they will be highlighted on the screen, and a preview of the bundle will update along the right side of the window. Figure 2-35 shows how I've filled in this form. Once my bundle is complete, I click on the "Save" button and I am returned to the "Manage Tag Bundles" page, which shows my one bundle (see Figure 2-36).

When I return to my bookmarks page, I see that my tags list is now a little different. Instead of just the "Top 10 Tags" and "All Tags" lists, I now have a "Bundles" list. By clicking on my "Classes" bundle, I can see a list of just the tags contained within that bundle. You are free to create as many bundles as you think you need, and a tag may appear in as many different bundles as necessary. For another example, let's say you have tags such as *arthistory*, *ushistory*, *europeanhistory*, *musichistory*, and *localhistory*. In this case, all of these history-related tags are nowhere near one another in your tags list. In this case, a bundle named *history* would do just the trick to bring them all together on the screen.

Now that we've got some links in your account and can move around within them, let's take a look at some of the more social aspects of Delicious.

People

The "People" button offers two choices: "My Network" and "Go to a User." Since one is much easier to explain than the other, let's examine these in reverse order.

Go to a User

As shown in Figure 2-37, this is a very simple page. All you need to do is type in the username of a Delicious user and press Enter (or click the left arrow) and you'll be sent to the public page of that user.

Unfortunately, there is no way to find a user based on his or her real name. So, for example, if you don't

(continued on p. 36)

Figure 2-31   The "Rename Tags" interface

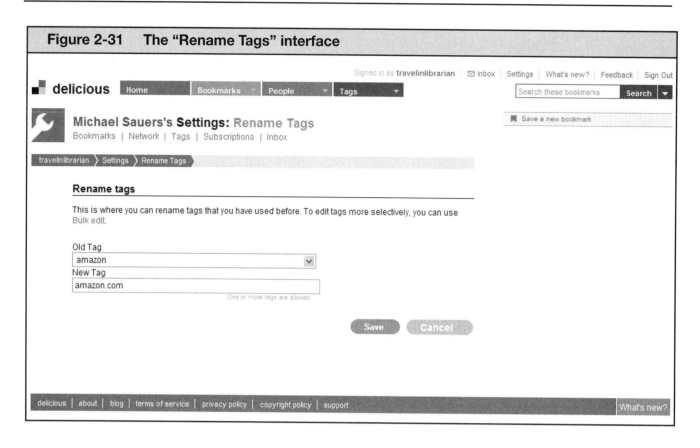

Figure 2-32   The "Delete Tags" interface

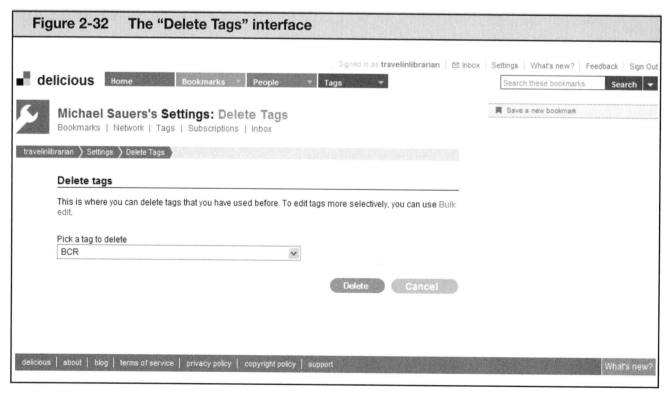

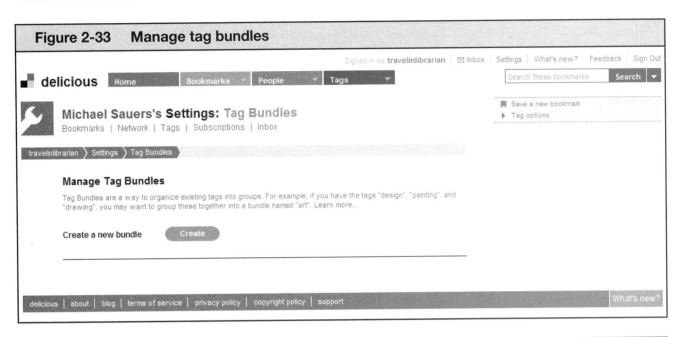

Figure 2-33   Manage tag bundles

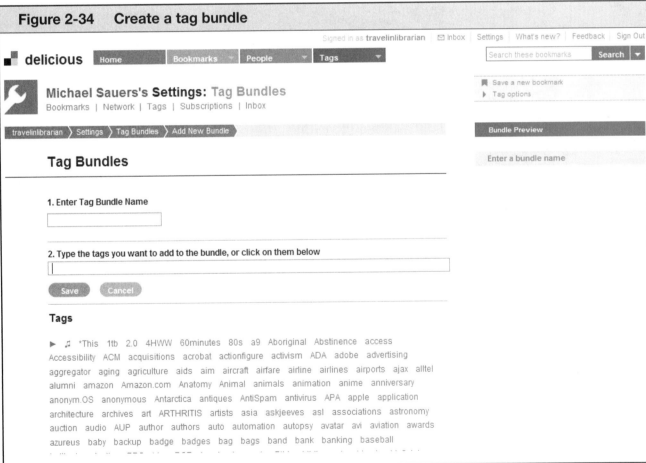

Figure 2-34   Create a tag bundle

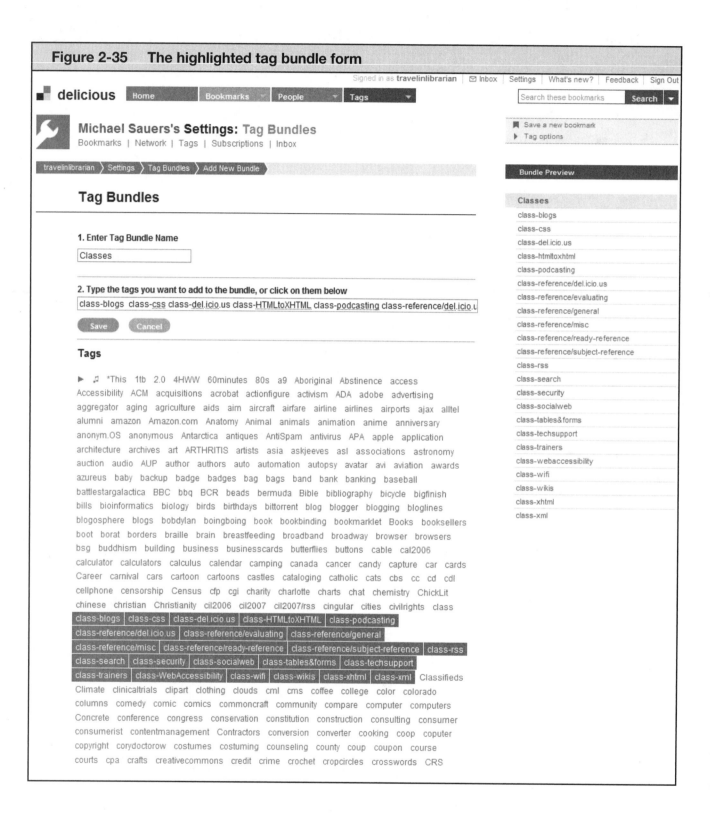

Figure 2-35   The highlighted tag bundle form

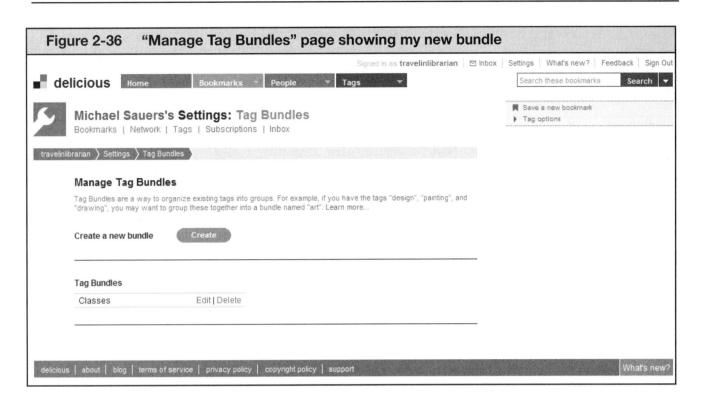

Figure 2-36   "Manage Tag Bundles" page showing my new bundle

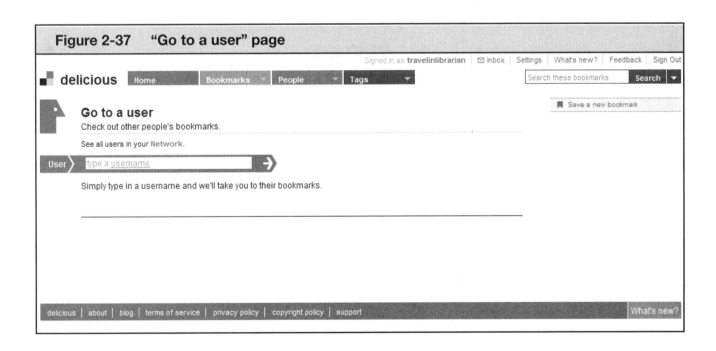

Figure 2-37   "Go to a user" page

know that my username is "travelinlibrarian," there's no way to find my public page within Delicious. So, yes, you need to ask people if they have an account and what their username is.

My Network

For those of you who are already familiar with the concept of "friends" in systems such as Facebook or MySpace, Delicious's network is very similar. To add someone to your network all you need to know is his or her username. Just select "My Network" from the "People" menu and then click "Add a user to Network." To the right a box will appear in which you enter a username and click the "Add" button. Once done, this user will be added to your network (see Figure 2-38). So, just what are the benefits of doing this? There are two of them.

The first is that you can easily track the new bookmarks that the user has added to his or her ac-count. Once you have other users in your network, when you select "My Network" from the "People" menu, you'll be presented with a list of bookmarks that have been recently added by those in your network, as shown in Figure 2-39.

The second benefit to adding individuals to your network is the ability to send them bookmarks that you think might interest them. Now when you add a new bookmark, the previously mentioned "People" tab will contain the list of users in your network. All you need to do to send someone a copy of this bookmark is to select his or her name and a *for:*username tag will automatically be added, as shown in Figure 2-40. Once you save the new link, it will appear in his or her inbox.[5] (I discuss the inbox in more detail later in this chapter.)

Once your library has an account, you can encourage your users not only to create their own Delicious accounts but to add the library to their

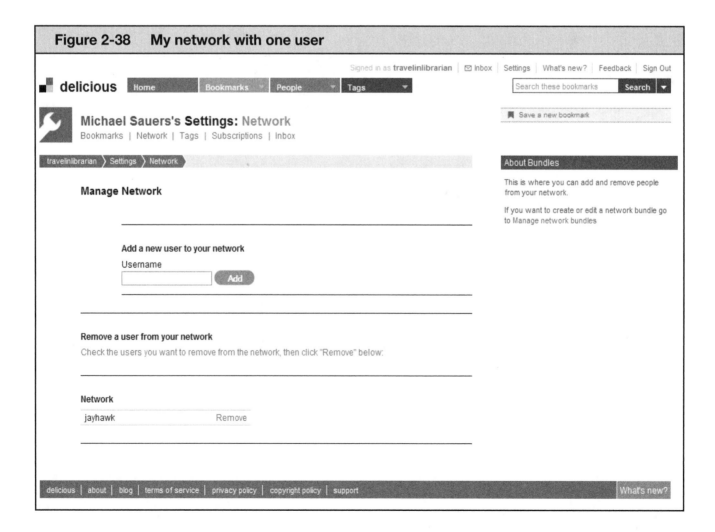

Figure 2-38   My network with one user

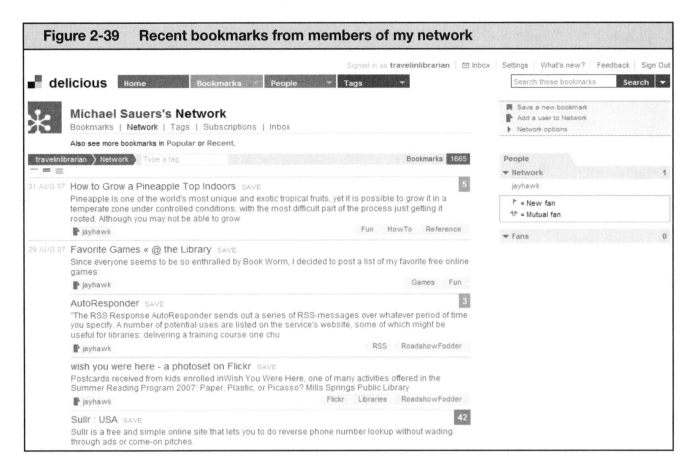

Figure 2-39   Recent bookmarks from members of my network

network, and then you can solicit resources from them for the library to consider adding to its account for the benefit of all of the library's users.

Tags

The Tags menu has three choices: "My Tags," "My Subscriptions," and "Explore." Let's see what these choices offer.

My Tags

Opening the "My Tags" page will, by default, show you an alphabetical tag cloud of your 200 most used tags, each one hyperlinked to that tag's page. Using the links at the top of the cloud, you can choose to show all of your tags instead of just the top 200 and you can switch from an alphabetical sort to a "By size" sort. Figures 2-41 through 2-44 show examples of these different views.

My Subscriptions

"My Network" is where you can track all new bookmarks from a particular user. "My Subscriptions" is where you can track all new bookmarks with a

particular tag, or, more specifically, you can track all new bookmarks with a particular tag from a particular user. The first time you go to the "Subscriptions" page, you'll see a brief introduction to how it works. Click on the "Add a subscription" button to get to the "Manage Subscriptions" page, as shown in Figure 2-45.

Once here you have two choices: add a new tag subscription or add a new tag for a specific user subscription.

* **Add a new tag subscription:**
  This is the field to use if you wish to know of any new bookmark added by any user that is assigned a specific tag. For example, if you're really interested in Abraham Lincoln, you could subscribe to the tag *abrahamlincoln*. You may also want to subscribe to the tag *"abraham lincoln"* (quotes included) for users who assign tags that include spaces. (If your tag contains spaces and you don't include the quotation marks, your words will be interpreted as multiple single-word tags instead of one multiword tag.)

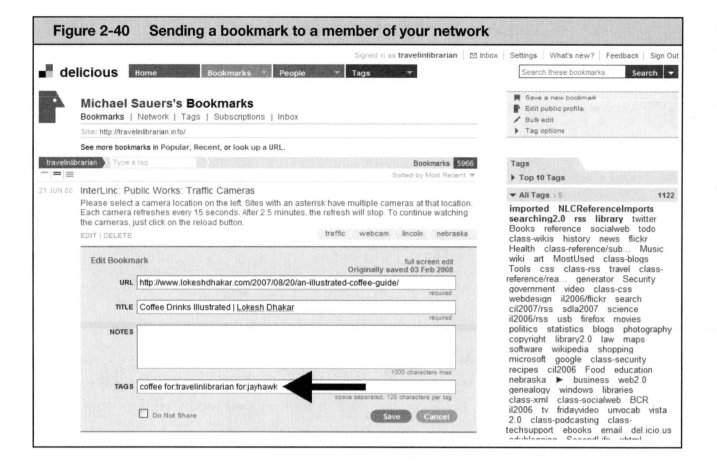

Figure 2-40   Sending a bookmark to a member of your network

- **Add a new tag for a specific user subscription:**

    As you explore Delicious further, you'll start to become familiar with other users who bookmark similar pages as you. Also, you might have real-life friends who also have accounts. Let's say you know of another user who is interested in many topics, but you and she have an overlapping interest in Cascading Style Sheets. After a little investigation you discover that she consistently adds interesting resources on that topic using the tag *css*. All you need to do to track these new bookmarks is to enter her username and the tag *css* and they'll be automatically tracked for you. Looking at it another way, if you're the library, you can encourage your users to get Delicious accounts and then track the new bookmarks that you add on the topics that interest them.

Once you've added a subscription or two, you can find the results back on your "Subscriptions" page. Figure 2-46 shows my updated subscriptions page with the results of several subscriptions.

To edit or remove an existing subscription, find it in the "Subscriptions" list on the right of the "Subscriptions" page, move your mouse pointer over it, and click on the pencil icon that appears. This will open the edit subscription interface, as shown in Figure 2-47.

To add a new subscription or create subscription bundles, which work similarly to tag bundles, select either the "Add a subscription" or "Subscription" bundles under the Subscription options link in the light blue box above your subscription list, as shown in Figure 2-48.

(*continued on p. 46*)

Figure 2-41   My tags, top 200, alphabetical

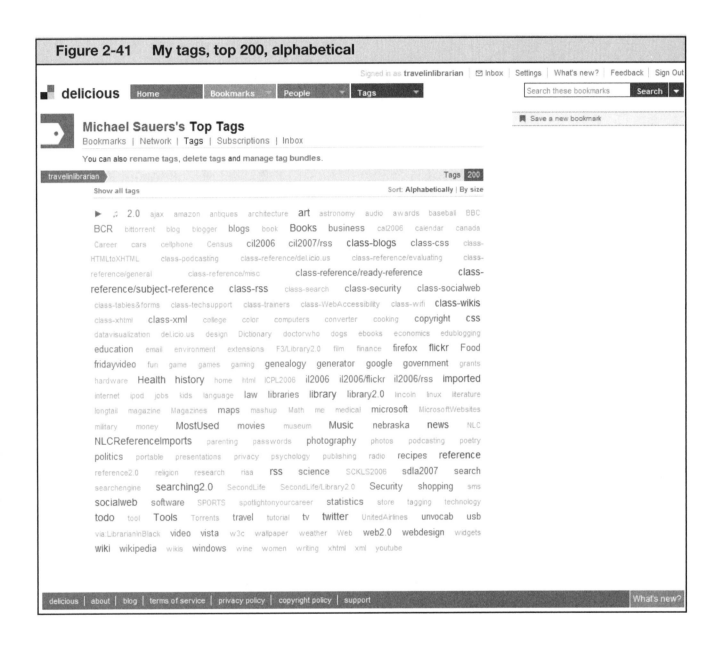

Figure 2-42   My tags, all tags alphabetical

Figure 2-43   My tags, top 200, most used

Figure 2-44   My tags, all tags, most used

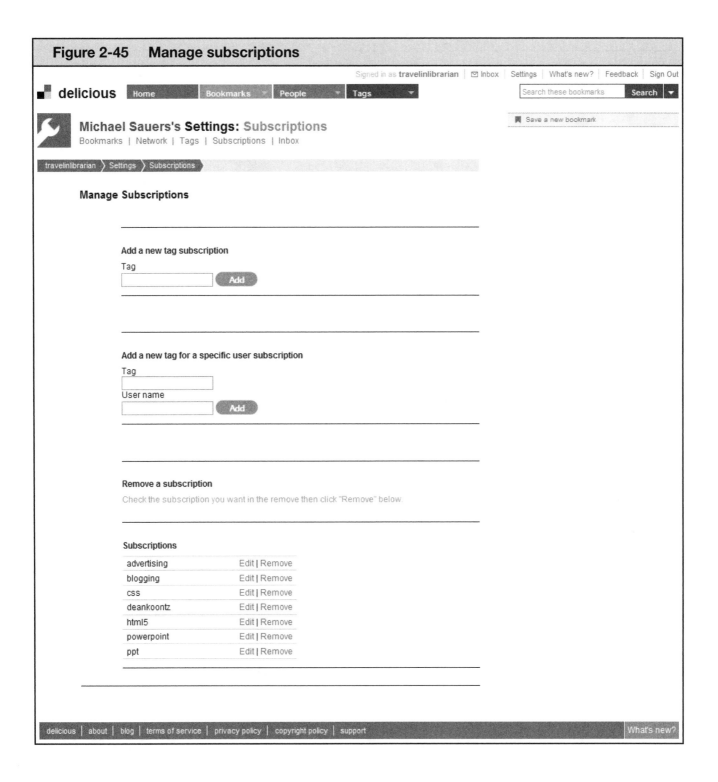

Figure 2-45   Manage subscriptions

Figure 2-46   My subscriptions with results

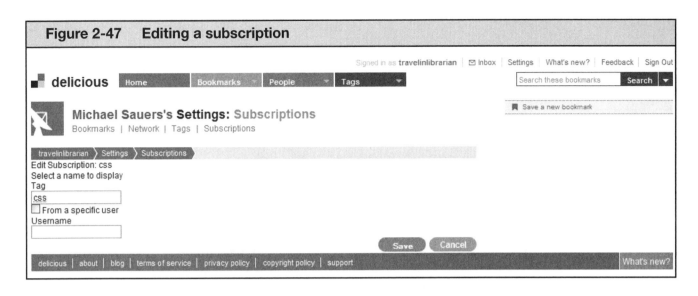

Figure 2-47   Editing a subscription

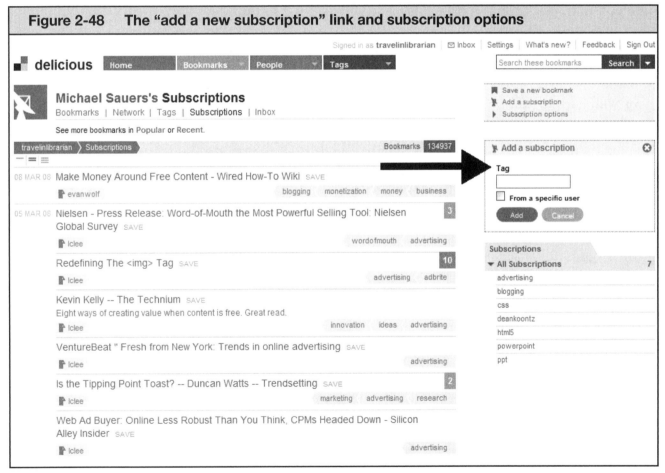

Figure 2-48   The "add a new subscription" link and subscription options

Explore

The "Explore" option takes you to a page with a layout and content similar to the "My Tags" screen. However, in this case, the tag cloud is based on tags from every Delicious user instead of just your own. You are presented with the top 200 tags, which you can display either by size ("most used," the default setting, as in Figure 2-49) or alphabetically (as in Figure 2-50). Tags in blue are tags that appear in your account; tags that appear in gray do not. As usual, all of the displayed tags are hyperlinked to that tag's page.

Inbox

The link to your inbox can be found near the top right corner of any Delicious page. This is where you'll find any bookmarks that have been sent to you via the *for*:username tag. If you have any new links that you have not yet seen, the link will read as "# *new*" instead of "inbox." Figure 2-51 shows my inbox with one new link.[6]

Settings

You can find a lot of choices within Delicious's settings page. Several of them have been previously discussed in this chapter, so I'll not cover them in much detail here. In all of those cases, the settings screen is just another way to access those same services.

Account

Here you will find options relating to your Delicious account.

- **Edit account info:**
  Here you can supply your first and last name and change the e-mail address associated with your account, as shown in Figure 2-52.
- **Change password:**
  Don't like the password associated with your account? Just supply your current password and then enter your new password twice. Upon clicking the "Save" button, your password will be updated. See Figure 2-53.

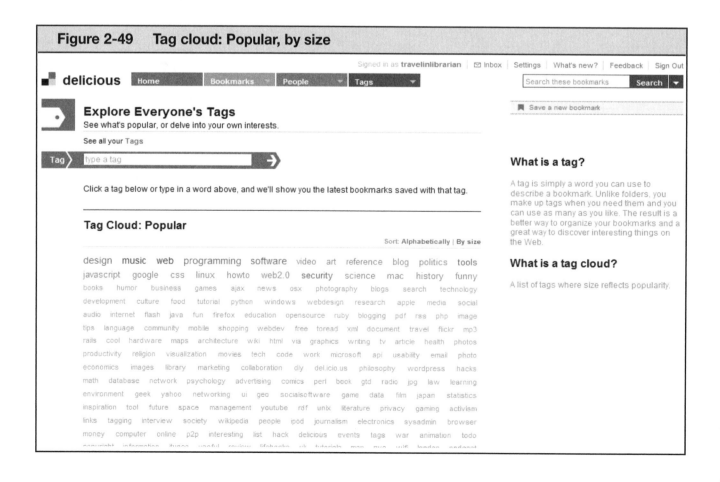

Figure 2-49   Tag cloud: Popular, by size

Figure 2-50 Tag cloud: Popular, alphabetical

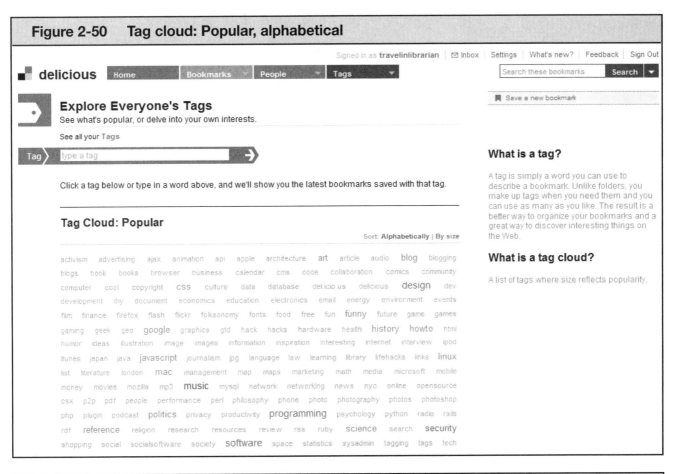

Figure 2-51 My inbox with one new link

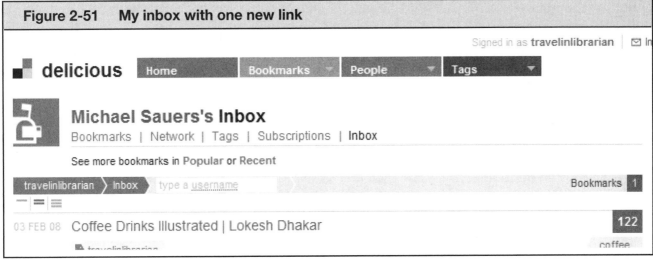

Figure 2-52   Edit account info

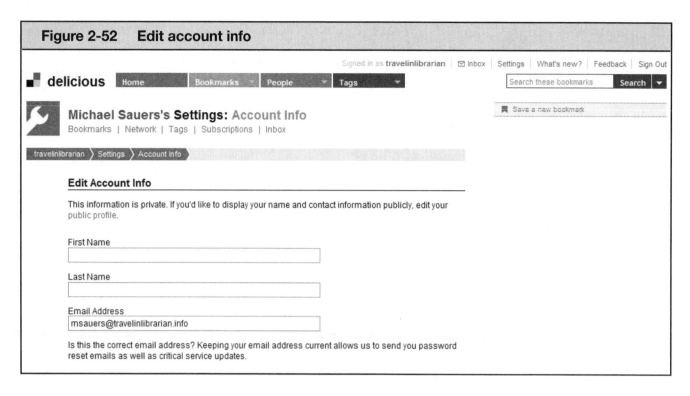

Figure 2-53   Change password

- **Edit public profile:**
  This takes you to the "Edit Public Profile" screen previously discussed.
- **Delete account:**
  Don't want your account anymore or just feel like starting over? Completely remove the account and all of its content here. Just confirm it's what you really want to do, enter your password, and click the "Delete" button. See Figure 2-54.

Bookmarks

Here are options for controlling the bookmarks that are contained within your account.

- **Import/Upload bookmarks:**
  You imported your home bookmarks at the beginning of this chapter, but now you want to import the bookmarks from work. Here's how you can get back to the page you need to do just that.
- **Export/Backup bookmarks:**
  Are you the type of person who doesn't trust online services not to lose all of your hard work? Maybe you've got a friend who would like a copy of all of your wonderful bookmarks. Choose this option and save a copy of your Delicious bookmarks to a file that can later be imported into a traditional browser-based bookmark file. If you'd like, the

backup file can also include your tags and your notes. Just check one or both, as shown in Figure 2-55.

- **RSS Feeds Rights/License:**
  Since users are able to subscribe to your bookmarks via an RSS feed, Delicious considers this to be "publishing" your bookmarks. As a result, Delicious gives you the ability here to assign a traditional copyright, all rights reserved license, or one of six different Creative Commons licenses that allow you to specify how you're willing to let others use your content—for example, whether you will allow commercial or noncommercial use of your bookmarks or declare that your work is in the public domain. (Detailed information about Creative Commons licenses can be found at http://creativecommons.org/.) Just make your choice from the drop-down list and click the "Save" button. See Figure 2-56.
- **Facebook Application:**
  If you have a Facebook account, you can install the Delicious application into your Facebook account. By doing this, you can have the newly posted bookmarks in your Delicious account appear automatically in your Facebook account. This page is shown in Figure 2-57.

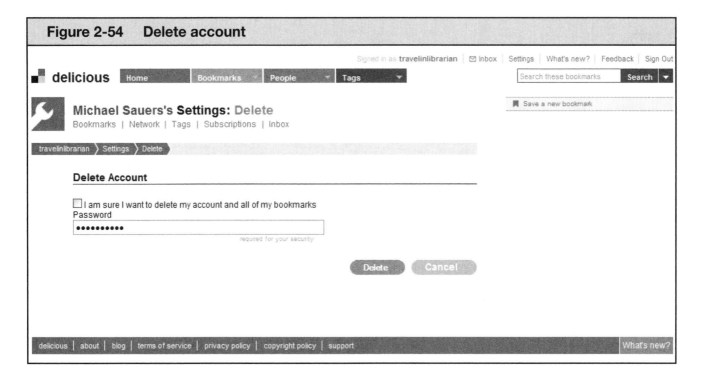

Figure 2-54 Delete account

Figure 2-55   Export/backup bookmarks

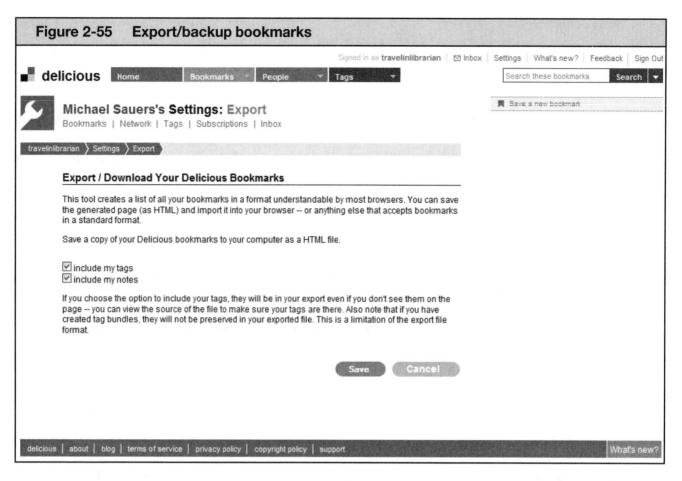

Figure 2-56   Rights/license

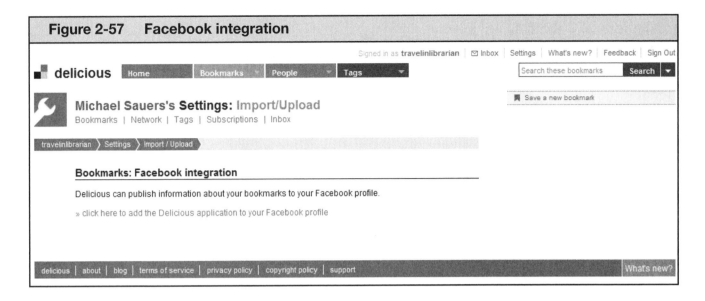

Figure 2-57   Facebook integration

People

Here are options for how your account interacts with the networking features of Delicious.

- **Edit Network:**
  This link will take you to the previously discussed "Manage Network" page.
- **Edit Network Bundles:**
  Here you can create bundles of network contacts similar to the way in which you can create tag bundles. For example, you could create bundles for coworkers, friends, and people you otherwise don't know in the real world. See Figure 2-58.

- **Set Network Privacy:**
  This screen, as seen in Figure 2-59, gives you the option to make your network contacts private. By doing so, other Delicious users will not be able to see your contacts.

Tags

Here are options for how to work with the tags in your account.

- **Rename Tags:**
  This is another way to reach the previously discussed "Rename Tags" screen.

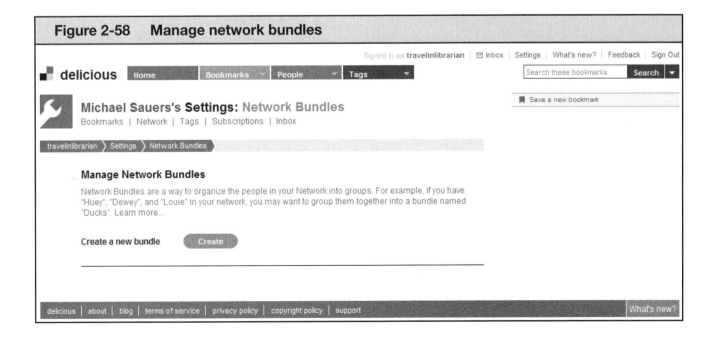

Figure 2-58   Manage network bundles

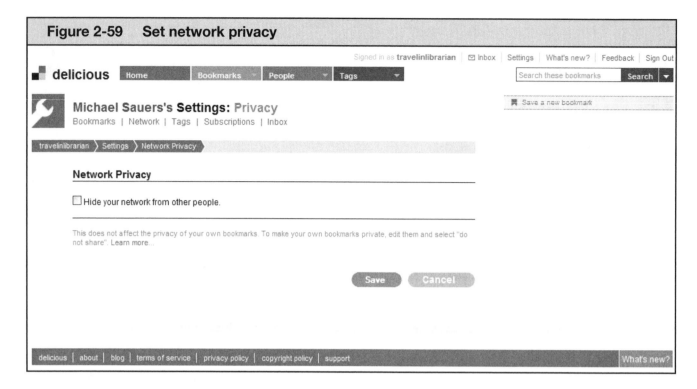

Figure 2-59   Set network privacy

- **Delete Tags:**
  This is another way to reach the previously discussed "Delete Tags" screen.
- **Edit Tag Bundles:**
  This is another way to reach the previously discussed "Manage Tag Bundles" screen.
- **Edit Tag Descriptions:**
  This is another way to change text descriptions of your tags.
- **Edit Subscriptions:**
  This is another way to reach the previously discussed edit subscriptions interface.
- **Edit Subscription Bundles:**
  This is another way to reach the previously discussed subscription bundles interface.

Blogging

Last, here is where you have the ability to integrate your Delicious account with your blog.

- **Network badges:**
  This option allows you to obtain and insert a graphic into your Web site that your readers can click on to automatically add a bookmark to your site into their Delicious account.
- **Link rolls:**
  This option allows you to create some HTML code

that, when inserted into your Web site, will automatically display a list of bookmarks that you've recently added to your Delicious account.

- **Tag rolls:**
  This option will allow you to create some HTML code that, when inserted into your Web site, will display a list of tags that you use in your Delicious account. Readers of your site can then click on those tags and be presented with the matching public page in your Delicious account.
- **Blog posting:**
  At the time of this writing, this was still listed as an "experimental" feature. The idea is that you can set up a "job" to automatically create a daily blog post that contains the new bookmarks that have been added to your Delicious account for that day.[7] The blog posting option is shown in Figure 2-60.

Searching Delicious

Even though the main point of this chapter was to show how you can use Delicious to organize your online resources, this is a book about searching. So, I can't end this chapter without pointing out that Delicious is completely searchable. What better way to look for great resources on a topic than to see what sites have been bookmarked by others.

The actual searching of Delicious couldn't be

Figure 2-60   Blog posting

Just find the search box in the upper right corner of any page (as shown in Figure 2-61), enter your search term(s), choose the type of search you wish to perform from the drop-down list associated with the search button ("My bookmarks," "My Network's bookmarks," or "Everyone's bookmarks," the default), and click the "Search" button.

The search results page will be similar to your bookmarks page, as shown in Figure 2-62. Each result presented will include a hyperlink to the page being bookmarked, the number of users who have bookmarked it, the username of the person who first saved it in Delicious, and its associated tags.

What you'll also see here is a "SAVE" link to the right of each result. This link actually appears whenever you see a bookmark in Delicious that is not already in your account. Clicking this link will open the "Save a new bookmark" interface, allowing you to easily add the bookmark to your account.

The last thing I'll note is that despite having performed my search against everyone's bookmarks, the first three results are from my account. I find this

very useful, especially when you have thousands of bookmarks. Many times I've found myself searching Delicious for information only to find that I already had the perfect resource in my account but had simply forgotten about it.

LIBRARIES USING DELICIOUS

Following is a brief sampling of libraries that are using Delicious actively.[8] These are great resources if you're looking for ideas about how to implement Delicious in your library or for ways to tag your resources. The name of the library and its location are listed, followed by the library's Delicious username.

* Bibliothèques de l'Université Paris-Sorbonne (Paris-IV): bibliparis4
* The College of New Jersey (Ewing, NJ): tcnjml
* Holdrege Public Library (Holdrege, NE): Holdrege Library
* La Grange Park Public Library (La Grange Park, IL): LaGrangeParkLibrary

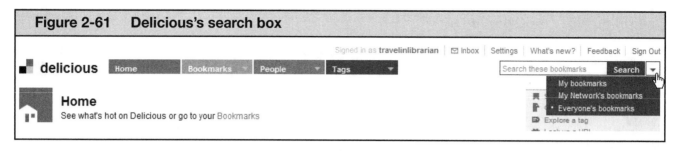

Figure 2-61   Delicious's search box

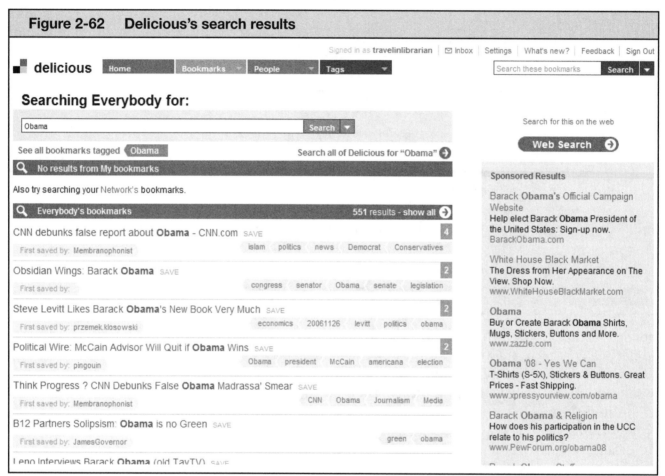

Figure 2-62   Delicious's search results

- Lansing Public Library (Lansing, IL): lansing publiclibrary
- Massachusetts Institute of Technology (Cambridge, MA): virtualref
- Maui Community College Library (Kahului, HI): mauicclibrary
- Nashville Public Library (Nashville, TN): nashpubya
- Nebraska Library Commission (Lincoln, NE): NLC_Reference

- OCLC list of the top 1000 titles: oclc2005top1000
- The Republican Valley Library System (Hastings, NE): rvls
- San Mateo Public Library (San Mateo, CA): SanMateoLibrary
- Seldovia Public Library (Seldovia, AK): seldovia.library
- Thomas Ford Memorial Library (Western Springs, IL): thomasford
- Thunder Bay Public Library (Thunder Bay, Ontario, Canada): TBPL

CONCLUSION

Searching is going to do you only so much good if you don't have a way to organize the answers and, more important, the resources you discover that may help you answer questions in the future. Today, social bookmarking services such as Delicious serve this need perfectly, giving you the ability to access your bookmarks from any computer and share them with your users through the benefits of the features of the social Web. Now that we've got a great way to organize our resources and easily share them with our users, let's move on and take a look at the state of the big players in Web search today.

EXERCISES

1. Create a Delicious account for yourself.
2. Install the browser buttons.
3. Import your browser's bookmarks into your Delicious account. Be sure to have the system add some tags for you.
4. Add some of your own tags to your newly imported bookmarks. If you have many bookmarks, start by adding tags to those you use the most often so they'll be the easiest to find.
5. Add a few new bookmarks to your account.
6. Find a colleague with a Delicious account and add him or her to your network. Feel free to use me for this step.
7. Send the link to one of your favorite sites to your new Delicious friend.

NOTES

1. I always love sharing the story of a librarian whom I met early in my training career. She was so familiar with the Dewey Decimal Classification (DDC) system that she used it to organize her bookmarks. She created ten top-level folders marked 000–900 and then ten subfolders under each one labeled 00–90. Whenever she added a bookmark, she placed it into the correct DDC folder.
2. Delicious, "About Delicious," http://www.delicious.com/about/.
3. Browser bookmarks allowed you to add additional searchable keywords though the description field, but I never met a single user who took advantage of this "feature." My guess is that since this text wasn't displayed in the bookmark list itself but had to be specifically accessed through several steps by the user, many users did not even know this option was available. Since Delicious displays this content up front, I find it much more useful and use it much more regularly.
4. The "*new* Firefox bookmarks extension" choice offers Firefox users the ability to completely replace their browser's bookmark interface with one that completely integrates with their Delicious account. I have played with this and still find it somewhat difficult to use. Additionally, I have yet to meet anyone else who has successfully implemented this feature. I encourage you to experiment, but I will not be covering it in any more detail. (Note that you can uninstall it and get all of your old bookmarks back should you decide you don't like it.)
5. You can always send another user a bookmark even if they aren't in your network by adding the tag *for*:username. This can be done either during the addition of a new bookmark or by editing an existing bookmark and adding the appropriate tag.
6. You may notice that the user identified as the sender of this link was me. Since I was using the preview version of Delicious I did not know any other users personally and therefore did not have anyone to ask to send me a link or two.
7. Just a heads-up, some blog readers do not like such posts (http://babyboomerlibrarian.blogspot.com/2007/12/blog-posts-with-no-content.html), while others, myself included, find them useful (http://www.travelinlibrarian.info/2007/12/what-is-content.html). Please keep your audience in mind if you decide to create such posts.
8. A much longer list can be found at http://angelacw.wordpress.com/2007/06/04/delicious-libraries/.

Chapter 3

Popular Search Engines

INTRODUCTION

This chapter presents an overview of the three most widely used search engines available today. Since these services are so extensive and could have entire books dedicated to them, I will cover only the topics that are relevant and pertinent to *Searching 2.0*, focusing on their major features to show how you can use them in your daily reference work.

I call each of these "major search engines" because their central purpose is to search the whole Web—as much as they can possibly index anyway. Most of them also have ways to search subsections of the Web or of certain types of material. For each of these services, I do not cover all of the available features here. In some cases, I cover topics in later chapters, such as media and local searching in Chapters 5 and 6, respectively. In other cases, since some features may not be as useful at the reference desk, I focus on only the most useful features of these services.

Many major search engines are available today, such as the old-timers like AltaVista[1], Lycos[2], and Ask[3] (formerly Ask Jeeves), along with newer contenders such as Clusty.[4] However, I decided to focus on Google, Microsoft's Live Search, and Yahoo! Search for several reasons. First, most of these are already familiar to my students. Second, despite the familiarity, I've found that a large proportion of students have never ventured past the search box on the homepage of each and are therefore unfamiliar with the advanced features of these services. Third, having watched the searching habits of public library patrons for the past two years, I've noticed that these are the three most commonly used search engines of

the "typical" patron.[5] With this in mind, let's begin with Google.

GOOGLE

Basic Search

Nearly every Internet user today is familiar with the Google homepage. But, just as a reminder, here it is again in Figure 3-1.

By default, any search performed from this page will search Google's database of Web content. From here you can also click on links to search various other Google databases, such as Images, Groups (the Usenet news archive), News, Froogle (to search for products you wish to purchase online), and Google Maps. Others are available through the "more" link, which I cover later in this chapter, along with the links for "Advanced Search," "Preferences," and "Language Tools." As of early 2006, Google also offers users the ability to customize their Google homepage through the "iGoogle" and "Sign in" links in the upper right corner of the page.

Basic searches are performed by entering your search terms, and any operators as needed, into the search box and clicking on one of the two available buttons. Those buttons are "Google Search" and "I'm Feeling Lucky." Clicking on the "Google Search" button, which can also be activated by pressing your Enter key while your cursor is in the search box, will perform your search and present you with a list of results. Clicking on "I'm Feeling Lucky" will perform your search, but instead of presenting you with a list of results, it will take you right to the page

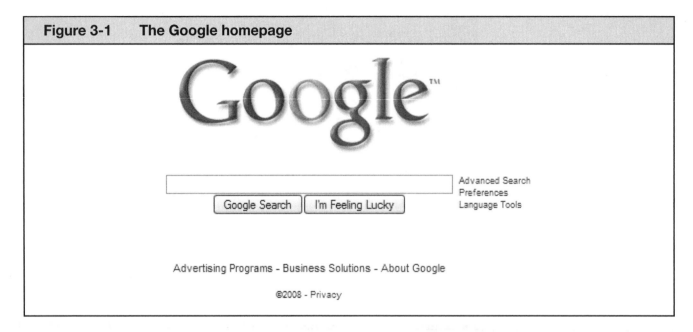

Figure 3-1   The Google homepage

that was the first result. This is as if you had clicked on Google Search, retrieved your list of results, and clicked on the first result yourself.

The "I'm Feeling Lucky" option works very well when you're pretty sure of where you're going to end up. For example, searching on such terms as *microsoft*, *nike*, or *wikipedia* will retrieve for you www.microsoft.com, www.nike.com, and www.wikipedia.org, respectively. However, if you're not sure of the end result, as with more complex searches, or if you don't want to take the chance of displaying something potentially inappropriate to a patron, the standard "Google Search" option is your better choice.

Advanced Search

Google's basic search simplicity is one of the reasons that Google became so popular so quickly. However, more options are available. The screen you'll get when you click on the "Advanced Search" link is shown in Figure 3-2.

As you can see, the available options are much more extensive on this screen. All of these options are available to you through the basic search, but you need to know the syntax necessary to access them. On this screen, you just fill out the fields you wish to use and click the appropriate search button. I'd also like to point out that what you see in Figure 3-2 is the result of my clicking the "+" to the left of the "Date, usage rights, numeric range, and more" link, about two-thirds down the page. By default, this area

is hidden until you do this. Let's take a look at each of the options.

The blue area at the top of the screen will show the Google syntax version of your search as you build it using this form. The first section of the form is designed to find Web pages that have the following:

- **All these words:**
  This field works as a Boolean "AND." Every word in this field will be considered in the search.
- **This exact wording or phrase:**
  This field is used in place of the standard quotation marks to form a phrase. All words in this field will be considered in the order given.
- **One or more of these words:**
  This field works as a Boolean "OR." Any word in this field will be considered in the search, but only any one word of the list need be considered.

The next section, "But don't show pages that have," will eliminate content:

- **Any of these unwanted words:**
  This field works as a Boolean "NOT" (AND NOT). Words in this field will be explicitly excluded from consideration in the results list.

You may have noticed that my wording was not exactly standard when it came to explaining the four items. Typically when describing a Boolean operator such as "AND" one would say that both words "must

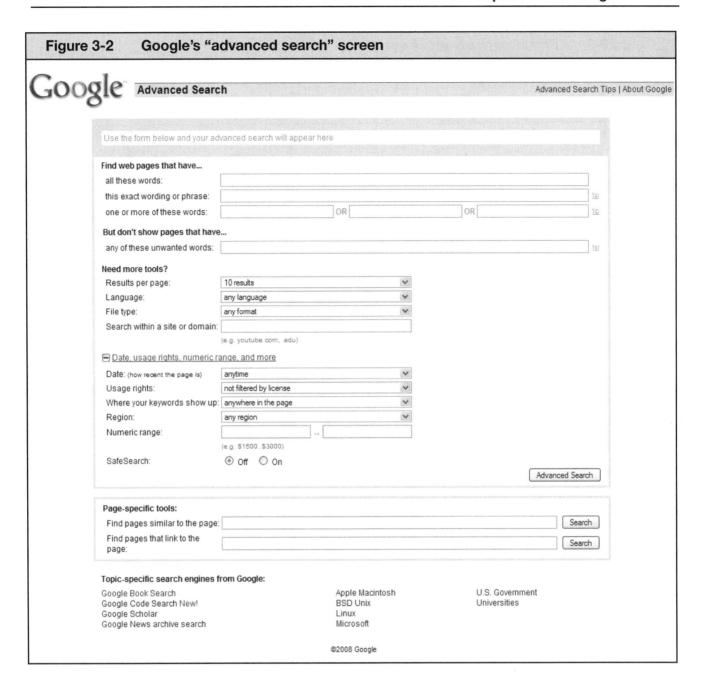

Figure 3-2   Google's "advanced search" screen

appear in the *result*." However, based on how Google's search algorithm works, at times you can require a word to be present but that word will not appear in the result.[6] Therefore, I needed to say that the words "will be *considered in the search*" as opposed to the more standard "must appear" language. For example, take a look at the search I've built in Figure 3-3.

Here's the Boolean equivalent: (*southern AND coast AND england AND "tide table") AND NOT new.* As previously mentioned, Google shows you, near the top of the screen, what you could type into its

basic search to get the same results. In this case, it is *southern coast england "tide table" –new.*

The next section of the form is "Need more tools?". Here you have four more options.

- **Results per page:**
  This field allows you to choose how many results appear on a single page. Any additional results will be displayed on additional pages.

- **Language:**
  This field allows you to limit your results to only

Figure 3-3   An example advanced search

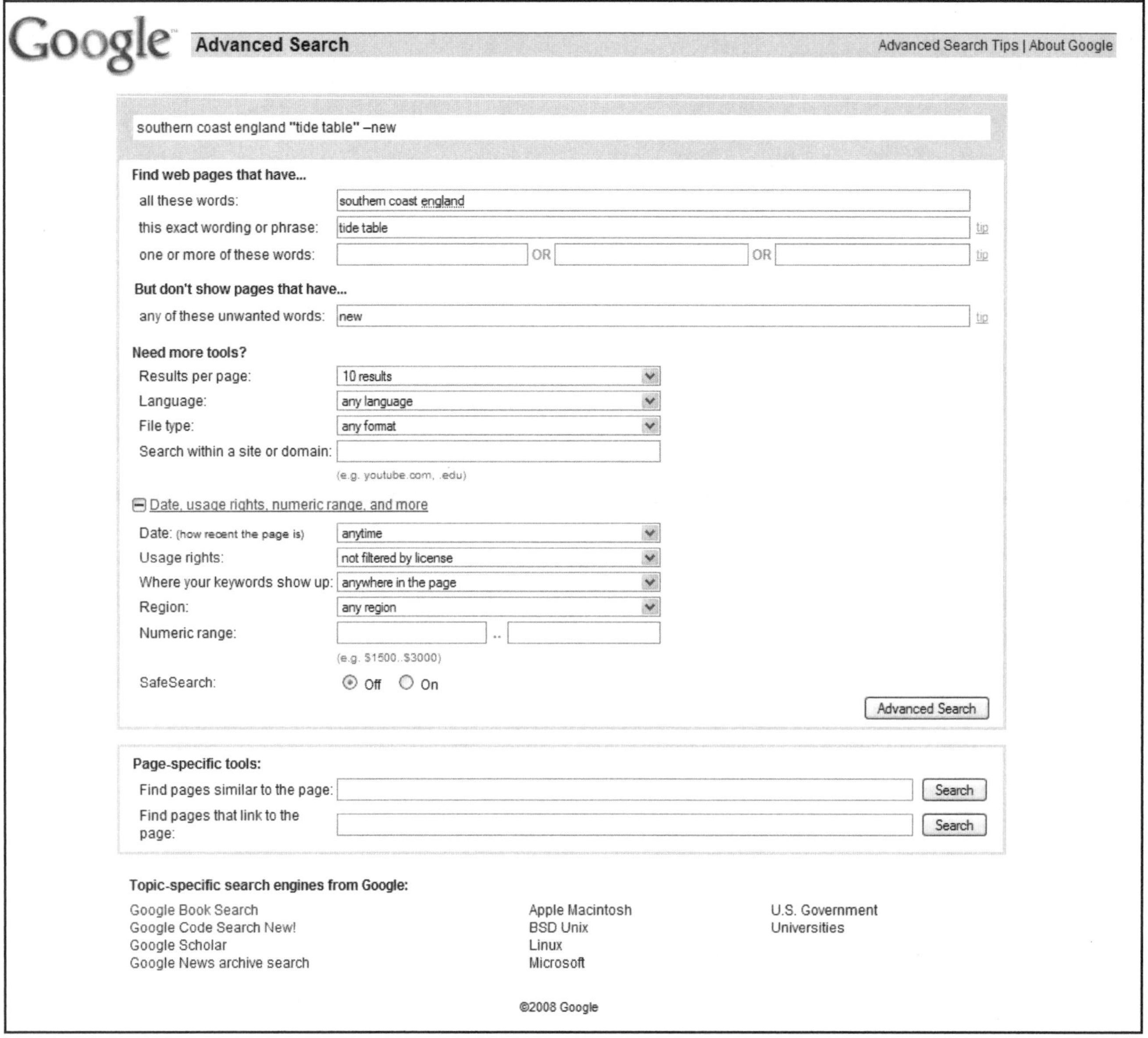

Google™ **Advanced Search**   Advanced Search Tips | About Google

southern coast england "tide table" –new

Find web pages that have...

all these words: southern coast england

this exact wording or phrase: tide table   tip

one or more of these words: OR   OR   tip

But don't show pages that have...

any of these unwanted words: new   tip

Need more tools?

Results per page: 10 results

Language: any language

File type: any format

Search within a site or domain:
                                    (e.g. youtube.com, .edu)

⊟ Date, usage rights, numeric range, and more

Date: (how recent the page is)   anytime

Usage rights: not filtered by license

Where your keywords show up: anywhere in the page

Region: any region

Numeric range: ..
                                    (e.g. $1500..$3000)

SafeSearch: ⊙ Off ○ On

                                                              [Advanced Search]

Page-specific tools:

Find pages similar to the page: [Search]

Find pages that link to the
page: [Search]

Topic-specific search engines from Google:

Google Book Search   Apple Macintosh   U.S. Government
Google Code Search New!   BSD Unix   Universities
Google Scholar   Linux
Google News archive search   Microsoft

©2008 Google

those in a particular language. At the time of this writing, there were more than 30 language choices ranging from Arabic to Turkish. The default is "Any language."

- **File type:**
  This field allows you to limit or exclude results in a particular file format. Available formats are PDF (portable document format), Postscript, Word, Excel, PowerPoint, and RTF (rich text format). For example, if you're looking for a government report, many of them are published in PDF format, so limiting to that format could make finding the report

you're looking for easier by removing all pages with links to it that are not in PDF format.

- **Search within a site or domain:**
  This field allows you to limit your results to a particular domain or top level domain. For example, to retrieve results from only U.S. government sites, enter *.gov*. To retrieve results from only Microsoft, enter *microsoft.com*.

The next section of the form is "Date, usage rights, numeric range, and more." If you haven't already, you'll need to click the "+" to the left to see these options.

- **Date (how recent the page is):**
  This field allows you to limit your results to pages that are from the previous three months, six months, or one year. Please keep in mind that this date is based on the date of the page when last indexed, not the date on the live page as it is today. (See Chapter 8 for more details on how dates and search engines work.)

- **Usage rights:**
  Creative Commons (http://creativecommons.org), a project started by Lawrence Lessig, allows content creators to assign a copyright-like license to their content, controlling attribution, commercial usage, and derivative creation. Once created, this license can be attached to the content, allowing users to know what permissions they do and do not have when it comes to using that content. Google, using the usage rights limiter, allows you to specify which type of content you wish to find based on those licenses. The default choice is "not filtered by license." The four limiters available to you are "free to use or share"; "free to use or share, even commercially"; "free to use, share, or modify"; and "free to use, share, or modify, even commercially." Although this option is very promising, the attachment of Creative Commons licenses is not yet truly common, so be aware that using this limiter repeatedly may quickly limit you to no results.

- **Where your keywords show up:**
  As mentioned earlier, Google considers many locations when looking for your search terms, including ones that are not even part of the documents returned as results. This field allows you to specify where you would like your terms to appear. These options are "anywhere in the page," "in the title of the page," "in the text of the page," "in the URL of the page," and "in links to the page."

- **Region:**
  Here you'll find a list of countries that Google can limit your results to, which is pretty much all of them, actually. Results in most cases will be from pages whose domain names contain the two-letter country code of the country you selected.

- **Numeric range:**
  This option is designed for searches typically involving numbers, such as lengths or currency. For example, if you're looking for reviews of digital cameras costing between $200 and $300, you could enter those values here.

- **SafeSearch:**
  SafeSearch is Google's technology for filtering out potentially offensive content. By default, this content is not filtered. You must select "on" to turn on that filter. Please be aware that no filter is perfect. Even Google says that "[w]e do our best to keep SafeSearch as up-to-date and comprehensive as possible, but inappropriate sites will sometimes slip through the cracks."[7]

After setting any or all of these limiters, just click the "Advanced Search" button at the bottom right of the page to execute your search.

Page-Specific Search

This section of the Google Advanced Search page has two additional search types, both of which work independently of each other and anything else you may do on this page. The first is a "find pages similar" search and the second is a "find pages that link" search.

SIMILAR SEARCH

To perform a "similar" search, first find the URL of the type of page you're seeking. For example, let's say I'm looking for the Web sites of other libraries in my area. I know that the URL for my home library is www.nlc.state.ne.us, so I enter that URL into the "similar" search box, click the search button off to the right, and receive the results shown in Figure 3-4.

As you can see from the results, I've been presented with a list of other libraries and library-like institutions in Nebraska and surrounding states. The list is not geographically limited (discussed in Chapter 6), but generally the farther down the list we go, the farther out into the rest of the state the libraries are located.

LINKS SEARCH

The "links" search gives you a list of results to pages

Figure 3-4   The results of a similar search for "http://www.nlc.state.ne.us/"

Web   Images   Maps   News   Shopping   Gmail   more ▼   Sign in

Google   related:http://www.nlc.state.ne.us/ | Search | Advanced Search
                                                                    Preferences

Web   Results **1 - 10** of about 27 similar to **http://www.nlc.state.ne.us/**. (0.25 seconds)

Nebraska State Historical Society Home Page
Your comments and suggestions about the website are appreciated and may be sent
directly to web@nebraskahistory.org. Nebraska State Historical Society ...
www.nebraskahistory.org/ - 5k - Cached - Similar pages

Nebraska Library Association
Internet Site Coordinator Job Announcement. The Executive Committee of NLA
continues to accept resumes for the purpose of future staffing of NLA's Internet ...
www.nebraskalibraries.org/ - 31k - Cached - Similar pages

Nebraska Department of Education
Dedicated to serving Nebraska schools with information and resources.
www.nde.state.ne.us/ - 14k - Cached - Similar pages

Nebraska Legislature - HOME
Current Activity The 100th Legislature, Second Session adjourned sine die on Thursday,
April 17, 2008. The 101st Legislature, First Session is scheduled to ...
www.unicam.state.ne.us/ - 27k - Cached - Similar pages

Nebraska Department of Health and Human Services
Offers assistance with Medicaid, vaccinations, medical licensing, disability support, child
protection, and communicable diseases.
www.hhs.state.ne.us/ - 15k - Cached - Similar pages

Nebraska Game and Parks Commission Homepage
Includes information on permits, seasons, hunter education and harvest outlook.
www.ngpc.state.ne.us/ - 14k - Cached - Similar pages

Texas State Library and Archives Commission (TSLAC) Home Page
TSLAC Star, Texas State Library & Archives Commission. Agency Information · Areas of
General Interest · Our Services to Librarians · Our Services to ...
www.tsl.state.tx.us/ - 25k - Cached - Similar pages

Nebraska Secretary of State - John A. Gale
Nebraska Secretary of State. - John A. Gale. Nebraska Secretary of State - John A. Gale.
Secretary of State Nebraska.gov ...
www.sos.state.ne.us/ - 36k - Cached - Similar pages

UNL | Libraries
Research affiliation: Association of Research Libraries.
iris.unl.edu/ - 34k - Cached - Similar pages

ISL: Home
Includes tour, information about the board, mission, history, reference materials, and
genealogical resources.
www.statelib.lib.in.us/ - 21k - Cached - Similar pages

Gooogle ▶
1 2 3   **Next**

related:http://www.nlc.state.ne.us/ | Search |

Language Tools | Search Tips | Dissatisfied? Help us improve | Try Google Experimental

Google Home - Advertising Programs - Business Solutions - Privacy - About Google

linked to the URL that you entered. For example, if I'd like to know what Web sites link back to mine, I would enter *http://www.travelinlibrarian.info/* into the "links" search field and click the search button to the right of that field. Figure 3-5 shows my results.

Be aware that the "links" search will search only for pages that link to the *exact* URL that you entered. Thus, for the previous example, I will get results that link only to my homepage but not to any other page on my Web site. To see links to any other page on my site, I would have to re-search using a new URL.

Beyond the advanced search features and additional database searches that Google makes available, Google provides many built-in shortcuts on its homepage. Here are a few of the more useful ones for the reference desk:[8]

- **Google knows math:**
  Just type in a mathematical formula or measurement conversion and you'll get your answer, as shown in Figure 3-6.
- **Google knows currency:**
  Need a quick currency conversion? Just type in the amount and currency, then *in,* then the new currency, as shown in Figure 3-7.
- **Google knows definitions:**
  Just type *define* followed by the word you want defined, as shown in Figure 3-8.
- **Google knows movies:**
  Can't remember the name of a film but you remember an actor and/or some plot points? Just start your search with *movie:* and you should get the results you're looking for, as shown in Figure 3-9.
- **Google knows phone numbers:**
  There are several ways to perform this search, mostly depending on how much information you already have, but the simplest way is to search *lastname, city, state.* Depending on whether you're searching for residential, business, or either, you'll need to start your search with *rphonebook:, bphonebook:,* or *phonebook:,* respectively. For an example, see Figure 3-10.
- **Google knows numbers:**
  Google can automatically recognize several types of numbers. These include UPS (United Parcel Service), FedEx, and USPS (United States Postal Service) tracking numbers; VINs (vehicle identification numbers), UPCs (Universal Product Codes), and FAA (Federal Aviation Administration) airplane registration numbers. Just type any of these into Google to get a link to the results you need. For an example, see Figure 3-11.
- **Google knows stocks:**
  Just type in the ticker symbol for the latest stock information. For an example, see Figure 3-12.
- **Google knows weather:**
  Just start your search with *weather,* followed by *city, state* or *zip code* to receive the current and forecasted weather for that area. For an example, see Figure 3-13.

Language Tools

Figure 3-14 shows you Google's Language Tools, which can be reached via the "Language Tools" link to the right of the search box on the Google homepage (or by going to www.google.com/language_tools). This page gives you the ability to do more specific searches based on language, perform online translations, change Google's interface language, and view versions of Google specific to a geographic region.

- **Search across languages:**
  This section of the page allows you to perform a search but limits the results to a particular language and/or specific country. For example, if you are looking only for pages in French, set the "Search pages written in" field to French. However, if you want only pages in French from France (as opposed to Quebec, for example), then you would also set the "Search pages located in" field to France. Then fill in the "Search for" field with your search terms and click the "Translate and Search" button. A good practice is to enter search terms in the same language as the results you're seeking. For example, searching on the term *love* might not retrieve any French results, but using *amour* will work much better, as shown in Figure 3-15.
- **Translate text:**
  This area includes two tools for performing translations. In the first larger box, you can type or paste in text in one language and instruct Google to translate it into another,[9] as shown in Figure 3-15. Additionally, you can have Google translate an

Figure 3-5   The results of a links search for "http://www.travelinlibrarian.info/"

Google [link:http://www.travelinlibrarian.info/] [Search] Advanced Search
                                                                Preferences

Web   Results **1 - 10** of about 645 linking to **http://www.travelinlibrarian.info/**. (**0.16** seconds)

Thingology (LibraryThing's ideas blog): December 2006
Language: English [others]. Albanian · Basque · Bulgarian · Catalan · Croatian · Czech ·
Danish · Dutch · English · Estonian · French · Finnish · German ...
www.librarything.com/thingology/2006_12_01_archive.php - 57k -
Cached - Similar pages

Baby Boomer Librarian: 2006-05-28
Random thoughts and ideas of a babyboomer librarian in the early years of the 21st
century. My name is Bill Drew. Inspired by innovation, change and ...
babyboomerlibrarian.blogspot.com/2006_05_28_archive.html - 553k -
Cached - Similar pages

2008 March « Impromptu Librarian
03.25.08. Build your Wild Self. Posted in Customer Service, Libraries and Librarianship,
Me and mine at by Mary Beth Sancomb-Moran ...
impromptu.wordpress.com/2008/03/ - 39k - Cached - Similar pages

InfoSciPhi Linkblog - Renegade Librarian
Comments:. Comment from: M. Johnson [Visitor] · http://bluerectangle.com/.
BlueRectangle.com offers some very interesting reviews of books... all watchable ...
infosciphi.info/index.php?blog=4&title=renegade_librarian&more=1&c=1&tb=1&pb=1 -
38k - Cached - Similar pages

CUESD InfoZone: December 2005
Thursday, December 15, 2005. Odds and Ends. Entries are posted to the CUESD
InfoZone blog on the days that Mike Garofalo works in his office (Maywood School ...
cuesiz.blogspot.com/2005_12_01_archive.html - 24k - Cached - Similar pages

Social Networking : RSS info via LibWorm - [Translate this page]
Read the latest items and get the RSS feed on: social,networking,social,networks,social,network.
Librarian news from over 1500 librarian sources is provided ...
www.libworm.com/rss/
search.php?qu=%22social+networking%22+%22social+networks%22+%22social+network%22&...
- 91k - Cached - Similar pages

2008 February 03 « Panorama of the Mountains
3 February 2008. Ireland/Britain 1998 day 15: Dublin & heading to The North. Tuesday
morning, 3 February 1998, I wandered around Dublin visiting the famous ...
othemts.wordpress.com/2008/02/03/ - 62k - Cached - Similar pages

The 'M' Word - Marketing Libraries: Branding war between J&J and ...
Talk about brand identity... J&J is suing the Red Cross over the, what else? The Red
Cross. Great article in the NY Times... read ...
themwordblog.blogspot.com/2007/08/branding-war-between-j-and-red-cross.html - 74k
- Cached - Similar pages

The Travelin' Librarian
"You Two! We're at the end of the universe, eh. Right at the edge of knowledge itself. And
you're busy... blogging!" — The Doctor, Utopia ...
www.travelinlibrarian.info/2003/07/gutenberg-bible-onlineever-wanted-peek.html - 13k -
Cached - Similar pages

LIScareer News: Feb 2008 LIScareer Articles
Updates about new LIScareer.com articles and website enhancements. Occasional
news about books and other information relating to library and information ...
liscareer.blogspot.com/2008/02/feb-2008-liscareer-articles.html - 17k -
Cached - Similar pages

Gooooooooooogle ▶
1 2 3 4 5 6 7 8 9 10   **Next**

[link:http://www.travelinlibrarian.info/] [Search]

Language Tools | Search Tips | Dissatisfied? Help us improve | Try Google Experimental

Google Home - Advertising Programs - Business Solutions - Privacy - About Google

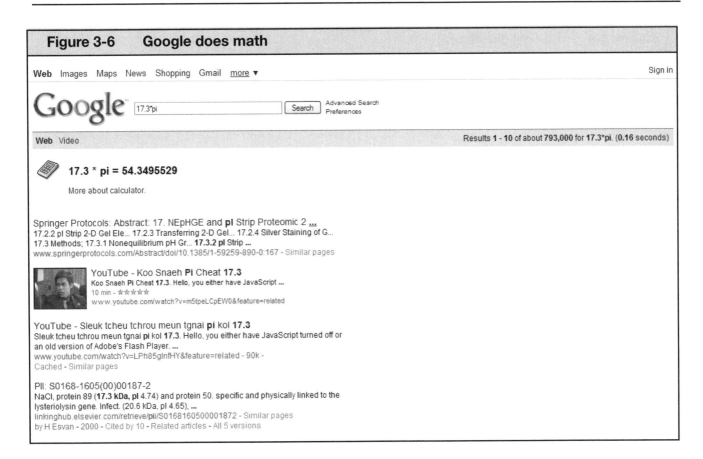

Figure 3-6   Google does math

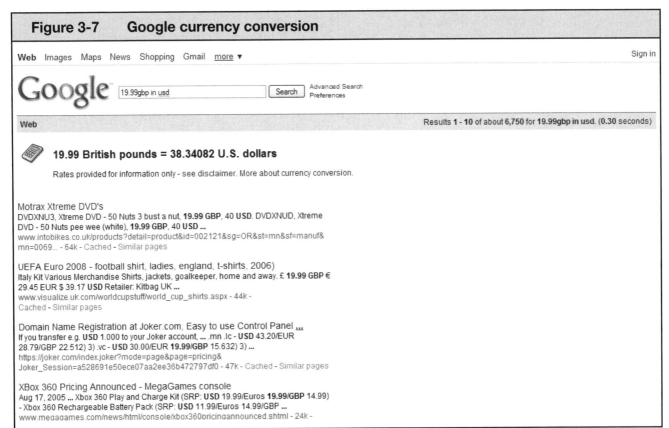

Figure 3-7   Google currency conversion

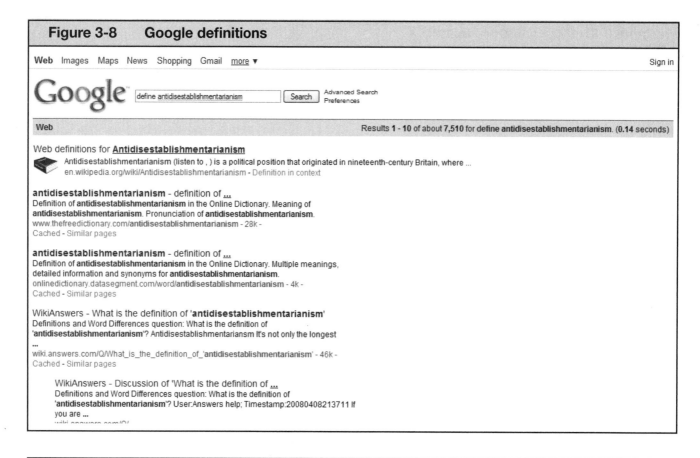

Figure 3-8   Google definitions

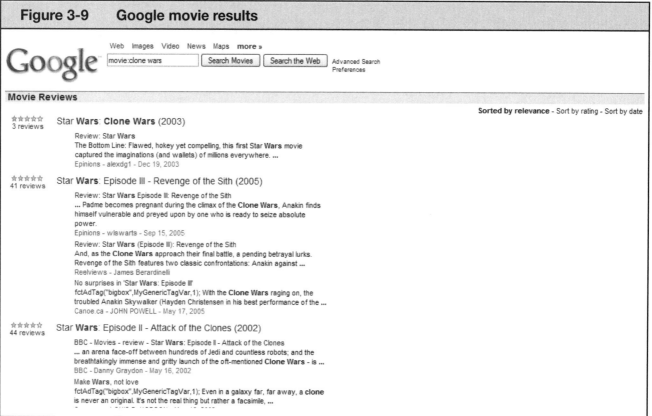

Figure 3-9   Google movie results

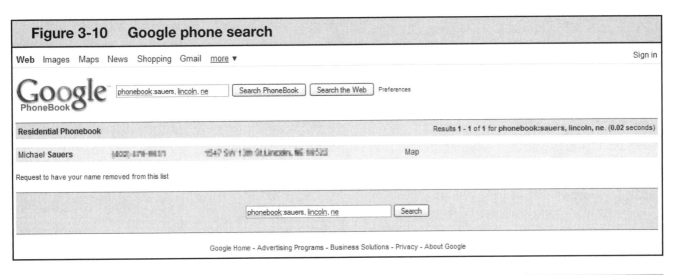

Figure 3-10   Google phone search

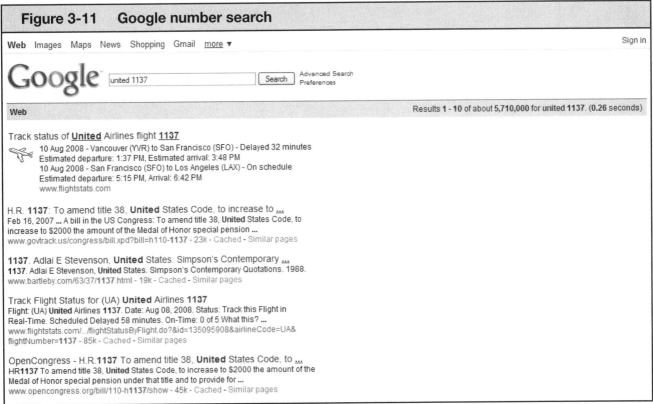

Figure 3-11   Google number search

entire Web page by entering the URL and selecting the appropriate translation (see Figure 3-16).

- **Use the Google interface in your language:**

  Currently, Google's interface is available in 118 different languages, ranging from Afrikaans to Zulu.[10] Clicking on a language in this list will take you to the version of Google in that language. This setting is not permanent (but can be done in the Preferences area, discussed later in this chapter),

and you will always have a "Google in English" link in all of the other languages. It is important to note that choosing a different interface language does not affect the results, just Google's words.

- **Visit Google's site in your local domain:**

  Google also has 165 different country/region-specific versions, ranging from Andorra to Zambia. Choosing one of these versions will both change the interface language to the one appropriate for

(continued on p. 72)

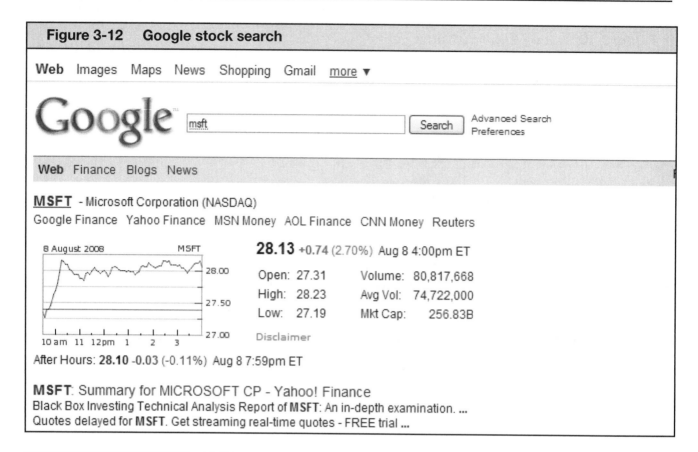

Figure 3-12   Google stock search

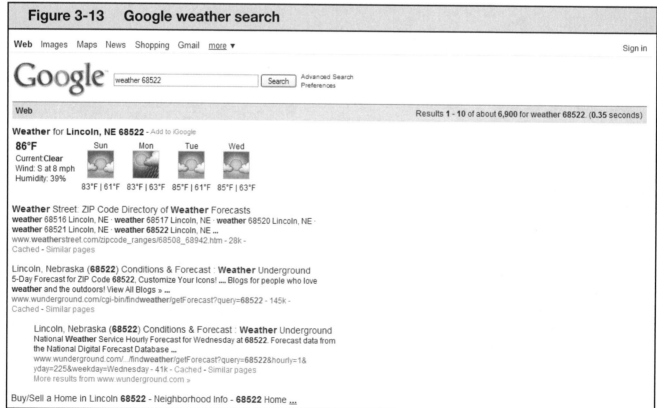

Figure 3-13   Google weather search

Figure 3-14   Google's language tools

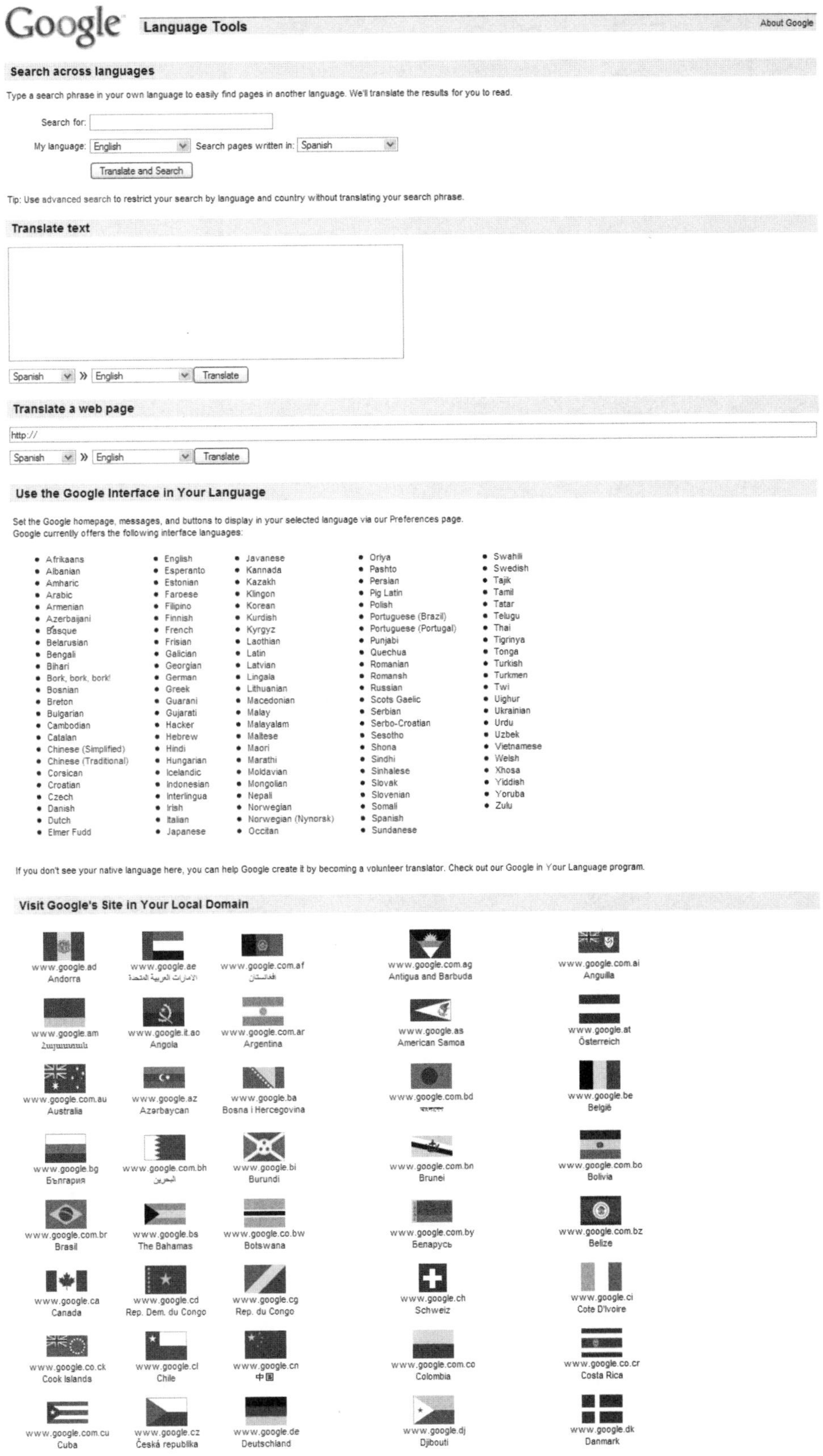

Google **Language Tools**   About Google

Search across languages

Type a search phrase in your own language to easily find pages in another language. We'll translate the results for you to read.

Search for: [   ]

My language: [English ▼]   Search pages written in: [Spanish ▼]

[Translate and Search]

Tip: Use advanced search to restrict your search by language and country without translating your search phrase.

Translate text

[   ]

[Spanish ▼] » [English ▼] [Translate]

Translate a web page

[http://   ]

[Spanish ▼] » [English ▼] [Translate]

Use the Google Interface in Your Language

Set the Google homepage, messages, and buttons to display in your selected language via our Preferences page.
Google currently offers the following interface languages:

- Afrikaans
- Albanian
- Amharic
- Arabic
- Armenian
- Azerbaijani
- Basque
- Belarusian
- Bengali
- Bihari
- Bork, bork, bork!
- Bosnian
- Breton
- Bulgarian
- Cambodian
- Catalan
- Chinese (Simplified)
- Chinese (Traditional)
- Corsican
- Croatian
- Czech
- Danish
- Dutch
- Elmer Fudd

- English
- Esperanto
- Estonian
- Faroese
- Filipino
- Finnish
- French
- Frisian
- Galician
- Georgian
- German
- Greek
- Guarani
- Gujarati
- Hacker
- Hebrew
- Hindi
- Hungarian
- Icelandic
- Indonesian
- Interlingua
- Irish
- Italian
- Japanese

- Javanese
- Kannada
- Kazakh
- Klingon
- Korean
- Kurdish
- Kyrgyz
- Laothian
- Latin
- Latvian
- Lingala
- Lithuanian
- Macedonian
- Malay
- Malayalam
- Maltese
- Maori
- Marathi
- Moldavian
- Mongolian
- Nepali
- Norwegian
- Norwegian (Nynorsk)
- Occitan

- Oriya
- Pashto
- Persian
- Pig Latin
- Polish
- Portuguese (Brazil)
- Portuguese (Portugal)
- Punjabi
- Quechua
- Romanian
- Romansh
- Russian
- Scots Gaelic
- Serbian
- Serbo-Croatian
- Sesotho
- Shona
- Sindhi
- Sinhalese
- Slovak
- Slovenian
- Somali
- Spanish
- Sundanese

- Swahili
- Swedish
- Tajik
- Tamil
- Tatar
- Telugu
- Thai
- Tigrinya
- Tonga
- Turkish
- Turkmen
- Twi
- Uighur
- Ukrainian
- Urdu
- Uzbek
- Vietnamese
- Welsh
- Xhosa
- Yiddish
- Yoruba
- Zulu

If you don't see your native language here, you can help Google create it by becoming a volunteer translator. Check out our Google in Your Language program.

Visit Google's Site in Your Local Domain

www.google.ad Andorra	www.google.ae الامارات العربية المتحدة	www.google.com.af افغانستان	www.google.com.ag Antigua and Barbuda	www.google.com.ai Anguilla
www.google.am Հայաստան	www.google.it.ao Angola	www.google.com.ar Argentina	www.google.as American Samoa	www.google.at Österreich
www.google.com.au Australia	www.google.az Azərbaycan	www.google.ba Bosna i Hercegovina	www.google.com.bd বাংলাদেশ	www.google.be België
www.google.bg България	www.google.com.bh البحرين	www.google.bi Burundi	www.google.com.bn Brunei	www.google.com.bo Bolivia
www.google.com.br Brasil	www.google.bs The Bahamas	www.google.co.bw Botswana	www.google.com.by Беларусь	www.google.com.bz Belize
www.google.ca Canada	www.google.cd Rep. Dem. du Congo	www.google.cg Rep. du Congo	www.google.ch Schweiz	www.google.ci Cote D'Ivoire
www.google.co.ck Cook Islands	www.google.cl Chile	www.google.cn 中国	www.google.com.co Colombia	www.google.co.cr Costa Rica
www.google.com.cu Cuba	www.google.cz Česká republika	www.google.de Deutschland	www.google.dj Djibouti	www.google.dk Danmark

Figure 3-14   Google's language tools *(Continued)*

©2008 Google

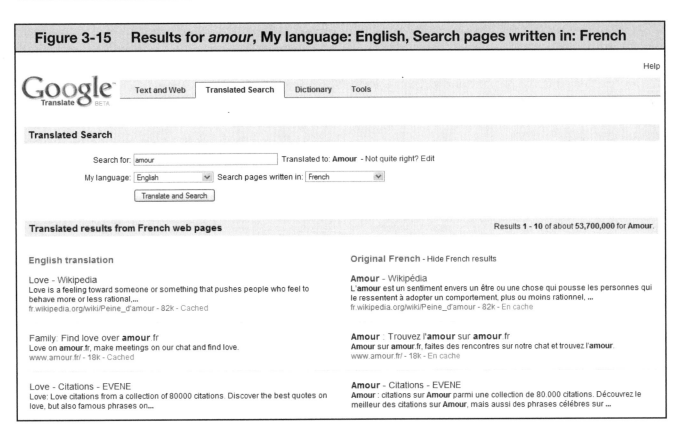

Figure 3-15   Results for *amour*, My language: English, Search pages written in: French

Figure 3-16   Using Google to translate a Web page

that country/region *and* limit the results of any search to resources from that country/region. As with the interface language section of this page, this setting is not permanent and can be easily changed back.

Google Settings

The "Preferences" link will take you to the Google Preferences page. Changing any of these settings means you are changing them indefinitely for the computer you are using. So, if you are on a computer

that is used by more than one person, you may want to consider your changes carefully. By signing in to Google, you can have these settings affect your own account as opposed to the particular computer. To reinstate your customized settings, just log in to your Google account.

As shown in Figure 3-17, six options are available to you in the Preferences area. These are "Interface Language," "Search Language," "SafeSearch Filtering," "Number of Results," "Results Window," and "Query Suggestions." To finalize any changes you

Figure 3-17   Google's preferences

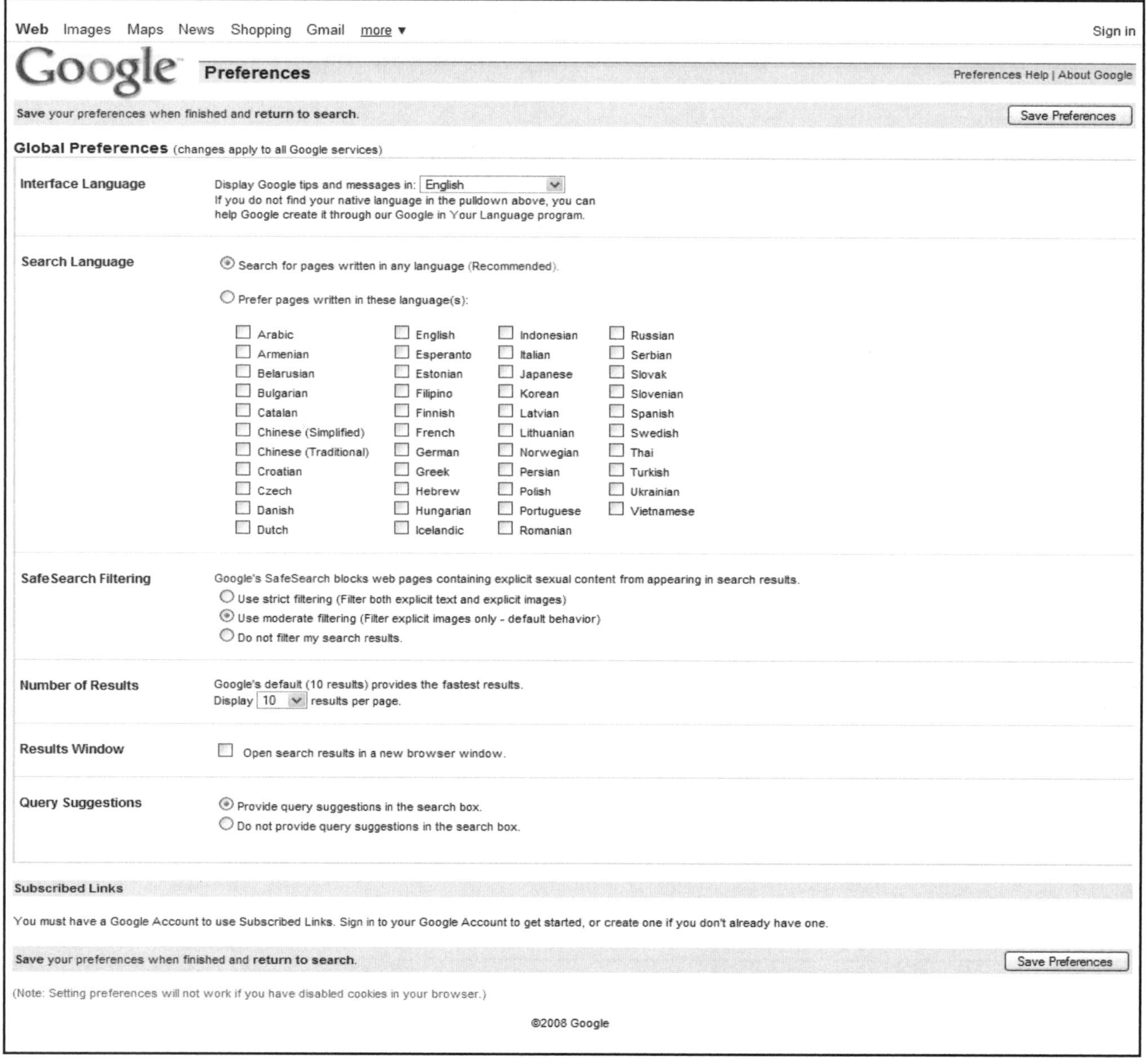

make on this screen, you will need to click on one of the "Save Preferences" buttons at the top or bottom of the screen.

- **Interface language:**

  As with the interface language option on the language tools page, you may choose whichever of the available languages you wish to use for Google's interface. However, unlike with the links on the language tools page, choosing an option here will "permanently" change Google's interface for your computer. From this point forward (until you change it again), when you go to www.google.com, you will be presented with the language you selected.

- **Search language:**

  The default setting for Google's search language is "Search for pages written in any language." This instructs Google to retrieve all relevant results regardless of the language the result is written in. By changing this setting to "Prefer pages written in these language(s):" you can then select one or more of the 43 languages listed to limit your results. Unlike the language-specific search on the language tools page, here you can limit your results to more than one language. However, you must remember that by choosing this option, Google will remember this limitation until you come back and change it again.

- **SafeSearch filtering:**

  I have already discussed the SafeSearch filter earlier in this chapter. Here is where you can turn this on "permanently" and choose from one of two levels of filtering. However, this is not a replacement for any filtering software you may be considering installing in your library. Anyone can easily get around this by coming back to this page and changing the setting.

- **Number of results:**

  Here you can set how many results you would like per screen. The default is 10, but if you would like more, you can change this to 20, 30, 50, or 100.

- **Results window:**

  When this option is selected, the result you click on will be opened in a new window or tab (if your browser supports tabbed browsing). This will allow you to open multiple results at the same

time instead of having to move back and forth between results and the Google results list. If you are not comfortable working with multiple browser windows or tabs, checking this option is not recommended.

- **Query suggestions:**

  This is a new feature you may have noticed if you use Google regularly. Once you begin to type in your search term, beginning with the first letter in most instances, Google will offer suggested terms that you can scroll down to and choose. For example, when I type in *li*, Google offers as the first three suggestions "limewire," "littlewoods," and "linens and things." It also displays the number of results available for that search term. As I continue to type in my term, the query suggestions narrow—*library* produces "library of congress" "library jobs," and "library things" as the top three suggestions. If you do not like this feature, here is where you can turn it off.

Last, you will see a section labeled "Subscribed Links." This feature requires you to have a Google account and thus will not be covered in this book.

MICROSOFT'S LIVE SEARCH

Google was the first major search engine to have a very sparse opening screen. Finally, most of the other search engines out there today are following Google's lead. Take a look at Figure 3-18, the Live Search homepage (http://search.msn.com), if you're not sure what I mean.

Granted, you might not agree with my definition of "sparse." What I mean is that the screen does not offer a lot of options and links. Yes, the background image may look busy, but you're still limited as to what you can actually do on this page.

As with Google, Live Search's default search is of the Web. Five other databases are available through links on the screen: images, video, news, maps (covered in Chapter 6), and more. Under the "More" option are health, local (also covered in Chapter 6), products, QnA, xRank, and a "see all" option.

To perform a basic Web search, just type your search terms (and any Boolean operators) into the search field and click on the search button, which contains a magnifying icon. Results will be displayed

Figure 3-18   The Live Search homepage

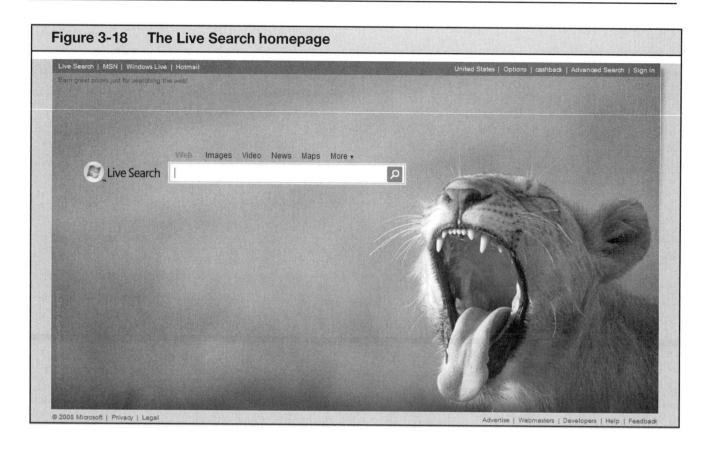

in a standard list format, with subpages nested beneath master pages. You'll also see a list of related searches to the right, as shown in Figure 3-19.

Advanced Search

Like Google's advanced search, Live Search's advanced search allows the searcher to enter search terms. Unlike Google, however, you do not actually perform the search based on these fields. Instead, you insert the relevant information into the form and then click the "Add to search" button, as seen in Figure 3-20. This turns what you've entered into correct syntax and places the new information into the main search field.

For example, Figure 3-21 shows the results of the following steps:

1. Entering the terms *dean koontz*
2. Selecting "This exact phrase"
3. Clicking "Add to search"
4. Clicking the "Country/Region" link
5. Selecting France
6. Clicking "Add to search" again

As you can see, the result is *"dean koontz" loc: FR* being displayed in the search field. If you were performing this search while reading the text, you should have noticed that each time you clicked "Add to search" not only did the syntax update itself in the search box but each stage of the search was actually performed and results displayed. Although this type of interface is not what most people are used to, in my experience, after a search or two most do become used to it. Let's take a look at each of the advanced search options individually.

- **Search terms:**
  Typing search terms into this field allows you to build your search by choosing from the four options of "All of these terms" (Boolean AND), "Any of these terms" (Boolean OR), "This exact phrase" (quotation marks), and "None of these terms" (Boolean NOT) (see Figure 3-22). To use more than one of these choices in your search, enter your first set of terms, choose the appropriate option, click "Add to search," and then repeat the process. For example, to create *"dean koontz" NOT husband* you would

Figure 3-19   A Live Search results page

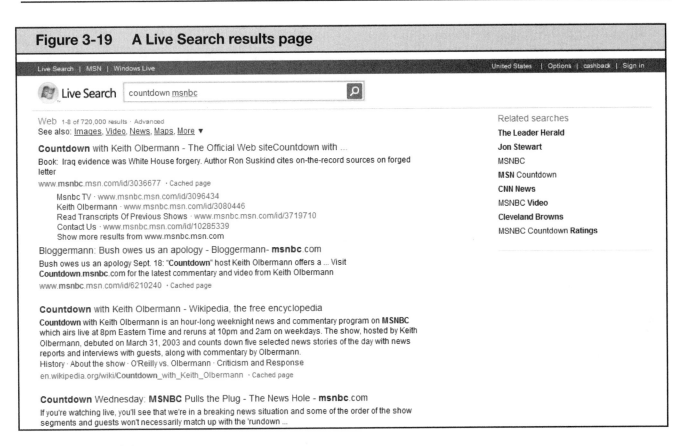

Figure 3-20   Live Search's advanced search

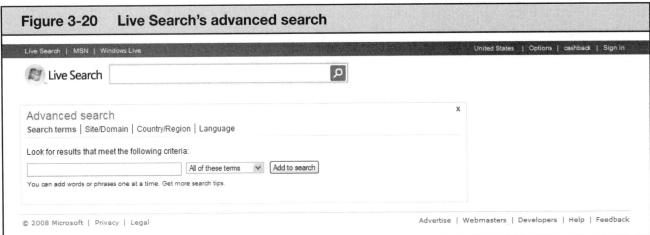

type *dean koontz*, choose "This exact phrase," click "Add to search," type *husband,* choose "None of these terms," and click "Add to search" again. The result will be *"dean koontz"–(husband).* Of course, in this example, for someone with experience in online searching, just typing *"dean koontz"–husband* would most likely be quicker.

- **Site/Domain:**
  The "Site/Domain" area (as shown in Figure 3-23) allows you to limit to or exclude results from

particular Web sites or top level domains. To limit to only U.S. educational sites, choose "Look for results only in the following site or domain" and enter *.edu* in the "field below. To exclude results from Microsoft, choose "Don't look for results from the following site or domain" and enter *microsoft. com* in the field below.

- **Country/Region:**
  This area, as shown in Figure 3-24, allows you to limit your results to any single country/region from

Figure 3-21   The results of using the "search builder" interface

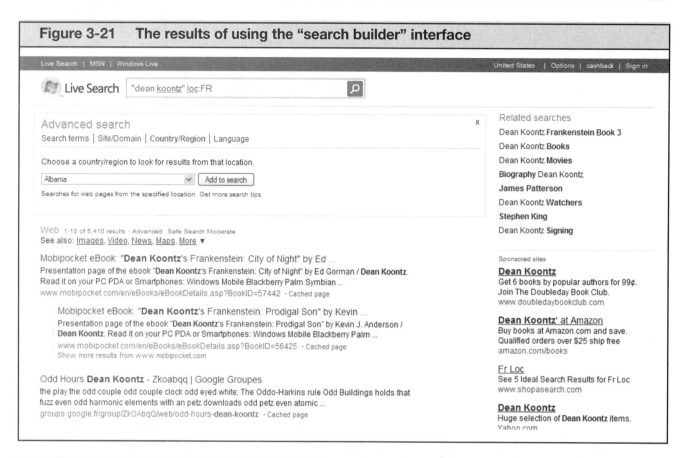

Figure 3-22   Search builder: Search terms

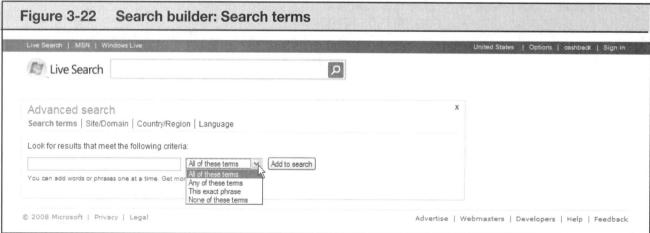

a list of almost 100, ranging from Albania to Yemen. Although in certain cases this may also limit your results to the language of the country/region you chose, this is only coincidental. To specifically limit by language, use the "Language" portion of the advanced search.

- **Language:**

  This setting, as shown in Figure 3-25, allows you to limit your results to a particular language. Over

30 languages are available, ranging from Albanian to Ukrainian.

Live Search Options

Live Search's options screen is similar to Google's preferences. Here there are five areas that you can adjust: SafeSearch, location, display, results, and search language, as shown in Figure 3.26. Just as with Google's preferences, any changes made here are considered "permanent" until changed again.

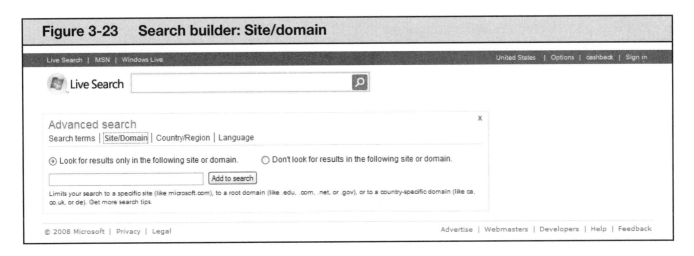

Figure 3-23   Search builder: Site/domain

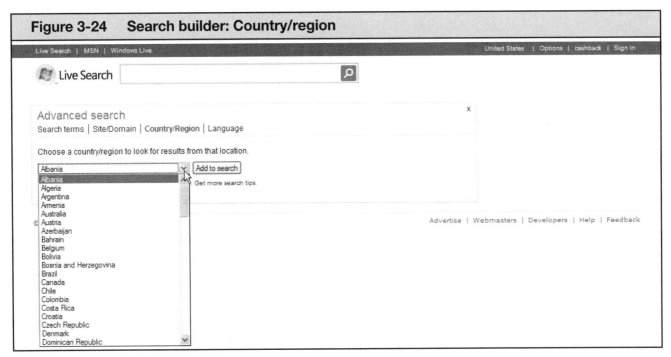

Figure 3-24   Search builder: Country/region

- **SafeSearch:**

  Here you can turn on and choose the level of content filtering applied to your search results. Just as with Google's SafeSearch, this is not a replacement for content filtering software, as it can be easily turned off by anyone who can get to this screen.

- **Location:**

  Here, you're asked to input your home city and state (country, if not the United States). This is because knowing your location sometimes helps to provide more relevant information. Unfortunately, I was unable to find anything more specific than this to explain how putting in the correct information helps.[11] If you're truly trying to perform a search

in which your results are based on your physical location, follow the recommendations in Chapter 6.

- **Display:**

  The display option allows you to change the language of the Live Search interface. There are 39 different language options, ranging from Basque to Ukrainian.

- **Results:**

  The results area gives you the option to change two different settings, both having an effect on the list of results from a search. The first allows you to change the number of results shown per screen. Your options are 10 (the default), 15, 30, and 50.

Figure 3-25   Search builder: Language

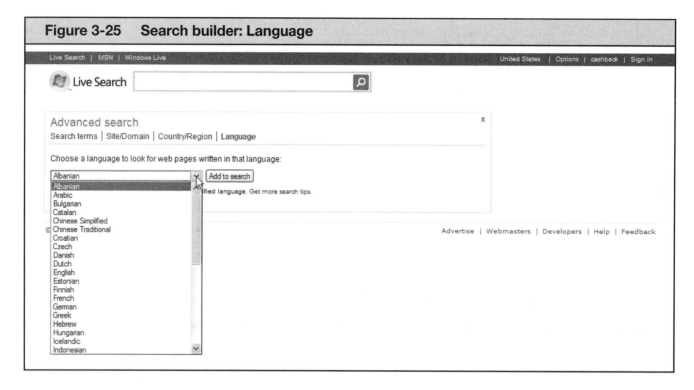

The second option in this section, when checked, opens links from results in a new window or tab, instead of opening the link in the same window.

- **Search Language:**

    Here you can choose one or more of the 41 different language options, ranging from Albanian to Ukrainian, to limit your search results. All you need to do is select "Limit my searches to pages written in the following languages:" and then check the appropriate languages from the list.

Once you have made your changes, click one of the "Save settings" buttons (located at the top right and bottom right corners of the page) to make your changes permanent.

YAHOO! SEARCH

After years of Yahoo! being a searchable directory of resources, finally in 2005 the company launched Yahoo! Search (http://search.yahoo.com), a full-featured Web search engine designed to compete with the likes of both Google and Live Search. Figure 3-27 shows the Yahoo! Search homepage. Since Yahoo! considers Google and Live Search the competition, you can quickly understand why its homepage is also sparsely designed.

In addition to the basic search box, which will search the Web by default, the homepage also offers links to the following other types of searches: images, video, local, shopping, and more. The "More" option contains sublinks to answers, audio, directory, jobs, news, and all search services.

As we did with Google and Live Search, let's jump directly into Yahoo! Search's advanced searching features, the link to which can be found by clicking on "Options" to the right of the search box.

Advanced Search

Most of the features of Yahoo! Search's advanced search screen are similar to those of both Google and Live Search. However, I cover here a few unique features, so you may not want to skim this part. Figure 3-28 shows you Yahoo! Search's advanced search interface.

The advanced search screen presents you with many options for manipulating your search, broken down into ten sections: "Show results with," "Updates," "Site/Domain," "Creative Commons Search," "File Format," "Same Search Filter," "Country," "Languages," "Subscriptions," and "Number of Results."

- **Show results with:**

    This section allows you to build your search without the need to know proper use of Boolean operators;

Figure 3-26   Live Search's settings

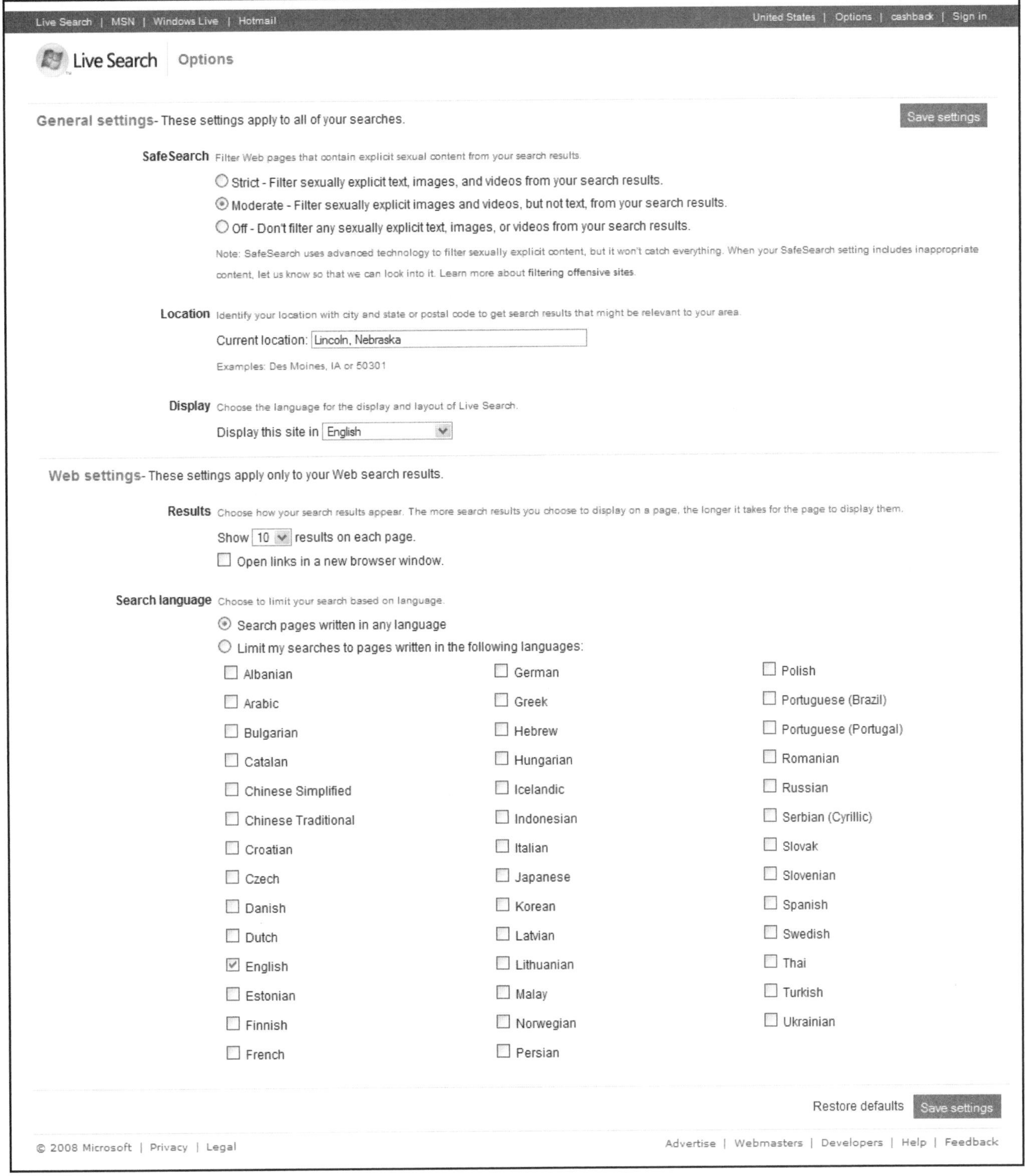

Live Search | MSN | Windows Live | Hotmail   United States | Options | cashback | Sign in

Live Search   Options

General settings- These settings apply to all of your searches.   [Save settings]

SafeSearch Filter Web pages that contain explicit sexual content from your search results.

○ Strict - Filter sexually explicit text, images, and videos from your search results.

◉ Moderate - Filter sexually explicit images and videos, but not text, from your search results.

○ Off - Don't filter any sexually explicit text, images, or videos from your search results.

Note: SafeSearch uses advanced technology to filter sexually explicit content, but it won't catch everything. When your SafeSearch setting includes inappropriate content, let us know so that we can look into it. Learn more about filtering offensive sites.

Location Identify your location with city and state or postal code to get search results that might be relevant to your area.

Current location: [Lincoln, Nebraska]

Examples: Des Moines, IA or 50301

Display Choose the language for the display and layout of Live Search.

Display this site in [English ▼]

Web settings- These settings apply only to your Web search results.

Results Choose how your search results appear. The more search results you choose to display on a page, the longer it takes for the page to display them.

Show [10 ▼] results on each page.

☐ Open links in a new browser window.

Search language Choose to limit your search based on language.

◉ Search pages written in any language

○ Limit my searches to pages written in the following languages:

☐ Albanian	☐ German	☐ Polish
☐ Arabic	☐ Greek	☐ Portuguese (Brazil)
☐ Bulgarian	☐ Hebrew	☐ Portuguese (Portugal)
☐ Catalan	☐ Hungarian	☐ Romanian
☐ Chinese Simplified	☐ Icelandic	☐ Russian
☐ Chinese Traditional	☐ Indonesian	☐ Serbian (Cyrillic)
☐ Croatian	☐ Italian	☐ Slovak
☐ Czech	☐ Japanese	☐ Slovenian
☐ Danish	☐ Korean	☐ Spanish
☐ Dutch	☐ Latvian	☐ Swedish
☑ English	☐ Lithuanian	☐ Thai
☐ Estonian	☐ Malay	☐ Turkish
☐ Finnish	☐ Norwegian	☐ Ukrainian
☐ French	☐ Persian	

Restore defaults [Save settings]

© 2008 Microsoft | Privacy | Legal   Advertise | Webmasters | Developers | Help | Feedback

---

Figure 3-27   The Yahoo! Search homepage

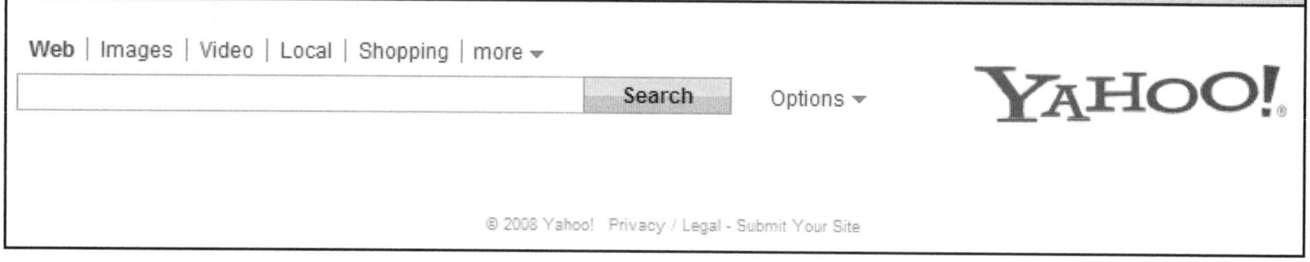

Web | Images | Video | Local | Shopping | more ▾

[   ]   [Search]   Options ▾   YAHOO!®

© 2008 Yahoo! Privacy / Legal - Submit Your Site

Figure 3-28   Yahoo! Search advanced search

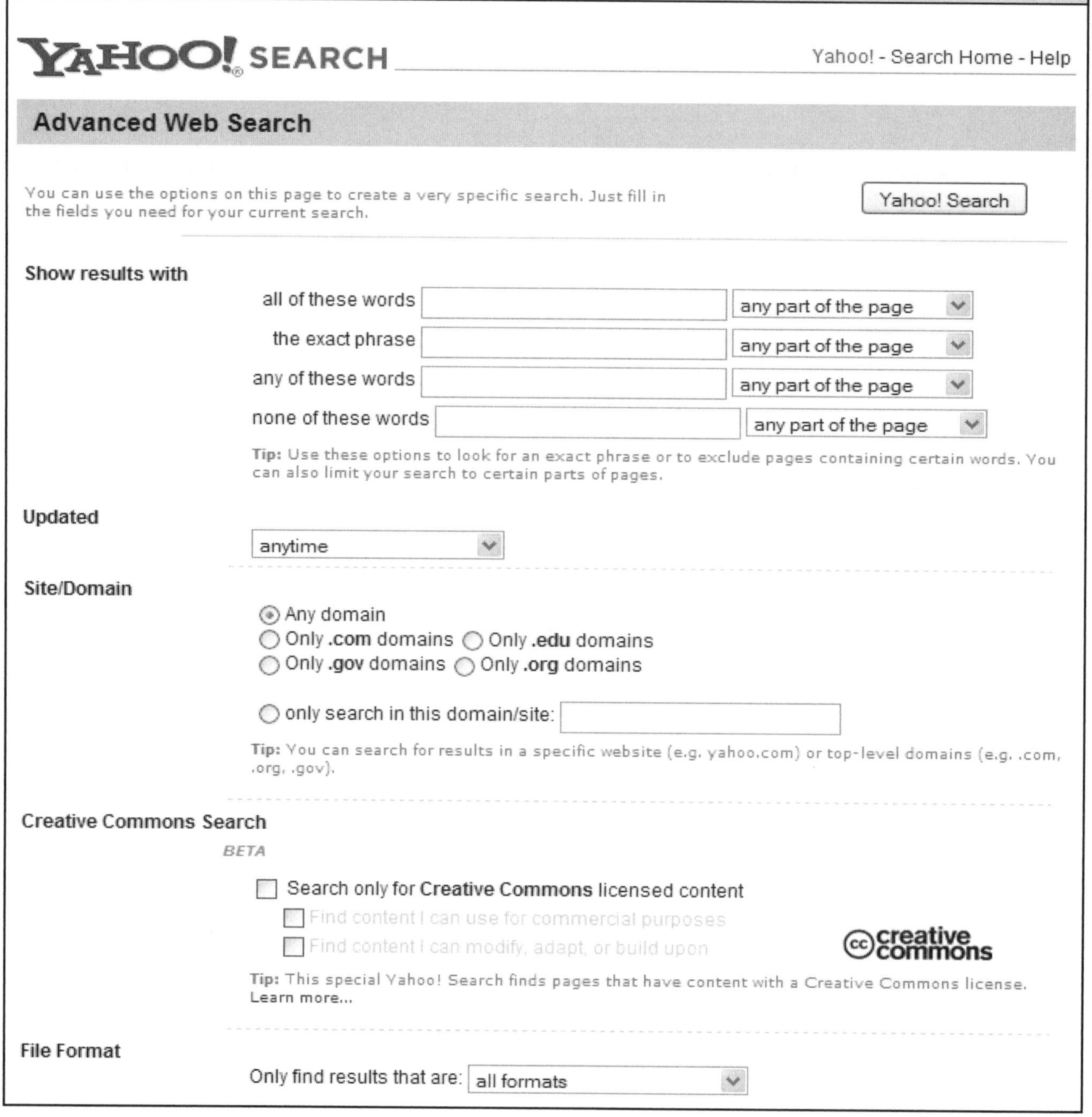

YAHOO!® SEARCH _____   Yahoo! - Search Home - Help

Advanced Web Search

You can use the options on this page to create a very specific search. Just fill in   [Yahoo! Search]
the fields you need for your current search.

Show results with

all of these words   [   ]   [any part of the page ▾]

the exact phrase   [   ]   [any part of the page ▾]

any of these words   [   ]   [any part of the page ▾]

none of these words   [   ]   [any part of the page ▾]

Tip: Use these options to look for an exact phrase or to exclude pages containing certain words. You can also limit your search to certain parts of pages.

Updated

[anytime ▾]

Site/Domain

⦿ Any domain
◯ Only **.com** domains ◯ Only **.edu** domains
◯ Only **.gov** domains ◯ Only **.org** domains

◯ only search in this domain/site: [   ]

Tip: You can search for results in a specific website (e.g. yahoo.com) or top-level domains (e.g. .com, .org, .gov).

Creative Commons Search

            BETA

☐ Search only for **Creative Commons** licensed content
   ☐ Find content I can use for commercial purposes
   ☐ Find content I can modify, adapt, or build upon   ©© **creative commons**

Tip: This special Yahoo! Search finds pages that have content with a Creative Commons license. Learn more...

File Format

Only find results that are: [all formats ▾]

Figure 3-28	Yahoo! Search advanced search *(Continued)*

SafeSearch Filter

Applies when I'm signed in:

○ Filter out adult Web search results - SafeSearch On
◉ Do not filter Web results (results may include adult content) - SafeSearch Off

Note: Any user signed in on your computer as 18 or older can change this setting. We recommend periodically checking the SafeSearch Lock settings.

Advisory: Yahoo! SafeSearch is designed to filter out explicit, adult-oriented content from Yahoo! Search results. However, Yahoo! cannot guarantee that all explicit content will be filtered out.

Learn more about protecting children online.

Tip: If you'd like to block explicit content for every search, you can set this in **preferences**. Keep in mind that this filter may not block all offensive content.

Country

[any country ▾]

Languages

Search only for pages written in:
◉ any language
OR
○ one or more of the following languages (select as many as you want).

☐ Albanian   ☐ German   ☐ Polish
☐ Arabic   ☐ Greek   ☐ Portuguese
☐ Bulgarian   ☐ Hebrew   ☐ Romanian
☐ Catalan   ☐ Hungarian   ☐ Russian
☐ Chinese (Simplified) ☐ Icelandic   ☐ Serbian
☐ Chinese (Traditional) ☐ Indonesian ☐ Slovak
☐ Croatian   ☐ Italian   ☐ Slovenian
☐ Czech   ☐ Japanese   ☐ Spanish
☐ Danish   ☐ Korean   ☐ Swedish
☐ Dutch   ☐ Latvian   ☐ Tagalog
☐ English   ☐ Lithuanian   ☐ Thai
☐ Estonian   ☐ Malay   ☐ Turkish
☐ Finnish   ☐ Norwegian   ☐ Vietnamese
☐ French   ☐ Persian

Subscriptions
BETA

Select from the sites below to include their content in your web search results.

To view content you will need a subscription to the site(s) below. For some sites you will need to pay for the subscription.

☐ Consumer Reports   ☐ FT.com (60 days)   ☐ Wall Street Journal (30 days)
☐ Factiva   ☐ LexisNexis
☐ Forrester Research ☐ TheStreet.com

Learn more about Yahoo! Search Subscriptions

Number of Results

Display [10 results ▾] per page.

[Yahoo! Search]

"all of these words" is your Boolean AND, "the exact phrase" is the same as using quotation marks, "any of these words" is a Boolean OR, and "none of these words" is a Boolean NOT. Any or all of these four options may be used in building your search. Additionally, each of the four options may be limited by choosing from the associated dropdown list to the right. Through these dropdown lists you can specify that the keywords appear in any part of the page (the default choice), in the title of the page, or in the URL of the page.

- **Updated:**
  Here you may limit your results to "anytime" (the default choice), "within the past 3 months," "within the past 6 months," or "within a year." As with the previously discussed search engines, please keep in mind the potential limitations of restricting search results by date, covered in Chapter 8.

- **Site/Domain:**
  This section allows you to limit your results to "any domain" (the default choice) or to one of the four preset top-level domains: .com, .edu, .gov, or .org. If you wish to limit to a top-level domain, such as .info, you can enter it into the "only search in this domain/site:" field. Additionally, you can use this field to limit to a domain such as "microsoft.com" or "usda.gov."

- **Creative Commons search:**
  As with Google, Yahoo! Search offers the ability to search for content that contains Creative Commons licenses. If you check "Search only for Creative Commons licensed content," you can then further limit your search to "Find content I can use for commercial purposes" and/or "Find content I can modify, adapt, or build upon."

- **File format:**
  Here you can limit your search results to content in only certain formats. The available choices are all formats (the default choice), HTML (hypertext markup language), Adobe PDF, Microsoft Excel, Microsoft PowerPoint, Microsoft Word, RSS (really simple syndication)/XML (extensible markup language), or text format (plain text). The ability to limit your results to XML does present a unique option here in that you can use Yahoo! Search to search specifically for content in RSS feeds, which are written using XML. Although there are

RSS-specific search engines on the Web, this is the only major search engine I am aware of that allows you to limit to this type of result.

- **SafeSearch filter:**
  As with the previous search engines in this chapter, you can instruct Yahoo! Search to filter out adult content. The filter here is no better or worse than those presented previously.

- **Country:**
  Yahoo! Search gives you a list of 99 preselected countries to choose from, ranging from Algeria to Zimbabwe, along with an "any country" default choice. Choose the country you would like to limit to from the list and then perform your search.

- **Language:**
  Here you may choose one or more languages to limit your search results to from a list of 41, ranging from Albanian to Vietnamese. To use this option, you must first choose the "one or more of the following languages" option and then select from the list of languages. If you select from the language list without changing this option, your selections will not be applied to your search.

- **Subscriptions:**
  Yahoo! Search has worked out deals with—at the time of this writing—seven third-party publishers (i.e., not Yahoo!) whose content can be included in Yahoo! search results.[13] For this to work, you must first create an account with the applicable content providers, which may involve subscription pricing. Once you have established an account, you can then select them from this list and have their content searched along with the content of Yahoo! Search's database.

- **Number of results:**
  Last, you can choose to set the number of results shown per page to 10 (the default), 15, 20, 30, 40, or 100.

Once you have filled in and/or chosen the options appropriate to your search, click on the Yahoo! Search button at either the top or bottom of the page to perform your search.

Yahoo! Search Preferences

To find the preferences area of Yahoo! Search, you need to head back to the search homepage and again click on "Options" to the right of the search box. There you'll find the "Preferences" link. Once at the preferences screen, as shown in Figure 3-29, the changes you can make are divided into eight sections: "Search Assist," "Enhanced Results," "SafeSearch," "SearchScan," "Languages," "Display & Layout," "Subscriptions," and "Multimedia Search." To change any of the options in this section, you need to click on the associated "Edit" link off to the right. A few of the options you can change—most specifically SafeSearch and Languages—are similar to the options in advanced search, but here the settings apply to all future searches (until the options are once again changed). This is instead of formatting preferences for the immediate next search.

After changing settings on any of these screens, you will need to click the "Finished" button at either the top or bottom right of the screen (see Figure 3-29). Failing to do so will prevent your changes from being saved. As Figures 3-30 through 3-37 show, to make most of these settings permanent across searching sessions, you will need to create work from a Yahoo! account.

- **Search assist:**

    Search assist is the function Yahoo! builds into its search box to provide you with suggestions while you're searching. As you type content into the search box, a drop-down list of suggested searches will appear based on this setting. The options are "Always: Show Search Assist whenever suggestions are available," "More: Show search suggestions as my typing slows" (the default), "Less: Show search suggestions when my typing pauses," and "Never: Do not automatically display search suggestions." This screen is shown in Figure 3-30.

- **Enhanced results:**

    This screen, as seen in Figure 3-31, allows you to add and remove content types from the search results screen. Types available include video, Yahoo! Travel, Flickr (photos), Yelp (business reviews), Yahoo! Local, and LinkedIn Public Profiles (a professional social network). As you may have guessed, all of these resources are Yahoo! corporate properties. You can remove individual types by clicking the appropriate "Remove" link. You can

also reorder these types by dragging and dropping them into your preferred order.

- **SafeSearch:**

    Here you may turn on SafeSearch at one of two levels: (1) for Web, video, and images results or (2) just image and video results. You can also turn of SafeSearch here. Additionally, you can lock this option, if you have a Yahoo! account, so that others using the computer cannot turn off Safe-Search without the correct password. This feature is unique to Yahoo! Search. See Figure 3-32.

- **SearchScan:**

    Yahoo!'s SearchScan uses McAfee antivirus technology to advance scan your search results for potentially harmful sites, such as those that may contain viruses or spyware. Your options here, as shown in Figure 3-33, are "Never display websites indicated as potentially harmful," "Alert me to websites indicated as potentially harmful" (the default), and "Do not alert me to websites indicated as potentially harmful."

- **Languages:**

    The options here (see Figure 3-34) work exactly as they do on the advanced search screen. Select the languages you wish to limit your searches to, but be sure to change the top option to "Search only for pages written in one or more of the following languages" or your language selections will not be applied.

- **Display and layout:**

    The options found here (see Figure 3-35) focus on how your search results are displayed and what options are available for manipulating those results.

    o **New window:**

        Selecting this option instructs Yahoo! Search to open a new window (or tab, depending on your browser) whenever you click on a search result's link.

    o **Results per page:**

        Here you may choose to display 10, 15, 20, 30, 40, or 100 results per page.

    o **More from this site:**

        Checking the "More from this site link" option will add an additional link to your search results when multiple results are from a single site. With this option, you'll see one to two results

Figure 3-29 Yahoo! Search preferences

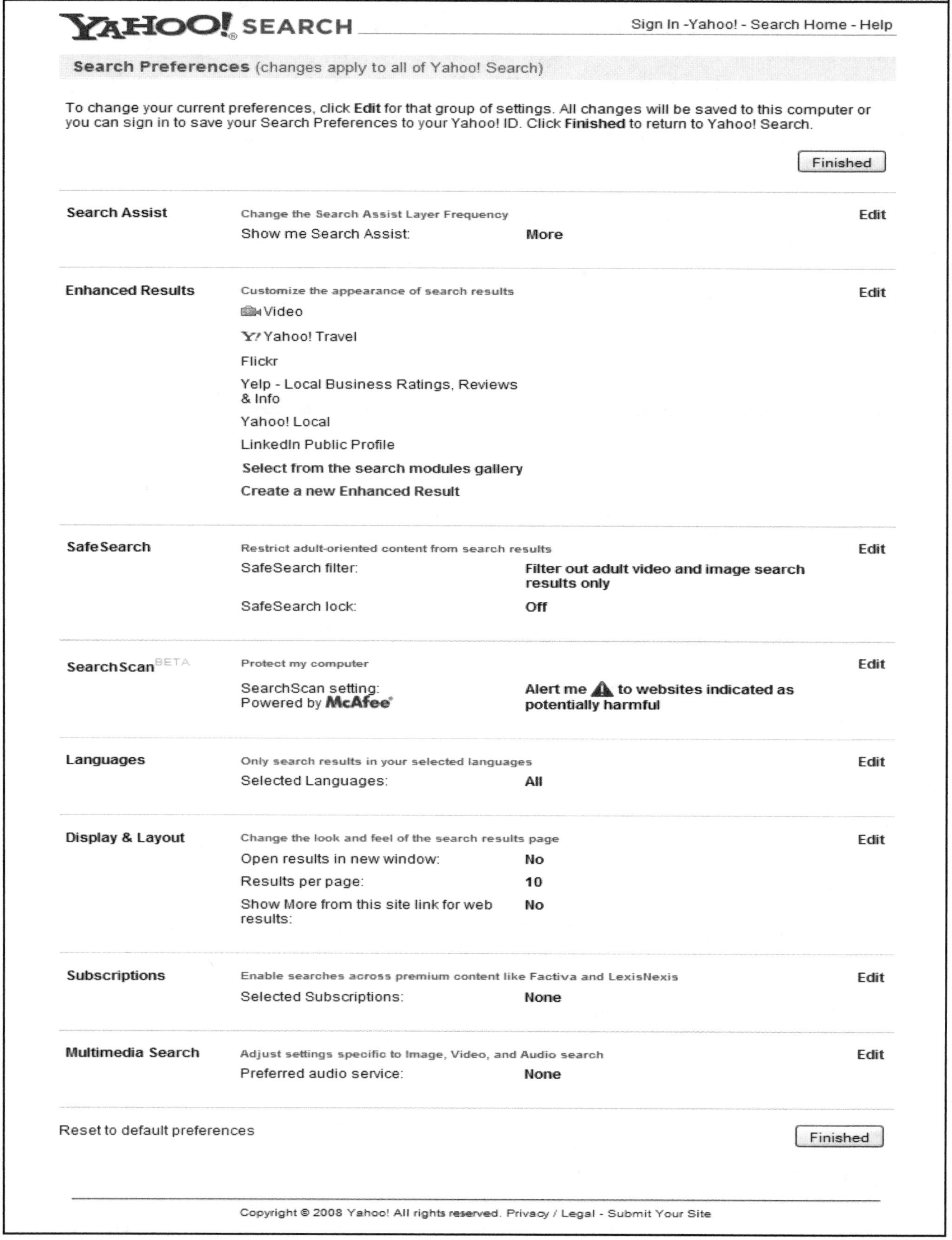
YAHOO! SEARCH — Sign In -Yahoo! - Search Home - Help

Search Preferences (changes apply to all of Yahoo! Search)

To change your current preferences, click **Edit** for that group of settings. All changes will be saved to this computer or you can sign in to save your Search Preferences to your Yahoo! ID. Click **Finished** to return to Yahoo! Search.

Finished

Search Assist	Change the Search Assist Layer Frequency		Edit
	Show me Search Assist:	**More**	
Enhanced Results	Customize the appearance of search results		Edit
	Video		
	Y! Yahoo! Travel		
	Flickr		
	Yelp - Local Business Ratings, Reviews & Info		
	Yahoo! Local		
	LinkedIn Public Profile		
	Select from the search modules gallery		
	Create a new Enhanced Result		
SafeSearch	Restrict adult-oriented content from search results		Edit
	SafeSearch filter:	**Filter out adult video and image search results only**	
	SafeSearch lock:	**Off**	
SearchScan BETA	Protect my computer		Edit
	SearchScan setting: Powered by McAfee	**Alert me to websites indicated as potentially harmful**	
Languages	Only search results in your selected languages		Edit
	Selected Languages:	**All**	
Display & Layout	Change the look and feel of the search results page		Edit
	Open results in new window:	**No**	
	Results per page:	**10**	
	Show More from this site link for web results:	**No**	
Subscriptions	Enable searches across premium content like Factiva and LexisNexis		Edit
	Selected Subscriptions:	**None**	
Multimedia Search	Adjust settings specific to Image, Video, and Audio search		Edit
	Preferred audio service:	**None**	

Reset to default preferences — Finished

Copyright © 2008 Yahoo! All rights reserved. Privacy / Legal - Submit Your Site

Figure 3-30   Search assist preferences

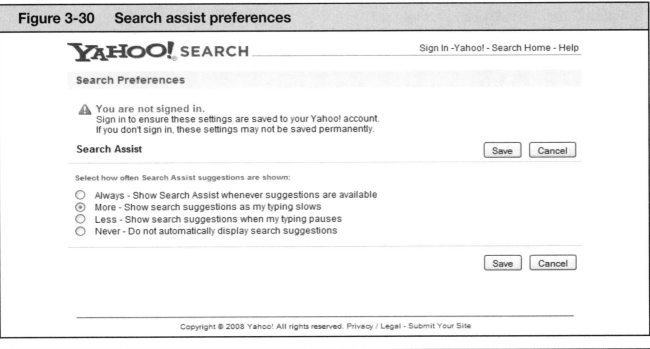

YAHOO! SEARCH   Sign In -Yahoo! - Search Home - Help

Search Preferences

⚠ You are not signed in.
Sign in to ensure these settings are saved to your Yahoo! account.
If you don't sign in, these settings may not be saved permanently.

Search Assist   [Save] [Cancel]

Select how often Search Assist suggestions are shown:

○ Always - Show Search Assist whenever suggestions are available
◉ More - Show search suggestions as my typing slows
○ Less - Show search suggestions when my typing pauses
○ Never - Do not automatically display search suggestions

[Save] [Cancel]

Figure 3-31   My enhancements

YAHOO! SEARCH   Sign In -Yahoo! - Search Home - Help

Search Preferences

⚠ You are not signed in.
Sign in to ensure these settings are saved to your Yahoo! account.
If you don't sign in, these settings may not be saved permanently.

My Enhancements   [Save] [Cancel]

✛	Name of Enhancements	Type	Settings
1.	🎥 Video	Default App	☒ Remove
2.	Y! Yahoo! Travel	Default App	☒ Remove
3.	Flickr	Default App	☒ Remove
4.	Yelp - Local Business Ratings, Reviews & Info Useful info about local businesses from Yelp.com. Get a preview of photos, reviews, rating, address, phone number & more while you search.	Default App	☒ Remove
5.	Yahoo! Local The Yahoo! Local Enriched Businesses application makes searching for local businesses faster, easier, and more fun by pulling in key info and reviews.	Default App	☒ Remove
6.	LinkedIn Public Profile Render LinkedIn Public Profiles in a richer and more compelling format within Yahoo! Search results. Currently, this plug-in is compatible only with the public profiles of LinkedIn members who have claimed a custom public profile URL.	Default App	☒ Remove

[Reset Preferences]   [Save] [Cancel]

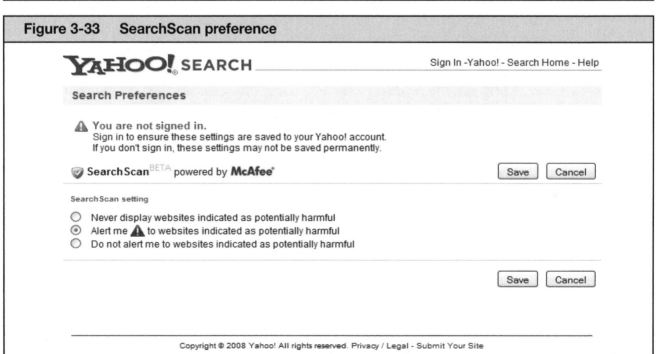

Figure 3-32   SafeSearch preferences

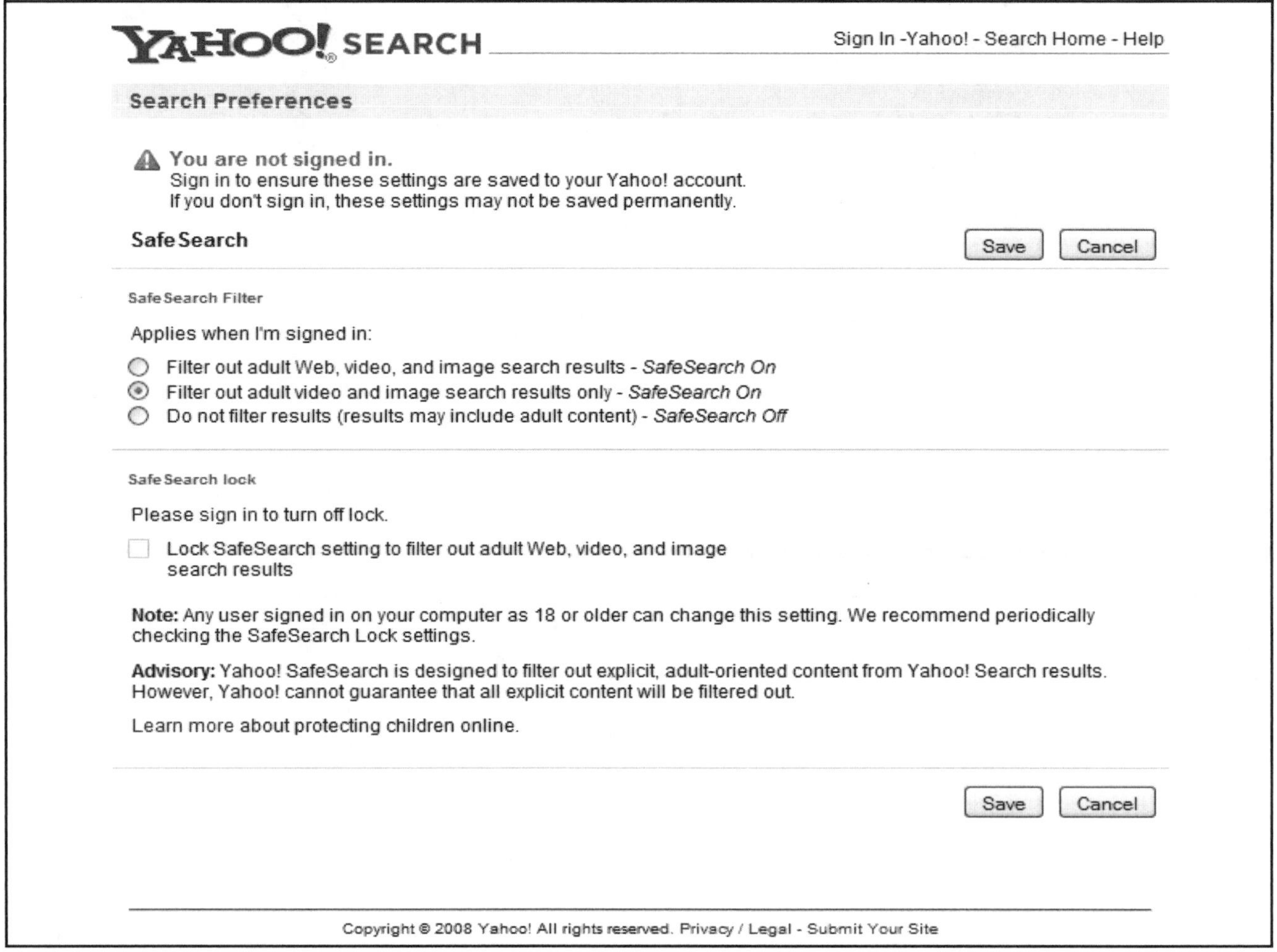

Figure 3-33   SearchScan preference

Figure 3-34   Language preferences

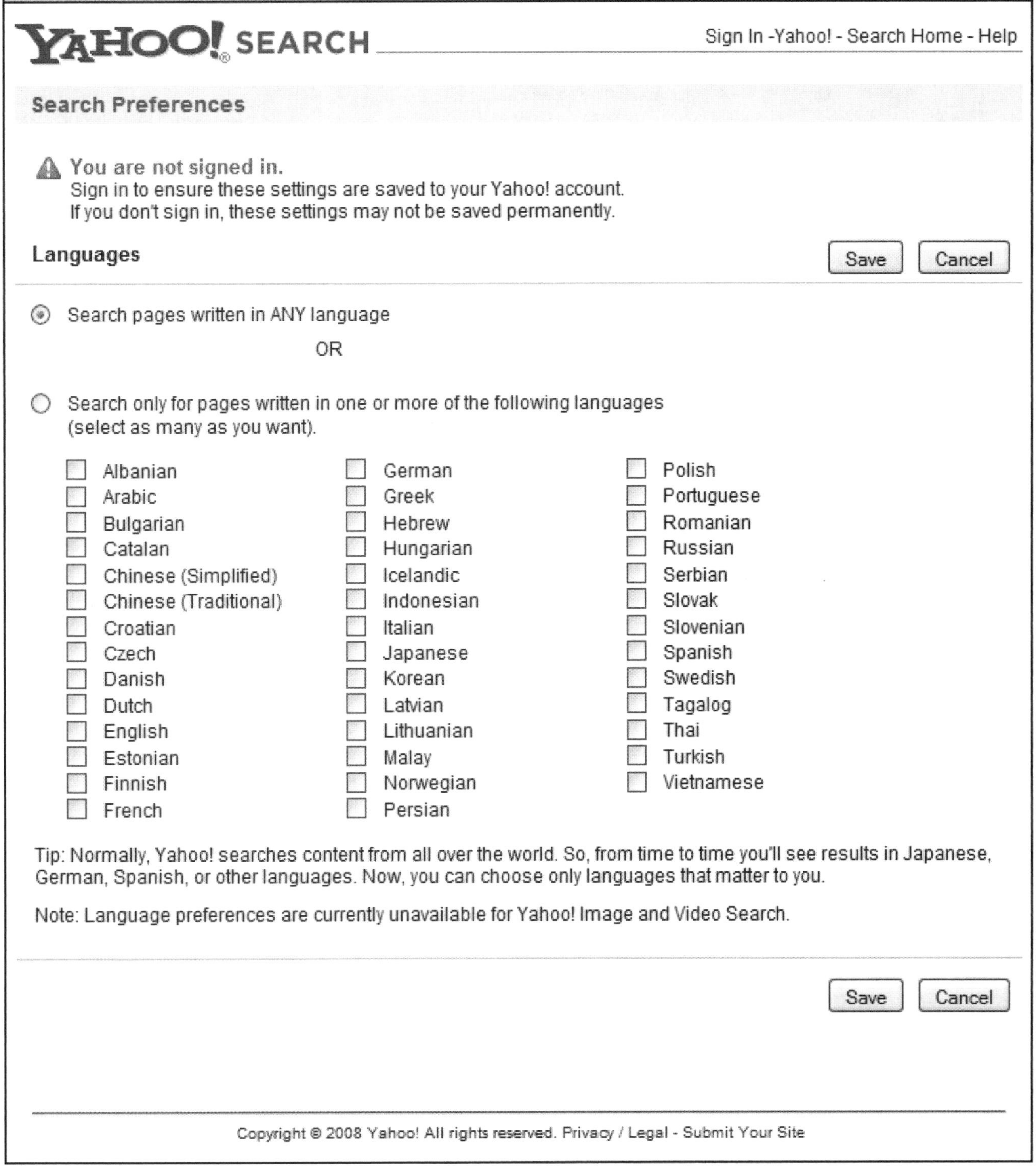

YAHOO! SEARCH

Search Preferences

⚠ **You are not signed in.**
Sign in to ensure these settings are saved to your Yahoo! account.
If you don't sign in, these settings may not be saved permanently.

Languages   [Save] [Cancel]

◉ Search pages written in ANY language

OR

◯ Search only for pages written in one or more of the following languages
(select as many as you want).

☐ Albanian	☐ German	☐ Polish
☐ Arabic	☐ Greek	☐ Portuguese
☐ Bulgarian	☐ Hebrew	☐ Romanian
☐ Catalan	☐ Hungarian	☐ Russian
☐ Chinese (Simplified)	☐ Icelandic	☐ Serbian
☐ Chinese (Traditional)	☐ Indonesian	☐ Slovak
☐ Croatian	☐ Italian	☐ Slovenian
☐ Czech	☐ Japanese	☐ Spanish
☐ Danish	☐ Korean	☐ Swedish
☐ Dutch	☐ Latvian	☐ Tagalog
☐ English	☐ Lithuanian	☐ Thai
☐ Estonian	☐ Malay	☐ Turkish
☐ Finnish	☐ Norwegian	☐ Vietnamese
☐ French	☐ Persian	

Tip: Normally, Yahoo! searches content from all over the world. So, from time to time you'll see results in Japanese, German, Spanish, or other languages. Now, you can choose only languages that matter to you.

Note: Language preferences are currently unavailable for Yahoo! Image and Video Search.

[Save] [Cancel]

Figure 3-35   Display and layout preferences

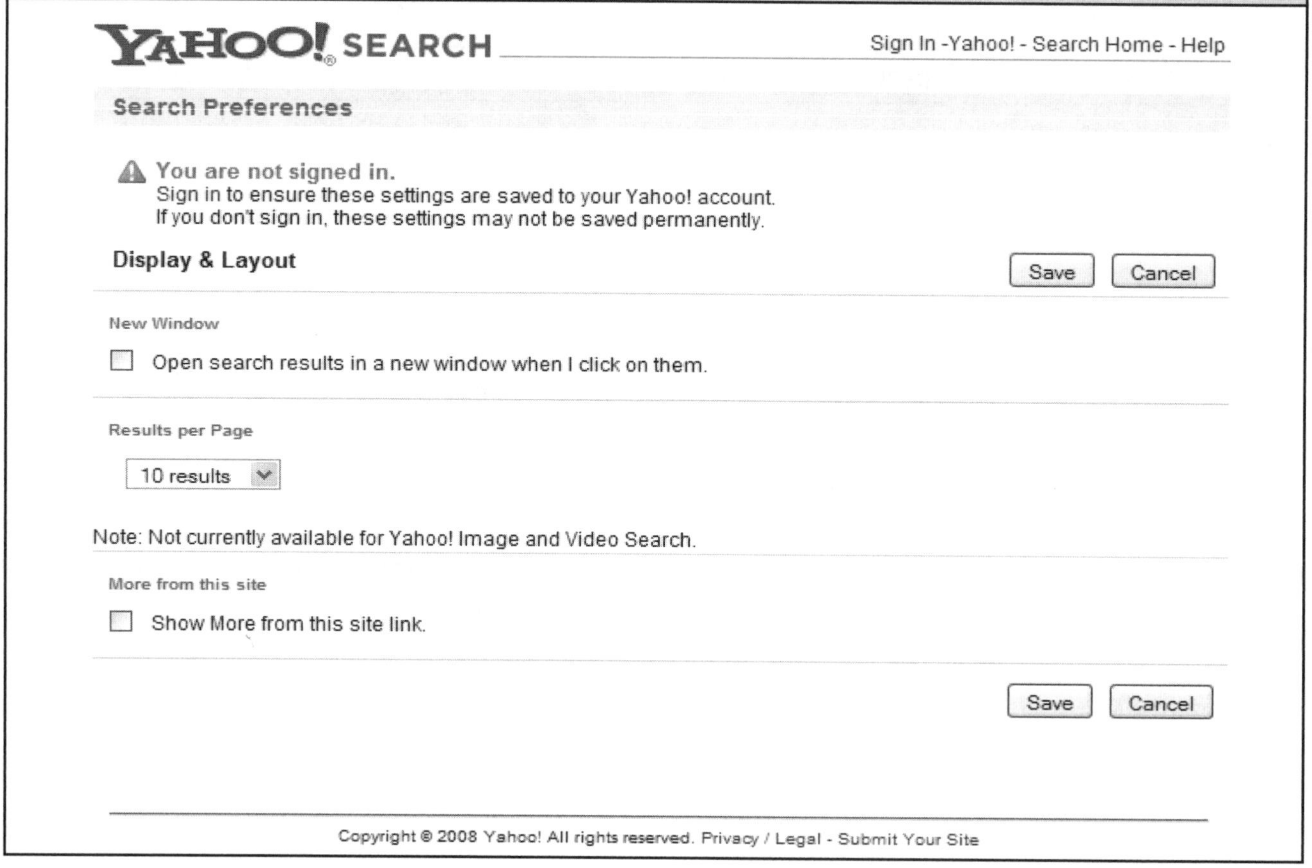

YAHOO! SEARCH   Sign In -Yahoo! - Search Home - Help

Search Preferences

⚠ You are not signed in.
   Sign in to ensure these settings are saved to your Yahoo! account.
   If you don't sign in, these settings may not be saved permanently.

Display & Layout   [Save] [Cancel]

New Window

☐ Open search results in a new window when I click on them.

Results per Page

[10 results ⌄]

Note: Not currently available for Yahoo! Image and Video Search.

More from this site

☐ Show More from this site link.

                                                                 [Save] [Cancel]

Copyright © 2008 Yahoo! All rights reserved. Privacy / Legal - Submit Your Site

---

Figure 3-36   Subscriptions preferences

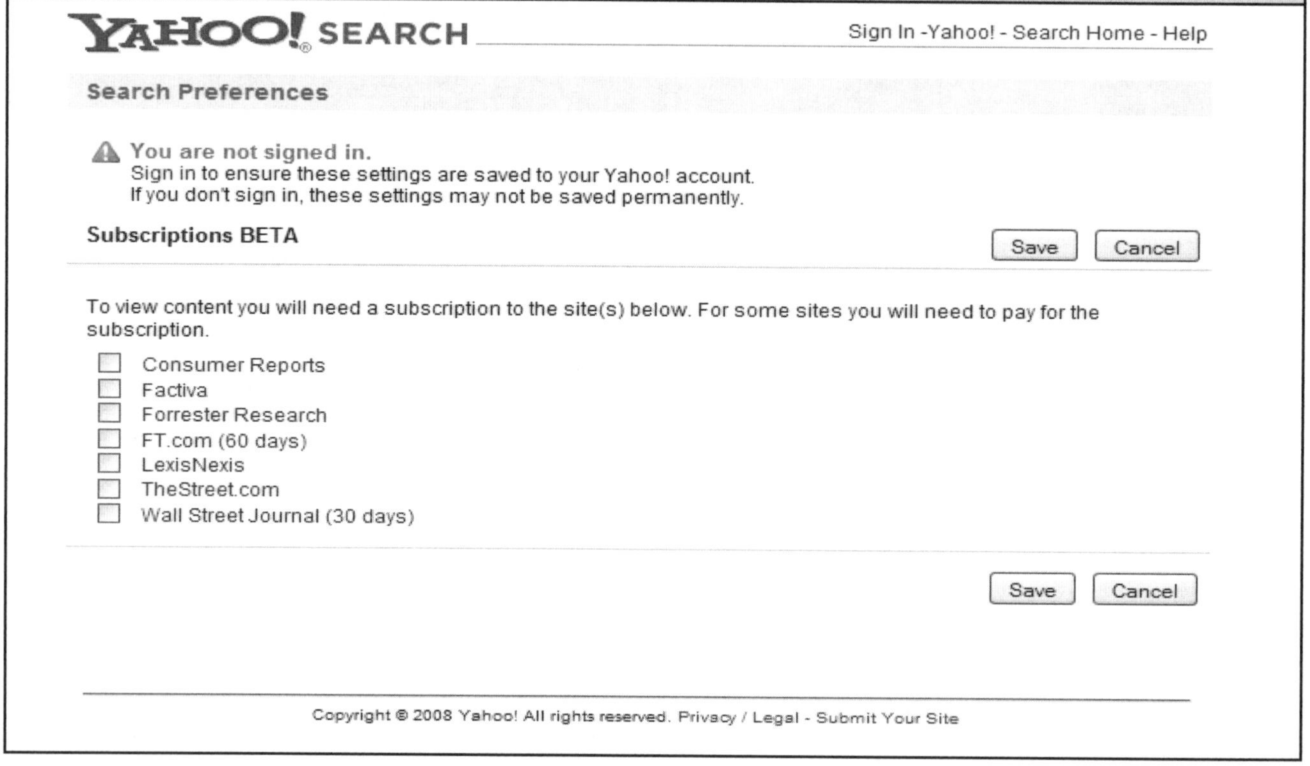

YAHOO! SEARCH   Sign In -Yahoo! - Search Home - Help

Search Preferences

⚠ You are not signed in.
   Sign in to ensure these settings are saved to your Yahoo! account.
   If you don't sign in, these settings may not be saved permanently.

Subscriptions BETA   [Save] [Cancel]

To view content you will need a subscription to the site(s) below. For some sites you will need to pay for the subscription.

☐ Consumer Reports
☐ Factiva
☐ Forrester Research
☐ FT.com (60 days)
☐ LexisNexis
☐ TheStreet.com
☐ Wall Street Journal (30 days)

                                                                 [Save] [Cancel]

Copyright © 2008 Yahoo! All rights reserved. Privacy / Legal - Submit Your Site

Figure 3-37   Multimedia search preferences

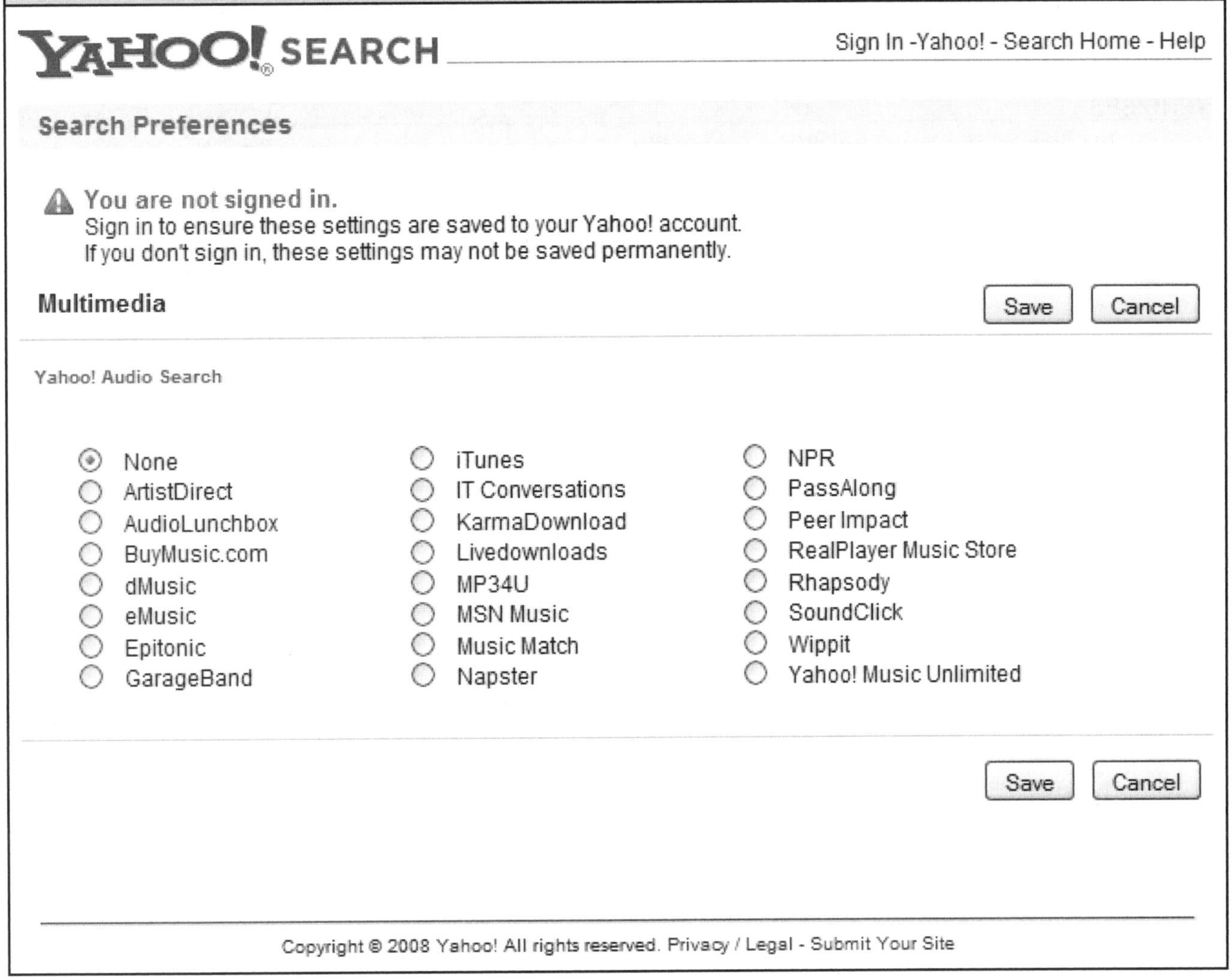

YAHOO! SEARCH   Sign In -Yahoo! - Search Home - Help

Search Preferences

⚠ **You are not signed in.**
Sign in to ensure these settings are saved to your Yahoo! account.
If you don't sign in, these settings may not be saved permanently.

Multimedia   [Save] [Cancel]

Yahoo! Audio Search

- ⦿ None
- ○ ArtistDirect
- ○ AudioLunchbox
- ○ BuyMusic.com
- ○ dMusic
- ○ eMusic
- ○ Epitonic
- ○ GarageBand

- ○ iTunes
- ○ IT Conversations
- ○ KarmaDownload
- ○ Livedownloads
- ○ MP34U
- ○ MSN Music
- ○ Music Match
- ○ Napster

- ○ NPR
- ○ PassAlong
- ○ Peer Impact
- ○ RealPlayer Music Store
- ○ Rhapsody
- ○ SoundClick
- ○ Wippit
- ○ Yahoo! Music Unlimited

[Save] [Cancel]

from a particular site, with a link to view the rest of the results from that site.

- **Subscriptions:**
If you have a subscription to any of the third-party content providers that Yahoo! Search supports, you may turn them on permanently here. This allows you to bypass the advanced search in order to search their content. With this option, as shown in Figure 3-36, content will be automatically searched whenever you use Yahoo! Search.

- **Multimedia search:**
This screen (see Figure 3-37) allows you to instruct which service Yahoo! Search should use whenever you perform an audio search. Audio searching via Yahoo! Search is not covered in this book. You

are presented with more than 20 choices, ranging from ArtistDirect to iTunes, NPR, and Yahoo! Music Unlimited.

Once you're done editing your preferences, click on either of the "Finished" buttons located at the top and bottom right of the Preferences page to return to the Yahoo! Search homepage.

CONCLUSION

Each of the three major search engines offer unique features that allow you to build and control your searches in different ways. It's likely that your current popular major search engine is Google. Hopefully, however, in addition to learning about a few new

Google features, you can now also see some uses for the features of Live Search and Yahoo! Search. Be sure to take time to experiment with each of them.

EXERCISES

Look for the answers to the following questions in each of the three search engines discussed in this chapter. Compare the results, looking for differences in the actual results and/or the different order of the same results.

1. What is the population of Buffalo, Wyoming?
2. What are the birth and death dates of Paul Newman?
3. How many public libraries are there in Nebraska?
4. I heard the TED conference will no longer be held in Monterey, CA. Where did it move to and what are the dates for the next one?
5. Where can I find a complete bibliography for the author Michael Moorcock?
6. How many episodes were there in the TV series *Galactica 1980*?
7. What is the lowest price for a 1TB SATA hard drive?
8. Who was the inspiration for the main character in the novel *Young Man with a Horn*? Have there been any other fictionalizations of his life?
9. What is the most recent animal to be declared extinct?
10. Who is Alan Smithee?

NOTES

1. www.altavista.com/
2. www.lycos.com/
3. www.ask.com/
4. http://clusty.com/
5. My evidence is anecdotal only. I have not been actually *watching* patrons perform searches, I've just been able to look up from the reference desk and have been able to tell which search engine they're using from a distance.
6. A perfect example of this was the widely publicized search of "miserable failure" that retrieved George W. Bush's official White House biography as the top result. This is because those terms appeared as links to that page as opposed to on the resulting page itself. More details can be found at: *Wikipedia, the Free Encyclopedia*, s.v. "Political Google Bombs in the 2004 U.S. Presidential Election," June 10, 2008, http://en.wikipedia.org/wiki/Miserable_failure.
7. Google, "Web Search Help," www.google.com/intl/en/help/customize.html#safe.
8. A complete list can be found at: Google, "Search Features: Improve Your Search Experience," www.google.com/help/features.html.
9. At the time of this writing, this feature covered more than 30 languages, ranging from Arabic to Vietnamese.
10. If you take a close look at this list, you will see that some languages are presented for fun. These include Klingon, Elmer Fudd, and "Bork, bork, bork!" (the language of the Swedish Chef from the *Muppet Show*).
11. When writing this portion of the book I was on a computer that was connected to the Internet via America Online. Because of this, Live Search thought I was in Mountain View, California.
12. Doing this will leave "show mail" and/or "show news" links on the page, allowing you to access these features.
13. Consumer Reports, *Financial Times*, Factiva, Forrester Research, IEEE Publications, LexisNexis, *New England Journal of Medicine*, TheStreet.com, and the *Wall Street Journal*.

Chapter 4

Wikipedia

INTRODUCTION

One of the prime technologies supporting the participatory nature of Web 2.0 is the wiki. A wiki is "a type of website that allows users to add, remove, or otherwise edit all content very quickly and easily, sometimes without the need for registration."[1] More simply stated, a wiki is a Web site that anyone can edit. This is, in my opinion, the most radical change in how individuals can use the Internet since the invention of the Web itself. The most well-known wiki on the Web today is Wikipedia. I feature Wikipedia in this chapter not only as an example of how wikis work but also as a resource that you'll want to use at your reference desk.

OVERVIEW AND HISTORY

Started in January 2001, "Wikipedia is an international Web-based cooperative free-content encyclopedia. It exists as a wiki, a web site that allows visitors to edit its content; the word *Wikipedia* itself is a portmanteau of *wiki* and *encyclopedia* and is often abbreviated to WP by its users. Wikipedia is written collaboratively by volunteers, allowing articles to be changed by anyone with access to the website."[2]

Wikipedia is run by the nonprofit Wikimedia Foundation and contains more than 10,000,000 articles in more than 260 languages (with more than 2.6 million articles in English),[3] on almost every conceivable topic. Users are encouraged to contribute content to the articles without opinion in a "neutral point of view." Discussion is encouraged, but it is done on "talk" pages where those editing a document can work toward a consensus before changing the article itself.

OPINIONS OF WIKIPEDIA

As Wikipedia becomes more popular and extends into the world's consciousness, those familiar with it tend to fall into one of three predictable categories: love it, not sure yet, and hate it. Those who fall into the middle category tend to, eventually, end up shifting to the love it or hate it categories. Let's take a look at the underlying opinions of each of the two end categories.

Love It

Those who love Wikipedia tend also to be those who participate in the project itself. They enjoy the ability to share knowledge that they have with others around the world. These folks also tend to view Wikipedia as accurate overall due to the concept of "the power of the many versus the power of the few," as proposed by James Surowiecki in his book *The Wisdom of Crowds.*[4]

Although Mr. Surowiecki doesn't address wikis specifically in his book, his underlying thesis is that any large group of people, despite their lack of expertise in a particular topic, will arrive at a conclusion that is just as accurate as the conclusion of any one expert on the same topic. Based on the evidence presented in the book, a resource such as Wikipedia, with a group of editors as large as it has, should contain correct and accurate information.

Most fans of Wikipedia will quickly admit that it is not perfect. Some articles contain incorrect and/or erroneous information, but those limited circumstances should not automatically invalidate the resource as a whole. Besides, once the inaccuracies are found, they can be easily and quickly corrected, unlike in a print publication that cannot make a correction until the next edition is published, often a year or more after the error is discovered.

Hate It

Those who don't like Wikipedia do so for at least one of several common criticisms. The first and most common criticism is one of the underlying principles of any wiki: that anyone can edit it. This concept flies in the face of the standard practice of information being created by experts who have gone through a peer review process to vet the information before presenting it as fact. How could a resource generated by (potentially) laypeople and edited by (potentially) laypeople be accurate? I add the word *potentially* to the argument since one never knows if the person is lay or an expert. People may state one thing or another, but they might be lying.

The second criticism is that Wikipedia contains inaccurate and erroneous information, therefore making the entire collection suspect. As noted earlier, some inaccurate information need not affect the system as a whole. What if I told you that the *Encyclopedia Britannica* contained inaccuracies? Would you remove it from your collection? (Think about that one for a few minutes. I'll be coming back to that issue shortly.)

The third and final criticism of Wikipedia is of the problem of vandalism. Since anyone can edit a wiki, the chances of someone adding or removing content for the express purpose of causing harm to the article is always a possibility and does occur. However, wikis allow for anyone not only to fix the vandalism but also to remove it by reverting to an earlier version of the article should the vandalism be more extensive. I have seen instances in which vandalism has occurred and is generally fixed within minutes.[5]

Not Sure Yet

In case my opinion of Wikipedia is not yet clear, please allow me to admit that I am biased and fall into the "love it" category. Many of the definitions used in this book come from either Wikipedia or one of its sister projects, such as Wiktionary (a wiki-based dictionary). Besides, if I didn't think it was a good, legitimate resource, I wouldn't devote an entire chapter to it. However, if my opinion isn't enough, let me present two scenarios that may help convince you. The first is from the journal *Nature*. The second is from a 12-year-old in the United Kingdom.

In December 2005, the journal *Nature* published the results of a study comparing Wikipedia to the *Encyclopedia Britannica* in the area of science.[6] In this study, *Nature* chose 50 scientific topics, retrieved the relevant article from both Wikipedia and *Encyclopedia Britannica*, and sent each pair of articles to an expert in the relevant field. Each expert was asked to review the articles and point out any incorrect or inaccurate information. Of the 50 articles sent out, 42 were received back. The results were surprising: "the average science entry in Wikipedia contained around four inaccuracies; Britannica, about three."[7] Previously, in January 2005, "Lucian George, 12, from north London, found five errors on two of his favourite subjects—central Europe and wildlife—and wrote to complain."[8] His complaint went to the editors of *Encyclopedia Britannica*.

These stories bring me back to my earlier question. If you knew, which you do now, that the *Encyclopedia Britannica* contained errors, would you stop using it or even go so far as to remove it from your collection? Of course not. So why, if Wikipedia contains errors in a number not much higher than the old standby *Encyclopedia Britannica*, would you not use it?

CONTROVERSIES

Even with all of the support for Wikipedia from around the world, it is not without controversy. In the past few years, there have been several high-profile controversies—all involving Wikipedia biographies of living individuals. Two of them involved Adam Curry[9] (a former MTV VJ) and Jimmy Wales[10] (cofounder of Wikipedia) editing their own biographies to depict themselves in a better light. Wikipedia has a guideline that states, in part, the following:

> It is a *faux pas* to write about yourself, according to Jimmy Wales, Wikipedia's founder. You should wait for others to write an article about subjects in which you are

personally involved. This applies to articles about you, your achievements, your business, your publications, your website, your relatives, and any other possible conflict of interest.[11]

The largest controversy, and one that illustrates several of the larger issues of Wikipedia, was the one over the biography of John Seigenthaler Sr. The easiest way to tell this story is to quote directly from Wikipedia about the incident.

The John Seigenthaler Sr. Wikipedia biography controversy arose when contributor Brian Chase anonymously posted a hoax in the Wikipedia entry for John Seigenthaler Sr. in May 2005. Chase had suggested that Seigenthaler may have had a role in the assassinations of both John F. Kennedy and Robert F. Kennedy. In September, Victor S. Johnson Jr., a friend of Seigenthaler's, discovered the entry. Demonstrably false statements in the article included claims that Seigenthaler lived in the Soviet Union from 1971 to 1984 and that he was the founder of a public relations firm. Seigenthaler's brother founded a public relations firm that bears the family name, but John Seigenthaler has no role in it.

After Johnson alerted him to the article, Seigenthaler e-mailed friends and colleagues about it. One colleague, Eric Newton from the John S. and James L. Knight Foundation, cut and pasted Seigenthaler's official biography into Wikipedia from the Freedom Forum Web site on 23 September 2005. Newton's copyright violation was soon replaced by a shorter biography that did not violate Wikipedia's policies. When Newton ran into Seigenthaler in November in New York at the Committee to Protect Journalists dinner, he told Seigenthaler he had replaced the vandalism with the official biography.

Seigenthaler himself contacted Wikipedia founder Jimmy Wales in October 2005, and Wales took the unusual step of having the false information hidden from the public in Wikipedia version logs. As a result, the unredacted versions of the article could be viewed only by Wikipedia administrators. The false statements were added on May 26, 2005, so they had remained uncorrected for almost four months. Several "mirror" Web sites not controlled by Wikipedia continued to display the inaccurate article for several weeks fol-

lowing Wikipedia's action. It is not known how many people actually saw the libelous entry before it was corrected.

On November 29, 2005, an op-ed article by Seigenthaler appeared in *USA Today*, describing the particulars of the incident. It included a verbatim reposting of the falsehoods in question:

John Seigenthaler Sr. was the assistant to Attorney General Robert Kennedy in the early 1960s. For a brief time, he was thought to have been directly involved in the Kennedy assassinations of both John and his brother Bobby. Nothing was ever proven.

An expanded version was published several days later in *The Tennessean* where Seigenthaler was editor-in-chief in the 1970s. Seigenthaler detailed his own failed attempts to identify the person who posted the inaccurate biography to Wikipedia anonymously. He reportedly asked the poster's Internet service provider, BellSouth, to identify its user. He criticized Wikipedia for offering inaccurate material to a wide audience. On 9 December, Seigenthaler appeared on C-SPAN's Washington Journal with Brian Lamb hosting. He said he was concerned that other pranksters would try to spoof members of Congress or other powerful figures in government, which may then prompt a backlash and turn back First Amendment rights on the Internet.

The audit log of Seigenthaler's Wikipedia page shows that a small number of posters are still re-adding the Kennedy assassination smears and other comments of a libelous nature on a regular basis, thereby providing further ammunition for Wikipedia's detractors.[12]

The fallout from this incident is still being felt today through the responsive Wikipedia policy that requires a user to have an account before creating a new article. Also in response, Wikipedia has increased the number of reviewers who look at new articles. The big question raised by this story is who was right and who was wrong. Everyone agrees that the creator of the article, later discovered to be "Brian Chase, a 38-year-old operations manager at Rush Delivery in Nashville," should not have created the article as he did despite his defense that he did it to "to play a joke on a colleague" as "one of Rush Delivery's clients was Seigenthaler's late brother Thomas." Despite this, many criticize Mr. Seigenthaler's handling of the situation. Both sides of the reaction can be divided into two camps: "old school" and "new school."

Mr. Seigenthaler definitely falls into the old-school camp. His reaction was to cry foul, complain to the host of the information, and take the matter public. Those in the old-school camp wouldn't have blinked at Mr. Seigenthaler as he decided to file a libel suit against Jimmy Wales, the Wikimedia Foundation, and the then unknown author of the article. This is exactly what has traditionally happened in the print media since the victim has no other method of recourse. For example, if I were libeled in the *Denver Post*, I would have no method of changing what the *Denver Post* had printed.

Most people who were already fans, and definitely those who were experienced in editing Wikipedia, fell into the new-school camp. They felt that Mr. Seigenthaler should have just edited the article himself (or had someone else do it for him so as to avoid the problems Messrs. Wales and Curry found themselves in) to correct any of the inaccurate information, thereby solving the problem in minimal time and causing the least disruption to the system. My feeling is to lean toward the side of the new-school camp. I do see where Mr. Seigenthaler was coming from, but since he disagreed with Wikipedia's premise in the first place,[13] he refused to learn how the system worked and adjust to the technology accordingly.

Ultimately, most fans of Wikipedia will agree that when it comes to scholarly research, Wikipedia should not be used as a primary resource. It's a place to start, just as any print encyclopedia is. Once you have a basic understanding of a topic, you can then move on to more specific and reliable resources. This also applies to many a reference interaction wherein librarians are presented with questions on topics on which they have no prior knowledge. Wikipedia can be a great resource for baseline information that can lead you to other resources.

Now that we have the larger issues concerning Wikipedia out of the way, let's take a look at the how and why of creating an account, how to search Wikipedia, and how to perform basic editing.

CREATING AN ACCOUNT

You are able to perform the most common functions in Wikipedia without creating an account. For example, you can read articles, search for articles, and even edit articles without signing in or even creating an account. However, a few additional benefits come along with creating and signing into your account:

- You're allowed to create new articles.
- You can create a "user page" that contains information about yourself and your library.
- When you do edit a page, your username will appear along with the edit instead of your computer's IP address. You will then also be able to easily track all of the edits you have made.
- You will be able to change your preferences, including the color scheme of Wikipedia.
- Most important, once you have an account, you will also have a "watchlist" to which you can add the articles you are interested in tracking. Your watchlist will inform you whenever an article you are tracking is edited.

To create an account, click on the "Log in/Create account" link in the upper right corner of any Wikipedia page. Once you are on the log-in page (see Figure 4-1), click on "Create one" to create a new account.

The "Create account" page (see Figure 4-2) will ask you to enter a username and a password (twice). You may also enter your e-mail address if you wish. Click on the "Create account" button to continue the process. You will then need to check your e-mail account for the verification e-mail that you've been sent. Once you click on the URL in that e-mail, your account will have been created and you will have the benefits of an account holder.

Once you're logged in you can add any article to your watchlist by clicking on the "watch" link at the top of the article (see Figure 4-3). To view your watchlist, click on the "my watchlist" link at the top of any page.

Figure 4-4 shows my watchlist page. The "My watchlist" page displays, by default, all of the pages that have been edited in the previous three days. On this page, you can change the length of time and types of edits displayed. You can also click on the

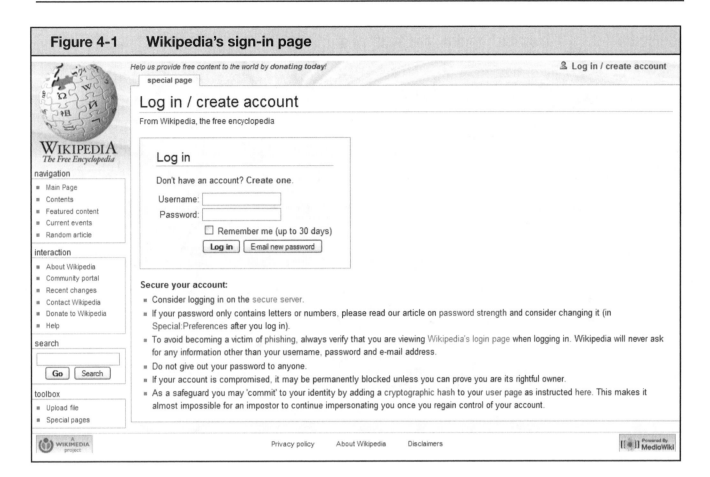

Figure 4-1   Wikipedia's sign-in page

"view and edit watchlist" link to see every page on your watchlist and remove them on a case-by-case basis.

Your preferences can be changed by clicking on the "my preferences" link at the top of any page (see Figure 4-5). Here you can change such settings as your profile, skin (color and font of Wikipedia), date and time format, and editing options.

Since we're focusing on searching, the only preference area that I wish to mention in detail is the "Search" area as shown in Figure 4-6. Here you can control which sections of Wikipedia are searched by default. To add a new section to your searches, just click on the appropriate box. To remove a section from a search, uncheck its box. Here you can also control how many hits are displayed on each result page and how much of the content of each result is displayed on the search results screen. The ability to edit pages is covered later in this chapter. The ability to see and compare earlier versions of Wikipedia articles is covered in Chapter 8.

SEARCHING WIKIPEDIA

When searching Wikipedia, you could receive three different types of search results: a perfect match, a list of relevancy ranked results, and a disambiguation page. Let me describe each of them to you in turn along with some examples.

A Perfect Match

All articles in Wikipedia have a title. For example, the title of the article on the author Dean Koontz is "Dean Koontz." The article for Denver is titled "Denver, Colorado." These titles are important and are rarely changed.[14] If you enter the name of an article in the search box and click the "go" button, Wikipedia will look for a single article with a title matching the keywords you typed in. Assuming a match is found you'll automatically be presented with that article.

For example, Figure 4-7 shows the results of a Wikipedia search for *dean koontz*. Since an article titled "Dean Koontz" exists, I've been presented with

Figure 4-2 **Wikipedia's "create account" page**

Figure 4-3   Wikipedia's "watch" and "my watchlist" links

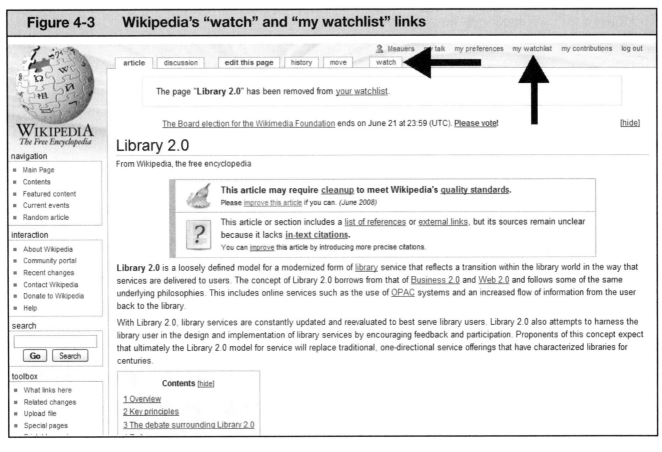

Figure 4-4   My watchlist page

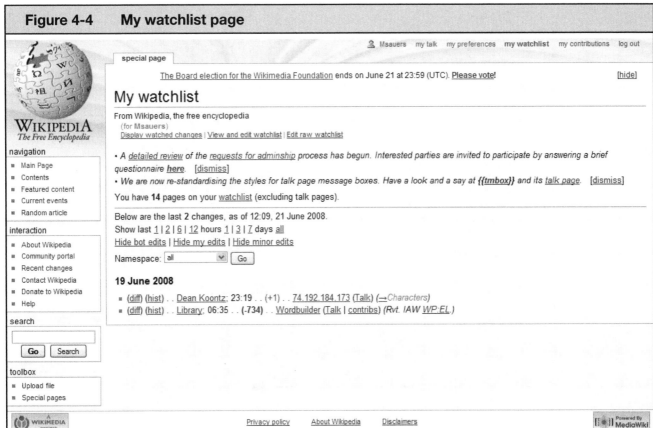

Figure 4-5	Wikipedia's "my preferences" page

  Msauers   my talk   **my preferences**   my watchlist   my contributions   log out

special page

The Board election for the Wikimedia Foundation ends on June 21 at 23:59 (UTC). **Please vote!**   [hide]

My preferences

From Wikipedia, the free encyclopedia

| **User profile** | Skin | Math | Files | Date and time | Editing | Recent changes | Watchlist | Search | Misc | Gadgets |

User profile

Username:	Msauers
User ID:	266856
Member of groups:	Autoconfirmed users, Users (User group rights)
Number of edits:	118
Global account status:	Not using unified account (Manage your global account)
E-mail (optional)*	msauers@travelinlibrarian.info

- E-mail (optional): Allows us to e-mail your password to you if you forget it. If you also "Enable e-mail from other users", then others can e-mail you from your **User** or **User talk** page by using the "E-mail this user" feature. Note that the sender's e-mail address will be visible to the recipient. If you change your e-mail address, you will need to reconfirm it.

Signature:	msauers

☐ **Raw signature** (If unchecked, the contents of the box above will be treated as your nickname and link automatically to your user page. If checked, the contents should be formatted with Wiki markup, including all links. **Do not use images, templates, or external links in your signature.**)

Language:	en - English

Change password

Old password:	••••••••
New password:	
Retype new password:	

☐ Remember my login on this computer

E-mail

Your e-mail address is not yet authenticated. No e-mail will be sent for any of the following features.
Confirm your e-mail address
☑ Enable e-mail from other users
☐ Send me copies of e-mails I send to other users

[Save] [Clear unsaved changes]

Note: After saving, you have to bypass your browser's cache to see the changes. In **Internet Explorer** and **Firefox**, hold down the Ctrl key and click the Refresh or Reload button. **Opera** users have to clear their caches through *Tools→Preferences*, see the instructions for Opera. **Konqueror** and **Safari** users can just click the Reload button.

WIKIPEDIA
The Free Encyclopedia

navigation
- Main Page
- Contents
- Featured content
- Current events
- Random article

interaction
- About Wikipedia
- Community portal
- Recent changes
- Contact Wikipedia
- Donate to Wikipedia
- Help

search

[   ]
[Go] [Search]

toolbox
- Upload file
- Special pages

WIKIMEDIA project   Privacy policy   About Wikipedia   Disclaimers   Powered By MediaWiki

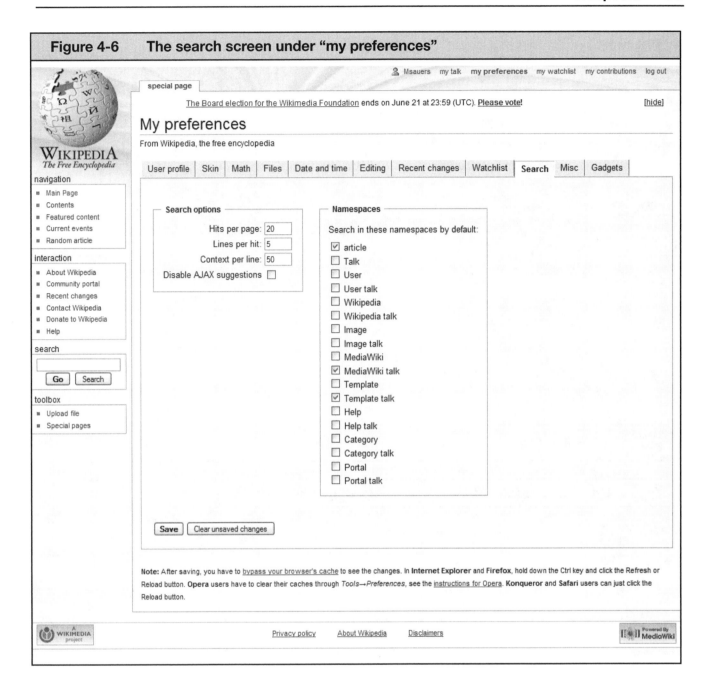

Figure 4-6   The search screen under "my preferences"

that article. Sometimes the matches aren't exact, but close enough. Figure 4-8 shows the results of a search on *science fiction authors*, which gets you the "List of Science Fiction Authors" article.

A List of Relevancy Ranked Results
If you enter search terms and click the "search" button or if you click on "go" and an exact match isn't found, you'll be presented with a list of relevancy ranked results as with most other search engines. For example, Figure 4-9 shows the results of a search for

punk rock pioneer, which retrieves a list of available articles, including "Punk Rock," "List of Brazilian Punk and Hardcore Groups," "Post-punk," and "The Lurkers."

A Disambiguation Page
In other situations, you'll search Wikipedia for a keyword that has multiple meanings depending on its context. A perfect example can be seen in Figure 4-10, which shows the resulting disambiguation page for a search on the term *boots*.[15]

Figure 4-7   The results of searching Wikipedia for *dean koontz*

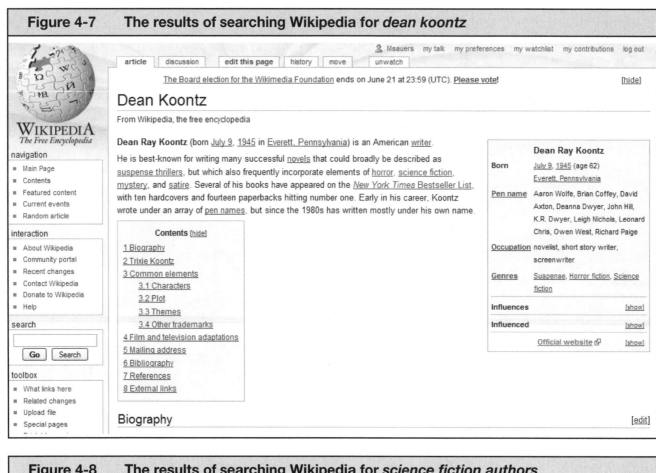

Figure 4-8   The results of searching Wikipedia for *science fiction authors*

Figure 4-9   The results of searching Wikipedia for *punk rock pioneer*

☻ Msauers   my talk   my preferences   my watchlist   my contributions   log out

WIKIPEDIA
The Free Encyclopedia

navigation
- Main Page
- Contents
- Featured content
- Current events
- Random article

interaction
- About Wikipedia
- Community portal
- Recent changes
- Contact Wikipedia
- Donate to Wikipedia
- Help

search

punk rock pioneer

[Go] [Search]

toolbox
- Upload file
- Special pages

special page

The Board election for the Wikimedia Foundation ends on June 21 at 23:59 (UTC). Please vote!   [hide]

Search results

From Wikipedia, the free encyclopedia

You searched for punk rock pioneer [Index]

No article title matches

No page with that title exists.

You can search again:

- Titles on Wikipedia are case sensitive, except for the first character; please check alternate capitalizations and consider adding a redirect here to the correct title.
- See all pages that begin with this prefix.
- See all pages within Wikipedia that link to this page.

You can create this article:

- Read Wikipedia:Your first article.
- Gather references to the source(s) of your information.
- Create the page including your references.

Or you can request that this page be created.

For more information about searching Wikipedia, see Wikipedia:Searching.

punk rock pioneer   [MediaWiki search ▾] [Search]

Showing below results **1 - 20** of **1040**

View (previous 20) (next 20) (20 | 50 | 100 | 250 | 500)

- **Punk rock**
  {{punkRockInfobox}} ... tripped-down instrumentation, and often political, anti-government lyrics. Punk embraces a [[DIY ethic|DIY]] (do it yourself) ethic, with many bands self- ...
  129 KB (19328 words) - 17:07, 21 June 2008

- **Punk rock subgenres**
  ... owever, sometimes a particular trait is common in several genres, and thus punk genres are normally grouped by a combination of traits and twee. ==Primary punk rock genres==
  10 KB (1503 words) - 20:19, 29 May 2008

- **History of the punk subculture**
  ... nd the globe and evolved into a number of different forms. The history of punk plays important part in the [[history of subcultures in the 20th century]] ... Several precursors to the punk subculture had varying degrees of influence on that culture.
  23 KB (3630 words) - 10:40, 5 June 2008

- **Pop punk**
  | name = [[Pop punk]] ... ic]] - [[Pub rock (UK)|Pub rock]] - [[Glam rock]] - [[Protopunk]] - [[Surf rock]]
  20 KB (3197 words) - 02:53, 17 June 2008

- **List of Brazilian punk and hardcore groups**
  The origin of [[punk rock]] and [[hardcore punk]] in [[Brazil]] was around the end of the 1970s, by the influence of bands ... ... only in the beginning of the 1980s that the scene grew, even with gangs of punks, specially in [[São Paulo]] city (and where "Restos de Nada" came from). ...
  9 KB (1425 words) - 18:09, 14 June 2008

- **Anarcho-punk**
  |name=[[Anarcho-punk]] |stylistic_origins= [[Punk rock]]
[[Street punk]]
  16 KB (2289 words) - 22:01, 20 June 2008

- **Post-punk**
  |name=Post-punk ... unk rock]], [[Glam rock]], [[Dub music|Dub]], [[Funk]], [[Reggae]], [[Krautrock]], {{nowrap|[[Avant-garde|Avant-garde art movements]]}}, [[Experimental mu ...
  10 KB (1406 words) - 08:32, 18 June 2008

- **List of rock and roll performers**
  {{See also|Rock and roll|Popular music|List of popular music performers|Country music|List ... This is a "list of rock and roll performers".
  18 KB (2622 words) - 05:43, 18 June 2008

- **List of punk bands, 0–K**
  :"See also [[List of punk bands, L–Z]]" ... 9 through K)" who have achieved notability. The bands listed have played punk music at some point in their career, although they may have also played ot ...
  28 KB (2924 words) - 12:51, 20 June 2008

Figure 4-9   The results of searching Wikipedia for *punk rock pioneer (Continued)*

- Rock music
  |name=[[Rock music]] |stylistic_origins=[[Rock and roll]]
[[Rockabilly]]
[[Jazz]]
  48 KB (7350 words) - 13:11, 21 June 2008

- Punk fashion
  ... re)|greasers]], and [[Mod (lifestyle)|mods]] have influenced punk fashion. Punk
  fashion has likewise influenced the styles of these groups, as well as tho ... ...
  supposedly managing the [[The New York Dolls]] (Note: In the documentary "Punk:
  Attitude", [[David Johansen]] said McLaren was never their manager, and ...
  19 KB (2860 words) - 12:44, 21 June 2008

- Argentine rock
  ... spañol]], and one of the most important non-English [[language]] forms of rock
  music in the world. ... it is known as "[[Rock Nacional]]" "/rok.nasjo'nal/", literally
  National Rock (not in a political way at all but as a local movement).
  78 KB (12500 words) - 22:10, 11 June 2008

- Brazilian rock
  | name = Brazilian rock stuff|bgcolor = navy | stylistic_origins = North American and
  British [[rock music]], [[samba]], [[forró]] and other [[Brazil]]ian genres
  28 KB (4151 words) - 18:10, 21 June 2008

- California punk scene
  ... moved: [[Image:Screamersgigposter.jpg|150px|thumb|Flyer for an late 70's punk
  show featuring The Screamers, with art by [[Gary Panter]]]]{{deletable imag ... The
  "California punk scene'" is a regional [[punk music]] scene that started in the late
  1970s and still exists today. It pr ...
  17 KB (2556 words) - 15:38, 15 June 2008

- Hardcore punk
  |name= Hardcore punk |stylistic_origins=[[Punk rock]]
  40 KB (6114 words) - 14:47, 21 June 2008

- List of post-punk bands
  ... , both from the original [[post-punk]] movement as well as from the [[post-punk
  revival]]. ... e mid-80's. These bands are often disputed as being truly part of the
  post-punk movement.
  18 KB (2442 words) - 06:31, 21 June 2008

- Brisbane punk rock
  ... generation."<ref name="EncylopediaP706">"The Encyclopedia of Australian Rock
  and Pop", p. 706</ref> ... o two categories; the [[hardcore punk]] and the [[post-
  punk]] punk or dark punk.
  16 KB (2578 words) - 18:58, 15 June 2008

- Queercore
  |name=[[Punk rock]] ... [[Psychedelic rock]] - [[Pub rock (UK)|Pub rock]] - [[Glam
  rock]] - [[Protopunk]]
  23 KB (3519 words) - 20:41, 11 June 2008

- Alternative rock
  {{Redirect3|Alternative music|For other "alternative" subgenres of non-rock genres,
  see [[alternative hip-hop]] and [[alternative country]]}} | name = [[Alternative rock]]
  34 KB (5068 words) - 19:16, 19 June 2008

- The Lurkers
  | Genre = [[Punk Rock]]
[[Pop punk]]
[[New Wave music|New Wave]] '''The
  Lurkers''' were a late [[1970s]] [[England|English]] [[punk rock]] group from
  [[Uxbridge]], West [[London]],<ref name="Larkin">Larkin, Coli ...
  11 KB (1579 words) - 22:13, 7 June 2008

View (previous 20) (next 20) (20 | 50 | 100 | 250 | 500)

┌─ Advanced search ──

Search in namespaces:
☑ article ☐ Talk ☐ User ☐ User talk ☐ Wikipedia ☐ Wikipedia talk ☐ Image ☐ Image talk ☐ MediaWiki ☑ MediaWiki talk
☐ Template ☑ Template talk ☐ Help ☐ Help talk ☐ Category ☐ Category talk ☐ Portal ☐ Portal talk
☐ List redirects

Search for [punk rock pioneer   ]   [Advanced search]

└──

Figure 4-10 The disambiguation page for "boot"

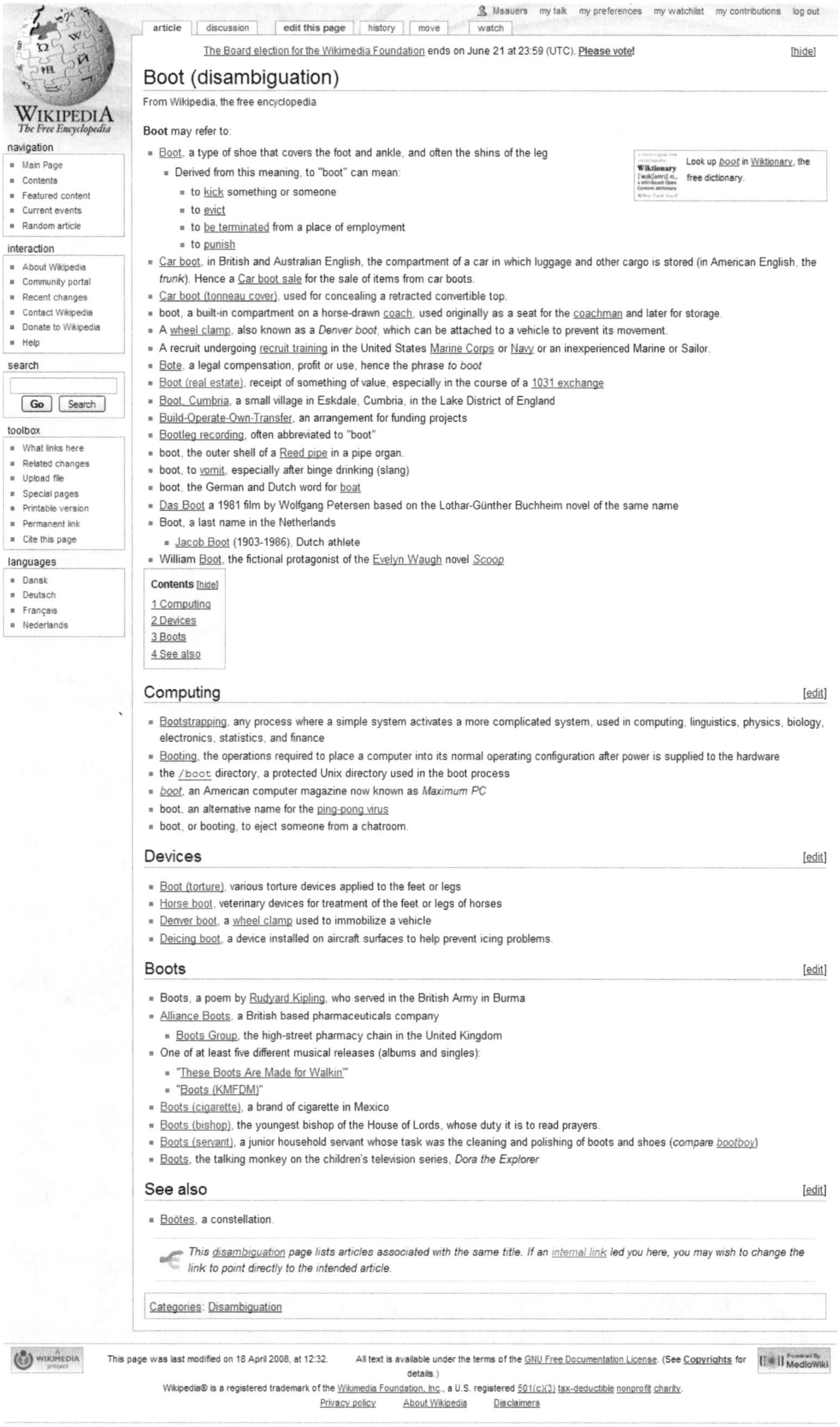

Msauers my talk my preferences my watchlist my contributions log out

article | discussion | edit this page | history | move | watch

The Board election for the Wikimedia Foundation ends on June 21 at 23:59 (UTC). Please vote! [hide]

Boot (disambiguation)

From Wikipedia, the free encyclopedia

Boot may refer to:

- Boot, a type of shoe that covers the foot and ankle, and often the shins of the leg
  - Derived from this meaning, to "boot" can mean:
    - to kick something or someone
    - to evict
    - to be terminated from a place of employment
    - to punish
- Car boot, in British and Australian English, the compartment of a car in which luggage and other cargo is stored (in American English, the *trunk*). Hence a Car boot sale for the sale of items from car boots.
- Car boot (tonneau cover), used for concealing a retracted convertible top.
- boot, a built-in compartment on a horse-drawn coach, used originally as a seat for the coachman and later for storage.
- A wheel clamp, also known as a *Denver boot*, which can be attached to a vehicle to prevent its movement.
- A recruit undergoing recruit training in the United States Marine Corps or Navy or an inexperienced Marine or Sailor.
- Bote, a legal compensation, profit or use, hence the phrase *to boot*
- Boot (real estate), receipt of something of value, especially in the course of a 1031 exchange
- Boot, Cumbria, a small village in Eskdale, Cumbria, in the Lake District of England
- Build-Operate-Own-Transfer, an arrangement for funding projects
- Bootleg recording, often abbreviated to "boot"
- boot, the outer shell of a Reed pipe in a pipe organ.
- boot, to vomit, especially after binge drinking (slang)
- boot, the German and Dutch word for boat
- Das Boot a 1981 film by Wolfgang Petersen based on the Lothar-Günther Buchheim novel of the same name
- Boot, a last name in the Netherlands
  - Jacob Boot (1903-1986), Dutch athlete
- William Boot, the fictional protagonist of the Evelyn Waugh novel *Scoop*

Look up *boot* in Wiktionary, the free dictionary.

Contents [hide]

1 Computing
2 Devices
3 Boots
4 See also

Computing [edit]

- Bootstrapping, any process where a simple system activates a more complicated system, used in computing, linguistics, physics, biology, electronics, statistics, and finance
- Booting, the operations required to place a computer into its normal operating configuration after power is supplied to the hardware
- the `/boot` directory, a protected Unix directory used in the boot process
- *boot*, an American computer magazine now known as *Maximum PC*
- boot, an alternative name for the ping-pong virus
- boot, or booting, to eject someone from a chatroom.

Devices [edit]

- Boot (torture), various torture devices applied to the feet or legs
- Horse boot, veterinary devices for treatment of the feet or legs of horses
- Denver boot, a wheel clamp used to immobilize a vehicle
- Deicing boot, a device installed on aircraft surfaces to help prevent icing problems.

Boots [edit]

- Boots, a poem by Rudyard Kipling, who served in the British Army in Burma
- Alliance Boots, a British based pharmaceuticals company
  - Boots Group, the high-street pharmacy chain in the United Kingdom
- One of at least five different musical releases (albums and singles):
  - "These Boots Are Made for Walkin'"
  - "Boots (KMFDM)"
- Boots (cigarette), a brand of cigarette in Mexico
- Boots (bishop), the youngest bishop of the House of Lords, whose duty it is to read prayers.
- Boots (servant), a junior household servant whose task was the cleaning and polishing of boots and shoes (*compare* bootboy)
- Boots, the talking monkey on the children's television series, *Dora the Explorer*

See also [edit]

- Boötes, a constellation.

This disambiguation page lists articles associated with the same title. If an internal link led you here, you may wish to change the link to point directly to the intended article.

Categories: Disambiguation

navigation
- Main Page
- Contents
- Featured content
- Current events
- Random article

interaction
- About Wikipedia
- Community portal
- Recent changes
- Contact Wikipedia
- Donate to Wikipedia
- Help

search

Go | Search

toolbox
- What links here
- Related changes
- Upload file
- Special pages
- Printable version
- Permanent link
- Cite this page

languages
- Dansk
- Deutsch
- Français
- Nederlands

This page was last modified on 18 April 2008, at 12:32. All text is available under the terms of the GNU Free Documentation License. (See Copyrights for details.)
Wikipedia® is a registered trademark of the Wikimedia Foundation, Inc., a U.S. registered 501(c)(3) tax-deductible nonprofit charity.
Privacy policy About Wikipedia Disclaimers

The boot disambiguation page contains links to no fewer than 20 different articles related to the concept of a boot. Topics listed range from the footwear to the computer term to a Denver boot to Nancy Sinatra to the film *Das Boot*. From here you can choose to view any of these articles by clicking on the appropriate link.

CITING WIKIPEDIA

Since Wikipedia articles are ever-changing, it is important that you cite Wikipedia properly. Every page in Wikipedia has a link on the left side of the screen that will take you to the proper citation for that page. Figure 4-11 shows the "Cite this article" link for the "Lincoln, Nebraska" article, while Figure 4-12 shows the citation page.

Citations are given in nine different formats, including APA, MLA, Chicago, and BibTex. Every citation format will include the date that the article was accessed when cited and a link to that version.

This allows interested individuals the ability to view the page as it looked when it was cited.

ADDING AND EDITING

Wikipedia has many help files, several of which are dedicated to how to edit articles.[16] Although this is not directly related to searching, I would like to present a brief overview and some pointers for editing articles in Wikipedia before we move on to the next chapter because, without editing, Wikipedia is not the participatory medium I make it out to be.

A few things to keep in mind when creating a new Wikipedia article and/or editing an existing article, known as The Five Pillars[17] of Wikipedia, are abridged here:

- Wikipedia is an encyclopedia incorporating elements of general encyclopedias, specialized encyclopedias, and almanacs. Wikipedia is not an indiscriminate collection of information.

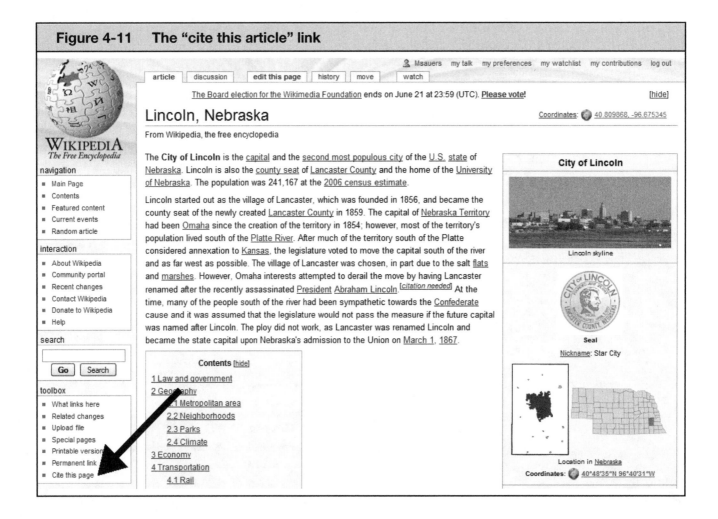

Figure 4-11   The "cite this article" link

Figure 4-12   The citation page for *Lincoln, Nebraska*

Maauers   my talk   my preferences   my watchlist   my contributions   log out

special page

The Board election for the Wikimedia Foundation ends on June 21 at 23:59 (UTC). **Please vote!**   [hide]

Cite

From Wikipedia, the free encyclopedia

Page: [Lincoln, Nebraska]   [Cite]

Contents: APA | MLA | MHRA | Chicago | CSE | Bluebook | AMA | BibTeX

IMPORTANT NOTE: Most educators and professionals do not consider it appropriate to use tertiary sources such as encyclopedias as a sole source for any information — citing an encyclopedia as an important reference in footnotes or bibliographies may result in censure or a failing grade. Wikipedia articles should be used for background information, as a reference for correct terminology and search terms, and as a starting point for further research.

As with any community-built reference, there is a possibility for error in Wikipedia's content — please check your facts against multiple sources and read our disclaimers for more information.

Bibliographic details for "Lincoln, Nebraska"

- Page name: Lincoln, Nebraska
- Author: Wikipedia contributors
- Publisher: *Wikipedia, The Free Encyclopedia.*
- Date of last revision: 9 June 2008 20:34 UTC
- Date retrieved: 21 June 2008 19:19 UTC
- Permanent link: http://en.wikipedia.org/w/index.php?title=Lincoln%2C_Nebraska&oldid=218248002
- Page Version ID: 218248002

Please remember to check your manual of style, standards guide or instructor's guidelines for the exact syntax to suit your needs. For more detailed advice, see **Citing Wikipedia**.

Citation styles for "Lincoln, Nebraska"

APA style

Lincoln, Nebraska. (2008, June 9). In *Wikipedia, The Free Encyclopedia.* Retrieved 19:19, June 21, 2008, from http://en.wikipedia.org/w/index.php?title=Lincoln%2C_Nebraska&oldid=218248002

MLA style

"Lincoln, Nebraska." *Wikipedia, The Free Encyclopedia.* 9 Jun 2008, 20:34 UTC. Wikimedia Foundation, Inc. 21 Jun 2008 <http://en.wikipedia.org/w/index.php?title=Lincoln%2C_Nebraska&oldid=218248002>.

MHRA style

Wikipedia contributors, 'Lincoln, Nebraska', *Wikipedia, The Free Encyclopedia,* 9 June 2008, 20:34 UTC, <http://en.wikipedia.org/w/index.php?title=Lincoln%2C_Nebraska&oldid=218248002> [accessed 21 June 2008]

Chicago style

Wikipedia contributors, "Lincoln, Nebraska," *Wikipedia, The Free Encyclopedia,* http://en.wikipedia.org/w/index.php?title=Lincoln%2C_Nebraska&oldid=218248002 (accessed June 21, 2008).

CBE/CSE style

Wikipedia contributors. Lincoln, Nebraska [Internet]. Wikipedia, The Free Encyclopedia; 2008 Jun 9, 20:34 UTC [cited 2008 Jun 21]. Available from: http://en.wikipedia.org/w/index.php?title=Lincoln%2C_Nebraska&oldid=218248002.

Bluebook style

Lincoln, Nebraska, http://en.wikipedia.org/w/index.php?title=Lincoln%2C_Nebraska&oldid=218248002 (last visited Jun. 21, 2008).

Bluebook: Harvard JOLT style

See Wikipedia, *Lincoln, Nebraska,* http://en.wikipedia.org/wiki/Lincoln%2C_Nebraska (optional description here) (as of Jun. 21, 2008, 19:19 GMT).

AMA style

Wikipedia contributors. Lincoln, Nebraska. Wikipedia, The Free Encyclopedia. June 9, 2008, 20:34 UTC. Available at: http://en.wikipedia.org/w/index.php?title=Lincoln%2C_Nebraska&oldid=218248002. Accessed June 21, 2008.

BibTeX entry

```
@misc{ wiki:xxx,
    author = "Wikipedia",
    title = "Lincoln, Nebraska --- Wikipedia{,} The Free Encyclopedia",
    year = "2008",
    url = "http://en.wikipedia.org/w/index.php?title=Lincoln%2C Nebraska&oldid=218248002",
    note = "[Online; accessed 21-June-2008]"
}
```

When using the LaTeX package url (\usepackage{url} somewhere in the preamble), which tends to give much more nicely formatted web addresses, the following may be preferred:

```
@misc{ wiki:xxx,
    author = "Wikipedia",
    title = "Lincoln, Nebraska --- Wikipedia{,} The Free Encyclopedia",
    year = "2008",
    url = "\url{http://en.wikipedia.org/w/index.php?title=Lincoln%2C Nebraska&oldid=218248002}",
    note = "[Online; accessed 21-June-2008]"
}
```

Privacy policy   About Wikipedia   Disclaimers   Powered By MediaWiki

- Wikipedia uses the *neutral point-of-view*, which means Wikipedia strives for articles that advocate no single point of view. Sometimes this requires representing multiple points of view; presenting each point of view accurately; providing context for any given point of view, so that readers understand whose view the point represents; and presenting no one point of view as "the truth" or "the best view."

- Wikipedia is free content, so all text is available under GNU's Free Documentation License (GFDL) and may be distributed or linked accordingly.

- Wikipedia follows the writers' rules of engagement: Respect your fellow Wikipedians even when you may not agree with them. Be civil. Avoid making personal attacks or sweeping generalizations.

- Wikipedia doesn't have firm rules besides the five general principles elucidated here. Be bold in editing, moving, and modifying articles, because the joy of editing is that although it should be aimed for, perfection isn't required.

As long as you keep these five pillars in mind, you shouldn't have any trouble contributing information to Wikipedia.

Beyond just mustering the courage to edit an article in Wikipedia, you then need to learn what is known as wiki syntax.[18] Learning wiki syntax is like learning HTML (hypertext markup language). Unfortunately, it doesn't look much like HTML at all. (In fact, from my experience, it's easier for those who have no HTML knowledge to learn wiki syntax than for those who do.) Even though it doesn't look like HTML, it still works on the same principle; add special codes (markup) to your text to get the system (the wiki) to present that text in a certain way.

To view the wiki syntax of an article, just click on the "edit this page" link at the top of the page. Figure 4-13 shows this link at the top of my user page (http://en.wikipedia.org/wiki/User:Msauers), while Figure 4-14 shows the editable wiki syntax for that page.

To make changes, edit the content of the large box at the top of the page. In most cases, you need only replace the incorrect content with the correct content or add new content in the appropriate location. However, you should familiarize yourself with some basic items of wiki syntax. The following are the most common:

Basic Wiki Terms

Wiki Syntax	Result
[[Librarian]]	Creates a hyperlink to the Wikipedia article titled "Librarian."
[[Cascading Style Sheets|CSS]]	Creates a hyperlink on "CSS" to the Wikipedia article titled "Cascading Style Sheets."
[http://www.nlc.state.ne.us/ Nebraska Library Commission]	Creates a hyperlink on "Nebraska Library Commission" to the URL given.
"No Limit"	*No Limit* (italics)
*One	• One
**Two	• Two
***Three	• Three
#One	1. One
#Two	1. Two
###Three	1. Three
-~~~~	Sign your work. This will insert your username and date/time stamp of the last edit.[19]

Figure 4-13   The "edit this page" link

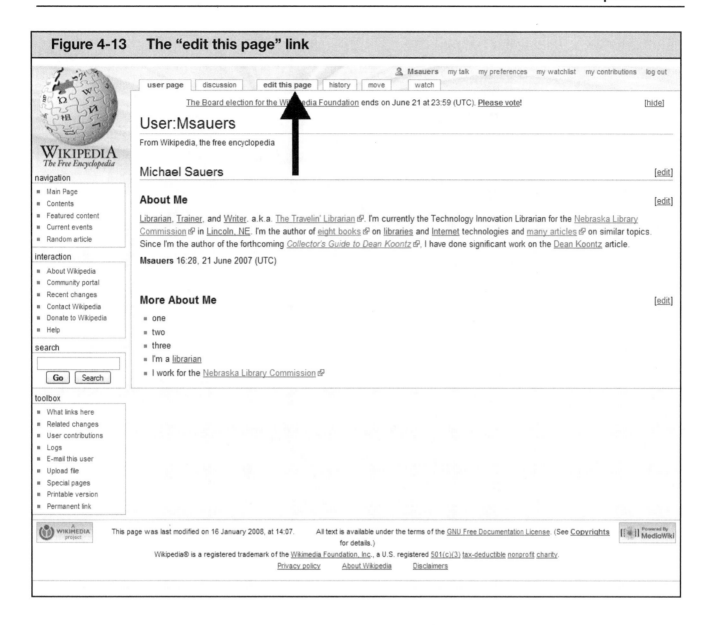

If you're looking for a place to practice editing, feel free to do so on your user page (http://en.wikipedia.org/wiki/User:*username*) or on Wikipedia's Sandbox page (http://en.wikipedia.org/wiki/Wikipedia:Sandbox). Before saving your changes to any page in Wikipedia, you are strongly encouraged to do the following:

1. Use the "Show preview" button to view the results of your edit before you save it. This is very important when you're first learning to edit. As you become more comfortable with editing it isn't as necessary but is still recommended. You can also use the "Show changes" button to see a side-by-side comparison of the current version of the article and your edits.

2. Write an edit summary. Although optional, writing an edit summary is a sign of a good editor. It doesn't need to be long and completely accurate. It just has to be enough to indicate the changes you made to someone looking at the article's history.

3. Mark your changes as a "minor edit" if appropriate. Minor edits include fixing grammar and spelling errors—edits that don't substantively change the content or layout of an article.

Once sure your edits are as you wish them to

Figure 4-14 **Editing user: Msauers**

WIKIPEDIA
The Free Encyclopedia

Msauers my talk my preferences my watchlist my contributions log out

user page | discussion | edit this page | history | move | watch

The Board election for the Wikimedia Foundation ends on June 21 at 23:59 (UTC). Please vote! [hide]

Editing User:Msauers

From Wikipedia, the free encyclopedia

```
==Michael Sauers==

===About Me===
[[Librarian]], [[Trainer]], and [[Writer]]. a.k.a. [http://travelinlibrarian.info/ The Travelin'
Librarian]. I'm currently the Technology Innovation Librarian for the [http://www.nlc.state.ne.us/
Nebraska Library Commission] in [[Lincoln, NE]]. I'm the author of [http://travelinlibrarian.info
/home/nonfic.html eight books] on [[libraries]] and [[Internet]] technologies and
[http://travelinlibrarian.info/home/articles.html many articles] on similar topics. Since I'm the
author of the forthcoming [http://cemeterydance.com/cgi-bin/miva?Merchant2/merchant.mv+Screen=CTGY&
Store_Code=CDP&Category_Code=KOONTZ ''Collector's Guide to Dean Koontz''], I have done significant
work on the [[Dean Koontz]] article.

[[User:Msauers|Msauers]] 16:28, 21 June 2007 (UTC)


===More About Me===

* one
* two
* three
* I'm a [[librarian]]
* I work for the [http://www.nlc.state.ne.us/ Nebraska Library Commission]
```

Content that violates any copyright will be deleted. Encyclopedic content must be verifiable. You agree to license your contributions under the GFDL.

Edit summary (Briefly describe the changes you have made):

☐ This is a minor edit (what's this?) ☐ Watch this page

Save page | Show preview | Show changes | Cancel | Editing help (opens in new window)

Do not copy text from other websites without a GFDL-compatible license. It will be deleted.

Insert: – — … ˈ ˌ ‘ ' ° " ' ″ ≈ ≠ ≤ ≥ ± − × ÷ ← → § **Sign your username:** ~~~~ (on talk pages)

Wiki markup: {{}} {{{}}} | [] [[]] [[Category:]] #REDIRECT [[]]   <s></s>   <code></code> <blockquote></blockquote> <ref></ref> {{Reflist}} <references/> {{DEFAULTSORT:}} <!-- --> <span class="plainlinks"></span> • (templates)

Symbols: ~ | ¡ ¿ † ‡ ↔ ↑ ↓ • ¶ # ½ ⅓ ⅔ ¼ ¾ ⅛ ⅜ ⅝ ⅞ ∞ ' ' " " « » ¤ ₳ ฿ ₵ ¢ ₡ ₢ $ ₫ ₯ € ₠ ₣ ƒ ₴ ₭ ₤ m₥ ₦ № ₧ ₰ £ ₨ ₪ Rp ₨ ₧ ฿ ₮ ₩ ¥ • ♠ ♣ ♥ ♦ m² m³

Characters: Á á Ć ć É é Í í Ĺ ĺ Ń ń Ó ó Ŕ ŕ Ś ś Ú ú Ý ý Ź ź À à È è Ì ì Ò ò Ù ù Â â Ĉ ĉ Ê ê Ĝ ĝ Ĥ ĥ Î î Ĵ ĵ Ô ô Ŝ ŝ Û û Ŵ ŵ Ŷ ŷ Ä ä Ë ë Ï ï Ö ö Ü ü Ÿ ÿ ß Ã ã Ẽ ẽ Ĩ ĩ Ñ ñ Õ õ Ő ő Ű ű Ÿ ÿ Ç ç Ģ ģ Ķ ķ Ļ ļ Ņ ņ Ŗ ŗ Ş ş Ţ ţ Ð ð Ů ů Ā ā Ĉ ĉ Đ ē Ė ė Ī ī Ĺ ŗ Ń ň Ő ő Ŕ Ŝ ŝ Ŧ ŧ Ū ū Ž ž Ā ā Ē ē Ī ī Ō ō Ū ū Ȳ ȳ Æ æ ű ů ǔ ǔ Ä ä Ë ë Ġ ġ Ĩ ĩ Õ õ Ő ů Ċ ċ Ė ė Ġ ġ ı ı Ż ż Ą ą Ę ę Į į Ǫ ǫ Ų ų Đ đ Ħ ħ Ŀ ŀ Į į Ł ł Ŧ ŧ Ṁ ṁ Ṅ ṅ Ŗ ŗ Ŗ ŗ Ş ş Ţ ţ Ł ł Ő ő Ũ ũ Ŀ ŀ Ħ ħ Đ ð Þ þ Œ œ Æ æ Ø ø Å å Ə ə • {{Unicode}}

Greek: Ά ά Έ έ Ή ή Ί ί Ϊ ΐ Ό ό Ύ ύ Ϋ ΰ ώ Α α Β β Γ γ Δ δ Ε ε Ζ ζ Η η Θ θ Ι ι Κ κ Λ λ Μ μ Ν ν Ξ ξ Ο ο Π π Ρ ρ Σ σ ς Τ τ Υ υ Φ φ Χ χ Ψ ψ Ω ω • {{Polytonic|}} • (polytonic list)

Cyrillic: А а Б б В в Г г Ѓ ѓ Ґ ґ Д д Ђ ђ Е е Ё ё Є є Ж ж З з Ѕ ѕ И и Й й І і Ї ї Ј ј К к Ќ ќ Л л Љ љ М м Н н Њ њ О о П п Р р С с Т т Ћ ћ У у Ў ў Ф ф Х х Ц ц Ч ч Џ џ Ш ш Щ щ Ъ ъ Ы ы Ь ь Э э Ю ю Я я

IPA: t d ɖ ɟ ɡ ɢ ʔ ɸ β ɱ ʃ ʒ ʂ ʐ ʝ ɣ ʁ ħ ʕ ɱ ɳ ɲ ŋ ɴ ʋ ɹ ɻ j ɰ ʙ ʀ ɾ ɽ l ɭ ʎ ʟ ɥ ʍ ɧ ʘ ɓ ɗ ʄ ɠ ʛ ⁿ | ‖ . ‿ ꜜ ꜛ ꜜ ꜛ ↓ ↑ → ↗ ↘ ɚ ɝ ɨ ʉ ʊ ɘ ɵ ɤ ʱ ʷ ˠ ˤ
• {{IPA|}}

Once you click the Save button, your changes will be visible immediately.

- For testing, please use the sandbox instead.

Please note:

- If you don't want your writing to be edited mercilessly or redistributed for profit by others, **do not submit it.**
- Only public domain resources can be copied without permission—this **does not include** most web pages or images.
- See our policies and guidelines for more information on editing.

^ GNU Free Documentation License, Version 1.2 or any later version published by the Free Software Foundation; with no Invariant Sections, with no Front-Cover Texts, and with no Back-Cover Texts.

A WIKIMEDIA project

Privacy policy   About Wikipedia   Disclaimers

Powered By MediaWiki

be and you've written your edit summary, click on the "Save changes" button to commit your edits to the article.

CONCLUSION

Despite all of the criticism of Wikipedia and of wikis in general, I believe that they can be used as perfectly legitimate resources for answering reference questions. As with any resource, you should double-check the information presented if you have any doubts as to its accuracy or if the topic being researched is even slightly controversial or quickly changing. As the *Nature* study and a 12-year-old in England showed, even the long-trusted *Encyclopedia Britannica* isn't perfect.

Whenever I get a chance, I survey rooms full of librarians regarding what they think of Wikipedia as a resource. When I started writing this book in 2005, the best I could hope for was 50 percent of the room approving of it. By summer 2008, when I surveyed a room full of university librarians (typically the most skeptical of Wikipedia, in my experience), not a single one indicated disapproval of Wikipedia as a resource. My, how times have changed in just three years when it comes to Wikipedia. Here we abandon the focus on searching for text-based results and, in the next chapter, switch gears to discover how to search for other types of media.

EXERCISES

1. If you haven't already, create a Wikipedia account for yourself.
2. Edit your user page, supplying some basic information about yourself and your interests within Wikipedia. Be sure to include links to some Wikipedia articles relating to you. (The page to the town/city in which you live or work would be an easy one.)
3. Edit at least one page within Wikipedia that isn't your user page. Pick a topic you know something about or are interested in.
4. If your library doesn't already have a Wikipedia article about it, create one. Be sure to link to it from the article about the town/city in which your library is located. If you're not sure what to include in the article, use the

one for the Lincoln City Libraries in Lincoln, Nebraska, as an example (http://en.wikipedia.org/wiki/Lincoln_City_Libraries).

NOTES

1. *Wikipedia, the Free Encyclopedia*, s.v. "Wiki," June 6, 2006, http://en.wikipedia.org/w/index.php?title=Wiki&oldid=57120412 (accessed June 6, 2006).
2. *Wikipedia, the Free Encyclopedia*, s.v. "Wikipedia," June 6, 2006, http://en.wikipedia.org/w/index.php?title=Wikipedia&oldid=57197030 (accessed June 6, 2006).
3. Wikimedia, "Wikipedia Statistics," May 31, 2008, http://stats.wikimedia.org/EN/Sitemap.htm.
4. James Surowiecki, *The Wisdom of Crowds* (New York: Doubleday, 2004).
5. While writing this chapter, the title of the Wikipedia article about Wikipedia was changed to "Wikipedia IS COMMUNISM" several times. Shortly thereafter, the article was "locked" by the Wikipedia administrators, preventing further edits from occurring. This is another response to vandalism that frequently occurs on pages dealing with controversial subjects such as abortion and the pages of presidential candidates.
6. Jim Giles, "Special Report: Internet Encyclopaedias Go Head to Head," Nature 438 (December 15, 2005): 900–901, http://www.nature.com/nature/journal/v438/n7070/full/438900a.html.
7. Ibid.
8. Justin Parkinson, "Boy Brings Encyclopaedia to Book," *BBC News*, January 26, 2005, http://news.bbc.co.uk/2/hi/uk_news/education/4209575.stm.
9. Daniel Terdiman, "Adam Curry Gets Podbusted" CNET News, December 2, 2005, http://news.com.com/2061-10802_3-5980758.html.
10. Evan Hansen, "Wikipedia Founder Edits Own Bio," *Wired*, December 19, 2005, http://www.wired.com/news/culture/0,1284,69880,00.html?tw=wn_tophead_2.
11. *Wikipedia, the Free Encyclopedia*, s.v. "Wikipedia: Autobiography," October 1, 2008, http://en.wikipedia.org/wiki/Wikipedia:Autobiography.
12. *Wikipedia, the Free Encyclopedia*, s.v. "John Seigenthaler Sr. Wikipedia Biography Controversy," June 7, 2006, http://en.wikipedia.org/w/index.php?title=John_Seigenthaler_Sr._Wikipedia_biography_controversy&oldid=57318828.
13. Ibid.
14. One title change I am aware of is on the Dean Koontz article. Originally it was titled "Dean R. Koontz," but since he'd not used the "R." in his name since the late 1980s, I suggested that the article's title be changed to reflect this fact. A consensus was reached and the article's title was changed. Searches on *dean r. koontz* will automatically redirect the user to the "Dean Koontz" article.
15. Searching the term *boot* will take you directly to the

footwear-related article that contains a link to the boot disambiguation page. Since no article titled "Boots" exists, you are directed to choices between "boot" and "boot disambiguation."

16. Most notably, *Wikipedia, the Free Encyclopedia*, s.v. "Wikipedia: How to Edit a Page," September 1, 2008, http://en.wikipedia.org/wiki/Wikipedia:How_to_edit_a_page, and *Wikipedia, the Free Encyclopedia*, s.v. "Image: Cheatsheet-en.png," February 8, 2008, http://commons.wikimedia.org/wiki/Image:Cheatsheet-en.png.

17. *Wikipedia, the Free Encyclopedia*, s.v. "Wikipedia: Five Pillars," October 5, 2008, http://en.wikipedia.org/wiki/Wikipedia:Five_pillars.

18. Different wikis will have different wiki syntax from others depending on the underlying software being used. Be sure to familiarize yourself with the syntax being used before editing a wiki.

19. Signing your edits should be done only on "talk" pages and on your personal page. You should not sign your work on article pages.

Chapter 5

Searching for Media

INTRODUCTION

With the advent of Web 2.0, many have noticed that creating content for the Web is no longer confined to just static or even dynamic Web pages. With digital stills and video cameras, simple video editing software, and simple audio editing and mixing software, combined with the new generation of point, click, and publish online platforms, creating and posting multimedia content online is easier than ever. With the explosion of this content, the need to find something from within this content also increases.

Text has always been very searchable with computers, as it is inherently indexable and therefore searchable. But when it comes to still images, audio, and video, in the past, these items were virtually unsearchable due to their lack of indexable text content. With newer services such as Flickr (for images), YouTube (for video), and Podscope (for audio and video), finding multimedia content is becoming much easier. This chapter introduces you to each of these services and shows you how to make the most of them. (In several cases, these services also allow you to post your own content. Since this is a book on searching, I do not focus on those features.)

FLICKR

Flickr is the single most popular service for posting images online today. Its simple interface for transferring images into the system and the ability to create photo sets, contribute to multiuser group pools, comment, tag, and leave notes on photos all lend to its popularity. With more than 3 billion photos and an average of more than 4,000 photographs being uploaded every minute, it is probably the single largest archive of images in the world. Chances are, if you need a photo of a person, place, or thing, you can find one on Flickr, whose homepage is shown in Figure 5-1.

Basic Search

To perform a simple search in Flickr, just go to the homepage (www.flickr.com) and enter your search terms in the search field and then click the search button. You will be presented with a list of results showing about 20 photos per page. Each result will include a small version of the image, the image's title, the date it was uploaded, the name of the user who contributed the image, and the first four tags of the photo (see Figure 5-2). To access a full result, click on the image. Additionally, other information such as the upload date, the username, and the tags are also clickable to retrieve the appropriate relevant information.

Search results are first presented in the "Most relevant" order. Relevancy is determined using the standard methodologies, including the appearance of your keyword(s) in the item's title and the number of appearances of your keyword(s). You may also have your results sorted by "Most recent" or "Most interesting." The "Most interesting" sort, if you'll excuse the redundancy, can sometimes be the most interesting way to view search results. In Flickr, "interestingness" is based on an unclearly defined list of factors, including the uniqueness of the tags associated with the photo, the number of comments and/notes that have been added with the photo, and the number of

Figure 5-1   Flickr's homepage

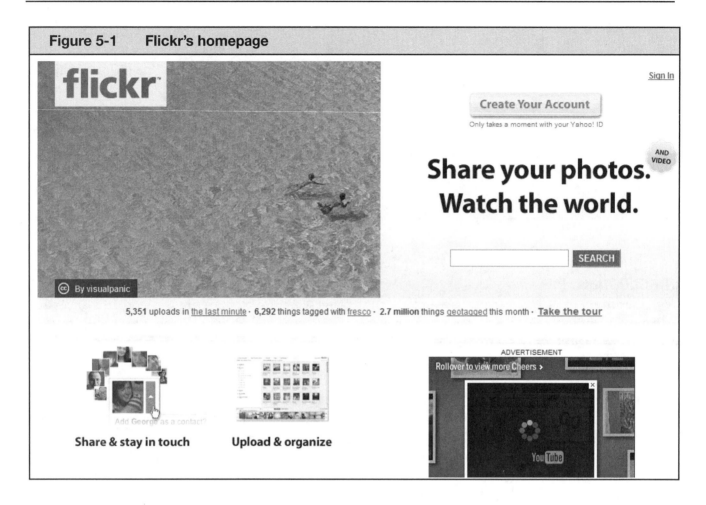

times the photo has been marked as a user's favorite. When you receive numerous results for a search and a recent photo is not one of your criteria, you may be surprised at the quality of results returned using the "Most interesting" sort option.

By default, as indicated by the selected "Full text" beneath the search box near the top of the search results page, your keywords are being run against a photo's title, tags, and description. To quickly change to a tags-only search, select "Tags only" and re-search. Every page in Flickr also has a search box in the upper right corner that, by default, does a full-text search across the whole system. The triangle to the right of the search button also gives you quick access to the group search, a Flickr members search, and location searches, all described later in this section.[1] Additionally, you can change your search to a groups or people search by selecting the appropriate tab above the search box. Let's turn to "Advanced

search" to the right of the search button to see the available search limiters.

Advanced Search

Unlike most of the advanced search pages described earlier in this book, Flickr's is not all that complex, having just five parts of your search that you can manipulate: "Search for," "Search by content type," "Search by media type," "Search by date," and "Creative Commons." Figure 5-3 is an example of the advanced search page.

- **Search for:**
  "Search for" allows some additional options beyond those of the basic search box. Here you enter your keywords in the first box and then you can choose to search for "All of these words" (Boolean AND), "The exact phrase" (with quotation marks), or "Any of these words" (Boolean OR). You can also choose between a "Full text" and "Tags only"

Figure 5-2   Basic Flickr search results

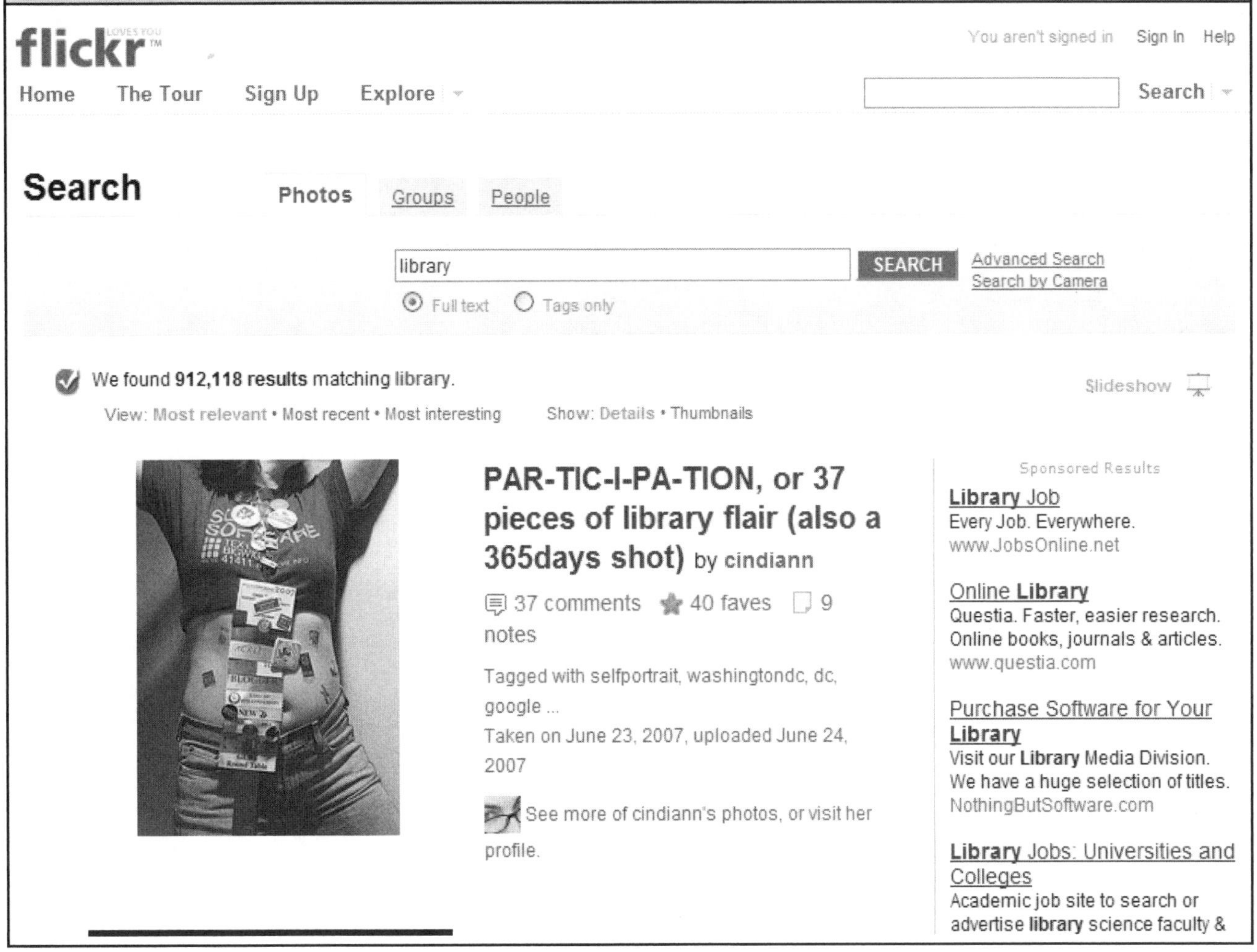

search using the radio buttons below the search box. Additionally, the "None of these words" box in this area allows you to enter keywords you wish to exclude from your search (Boolean NOT).

- **Search by content type:**
Flickr is meant to be a site for contributing and sharing photographs, but many users (myself included) also contribute screenshots, sketches, and other images that are not technically photographs. Although discouraged, Flickr allows this to a certain extent because, clearly, this is something a proportion of Flickr users want to do. As a result, users can mark specific images as a screenshot or other art when making a contribution. Flickr, by default, does not return images marked as one of these two categories as search results. To add these to your

search results, or to specifically retrieve only one of these categories, check and/or uncheck these options as appropriate. In my experience, however, although the option of marking an image as a screenshot or other art is available, many users do not do so. Thus, you may receive screenshots or other nonphotographs in search results even if you have not opted to do so.

- **Search by media type:**
In the spring of 2008, Flickr added the ability for users to upload videos of up to 90 seconds in length to their accounts. Although this has become popular with some users, other users view it as a violation of the central purpose of Flickr: hosting images. No matter how you feel about this, here you can choose to search both images and video

Figure 5-3 Flickr's advanced search page

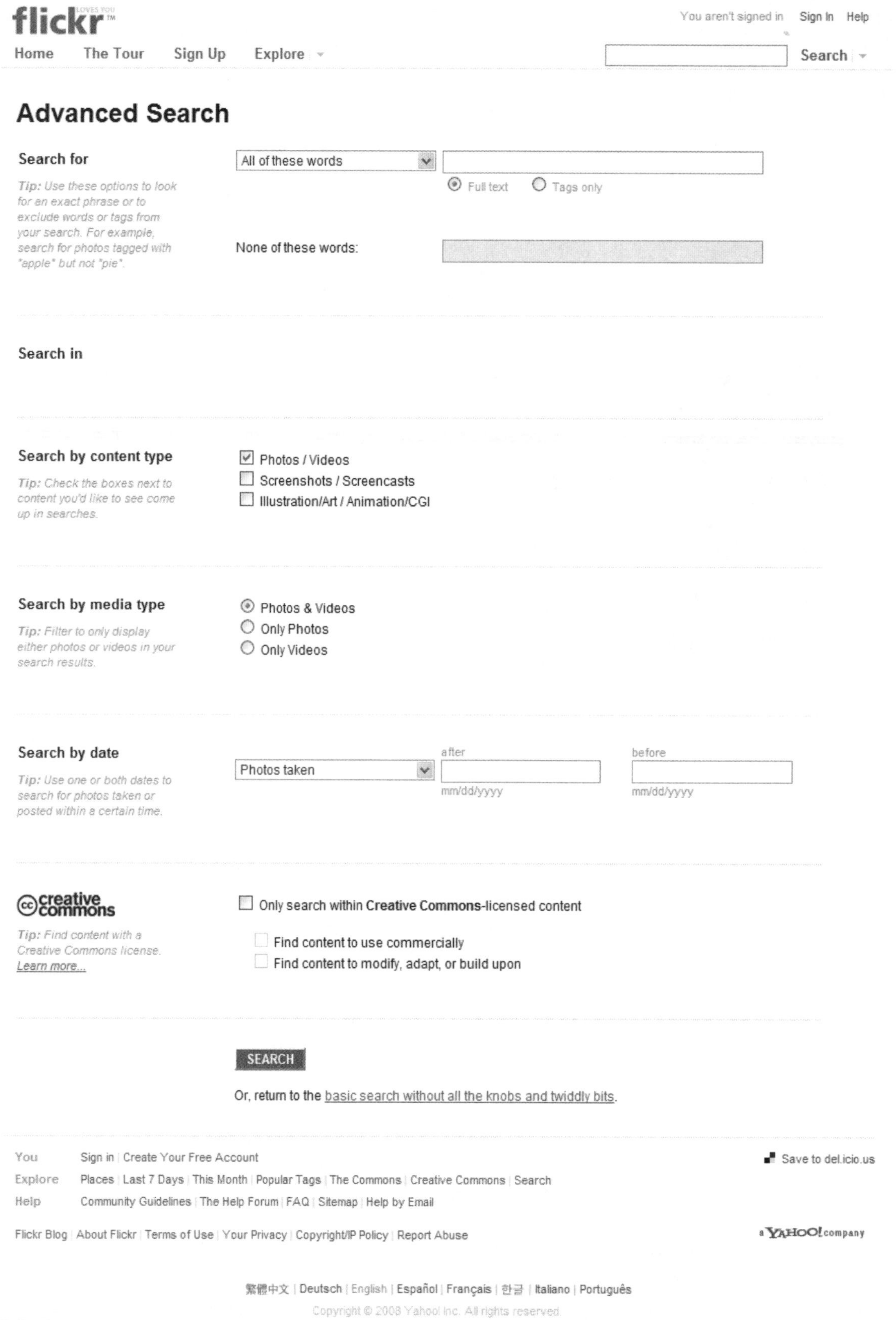
flickr
You aren't signed in
Sign In
Help
Home
The Tour
Sign Up
Explore
Search
Advanced Search
Search for
Tip: Use these options to look for an exact phrase or to exclude words or tags from your search. For example, search for photos tagged with "apple" but not "pie".
All of these words
Full text
Tags only
None of these words:
Search in
Search by content type
Tip: Check the boxes next to content you'd like to see come up in searches.
Photos / Videos
Screenshots / Screencasts
Illustration/Art / Animation/CGI
Search by media type
Tip: Filter to only display either photos or videos in your search results.
Photos & Videos
Only Photos
Only Videos
Search by date
Tip: Use one or both dates to search for photos taken or posted within a certain time.
Photos taken
after
before
mm/dd/yyyy
mm/dd/yyyy
creative commons
Tip: Find content with a Creative Commons license.
Learn more...
Only search within Creative Commons-licensed content
Find content to use commercially
Find content to modify, adapt, or build upon
SEARCH
Or, return to the basic search without all the knobs and twiddly bits.
You
Sign in | Create Your Free Account
Explore
Places | Last 7 Days | This Month | Popular Tags | The Commons | Creative Commons | Search
Help
Community Guidelines | The Help Forum | FAQ | Sitemap | Help by Email
Save to del.icio.us
Flickr Blog | About Flickr | Terms of Use | Your Privacy | Copyright/IP Policy | Report Abuse
a YAHOO! company
繁體中文 | Deutsch | English | Español | Français | 한글 | Italiano | Português
Copyright © 2008 Yahoo! Inc. All rights reserved.

(the default option) or limit your search to screenshots/screencasts or illustration/art/animation/CGI. Throughout this chapter, I focus only on searching for images.

- **Search by date:**

    Here you can limit your search results to a specific time frame. In the case of Flickr, however, each photo can have two different dates associated with it: the date taken and the date posted. For example, I may have taken a photo on Monday, September 10, 2007, but did not upload it into my Flickr account until Saturday, September 15, when I returned home from a trip. Flickr makes note of both of these dates and allows you to specify whether you're searching based on the date the photo was taken or on the date it was uploaded into the system. As another quick example, if you're looking for photos from a town's recent Fourth of July parade, you should probably search for photos uploaded after July 3 but before July 10, to take into account that not everyone uploads their photos promptly.

- **Creative Commons:**

    Chapter 4 gave an overview of Creative Commons (CC) licenses, so I won't repeat myself here other than to say that Flickr allows all account holders to set a CC license on any or all of the photos they upload. Here you can specify which license you want to appear on your search results. In the case of image searching, this is an important factor because it is highly probable that patrons who are looking for images wish to reuse whatever images they find. By specifying that all results must have a CC license attached, you can be comfortable presenting these results to a patron for their reuse.

Up until this point, a Flickr account was not required to search for content. However, to be able to perform the additional search types discussed in the following sections, you must have an account and be logged in. Accounts are free and can be created by clicking on the "Create Your Account" link at the top of the page and then following the onscreen instructions. If you already have a Yahoo! account, you can use that log-in information to quickly create a Flickr account. From here on out, I'll be using my Flickr account.

Groups Search

Groups are collections of Flickr users and photographs around a particular topic such as an event, location, theme, or activity. There are groups for quilters, conferences, people who like to take photos of airplane contrails, cities, and photos of vanity license plates. Each group has a group "pool," the collection of contributed photos from the group members, and a group discussion in which group members can discuss their topic. The group search allows you to search groups based on the keywords of your choice. You can search either the "Group Names & Descriptions" or "Group Discussions," as shown in Figure 5-4. Note that in either type of group search your results will not be photographs but a list of either relevant groups (as in Figure 5-5) or group discussion topics (as in Figure 5-6), respectively.

People Search

As with the groups search, a people search, as shown in Figure 5-7, will not find photos but Flickr users. The people search is just as simple as the group search. In this case, you can choose to search by a user's name or e-mail address (real name and/or username) to find a particular user (see Figure 5-8) or by interests, which will search the public profiles of Flickr users (not all of whom provide such information).

An interest-based people search can be an alternate way to find a particular image, as those who are interested in vanity license plates, for example, and mentioned this in their profile on a photo-sharing site likely take a lot of photos of that subject. Figure 5-9 shows the results of a search for people interested in "libraries."

Location Search

Flickr gives its users the ability to "geotag" their photos. This means that uploaded photos can be placed on a map to within just a few feet of where they were taken. Once a geotag has been added to a photo, users can search for photos based on location. Not every user takes advantage of this feature, but at the time of this writing, just short of 2.8 million photos had been geotagged, still a worthy collection to search. To access the location search, select "For a location" from the search dropdown list, as shown in Figure 5-10.

Figure 5-4   Group search

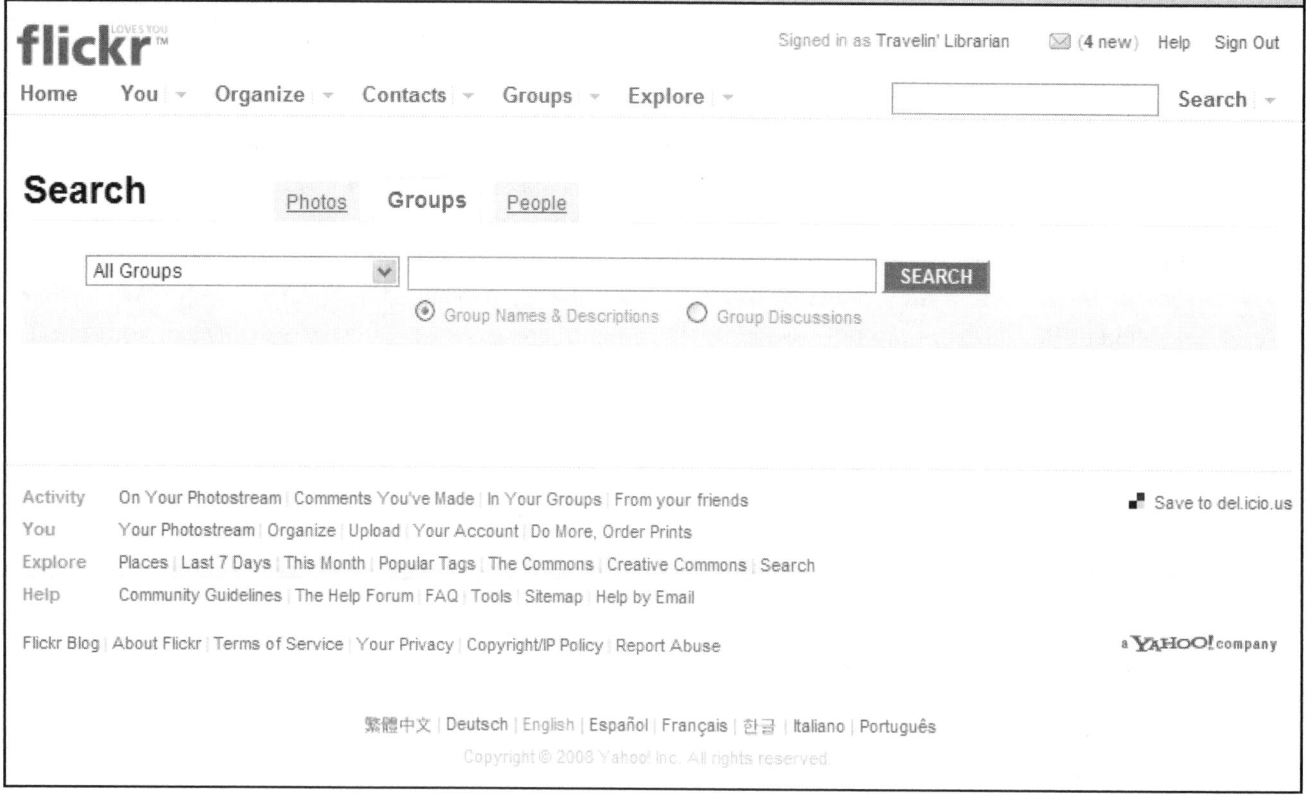

You'll then be presented with a world map (see Figure 5-11). Don't let the small numbers displayed here fool you. The more you zoom in, the more photos you'll find. From this map, you can perform a keyword search (at the bottom) or browse by panning and zooming using the controls on the right side of the screen. For example, if you'd like to look for photos taken in Lincoln, Nebraska, you could just enter *lincoln, ne* into the search box to retrieve the results shown in Figure 5-12.

Near the bottom of the map will be a scrollable list of the results that match the dots on the map. Selecting either a dot or one of the results will highlight both the dot and the image, as shown in Figure 5-13. Clicking on a highlighted photo will open that photo's page. Using the pan and zoom features of the map, the further you zoom in, the more specific the location markers will become. As you can see in Figure 5-14, by the time you get to the street level, more discrete locations and smaller collections of photos are present and accessible. You can also switch the map to a satellite view or map/satellite hybrid version.

Searching by Camera

Admittedly, this is probably the least useful type of search for the reference librarian, but I'd consider my coverage of Flickr to be incomplete if I failed to mention it. The camera search can be accessed through the "Search by Camera" link to the right of the search box on any search results page (see Figure 5-15). Here you can find photos that have been taken with a particular model of camera.

First, select the camera manufacturer, and then select the particular model you're interested in (see Figure 5-16). Last, enter your search keywords, and your results will be limited to only photos taken with that particular camera (see Figures 5-17).

In all honesty, the search page for a particular camera is probably useful at the reference desk more to answer questions from those looking to purchase a digital camera than to find a photo, as the page

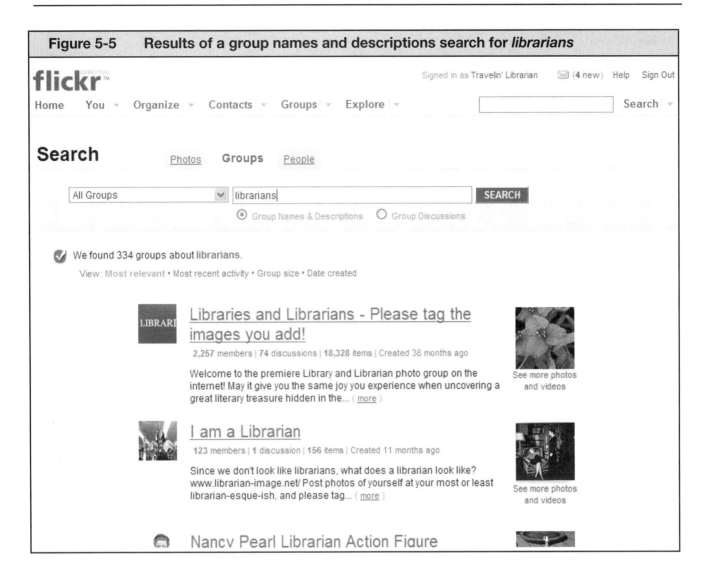

Figure 5-5   Results of a group names and descriptions search for *librarians*

offers links to the camera's full specifications, price comparisons, and user reviews.

YOUTUBE

When searching for a video of a particular recent event, a classic television commercial, or a clip from a news program from the past year or two, the best place to go is often YouTube. Yes, a lot of user-generated content on YouTube will probably not be of use in many reference situations, but you never know.

Before I cover searching YouTube, I would like to take a moment to mention copyright issues related to YouTube. Granted, most of the examples I gave at the beginning of this section have not been posted legally, but I believe that they should be considered as legitimate resources when attempting to answer a patron's question. For example, say your patron is

researching recent changes in U.S. economic policy and is interested in what administration officials said on the previous Sunday's morning talk shows, along with the reaction to the changes on that week's late-night talk shows. Chances are, in both cases, clips from those shows will be available on YouTube. Even though those clips may have been posted without the permission of the network, would you tell your patron that you can find the information he or she is looking for but you can't show them where it is because it may violate the network's copyright? I don't believe so.[2]

Basic Search

Searching YouTube is simple and straightforward. The search box is located at the top center of the homepage (see Figure 5-18). Just enter your key-

Figure 5-6   Results of a group discussions search for *librarians*

words and click the search button. Searches are performed against video titles, descriptions, and tags.

Figure 5-19 shows a search for *economy* that presented me with more than 6,600 results. By default, results are sorted by relevance and in the "list view." Figure 5-20 shows the same results in the "grid view." The grid view shows significantly less information on the screen but allows you to see more results with less scrolling.

You can also sort your results by date added (see Figure 5-21), view count (see Figure 5-22), and rating (see Figure 5-23), by clicking on the appropriate links just above the results list.

To view a particular video, its complete information—including description, date uploaded, and tags—and all associated comments, just click on the thumbnail image for that video or the video's title, as shown in Figure 5-24.

Clicking on the contributor's username will take you to that user's YouTube homepage, which will include information about that user, links to the user's other contributed videos, and any comments left about that user, as shown in Figure 5-25.

Channel Search

In YouTube parlance, a channel is the collection of videos created by a single user. So, in YouTube, searching for a channel is to search for a particular user. You can perform a channel search from any search box by changing the search type from "Videos" to "Channels" (see Figure 5-26). Figure 5-27 shows the results for a *library* channel search, while Figure 5-28 shows the results for a *nebraskaccess* channel search. Figure 5-27 shows the multiple results I received due to many different accounts having the word "library" in their name. In Figure 5-28, you'll

Figure 5-7   People search

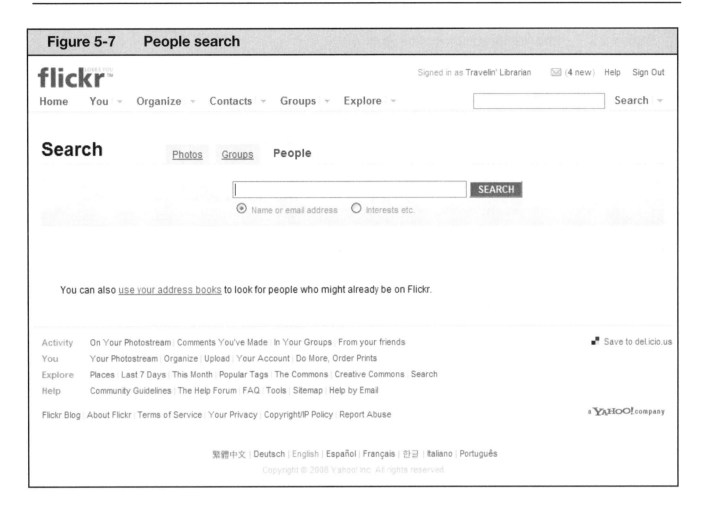

see that I've searched for a particular known user-name and received the single matching result.

Advanced Search

If you would like more control over your YouTube searching, click on the "advanced" link to the right of any search box, as shown in Figure 5-29. This will open a light blue box on the screen that gives you two search settings: (1) display query suggestions as I type and (2) filter videos that may not be suitable for minors; it also offers search options in two categories: (1) filter results and (2) refine further by, as shown in Figure 5-30. Let's take a look at the search settings in more detail.

Settings

Again, the available settings are "Display query suggestions as I type" and "Filter videos that may not be suitable for minors."

- **Display query suggestions as I type:**
  As with Google's new feature, as you're typing in a search box, YouTube will automatically suggest search terms to you. These suggestions can easily be selected using your mouse, saving you some typing. If you do not like this feature, you can turn it off here by unchecking this option.
- **Filter videos that may not be suitable for minors:**
  By default, YouTube will not return results that are marked as being for adults or if they might generally be considered to be adult in nature. Be aware, however, that videos do slip through, and one person's idea of "not suitable for minors" may not be the same as someone else's. To turn this limiter off, uncheck this option.

Advanced Search Options

The first category of advanced search options is

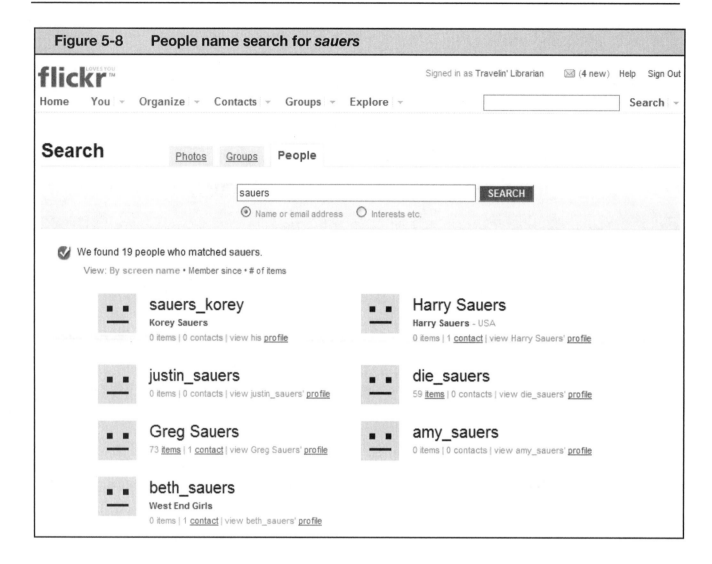

Figure 5-8   People name search for *sauers*

"Find Results." This category includes "with all of the words" (the default Boolean AND search), "with the exact phrase" (searching as if your terms were enclosed in quotation marks), "with at least one of the words" (Boolean OR), and "without the words" (Boolean NOT). You can also search by location. Over in the "Refine further by" category there are additional ways to limit your search results. These include "Duration," "Language," "Category," "Sort Results By," and "Uploaded." Let me briefly describe each of these options in turn.

- **Duration:**
  Here you can limit your results to videos of any length (the default), short (less than 4 minutes), medium (4–20 minutes), or long (more than 20 minutes).

- **Language:**
  Here you can limit your results to videos in any language (the default) or any one of more than 30 languages, ranging from Arabic to Turkish.

- **Category:**
  Here you can limit your results to videos in all categories (the default) or one or more specific categories. To see the categories list, select the "specific categories" option, which will provide a list of 15 different categories. Check the boxes for the categories to limit your results.

- **Sort results by:**
  Here you can change the sort order of your results. Your choices are relevance (the default), date added, view count, and rating.

(continued on p. 132)

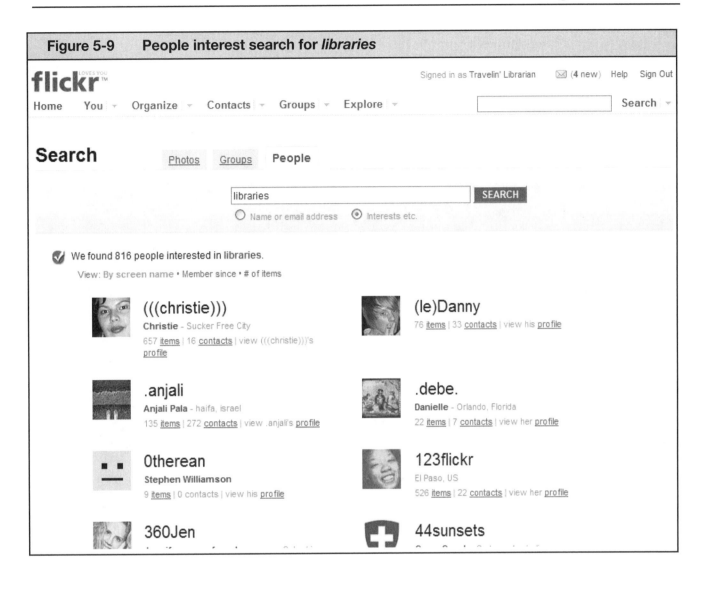

Figure 5-9   People interest search for *libraries*

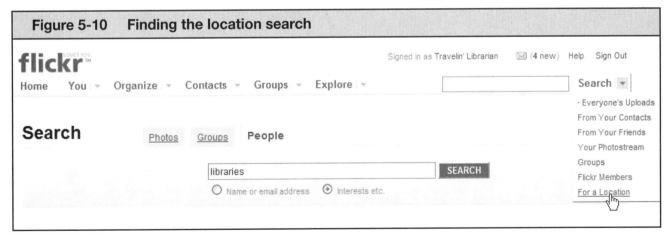

Figure 5-10   Finding the location search

Figure 5-11   Location search

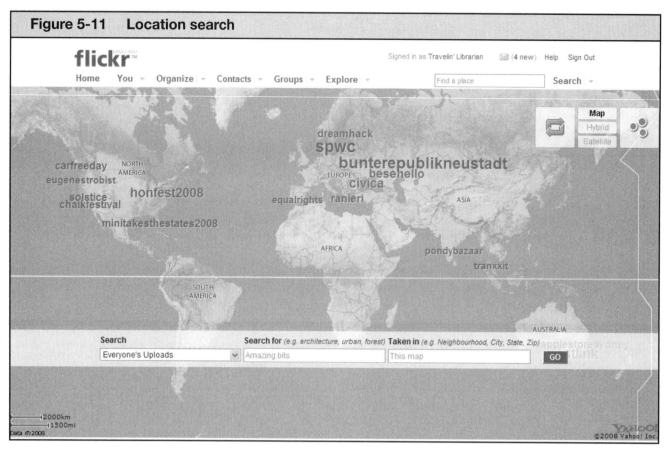

Figure 5-12   Initial results for a *lincoln, ne* location search

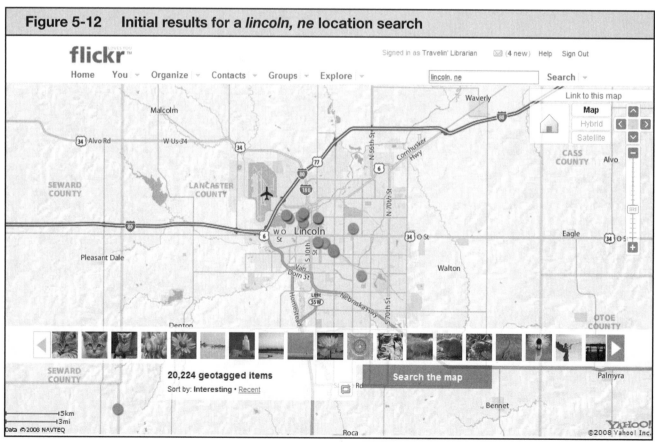

Figure 5-13   Highlighting a particular map-based result

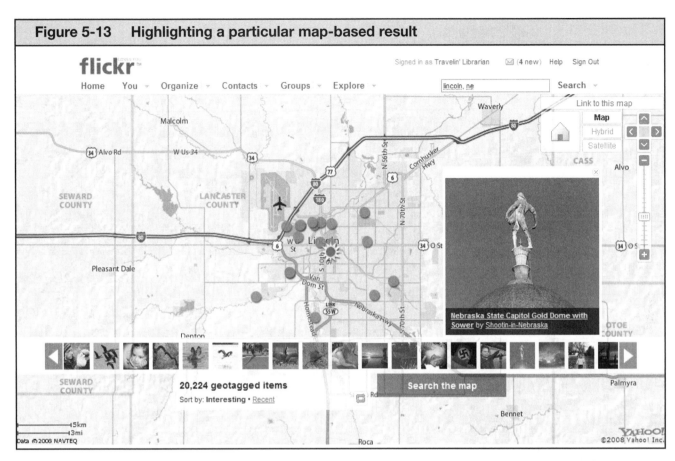

Figure 5-14   A street-level view of our search results

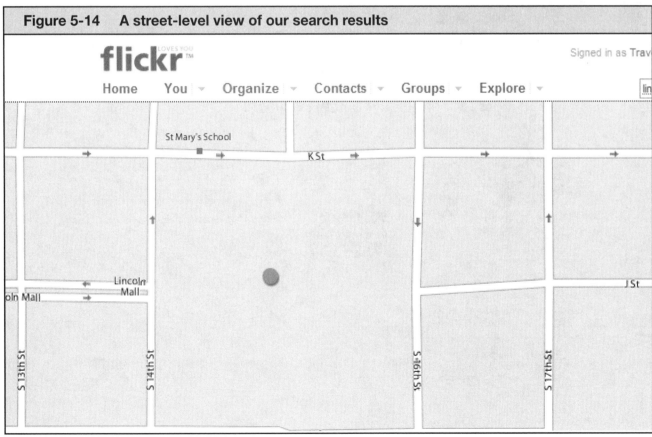

Figure 5-15 **Search by camera**

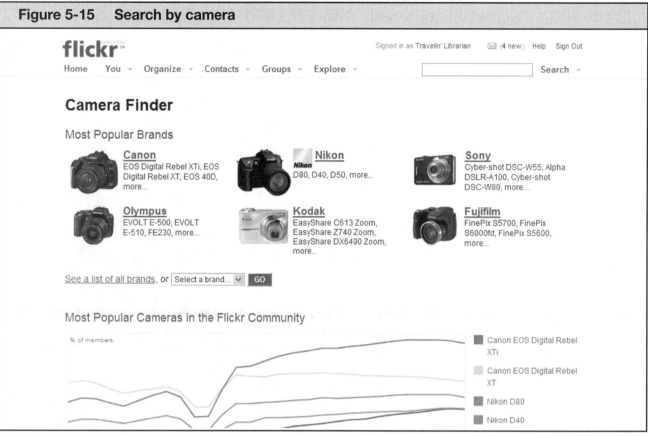

Figure 5-16 **Search page for the Fuji FinePix S8000fd camera**

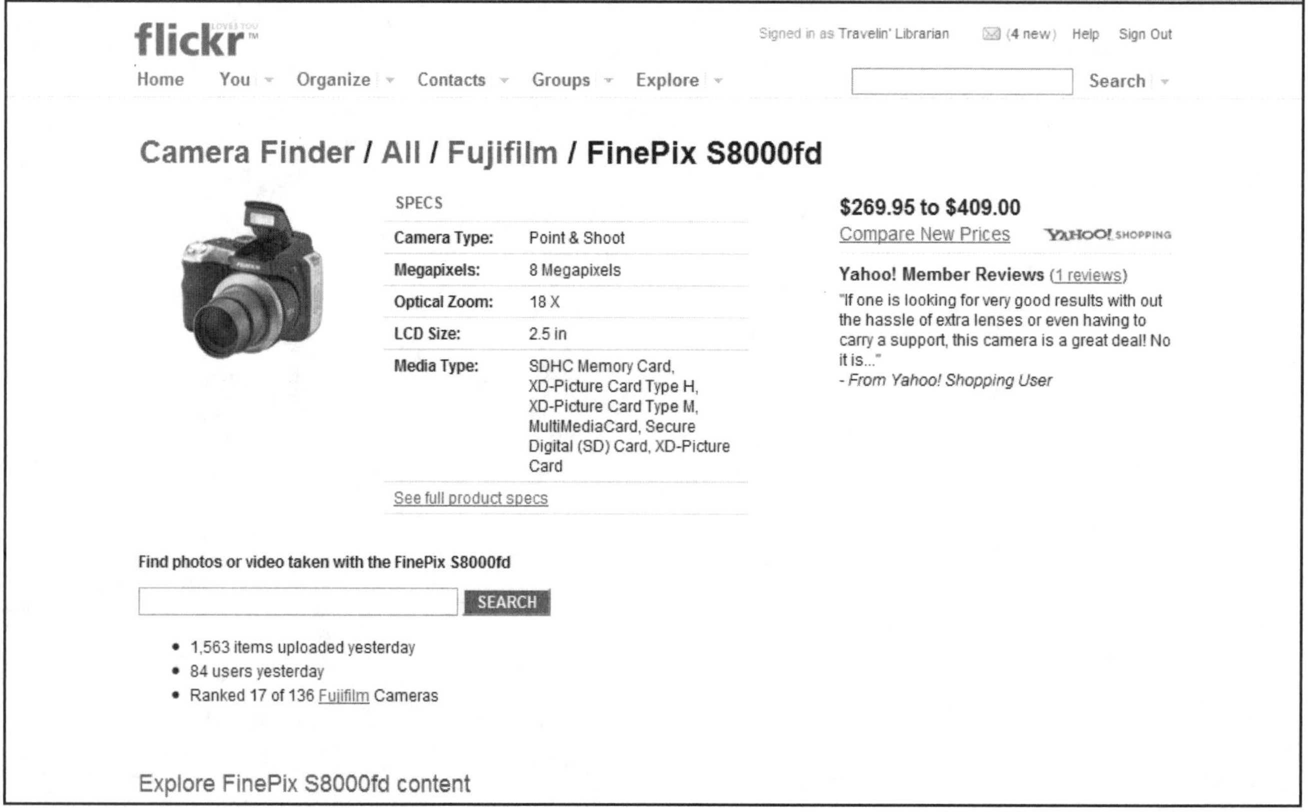

Figure 5-17   Search results for *sunset* from the Fuji FinePix S8000fd camera

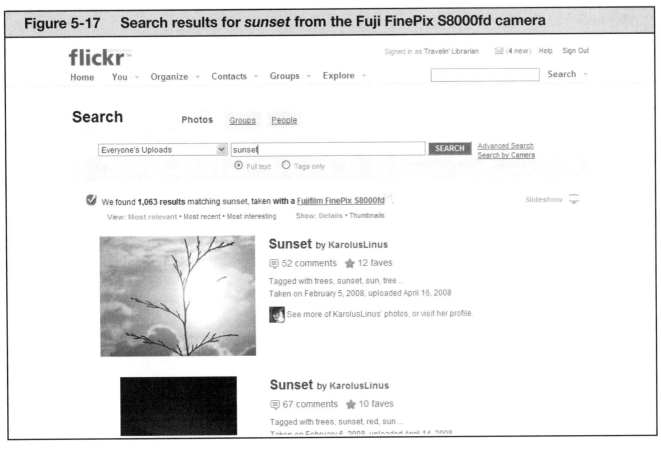

Figure 5-18   YouTube's homepage and search box

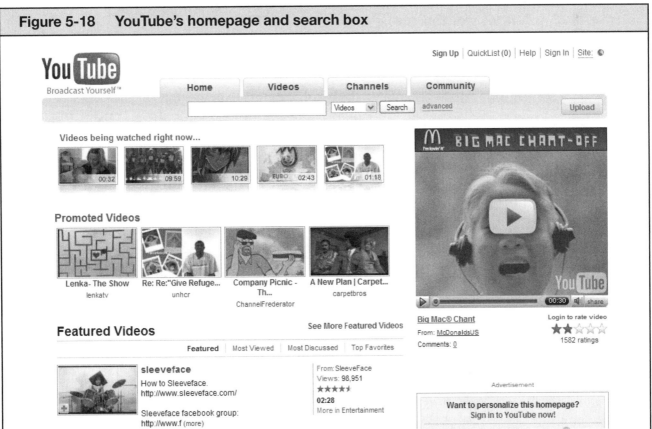

Figure 5-19   List view of YouTube search results

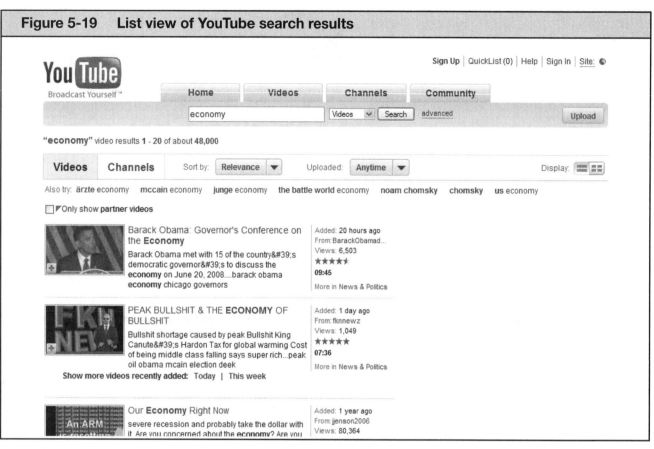

Figure 5-20   Grid view of YouTube search results

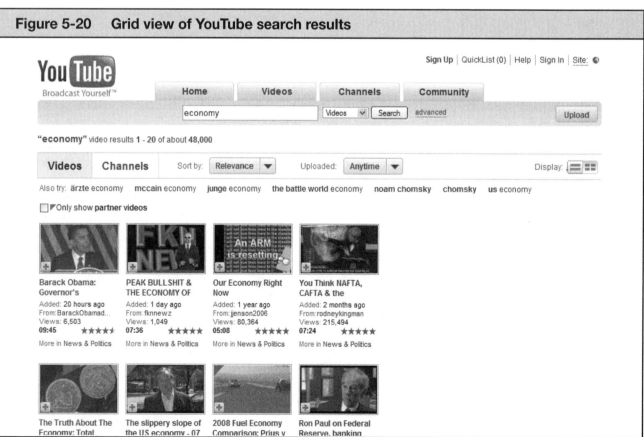

Figure 5-21   "Date added" results sort

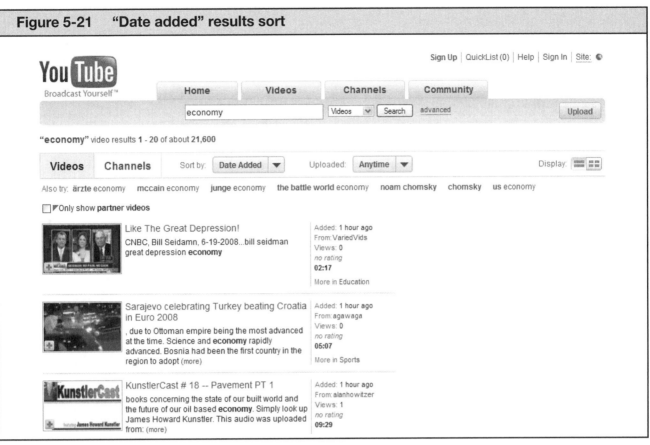

Figure 5-22   "View count" results sort

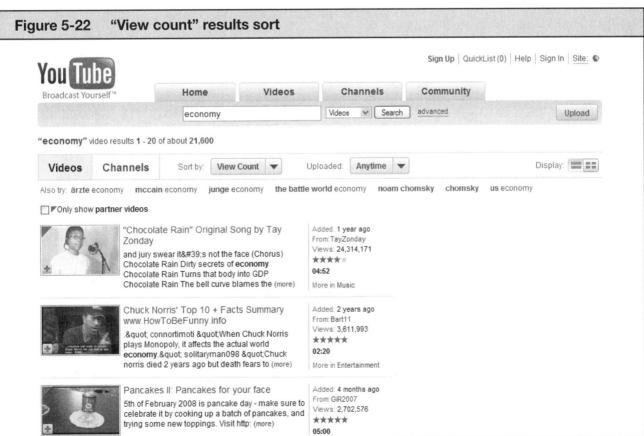

Figure 5-23   Rating results sort

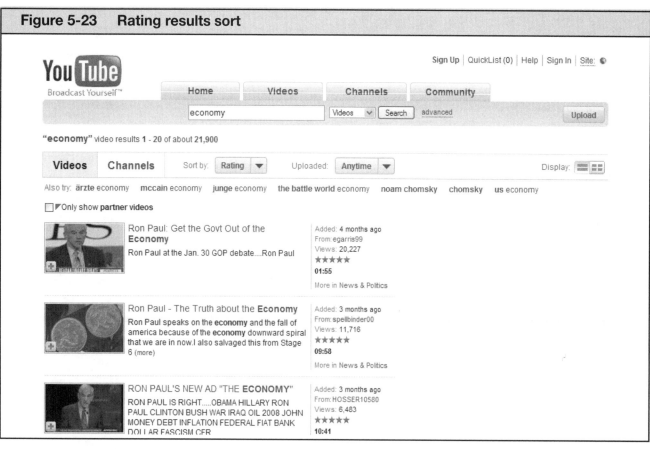

Figure 5-24   A YouTube video's page

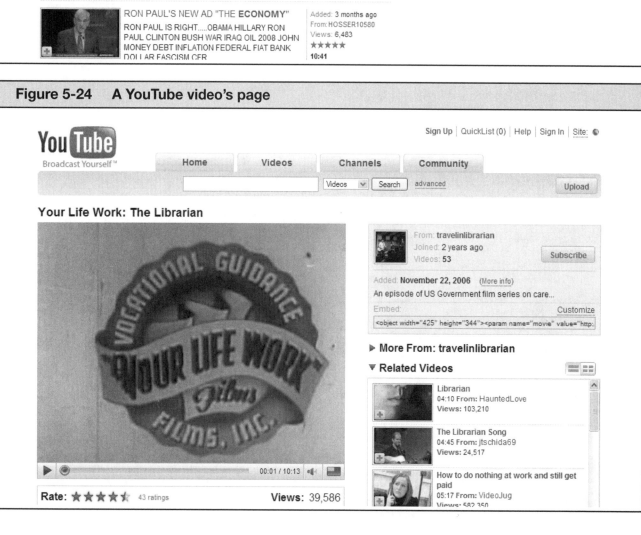

Figure 5-25   A YouTube user's homepage

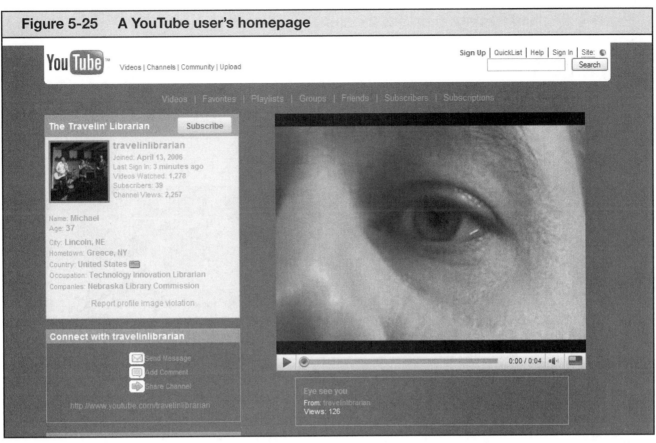

Figure 5-26   Changing to a channel search

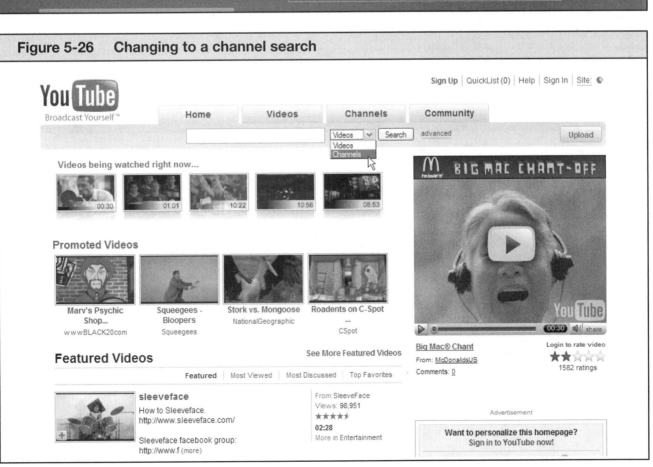

Figure 5-27   Channel search results for *library*

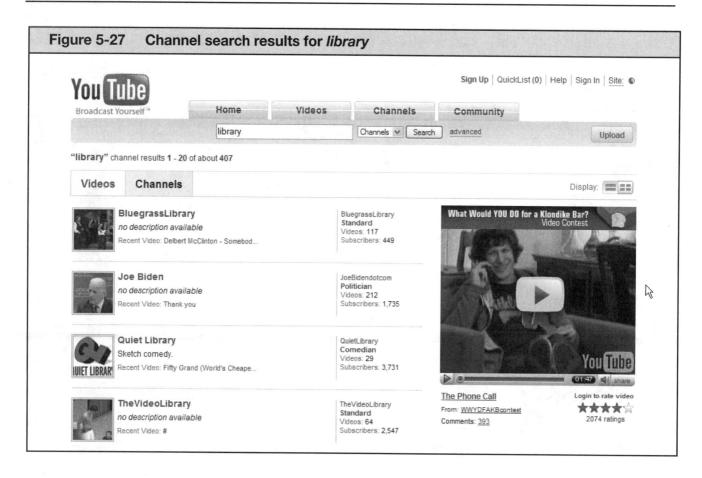

Figure 5-28   Channel search results for *nebraskaccess*

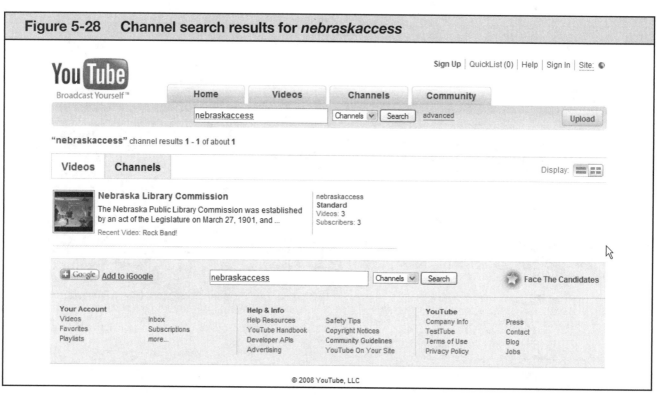

Figure 5-29   The advanced link

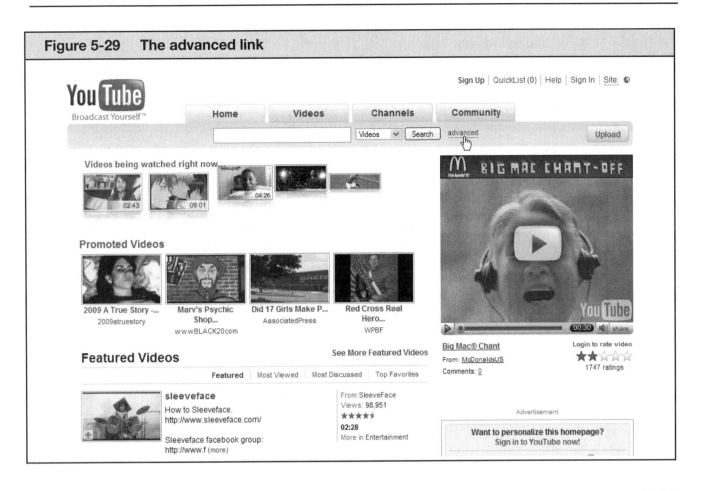

Figure 5-30   The advanced settings and search options

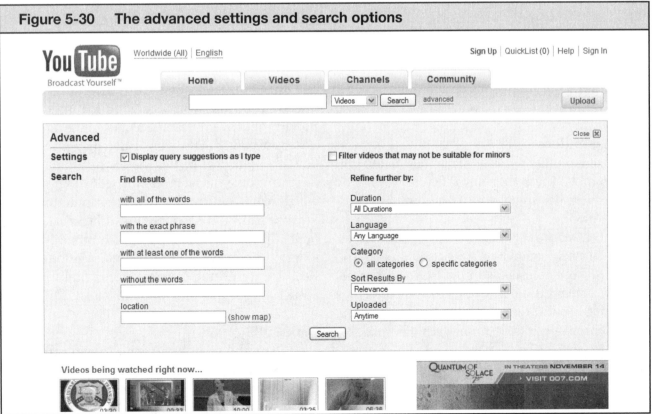

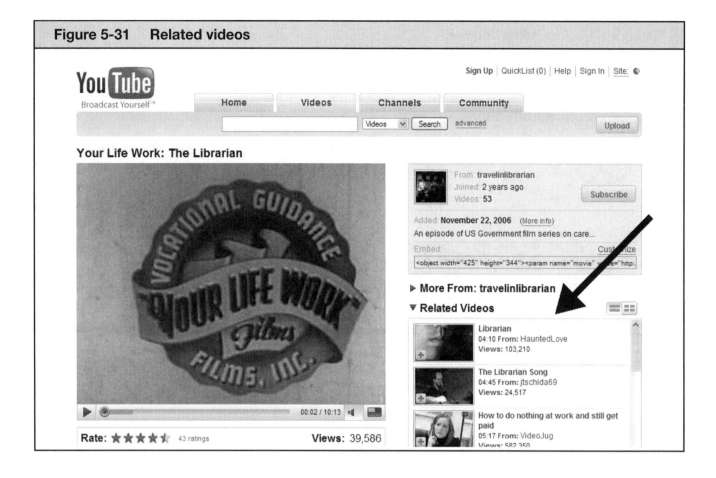

Figure 5-31   Related videos

- **Uploaded:**
  Here you can limit your results based on date. Choose between videos that have been added to YouTube anytime (the default), this month, this week, or today.

Browsing YouTube

You can also browse YouTube if you prefer not to start with a search. There are many different ways to do this. Here are just some of the more popular ones:

- Each video's page includes a list of "related videos" on the right side of the screen (see Figure 5-31).
- Sometimes users will post "video responses" to other videos. Links to those responses—or the original, if the video you're viewing is a response—can be found beneath the video (see Figure 5-32).
- The four blue tabs across the top of the page ("Home," "Videos," "Channels," and "Community") will take you to the homepages for each of those

four YouTube areas. From there you may browse accordingly (see Figure 5-33).

Two final notes about YouTube search results: First, if the video you're looking for is extremely popular or of a significant recent event, several if not dozens of copies of the same video may exist within YouTube. Since some will be shorter than others, be sure to note the length of the video to determine which might contain the most relevant information for your patron. Second, because YouTube generally limits uploaded videos to a length of ten minutes, longer videos may be split into multiple shorter clips. Keep an eye on the "related videos" links and the user's homepage to find all of the parts.

PODSCOPE

With more and more audio content being presented via RSS (really simple syndication), known as podcasting and then archived online, a need for being able to search the content of audio files has become

Figure 5-32   Response links

necessary. Podscope is one of the best ways to do that. Although Podscope indexes the audio content of both audio and video files, in my experience, the majority of results presented are audio only, so I will focus on that.

Unlike YouTube for video, Podscope has several important differences:

- YouTube accepts uploaded content from users and allows you to search for that content. Podscope,

Figure 5-33   YouTube section tabs

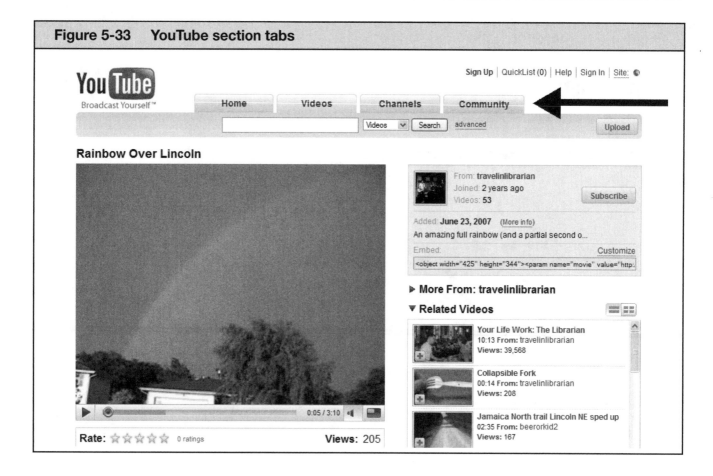

on the other hand, is a pure search engine, not accepting content, but instead crawling and indexing other online audio and video content.

- While YouTube allows you to search indexes of titles, tags, and descriptions, Podscope actually indexes the audio content of the files.

This second difference is the more important of the two. Instead of searching for content by title and other metadata, you are actually searching what is being said in the audio of the file. So, if you're looking for audio content that mentions, for example, Hurricane Katrina, Podscope will find those files for you. See Podscope's homepage in Figure 5-34.

Searching Podscope is very simple. Just enter your keywords into the search box, choose whether you want audio, video, or all (the default), and click the search button. By default, results are sorted by date, as shown in Figure 5-35. Results can also be sorted by relevance by clicking on the "score" link above the results list, as in Figure 5-36.

Each result will include the title of the file and the file's description, which are important enough, but the interesting parts of the results are the buttons and links to the left of each result's description, as highlighted in Figure 5-37.

When Podscope indexes audio content, it is also able to mark where within a file each word has been said. In other words, Podscope knows when in each audio file your keywords appear. Each instance of your keyword(s) is listed in a small box underneath the buttons and appears as a time code in the file where it appears. For example, in the first search result for our search shown in Figure 5-37 the phrase *libraries* occurs at 14:09, 14 minutes and 9 seconds, into the file.

Traditionally at this point, we would need to download the audio file to our computer, run the correct audio software, and then advance through the file to the right point in time to find the context of our keyword. Podscope saves us that trouble. All we need to do is to select the appropriate time code

Figure 5-34   The Podscope homepage

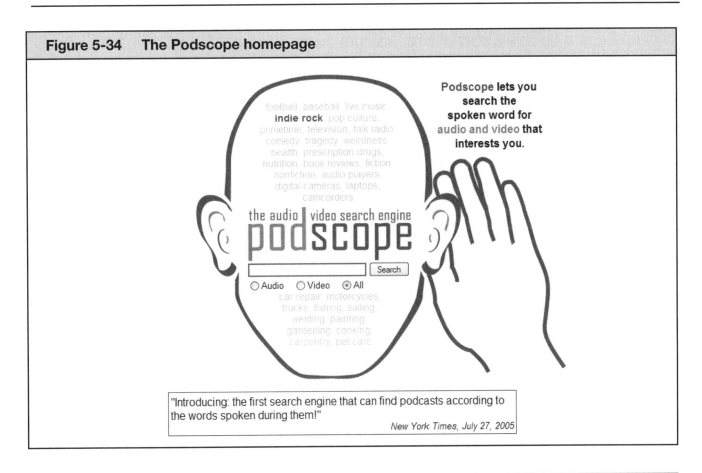

Figure 5-35   Podscope results for *libraries* sorted by date

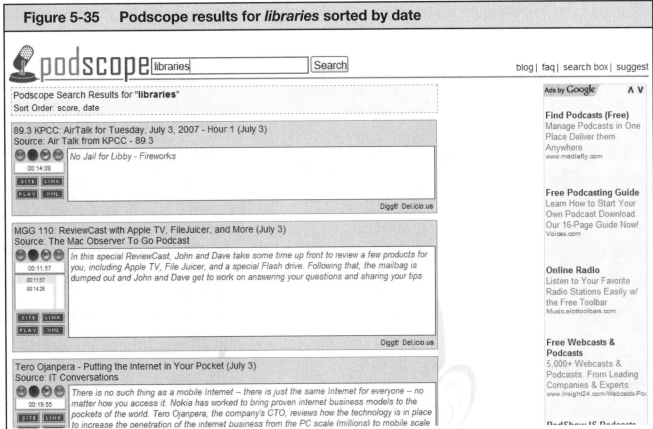

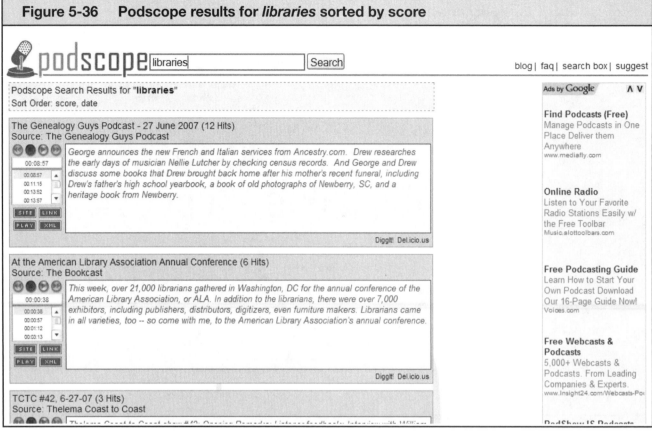

Figure 5-36   Podscope results for *libraries* sorted by score

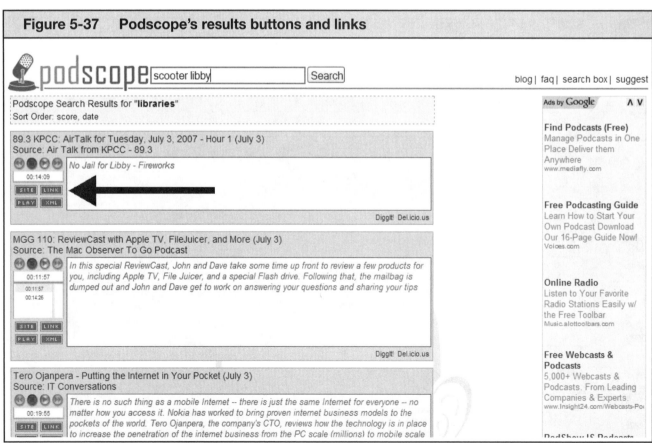

Figure 5-37   Podscope's results buttons and links

(assuming there is more than one) and click the green play button. After a few seconds, depending on your Internet connection speed, you will hear an approximately ten-second clip of the file containing your search term, giving you the context that should help you decide if you wish to hear the whole file. The other buttons are rewind, stop, and advance, respectively.

The following four linked buttons give you additional access to the complete audio file and related resources:

- **Site:**
  The site link will take you to the homepage of the podcast for the result.
- **Link:**
  This button will take you to the Web page for the particular episode that matches your search result.
- **Play:**
  Unlike the green "play" icon, this link will take you to a new page that contains the podcast's homepage

at the top of the screen and an embedded audio player at the bottom of the screen. Once you have chosen between the Windows Media Player and the Quicktime player (see Figure 5-38) the whole audio file will be played for you without the need to download the complete file (see Figure 5-39).

- **XML:**
  The XML (extensive markup language) link is to the RSS file for the associated podcast. This is the URL that you need to use should you wish to subscribe to that podcast.

I feel the need to mention just one more thing. There is a "search box" link in the upper right corner of the Podscope pages. Following this link gives podcasters the ability to create a Podscope search box for their Web site that links directly to their podcast. It is not relevant to a non-podcasting searcher.

CONCLUSION

With the advent of Web 2.0, it is becoming easier every day for regular people to create multimedia con-

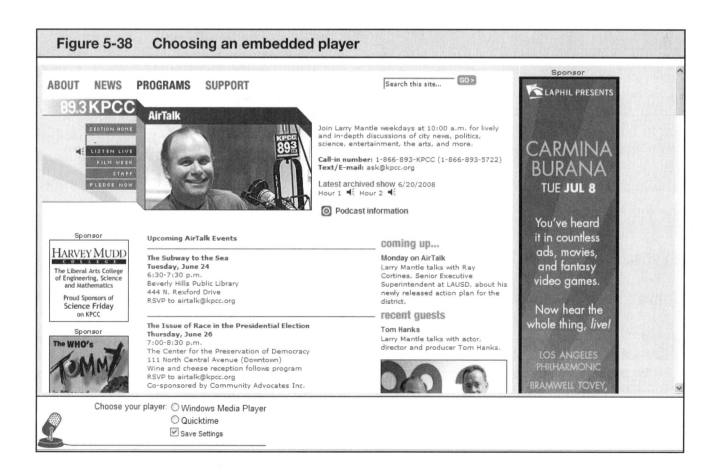

Figure 5-38   Choosing an embedded player

Figure 5-39   Listening to a podcast via Podscope

tent. Whether a still photograph posted to Flickr, a video posted to YouTube, or a weekly audio podcast, media are being created every second of every day. As more media are created, more library users will be looking for that content. Having a basic knowledge of how to find media content online should be considered a requisite skill for today's reference librarian. In the next chapter, we turn to finding out how to use the Web to find things in our own backyard using what's known as "local search."

EXERCISES

1. Search Flickr for photos of your library. You might be surprised at how often I've had librarians insist that there weren't any photos of their library online only to find out that a patron or traveler took a photo or two of the outside, or even the inside, of their library and posted them on Flickr.

2. Think of something that you've been meaning to learn how to do. This could be anything from using Windows Vista to wood carving. Search for a how-to video on that topic using YouTube.

3. Pick one of your hobbies and search Podscope for a related podcast that you might be interested in hearing.

NOTES

1. If you have a Flickr account and are logged in, you will also see options to search "Your contacts' photos," "Your friends' photos," and "Your photos." Since I am not assuming that all readers have or even wish to have an account, I do not cover these three searches.

2. However, I wouldn't encourage you to make a copy of said video clip and hand it over to the patron. That would be ethically questionable. All I'm suggesting is that you find what they're looking for and show them where it is. What they do with it is up to them.

Chapter 6

Local Search

INTRODUCTION

Several times in the past decade, I've insisted that I can't look up a movie time or a company's phone number because my Internet connection is down. As for the movie times, I've not subscribed to a newspaper for years. That's my defense and I'm sticking to it. As for a phone number, the typical response from whomever I'm speaking to is, "So, look it up in the phone book, dummy." Touché, but these days I'm tired of having a phonebook collection sitting on top of my fridge collecting dust. Now when I get one, it immediately goes into the recycling pile. Sorry folks, but I just don't have a phone book anymore.

Even if I did, using a phone book to pick a restaurant based on the size of its listing (meaning more money available to spend on advertising) just isn't reliable, if it ever was. I want to know how long it's going to take me to get there, see a menu, and read some reviews—from customers, not from someone who gets paid to write reviews—before I decide to head out the door. Taking it a step further, if I want to find something to do while I'm already out, I no longer need to call "information." I open up my cell phone's browser and get the information I need within seconds. "Local" search engines let me do all of this and more.

Two of the most popular local search services today are Google Maps and Windows Live Local. Although in many cases their features are built into the companies' main search engines (for example, if you include a zip code or "city, state" in a Google search you'll be presented with local results before

Web results), in this chapter, I focus on the local interfaces that each service provides.

A Few Notes on the Map Interfaces

First-time users of map/local sites such as the three discussed in this chapter tend to quickly notice that these pages do not work the same as the more traditional Web pages to which we've all become accustomed. To add to some users' frustration, the mouse doesn't always do what they expect. Before we get into searching Google Maps, let me point out a few things that will save you a certain amount of frustration in the long run.

First, there are typically zooming controls located in the upper left corner of the map. These traditionally contain plus (zoom in) and minus (zoom out) buttons. More advanced interfaces will also include a slider bar on which you can drag a marker up or down to zoom in and out, respectively. Using these methods will zoom on the current center of the map.

However, when the mouse pointer is on these maps, in most cases the mouse's scroll wheel also acts as a zoom controller, scrolling forward (away from you) to zoom in and scrolling back (toward you) to zoom out. Also, zooming with the scroll wheel tends to zoom in on the point where the mouse pointer currently is, not on the center of the map. When the mouse pointer is not on the map, the scroll wheel will act normally and scroll the page. Also, in some systems, double-clicking the left mouse button while on the map will zoom in one level on wherever your pointer was, and double-clicking the right mouse button will zoom out one level.

Second, when the mouse pointer is over a map, it will generally turn into a hand. This indicates that you may drag the map in any direction within the display window. For example, Google Maps starts by showing me the United States since that's where I am. If I want to see Europe, the easiest way is to move my mouse pointer over to the east (right) side of the map, press and hold down my left mouse button, and drag the map to the west (left) until I see Europe on the screen. Keep in mind that it may take a few seconds for the new areas of the map to load, so don't be worried if it looks like a part of the world has fallen off the map.

Third, a word of warning, avoid using your back button. Most map services are designed using newer coding methods, and despite what you do on the screen, you have not actually changed pages or gone "forward" to another page. A few times when working on a map site for 15 or 20 minutes, I've clicked the back button only to end up on the page I was on before I went to the maps site. As a result, I had

to click forward and start all over again. In some cases, the back button will work, but it's better to get into the habit of not using it and using the in-page controls instead.

Last, most mapping services have three to five different views available to you. The first traditional three are map, satellite, and hybrid. Newer services from larger companies such as Google Maps and Live Search Maps are also starting to offer "street view" and "traffic" versions in major cities (though mostly limited to those in the United States at the time of this writing). You may switch between these views by using the buttons typically located in the upper right corner of the map. Here's a brief description and example from Google Maps of each view. Some of them are of Times Square in New York City, while others are of Denver, Colorado, and Los Angeles, California.

- **Map:**
  The map view (see Figure 6-1) shows a basic colored line drawing map of the area. Streets are labeled, and one-way streets are indicated.

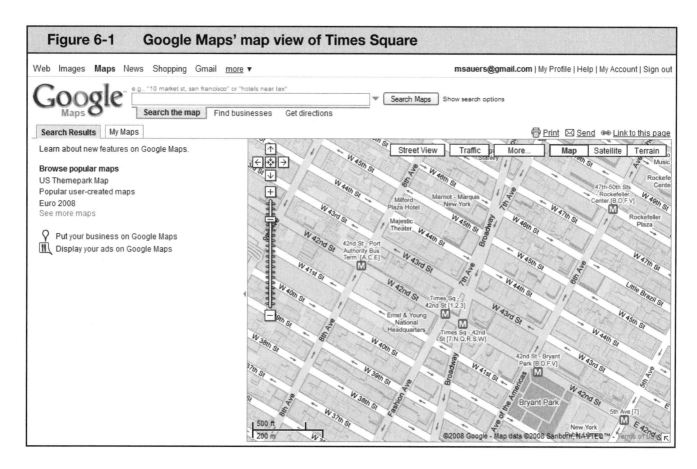

Figure 6-1   Google Maps' map view of Times Square

- **Satellite:**

  The satellite view (see Figure 6-2) shows a photographic view of the area from above. Satellite images can be as much as months or years out of date, and not all areas are covered. In addition, some areas considered "sensitive," such as the U.S. Capitol Building, are intentionally blurred. Nothing is labeled in the satellite view.

- **Terrain:**

  The terrain view (see Figure 6-3) shows the detailed terrain and elevation of the area. (I've switched to *Denver, CO* here since there isn't much terrain to speak of in Manhattan.)

- **Street view:**

  With recent advances in technology and digital storage, companies such as Google and Microsoft are investing millions of dollars in bringing local search to the street level (see Figure 6-4). Right now, this involves specially fitted vehicles driving through major metropolitan areas and photographing what they see every few feet. These photographs are then pieced together and rendered in the street view as if you were driving down the street yourself. This button will appear only if street view data are available. (If you're impressed with the results now, just wait. As the technology improves, this will only get better and more areas will be covered.)

- **Traffic:**

  As with street view, when this button is available you can overlay real-time traffic speeds on your current view. This typically works only for highways and color-codes the current speeds. In Google Maps the colors are "Green: more than 50 miles per hour," "Yellow: 25–50 miles per hour," "Red: less than 25 miles per hour," and "Gray: no data currently available." For an example, see Figure 6-5.

Despite having used Google Maps for my examples of the different map views, the results are similar in all three search engines discussed in this chapter. I picked just one to display here so as to avoid overt repetition.

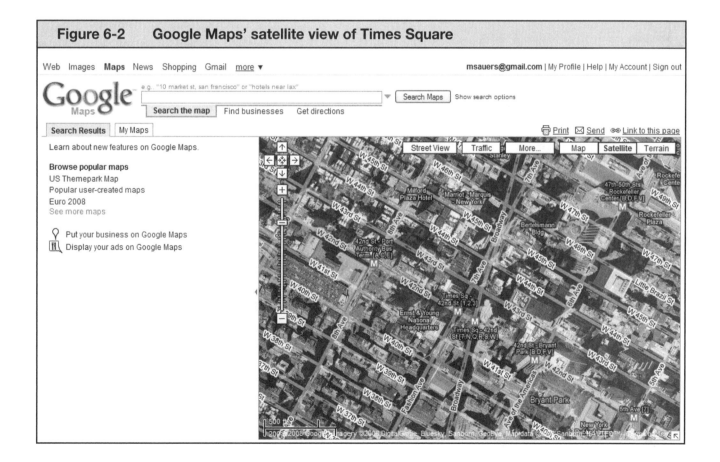

Figure 6-2   Google Maps' satellite view of Times Square

Figure 6-3   Google Maps' terrain view of Denver, Colorada

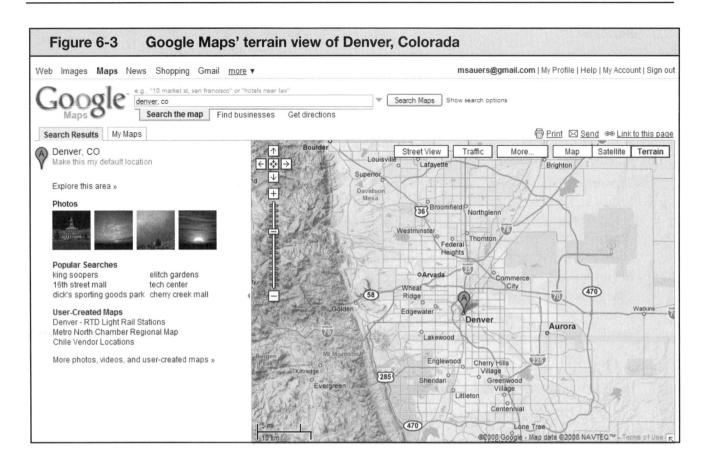

Figure 6-4   Google Maps' street view of Times Square

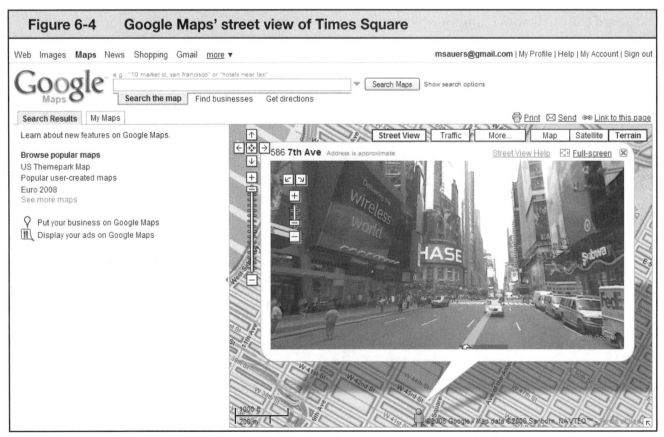

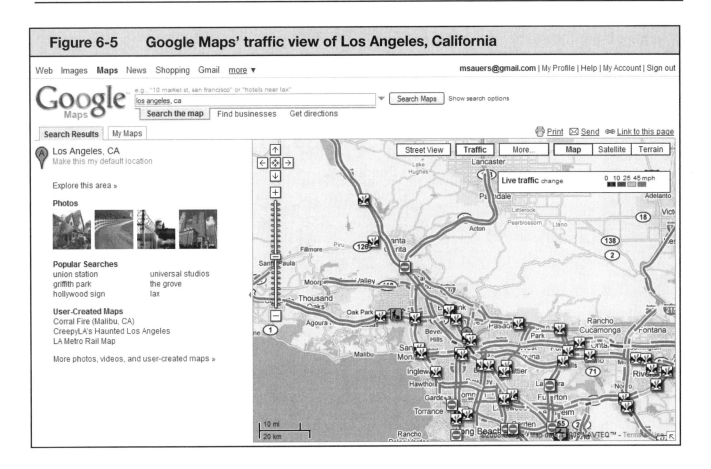

Figure 6-5   Google Maps' traffic view of Los Angeles, California

GOOGLE MAPS

Today, Google Maps is the single interface to what used to be two separate searching interfaces, Google's mapping service and the Google Local searching service. So you can use either http://maps.google.com/ or http://local.google.com/ to get to the service's homepage, as shown in Figure 6-6.

Once there you'll be presented with a map of the United States on which you can pan and zoom as described in the previous section. (You can change this view to your immediate area by using the "Set default location" link.) At the top of the page, you'll see a link that says "Show search options." Clicking this opens a drop-down menu to choose locations, businesses, user-created content, mapped Web pages, and real estate. A "Get Directions" link is available on the top left. Each of these represents a different method of searching Google Maps. Using this search box, you can actually change the method of your search through the way you type your search. For example, typing an address will do a map search,

while typing two addresses with the word "to" between them will do a directions search. However, for simplicity's sake, let's take a look at a locations search, a business search, and driving directions.

Locations Search

A map search is designed to accept a location as your search term. A location can be formatted in a number of different ways. For example:

- Zip code (68508 in Figure 6-7)
- City, state (Lincoln, NE, in Figure 6-8)
- Street and zip code (1200 N St, 68508, in Figure 6-9)
- A full address (1200 N St, Lincoln, NE 68508 in Figure 6-10)

Entering your search in any of these four formats will return to you a single match with the map zoomed in to the appropriate level with a marker on the location of your result. A balloon with a brief

Figure 6-6   The Google Maps homepage

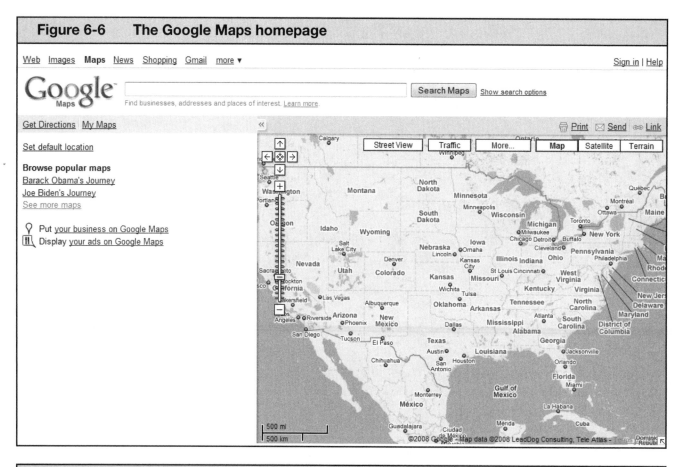

Figure 6-7   Zip code search results

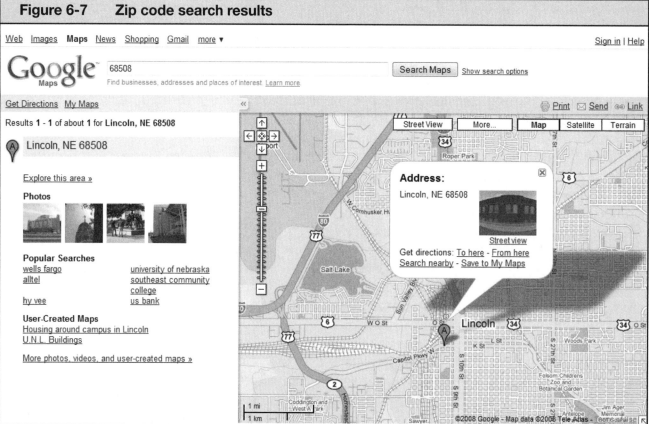

Figure 6-8   City, state search results

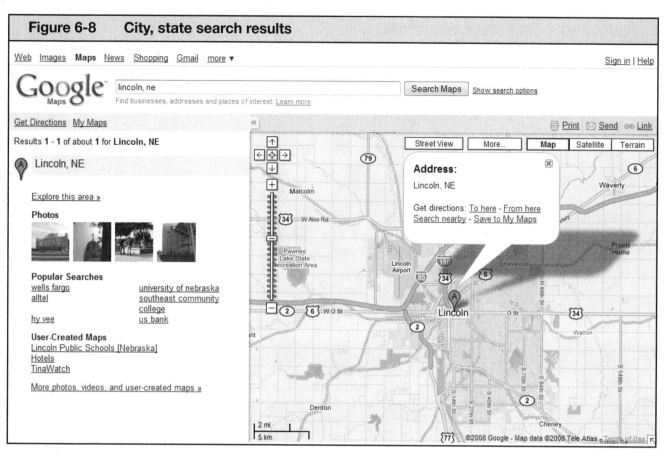

Figure 6-9   Street and zip code results

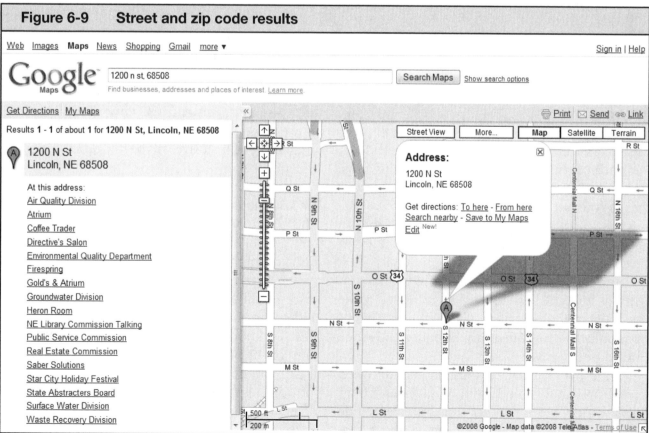

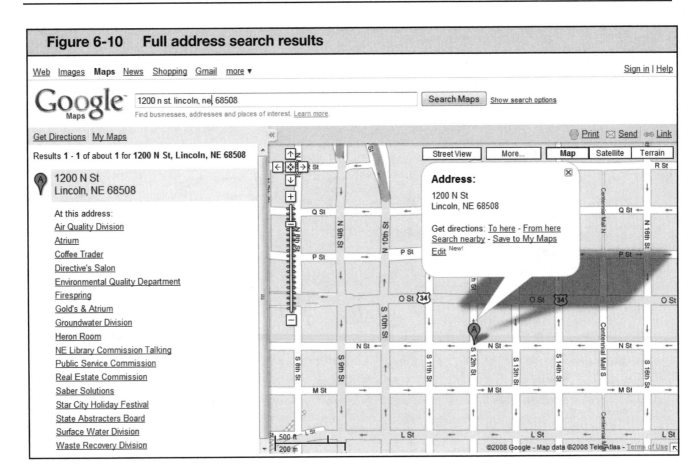

Figure 6-10   Full address search results

description of your result and links for more options—directions to/from here, search nearby, and save to my maps—will also appear. You can close this balloon by clicking the "x" in its upper right corner.

If you type in what Google considers to be an incomplete location—for example, just a street address but not a city/state or zip code, the first thing it will do is look for that address in the same geographic area of your last search. For example, since I've been recently searching for locations in Lincoln, Nebraska, a search for *1200 o st* will retrieve me that address in Lincoln, Nebraska (see Figure 6-11).

However, if I were to search for *10 belleview st* it will not find any such address in the Lincoln, Nebraska, area and return me a list of possible results from a much larger search area, in this case Belleview, Florida (see Figure 6-12).

Using the "Set default location" option (mentioned previously; see Figure 6-6) makes Google Maps work a little smoother. For example, my default location has been set to Lincoln, Nebraska (see

Figure 6-13). From this point forward, whenever I come back to Google Maps, the map will start with that location, and any searches I do will assume that I'm looking for things within the Lincoln area first. I suggest that you use your library's address as the default, assuming that most of the reference questions you'll receive will be for addresses in your general vicinity.

Find Businesses

The businesses search is for when you're looking for a type of or specific business in a particular area. For example, say your patron is looking for a good Indian restaurant in town. In this case you would enter *indian* and your general location (city, state, and/or zip code) (see Figure 6-14). If you've set a default location, this will automatically be the location for the business search. You can change this if it isn't appropriate for your search.

Your results will be presented to you in groups of ten to the left of the map, as seen in Figure 6-15. Each result will be labeled with a letter: A–J for the

Figure 6-11   Results for *1200 o st*

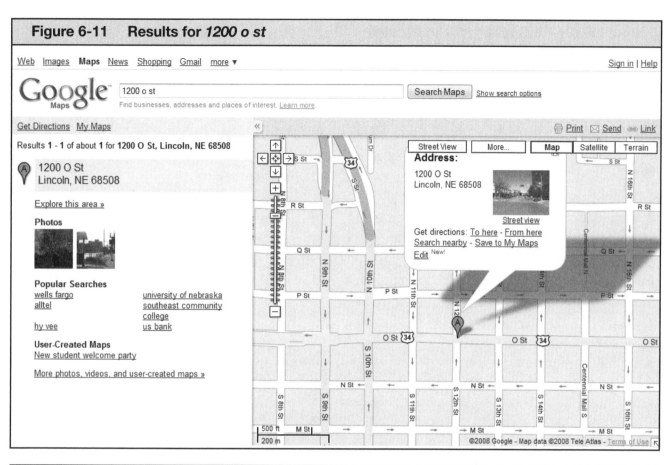

Figure 6-12   List of possible results for *10 belleview st*

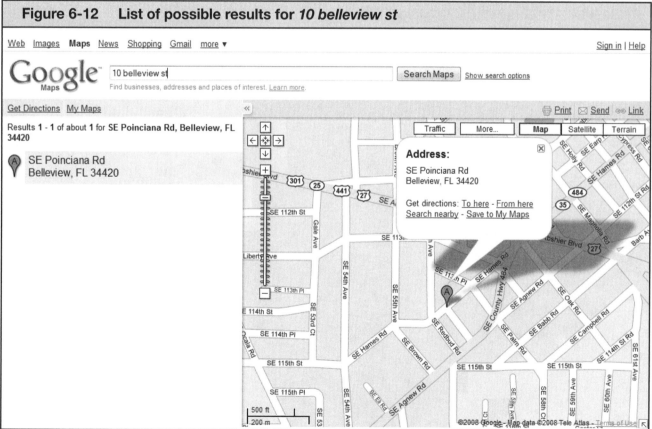

Figure 6-13   My default location setting

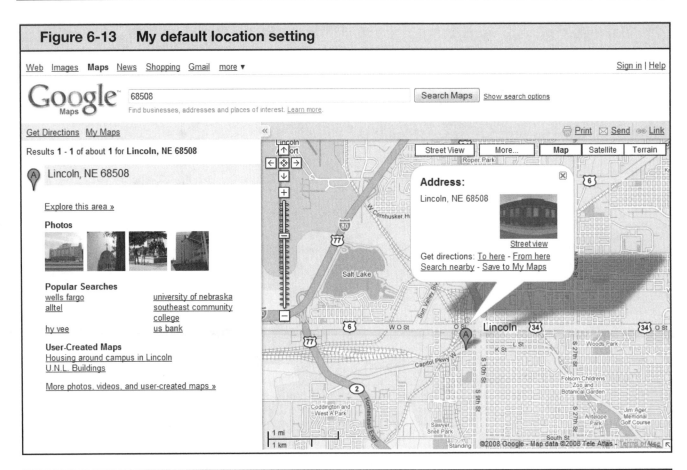

Figure 6-14   Search for a business

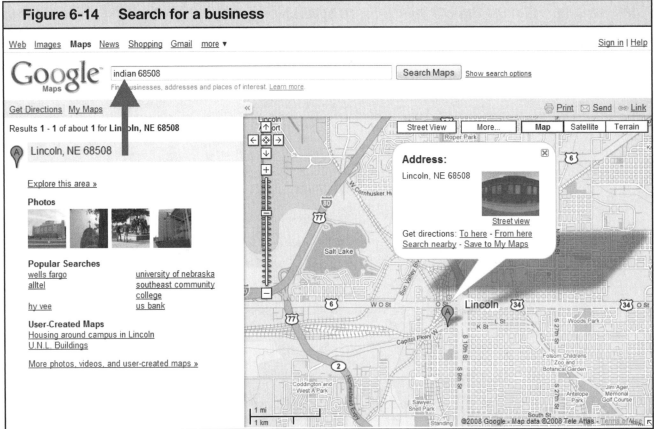

first ten, K–T for the next ten, etc., which will match a lettered pointer on the map.

Clicking on any of the pointers in the results list or on the map or the name of a result will open the descriptive balloon for that pointer on the map. The balloon will generally include the name of the business, a rating, links to the business's Web site and reviews, the full address, a photo of the business, and links for directions, search nearby, save to my maps, and send to phone (via SMS), e-mail, car, or GPS. I find the phone option very handy. The amount of information in this balloon will vary from business to business based on the information available to Google. Figure 6-16 shows the balloon for one of my results: The Oven. (Be sure to stop by if you're ever in town. I highly recommend it.)

If you don't like viewing the small list of text results along with the large map, you can click the "Text View" link at the top of the search results. This will rearrange the results page, giving you more text-based information and less map information (see

Figure 6-17). In this view, you can easily change the radius of the search to 1 mile, 5 miles, 15 miles, 45 miles, or 90 miles using the "Refine by: Distance" option near the top of the page.

Driving Directions

Once you've found the business you want to go to, or if you already know the address of where you want to end up, the "Get Directions" search is your final step. First let me cover "Get Directions" from the link at the top.

Selecting "Get Directions" will change the search interface at the top left of the page to give you two search boxes, A and B. If you have set a default location, it will automatically be filled in as your start address. Enter a destination address and you'll be presented with driving directions and a map to your destination, as shown in Figure 6-18.

If you wish to get return directions, you can click on the double arrow located between the start and end address fields to swap the start and end address-

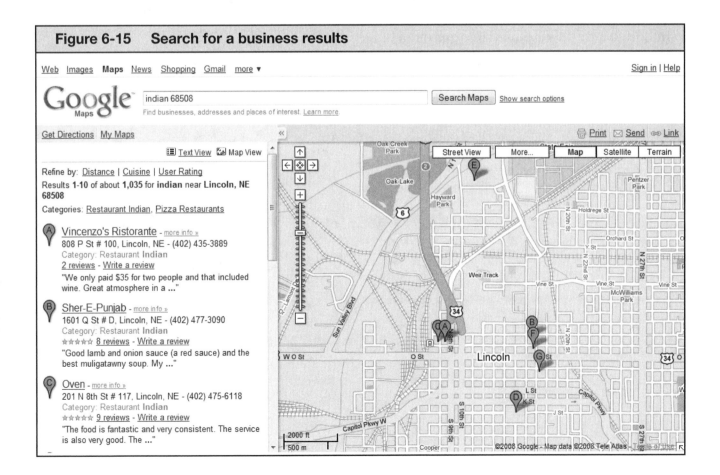

Figure 6-16   Details for "The Oven" business search results

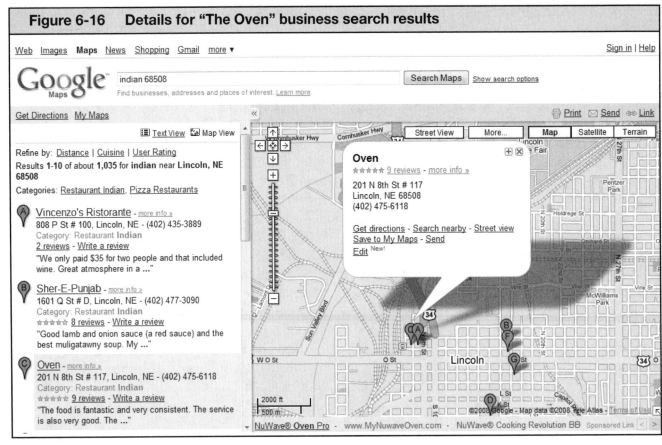

Figure 6-17   Text view of the search results

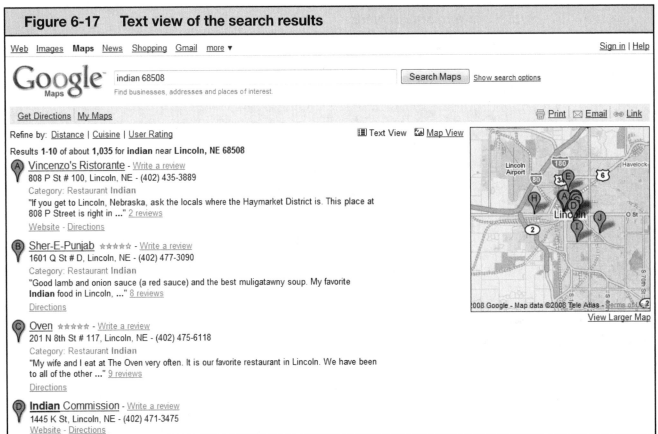

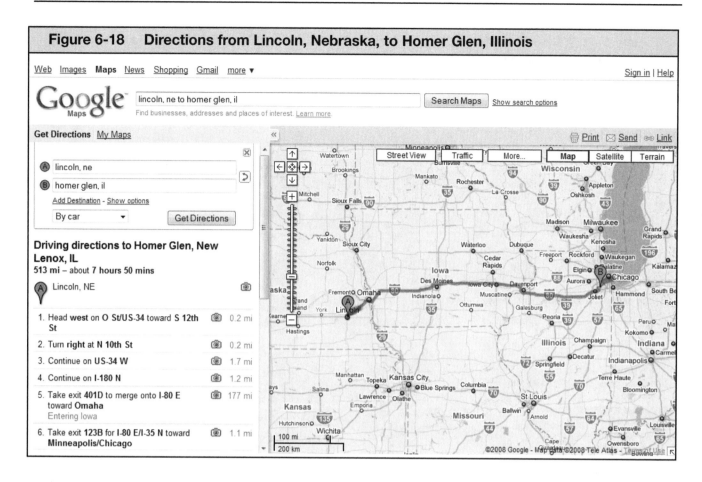

Figure 6-18   Directions from Lincoln, Nebraska, to Homer Glen, Illinois

es. Click the arrow and the directions reverse. This is also handy if you wish to get directions from your first destination to a second destination. Perform the switch then type in a new end address.

Once you have your route, you have a few options for customizing it. First click on the "Show options" link under box B. You can check the "Avoid highways" option if you would like a more scenic route, as shown in Figure 6-19.

Second, if you wish to stop in a particular location that isn't included on the route that Google provided, you can drag a spot on the blue route line to the location you wish to include, thereby changing the route, and new directions will be provided. For example, Figure 6-20 shows my route from Lincoln, Nebraska to Homer Glen, Illinois, with a stop in Waterloo, Iowa. You can click the "add a destination" link, which provides additional search boxes (box C, box D, etc., up to box Y) for directions to stops along the way.

These last options can be most useful when planning a multilocation trip. Start by finding the directions from your start to the furthest location, and then customize (drag) your route to include the additional places you wish to stop (see Figure 6-21), or enter the extra stops into the extra "add a destination" boxes. If on your return trip you wish to take a completely different route, just reverse the directions and move your route accordingly (see Figure 6-22).

As you may have noticed, if you're on a balloon for a particular location you can click on "Get directions" in the balloon to also access this search. When you select "Get directions" in a balloon it will give you a "Start address" box (with your default location presupplied if you've set one), as shown in Figure 6-23. This assumes that you're traveling to that location. If you wish to get directions from that location, click on the "From here" link to change the box to "End address," as in Figure 6-24.

Figure 6-19 Directions from Lincoln, Nebraska, to Homer Glen, Illinois, while avoiding highways

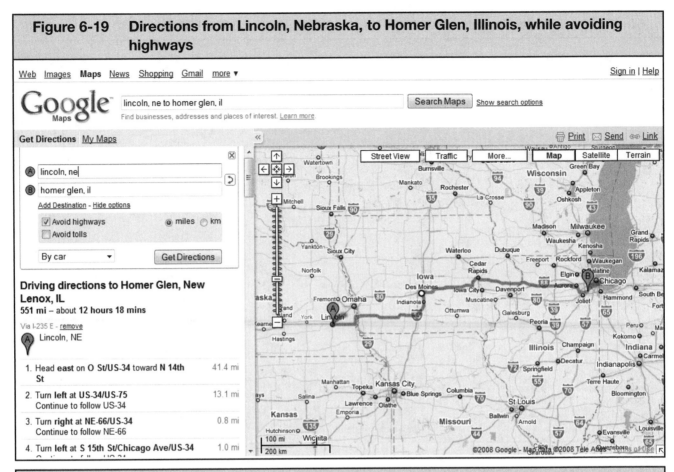

Figure 6-20 Directions from Lincoln, Nebraska, to Homer Glen, Illinois, with a stop in Waterloo, Iowa

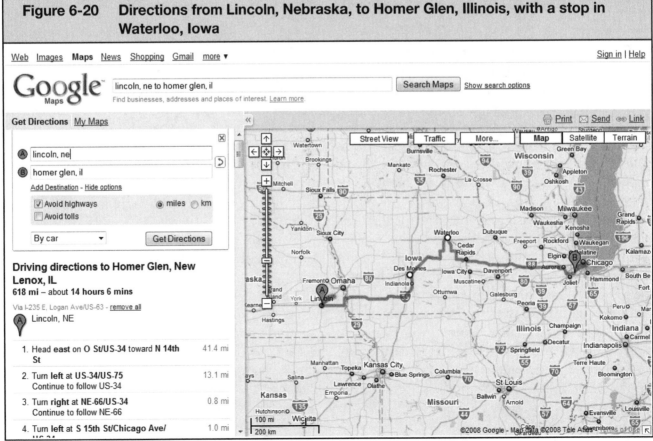

Figure 6-21   Directions from San Francisco, California, to New York City via a northern route

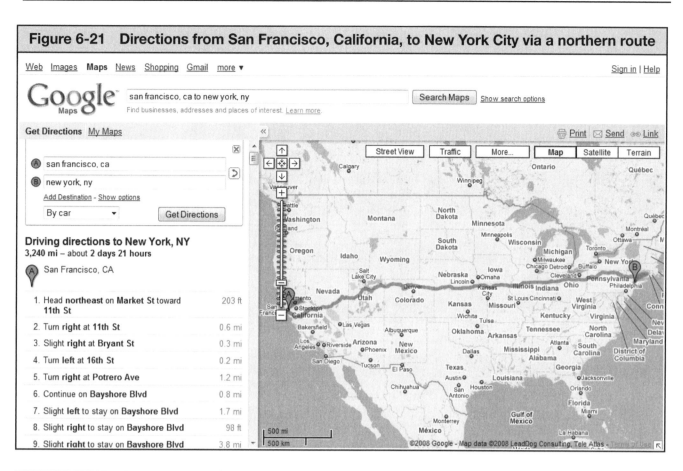

Figure 6-22   Directions from New York City to San Francisco, California, via a southern route

Figure 6-23   Accessing "get directions" from a location balloon

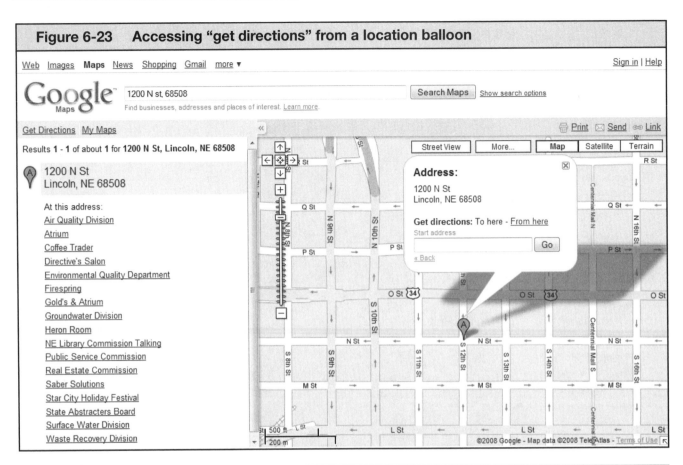

Figure 6-24   Changing to "from here" in a location balloon

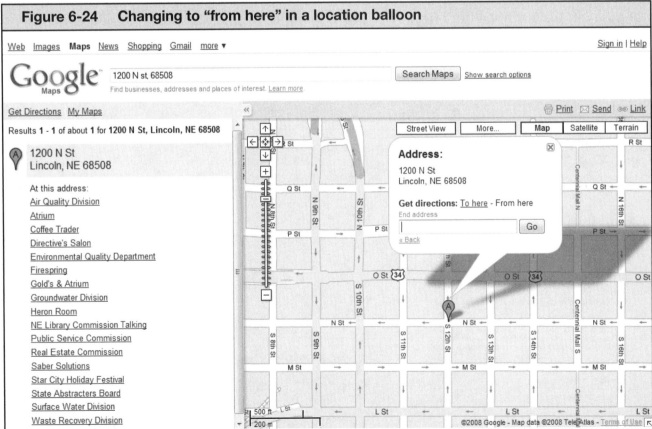

Output Options

Once you have chosen the map view that works best for you (see earlier in this chapter), you need to choose which output method you wish to use. Your three choices are "Print," "Send," or "Link" to this page.

- **Print:**

  Whether you have a map of an area, the location of a business, or directions from point A to point B, you're most likely going to want a printed copy. Unfortunately, what you're looking at on the screen is in landscape (especially if you're using a widescreen monitor) and by default, your printer prints portrait. The best way to handle this is not to use the print button built into your browser. Instead, use the print link located above the map on the right. This will open a new window for you, formatted for the correct orientation, with a map that correctly fits the piece of paper. Figures 6-25 and 6-26 show the print results for an area and a business.

  Figures 6-27 through 6-30 show the print views for directions. The three main print views are "Text only" (Figure 6-27); "Maps," which will show a map for each turn (Figure 6-28); and "Street view," which will display images of the area as if you were looking out your car window, if available (Figure 6-29). In addition, you can check the "Include large map" option on any of these three views to have a trip overview map included at the beginning of your directions (Figure 6-30).

- **Send:**

  The send option is great for when your patron is not in front of you but has e-mail access. When you click "send," a small window will appear on your screen, as in Figure 6-31, asking you which information you want to include in the e-mail to be sent—all results or a particular result from a business search, for example, the to and from e-mail addresses (including the option to cc: yourself on the e-mail), and a message including a link to the map you're viewing. You can add additional text to the body of the message if you wish. Just fill out the form and send.

- **Link to this page:**

  Because of the nature of the technology running

Google Maps, the URL of the page does not change all that often while you're navigating the site. (This is why I suggest not using the browser's back button while in these sites.) As a result, bookmarking what you're looking at or attaching the URL of your map in a regular e-mail is rather difficult. To do either of these things, you first need the real URL of what's on the screen. To get this, click on the "Link to this page" link. This will give you two pieces of information: the URL of this page that you can use as a bookmark, paste as a hyperlink in a Web page, regular e-mail, or instant message, and an HTML code needed to embed this map into a Web page. This is shown in Figure 6-32. To embed the map, just copy and paste the code into your Web page. If you wish to change the size of the map that you're embedding, click the "Customize and preview embedded map" link and a new window will appear allowing you to change the size and receive a revised embedding code, as in Figure 6-33.

My Maps

If you find yourself regularly giving out the same map-based information or wish to create a highly detailed map that you can access in the future, choose the "My Maps" option. The simplest way to use this feature is first to perform your search and customizations and then click on the "My Maps" tab above the search results. Click the "Create new map" link, give your map a name and a description, and then click the "Save button" (see Figure 6-34).

Once you've done this, your map is now listed and easily retrievable from your list in the future. Additionally, your map now has a few new buttons on it, located in the upper left corner, which allow you to add place pointers, draw lines, and draw shapes. This is a bit beyond the scope of this book, so I won't go into details on these abilities.

Saved Locations

Last, there is a hidden "Saved Locations" option. One thing Google Maps does (without explicitly telling you) is to make a list of all of your searched-for locations. This list can be accessed via the ▼ to the right of the search box (see Figure 6-35). Click that icon and then click "Edit saved locations." Once there

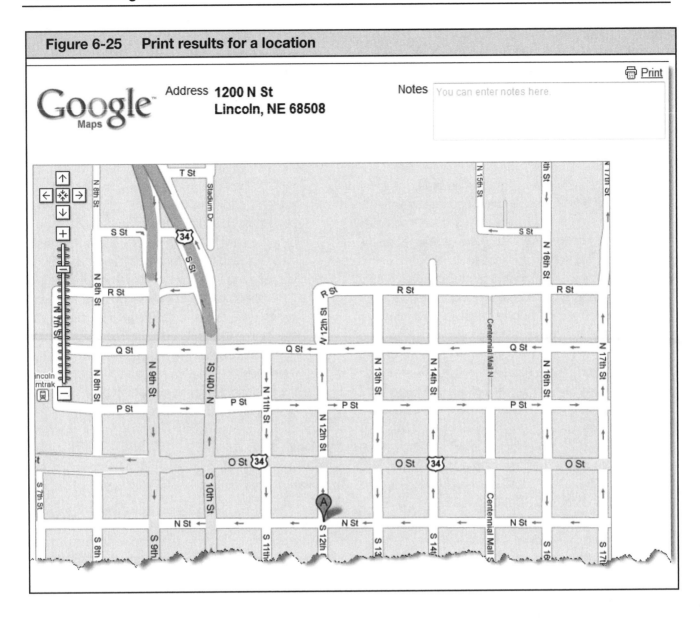

Figure 6-25　Print results for a location

you'll see a list of your searches along with the ability to add new locations manually via the "New locations" boxes at the top of the list (see Figure 6-36).

By clicking on the name of a location in this list you'll be taken to a map of that location. To delete one or more locations from your list, click the "Edit saved locations" link at the bottom of the list. On the next page check the box for the appropriate locations and click the "Delete" button. To change your default location, click on the arrow to the left of the location. The arrow will then turn solid green. Last, you can click on the "Edit" link to the far right of a location to change the location's address and/or add a label (see Figure 6-37).

The benefit of adding a label to a location is that when searching you can type in the label instead of the address. For example, if I want directions from work to a new bookstore in town and I've labeled my office address as "work," instead of typing the office's address into the start address field, I can just type *work*. Figure 6-38 illustrates this option. *Work* is automatically replaced with *1200 N St, Lincoln, NE 68508 (work)*.

LIVE SEARCH MAPS

Microsoft's Live Search Maps (http://maps.live.com/) is a little more interactive than Google Maps, so it creates a nice contrast for the second half of this chapter. As with Google Maps, Microsoft Live Search Maps contains a two-dimensional map that you can navi-

Figure 6-26   Print results for a business

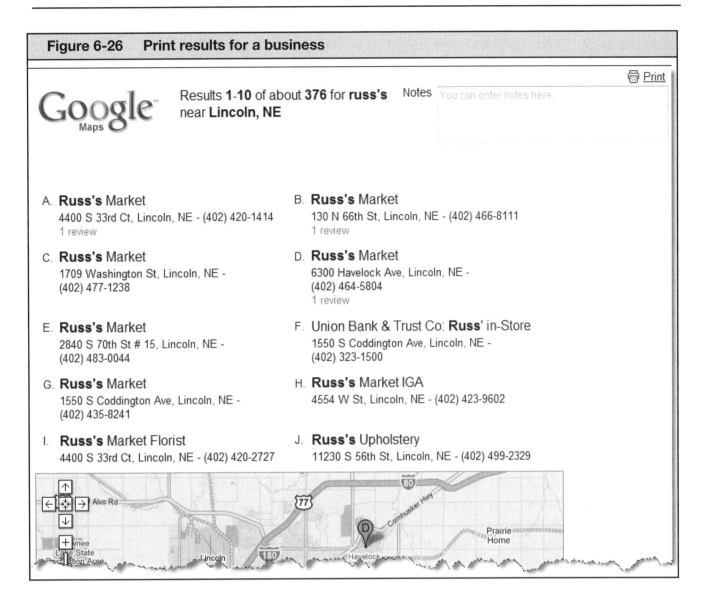

gate and pinpoint locations through search. Additionally, with the installation of some extra software, Microsoft's Virtual Earth 3D, you can switch from a 2-D environment to a 3-D one. I'll briefly cover the 3-D aspect at the end of this section, but for the rest of it I'll be working in the regular 2-D environment, as in Figure 6-39.

Search the Map

Live Search Maps has five different basic searches: Businesses, People, Collections, Locations, and Web. Each of these can be accessed via the links located beneath the search boxes at the top of the page. The businesses search is the default. Let's take a look at

how the businesses, people, and location searches work. (I discuss Collections later, and the Web option takes you to Microsoft Live Search, discussed previously in Chapter 2.)

Find Businesses

The businesses search gives you three search fields in which to enter information: business, category, or location. You can use one, two, or all three. Using all three will get you the most narrowed results. Enter the name of a business (e.g., Lincoln City Libraries) or a category (e.g., library). You can also enter a varied amount of information such as a city/state, zip code, or "landmark." Great examples of landmarks

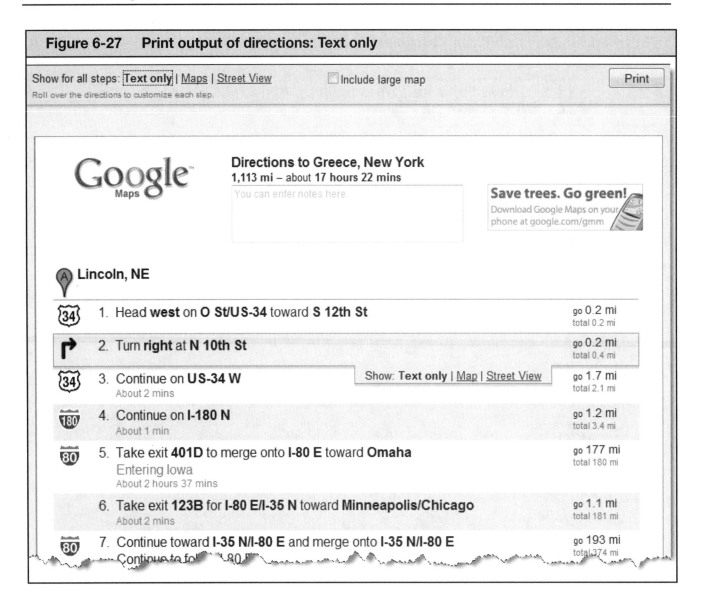

Figure 6-27   Print output of directions: Text only

Show for all steps: Text only | Maps | Street View   ☐ Include large map   [Print]
Roll over the directions to customize each step.

Google Maps

Directions to Greece, New York
1,113 mi – about 17 hours 22 mins

You can enter notes here.

Save trees. Go green!
Download Google Maps on your phone at google.com/gmm

Ⓐ **Lincoln, NE**

(34)	1. Head **west** on **O St/US-34** toward **S 12th St**	go 0.2 mi total 0.2 mi
↱	2. Turn **right** at **N 10th St**	go 0.2 mi total 0.4 mi
(34)	3. Continue on **US-34 W** About 2 mins Show: **Text only** | Map | Street View	go 1.7 mi total 2.1 mi
(180)	4. Continue on **I-180 N** About 1 min	go 1.2 mi total 3.4 mi
(80)	5. Take exit **401D** to merge onto **I-80 E** toward **Omaha** Entering Iowa About 2 hours 37 mins	go 177 mi total 180 mi
	6. Take exit **123B** for **I-80 E/I-35 N** toward **Minneapolis/Chicago** About 2 mins	go 1.1 mi total 181 mi
(80)	7. Continue toward **I-35 N/I-80 E** and merge onto **I-35 N/I-80 E** Continue to fol~~~ I-80 E~~~	go 193 mi total 374 mi

are airports. Once you've filled in your search fields click the search icon (the magnifying glass) to perform your search.

Your results will include an updated map with numbered markers that match the text-based results on the left of your screen. The text results can be sorted by either relevance (the default) or by distance using the "Sort by" drop-down menu above the text results, as shown in Figure 6-40.

The text-based results do include more than just the businesses that are marked on the map. First you'll see a few sponsored listings by Yellowpages.com. Next you'll see your mapped results. The markers that are bright in color are the ones that you can currently see on the map. The markers that are lighter

in color are on the map but outside of your current map's boundaries and therefore not displayed on the map. As you zoom and/or pan the map, when new results become visible the light markers will brighten.

To view the details of any of your mapped results, move your mouse pointer over either the text result or the on-map pointer. When you hover over the text result, the icon's color will change both to the left of the text result and on the map (see Figure 6-41). Hovering over the icon on the map will also change colors and display a balloon of additional details, as in Figure 6-42. This allows you to visually match details from the text results to the map and vice versa. (I realize that I've not been too specific about

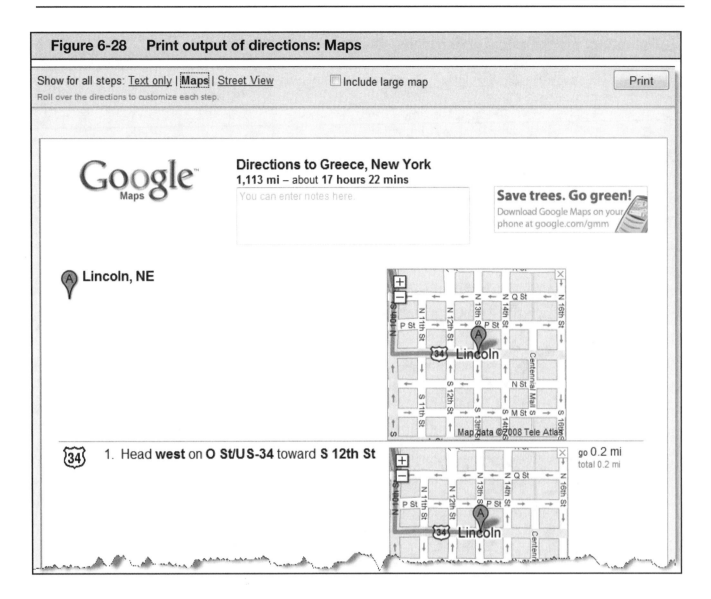

Figure 6-28   Print output of directions: Maps

Show for all steps: Text only | **Maps** | Street View   ☐ Include large map   Print

Roll over the directions to customize each step.

Google Maps

Directions to Greece, New York
1,113 mi – about **17 hours 22 mins**

You can enter notes here.

Save trees. Go green!
Download Google Maps on your phone at google.com/gmm

Ⓐ **Lincoln, NE**

㉞   1. Head **west** on **O St/US-34** toward **S 12th St**   go 0.2 mi
total 0.2 mi

the colors being used for the markers. I'll explain why shortly.)

Within each detail balloon you'll have many different options: "Send to," "Add to collection," "Drive from," "Drive to," or "Zoom to: street / city / region." Here's the skinny on each of them.

- **Send to e-mail:**
  Selecting this option will generate an outgoing e-mail message (using whichever e-mail client previously specified in your browser's settings) that contains the business's name in the subject line and the business's name and address in the body. The body will also contain a link back to your map.

Just enter the recipient's e-mail address and click "Send."

- **Send to mobile:**
  Selecting this link will open a window in which you can enter a cell phone number to which you would like to send the business's address and phone number via an SMS (short message service) text message (see Figure 6-43). This text message will also include a link to "more information" for phones that have built-in Web browsers. One important note: While this window is open, do not move your mouse pointer. If you move your mouse pointer off of the window, it will disappear; therefore, you must use your keyboard to maneuver within this

Figure 6-29   Print output of directions: Street view

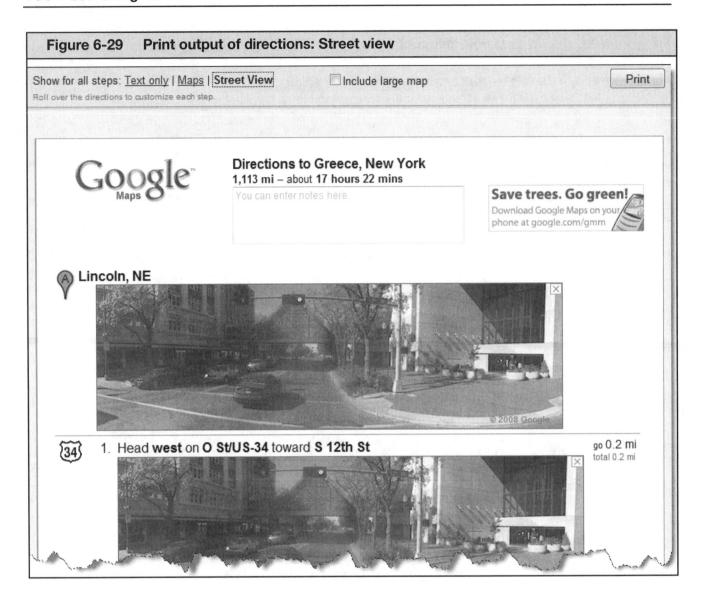

tool. Use your Tab key to move from field to field, and your Enter key to submit your request.

- **Send to GPS:**

  If you own a GPS device, you can send the location information to that device. To do so, choose this option and then choose whichever delivery method (wirelessly with MSN direct or with USB) is appropriate for your device (see Figure 6-44).

- **Add to collection:**

  Selecting "Add to collection" allows you to save this business/location to your account (see Figure 6-45). To take advantage of this feature, you must sign up for and log into a Windows Live account. I discuss collections later in this chapter.

- **Drive from or drive to:**

  These options change the left side of your screen into a directions search interface with the address of the business presupplied in the "Start" (see Figure 6-46) or "End" (see Figure 6-47) field. Just add the other address as needed, choose "Shortest time" or "Shortest distance," and click "Get directions." I also cover directions searches later in this chapter.

- **Zoom to street, city, or region:**

  The three zoom options give you quick access to different maps containing your results. For example, say you've searched for all of the quilt shops in the state of Washington. Figure 6-48 shows you

(continued p. 170)

Figure 6-30   Print output of directions: Trip overview map

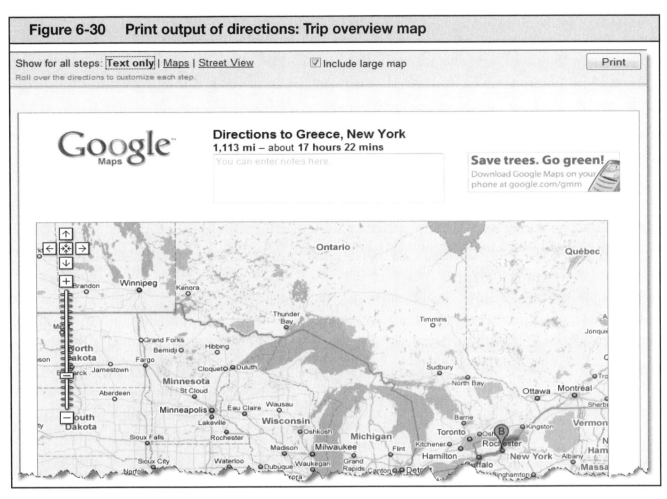

Figure 6-31   Send output

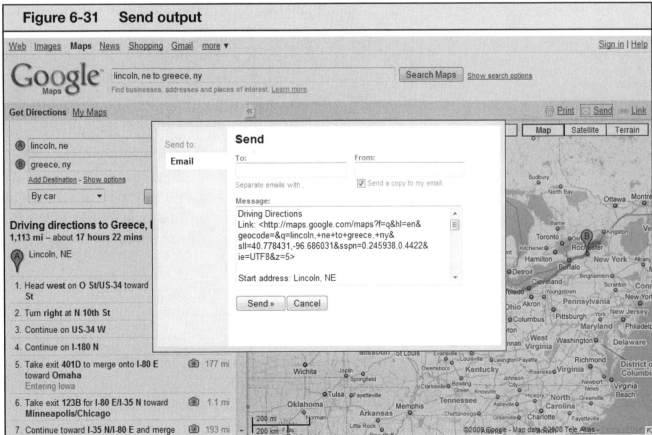

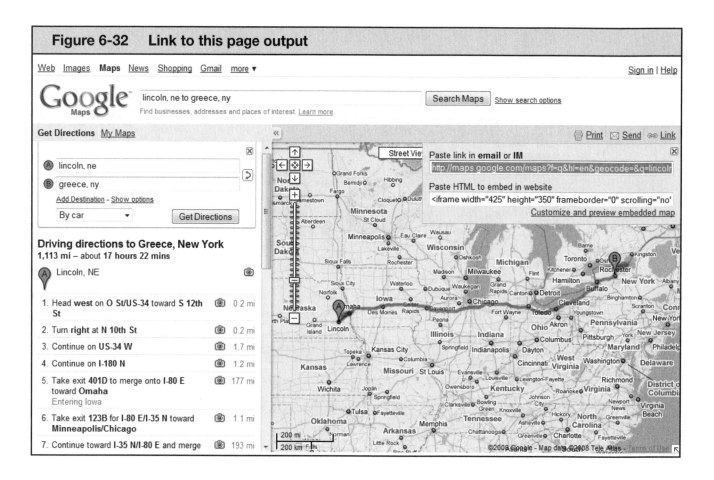

Figure 6-32   Link to this page output

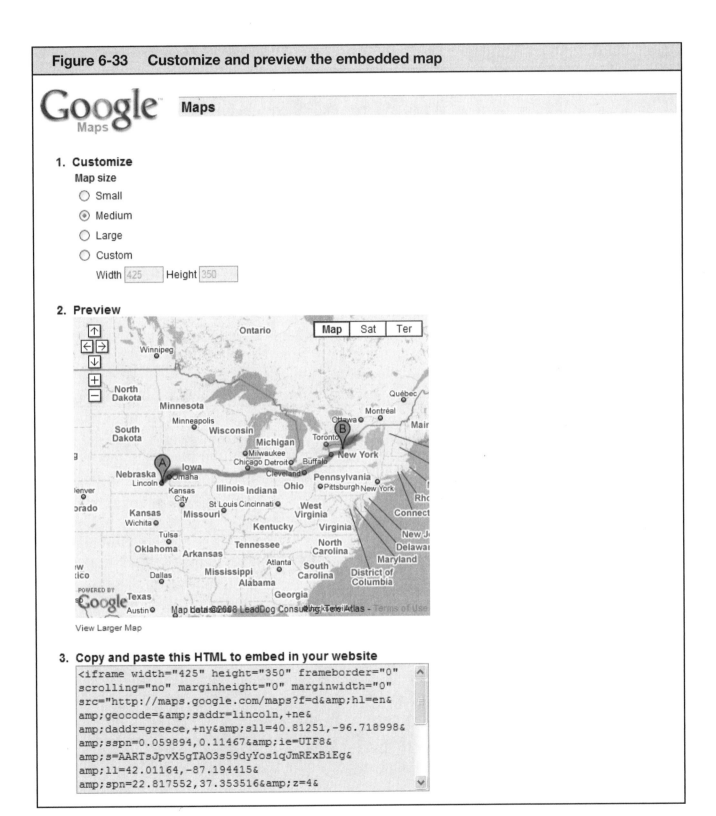

Figure 6-33   Customize and preview the embedded map

Figure 6-34   My maps: Creating a new map

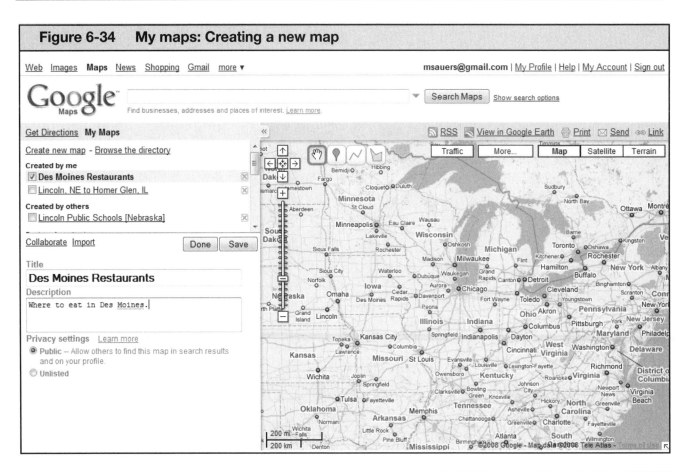

Figure 6-35   The hidden "saved locations" options

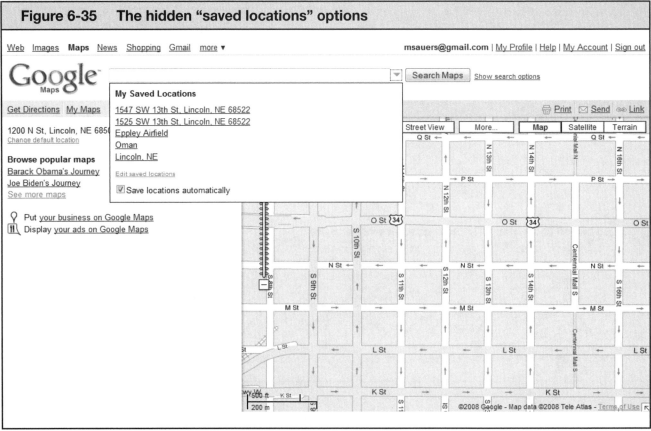

Figure 6-36   Saved locations

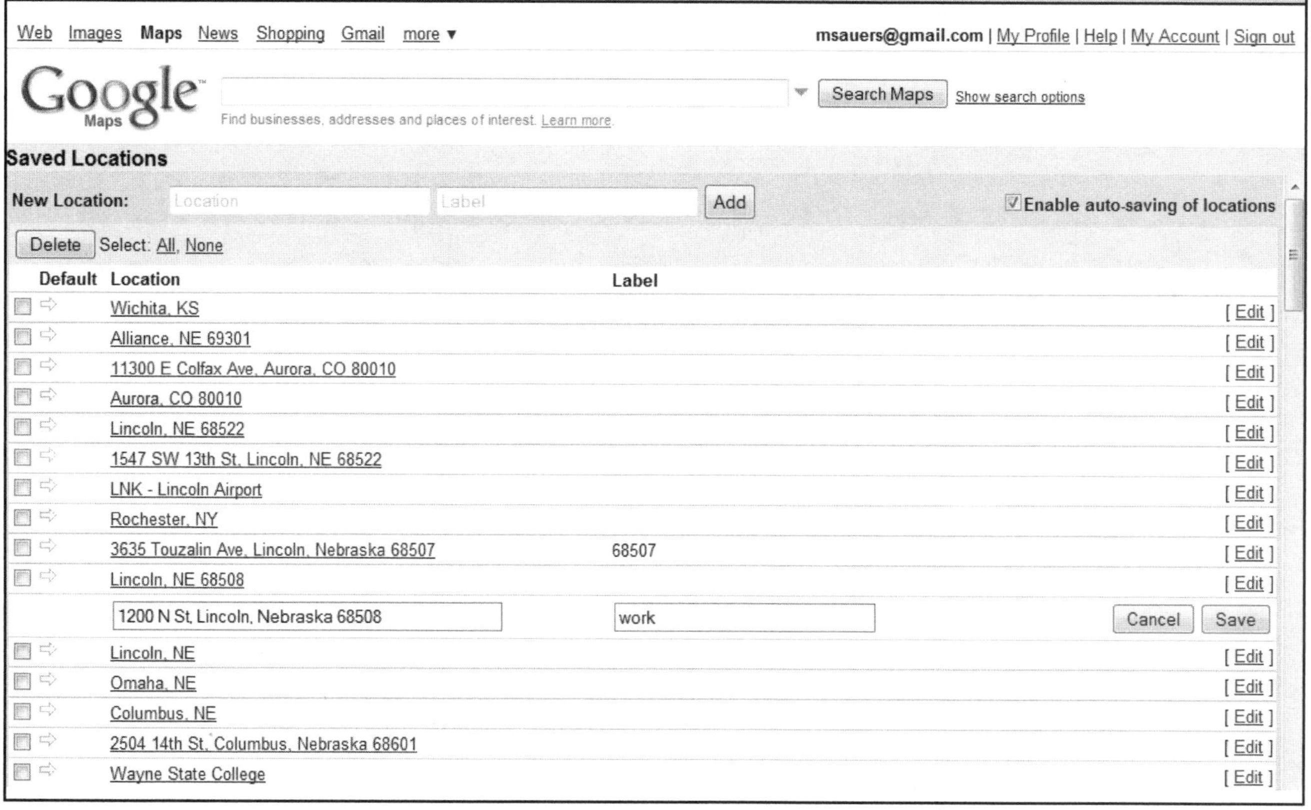

Web Images **Maps** News Shopping Gmail more ▼

msauers@gmail.com | My Profile | Help | My Account | Sign out

Google Maps

[   ] ▼ [Search Maps] Show search options

Find businesses, addresses and places of interest. Learn more.

Saved Locations

New Location: [Location] [Label] [Add]   ☑ Enable auto-saving of locations

[Delete] Select: All, None

Default	Location	Label	
☐ ⇨	Wichita, KS		[Edit]
☐ ⇨	Alliance, NE 69301		[Edit]
☐ ⇨	11300 E Colfax Ave, Aurora, CO 80010		[Edit]
☐ ⇨	Aurora, CO 80010		[Edit]
☐ ⇨	Lincoln, NE 68522		[Edit]
☐ ⇨	1547 SW 13th St, Lincoln, NE 68522		[Edit]
☐ ⇨	LNK - Lincoln Airport		[Edit]
☐ ⇨	Rochester, NY		[Edit]
☐ ⇨	3635 Touzalin Ave, Lincoln, Nebraska 68507	68507	[Edit]
☐ ⇨	Lincoln, NE 68508		[Edit]
	[1200 N St, Lincoln, Nebraska 68508]	[work]	[Cancel] [Save]
☐ ⇨	Lincoln, NE		[Edit]
☐ ⇨	Omaha, NE		[Edit]
☐ ⇨	Columbus, NE		[Edit]
☐ ⇨	2504 14th St, Columbus, Nebraska 68601		[Edit]
☐ ⇨	Wayne State College		[Edit]

Figure 6-37   Editing a saved location

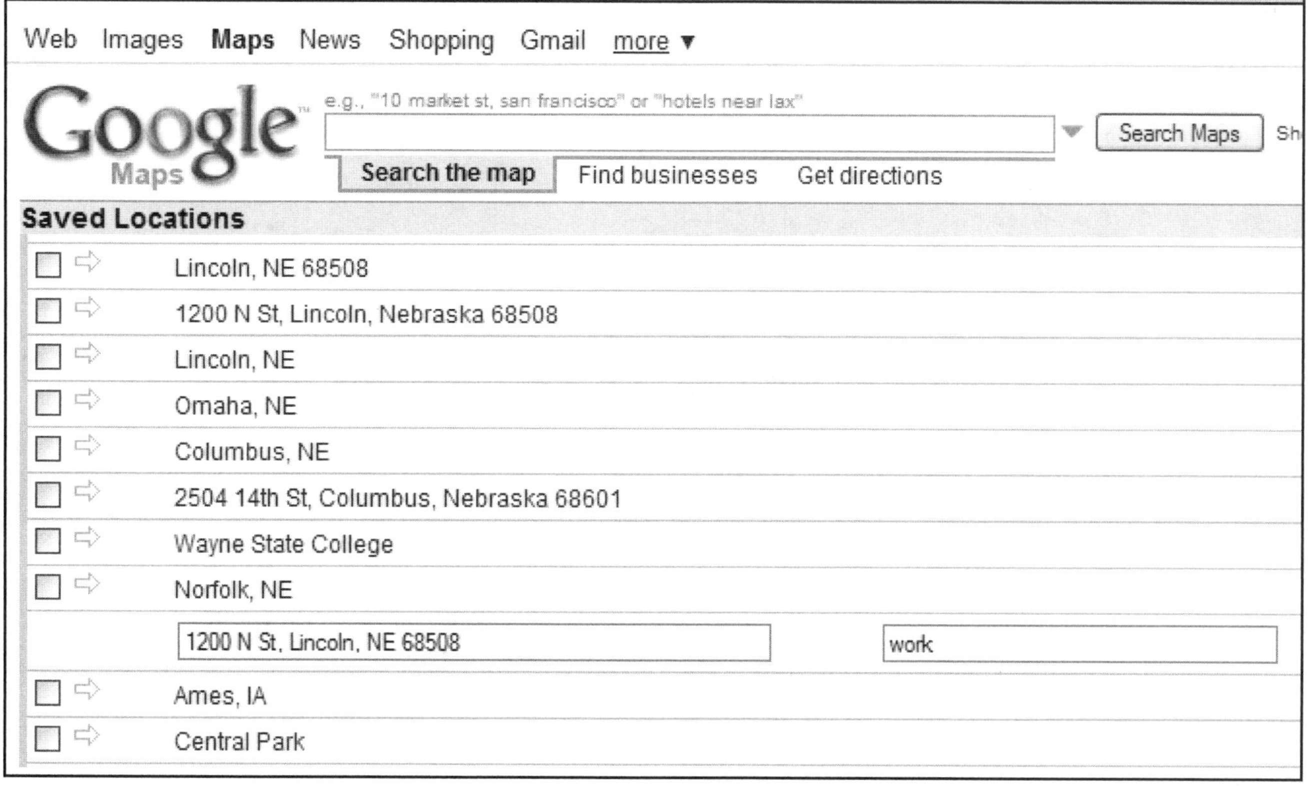

Web Images **Maps** News Shopping Gmail more ▼

Google Maps

e.g., "10 market st, san francisco" or "hotels near lax"

[   ] ▼ [Search Maps] Sh

[Search the map] Find businesses   Get directions

Saved Locations

☐ ⇨	Lincoln, NE 68508	
☐ ⇨	1200 N St, Lincoln, Nebraska 68508	
☐ ⇨	Lincoln, NE	
☐ ⇨	Omaha, NE	
☐ ⇨	Columbus, NE	
☐ ⇨	2504 14th St, Columbus, Nebraska 68601	
☐ ⇨	Wayne State College	
☐ ⇨	Norfolk, NE	
	[1200 N St, Lincoln, NE 68508]	[work]
☐ ⇨	Ames, IA	
☐ ⇨	Central Park	

Figure 6-38   Using labels instead of addresses

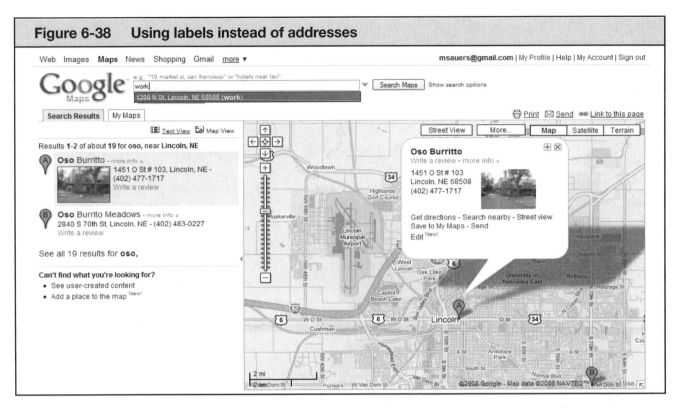

Figure 6-39   The Live Search Maps homepage

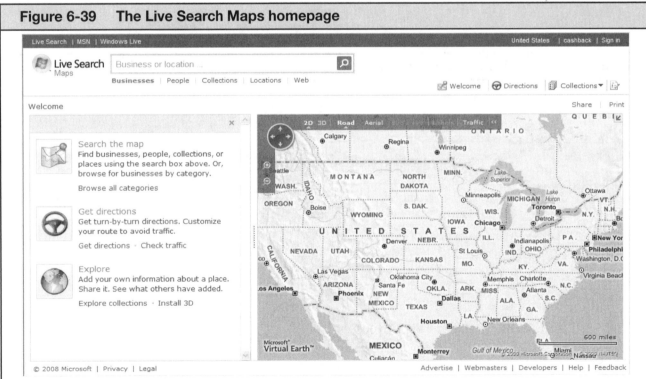

Note: Maybe because it is a Microsoft service, to me it seems to work just a bit smoother in Internet Explorer than it does in other popular browsers such as Firefox and Opera. Because of this, all of the screenshots of Live Search Maps have been created using Internet Explorer 7 instead of Firefox 3 as in the rest of this book. Using this service in Internet Explorer does have one annoying side effect: the service is ad-supported and the ads automatically update themselves every 15–30 seconds. Whenever this happens, the audible Internet Explorer "click" happens as if you'd clicked on a link. After working on this section of the chapter for about 30 minutes, I couldn't stand it anymore and had to turn off my speakers. Had I been using Firefox, this wouldn't have happened.

Figure 6-40   A business search and the results

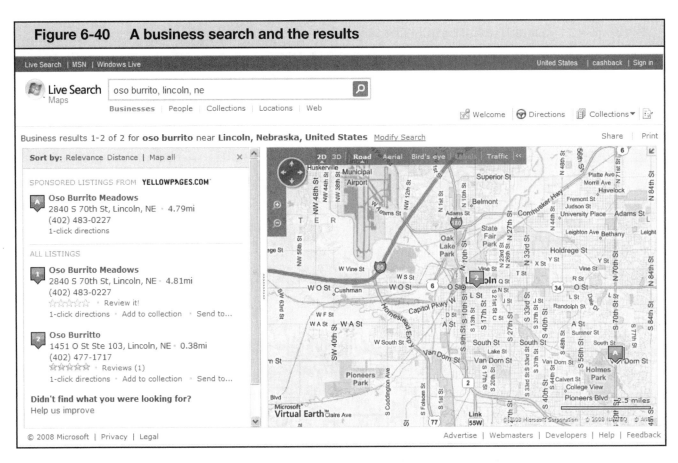

Figure 6-41   Search result details from the text-results list

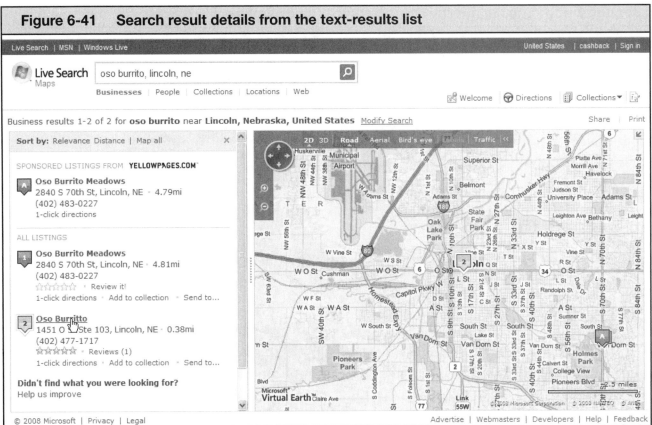

Figure 6-42   Search result details from the map

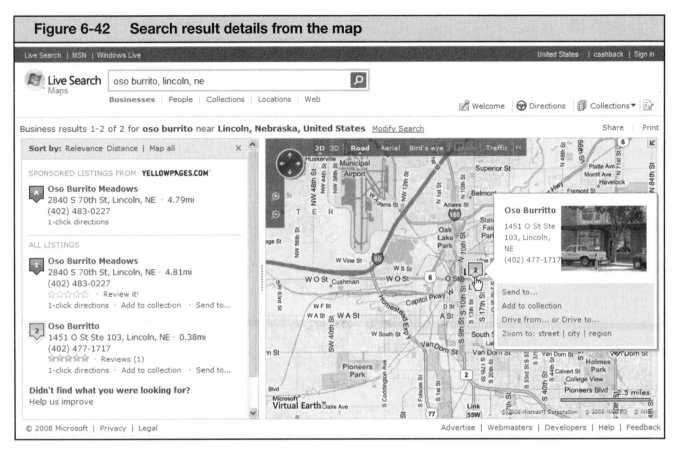

Figure 6-43   Send to mobile

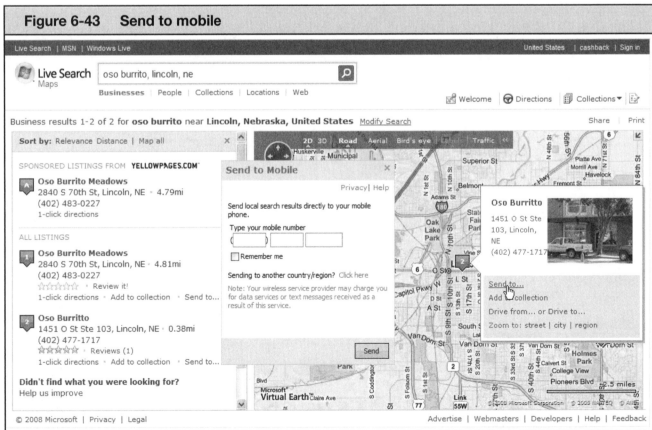

Figure 6-44   GPS delivery options

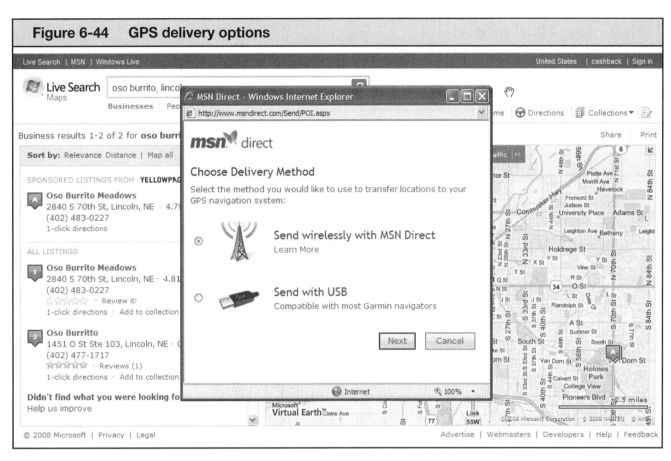

Figure 6-45   Add to collection

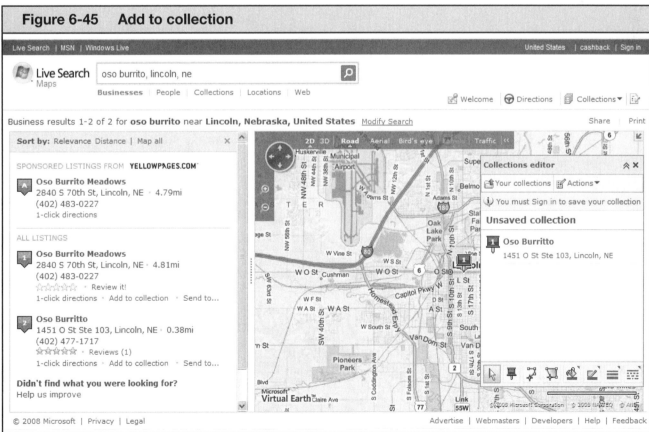

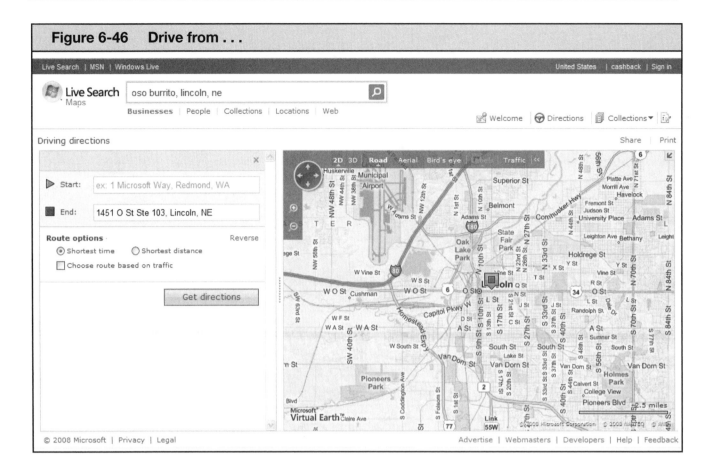

Figure 6-46   Drive from . . .

those results. As you can see, results appear for different areas of the state. Selecting "Zoom to city" on one of those choices will allow you to focus your results (see Figure 6-49). Choosing "Zoom to street" on one of the city-based results will allow you to see the exact location of a particular business (see Figure 6-50).

To view the business's details, click on the business's name. A new window will open with a more complete listing for that business. Details will include business name, phone number, address, a street-level map, links for driving directions, related categories, nearby related businesses, and how to report incorrect information, reviews, and Web search results (see Figure 6-51).

People Search

The people search asks you to enter a person's name and optional location. Additionally, if you search on a name, you can limit your results by entering a city, state, and/or zip code. To be honest, the results of my testing this search were not exactly spectacular. It didn't find me, but then again I had changed my address just six months prior. I was able to find some people I knew who'd been at their residence for several years or more, but those results were spotty. It was also unable to find many of the phone numbers I tried, but maybe the numbers of many of my friends are unlisted. Of course, your results may vary. I have not included a screenshot of any of my successful results out of respect for people's privacy.

Locations Search

Use a locations search when you're interested in finding a particular location but not necessarily associated with a particular business. You just need a map of a town for example. In this case, you're asked for an address, location, or landmark. You can put a full address or other combination of city, state, and zip. See Figure 6-52 for an example of the results.

When you type in a search for which multiple

Figure 6-47 Drive to . . .

Figure 6-48 Results of searching for *quilt* in Washington State

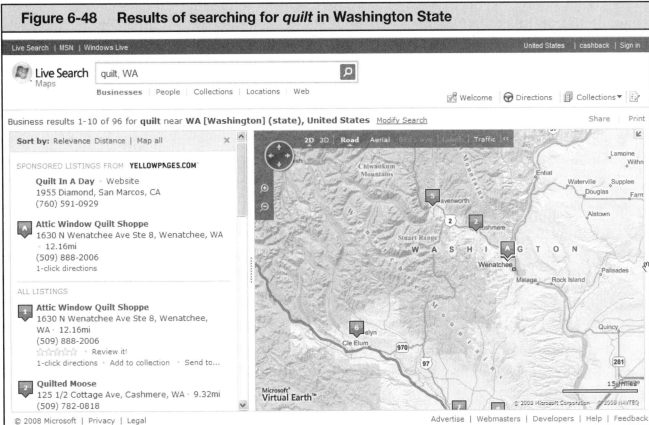

Figure 6-49   The results of choosing "zoom to city"

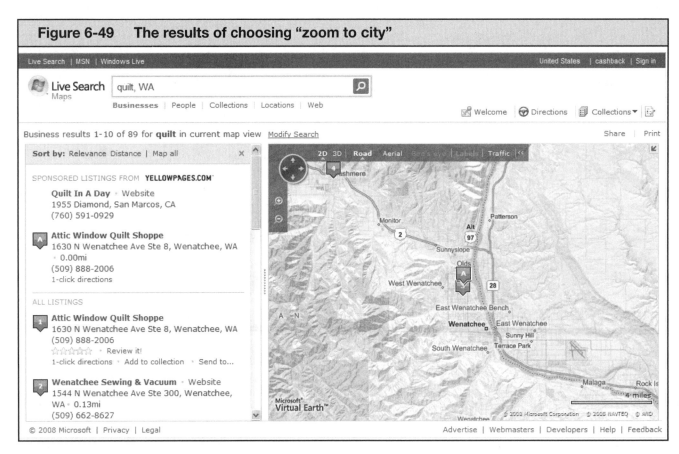

Figure 6-50   The results of choosing "zoom to street"

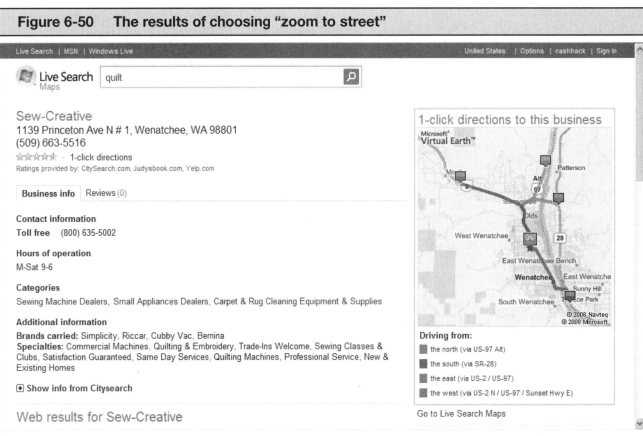

Figure 6-51   Business details

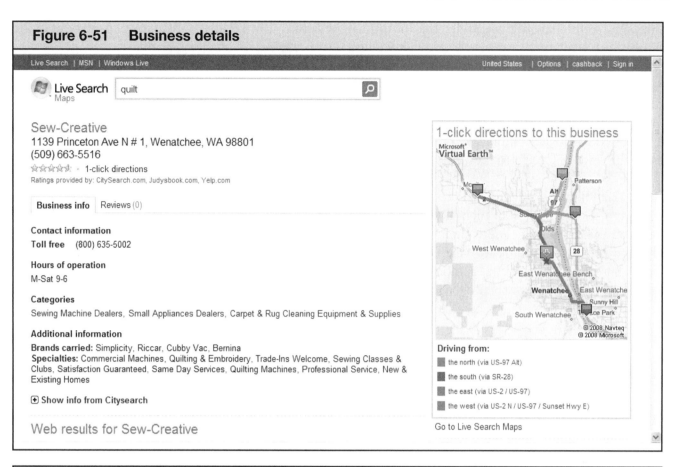

Figure 6-52   A maps search and the results

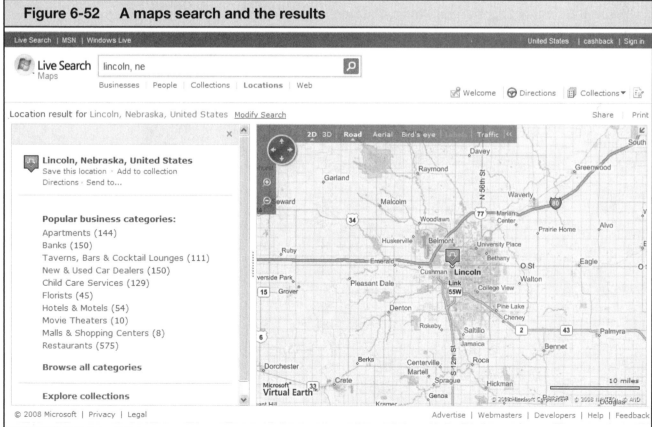

locations match, the site will offer the location it thinks you want based on previous searches and where you were on a map immediately prior to the search. For example, when I search for *rochester,* my hometown in New York, I usually get Rochester, New York, as a result (see Figure 6-53). However, if I wanted Rochester, Minnesota, I would need to enter the state to force it to find that city.

Driving Directions

Choosing "Directions" from the link on the left will give you the driving directions interface in the text area to the left of the map. Here you have two search fields: Start and End. Fill in each box with the information you have and then choose whether you want the resulting route to be based on shortest time or shortest distance. Figures 6-54 and 6-55 show the results for a drive from Lincoln, Nebraska to Rochester, New York, the first by shortest time and the second by shortest distance.[1] Your text results will include turn-by-turn directions, with each step numbered to match numbered points on the map.

Clicking the "Reverse" link at the bottom right of the text results will display a reverse route.

Last, a "Send to" link available at the top of your text search allows you to send the results to e-mail, mobile phone, or GPS. To the top right of the map are "Share" and "Print" links, both of which I discuss later in this chapter.

Traffic

The "Check traffic" option gives you access to live traffic information in over 50 cities across the United States. Figure 6-56 shows the coverage, with each city marked with a small traffic signal icon. Hovering over one of those icons will name the city and give you a link to "Zoom in for traffic details."

Once you've zoomed in to the city view, a map appears with major roads color-coded for speed: red for 0–25 mph, yellow for 25–45 mph, and green for 45+ mph. There are also markers for "incidents" ranging from minor to moderate to serious, as shown in Figure 6-57.

Once you've found an incident or construction

Figure 6-53   My search result for *rochester*

Figure 6-54   The shortest time from Lincoln, Nebraska, to Rochester, New York

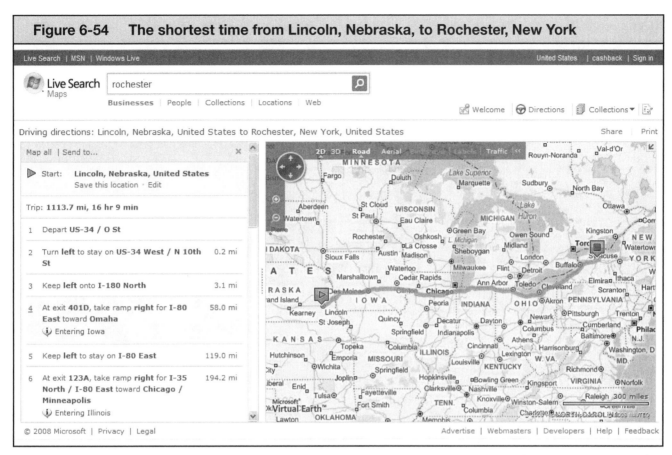

Figure 6-55   The shortest distance from Lincoln, Nebraska, to Rochester, New York

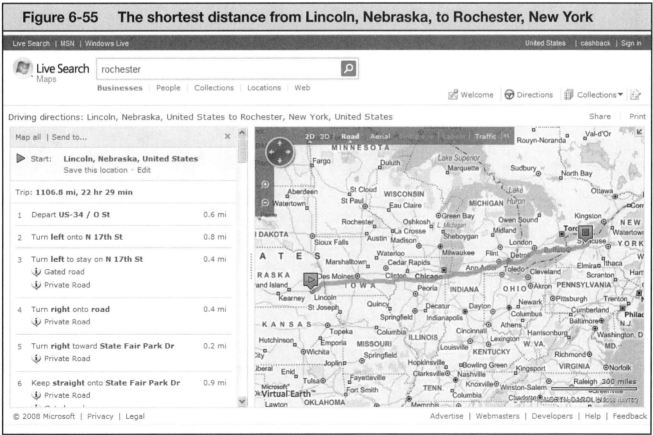

Figure 6-56   Live Search Maps traffic coverage in the United States

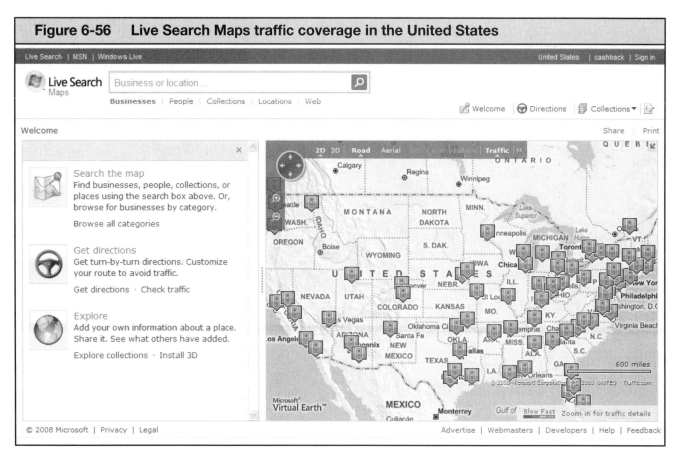

Figure 6-57   Traffic map for San Francisco, California

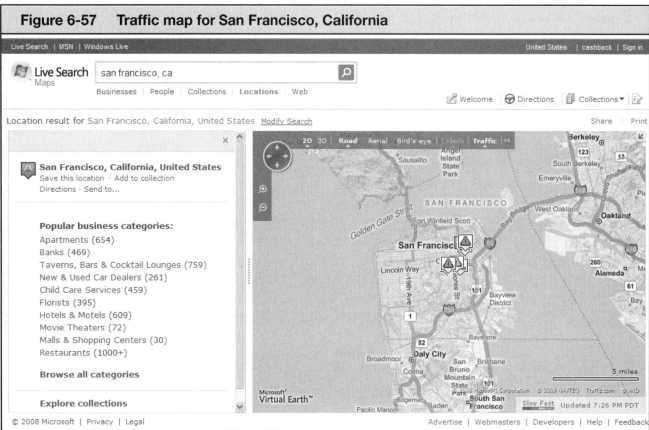

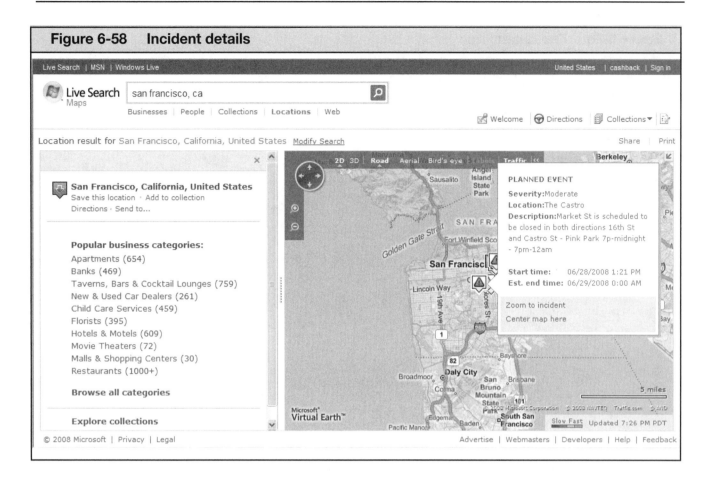

Figure 6-58   Incident details

marker that's relevant to you, hover over it to see a balloon containing further details, including its type, severity, location, description, start time, and end time. Links to "Zoom to incident" and "Center map here" are also available, as in Figure 6-58.

Share

Once you've retrieved the map that you need, you might want to share it with others. Live Search Maps offers you two methods for doing just that: "Send an e-mail" or "Blog it" (see Figure 6-59). Here's what each of these options allows you to do.

- **Send an e-mail:**
  Selecting this option will automatically generate an outgoing e-mail message in your e-mail client, whichever one has been specified in your browser's settings (see Figure 6-60). The subject line will be "Live Search Maps" and the body will contain "Live Search Maps" and the URL (permalink) of the map you are currently viewing.

- **Blog it:**
  This feature had a lot of potential when I first saw it. I loved the idea that I would be able to take my map and in a few clicks embed it into a blog post. Unfortunately, my dreams were much more than reality. My first disappointment was that "blog it" works only with Microsoft's Live Spaces blogging platform. If you don't have an account, or have an account but don't blog using that service, then this feature apparently will not work. The other disappointment was that even when it did work, the result wasn't what I expected. Instead of embedding a wonderful interactive map into my blog post, all I got was a link back to the map (see Figure 6-61).

Output Options

Once again, most people prefer their maps to be on paper rather than on a computer screen, especially if they're planning to use a motor vehicle to get from point A to point B. As with Google Maps, just clicking

Figure 6-59   The "share" link

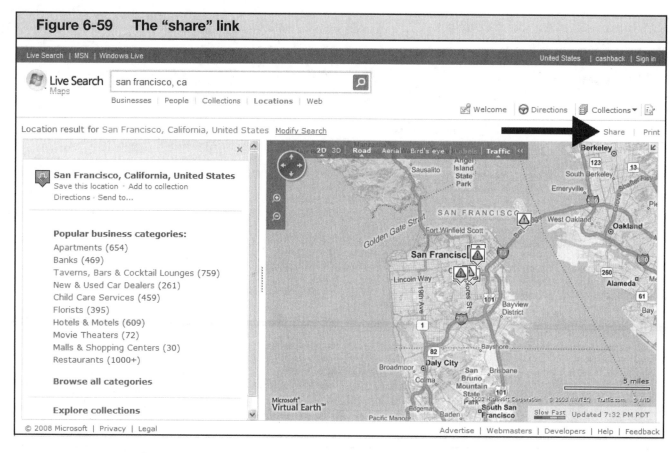

Figure 6-60   The "send an e-mail" button

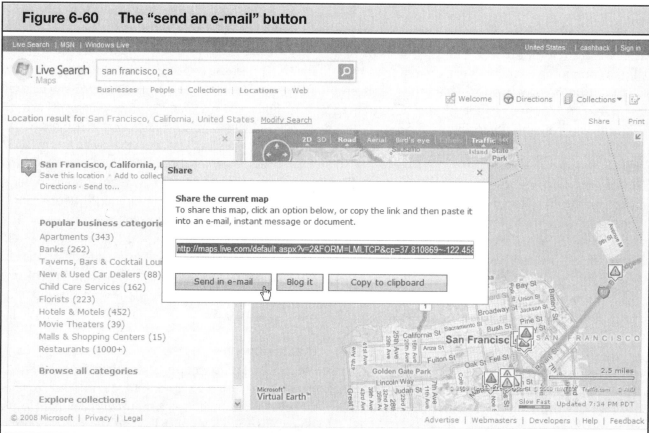

Figure 6-61   Results of "blog it"

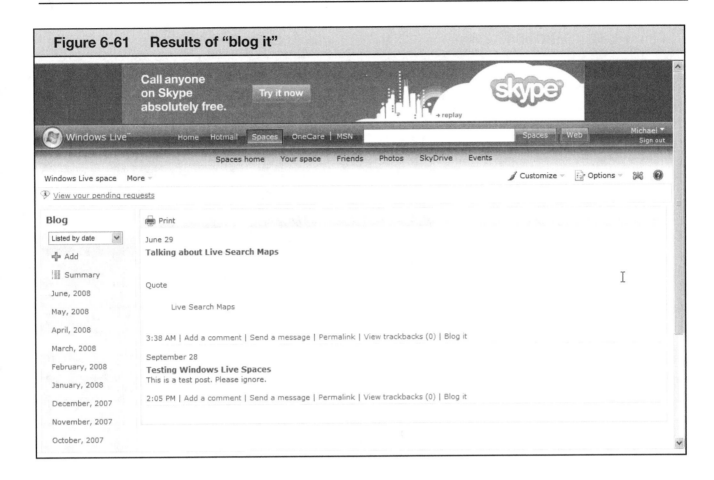

your browser's print button is not necessarily the best solution for printing your results. With Live Search Maps, printing options can be found by clicking the "Print" in the upper right corner (see Figure 6-62). Depending on the type of map you're printing, you may have up to four options: "Map and text," "Map only," "Text only," and "Custom." As with Google Maps, when you choose to print your map, a new window will open with a reformatted map suitable for printing (see Figure 6-63). A small area for notes is made available to you for adding content before sending the map to the printer.

Collections

For you to take full advantage of the Collections feature of Live Search Maps, you'll need to have a Windows Live account. For this section of the book, I'm going to assume that you have signed up for an account and have logged in as I have done.

Collections are maps you have created that you wish to refer to again. Ultimately, there isn't much difference between adding a bookmark for a map and adding it to your collection, but there are both benefits and downsides to doing it this way. One benefit is that if you've added a map to a collection you can now access it from any Internet-connected computer, unlike a bookmark saved in your browser. The other benefit is that you can share your collections (there's that social Web again!) and allow others to search for and access them. As a result, your work adds to the collective resources of the system.

One downside is that adding a bookmark is easy, while creating a collection takes a bit more work. For example, with a map of all of the pizza places in town, to bookmark it, you just need to select "Share," then copy the URL provided, open a new page with that URL, and bookmark it. To save a collection, you'll need to select each marked result, click "Add to collection," and then save your new collection. If there are only four pizza places in town, this isn't too difficult. If there's a few dozen, this process will become tedious. What I would like to see added to

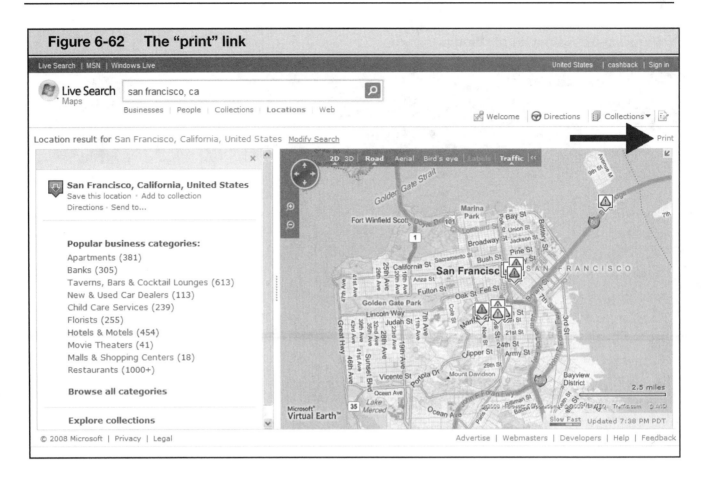

Figure 6-62   The "print" link

the collections feature is the ability to save maps that are a result of a search. For example, instead of having to place pushpins for every coffee shop in town, I'd rather be able to search for *coffee* and save that map to my collection instead of having to add each result one by one to a collection. Maybe this will be added in the future.

Once you have a map you wish to save, click on the "Add to collections" under the text field. Once the collections editor is displayed, click "Save it now" to add it. Give your map a title, add some notes if you wish, and add some tags (see Figure 6-64). You'll also want to choose whether to make this map public or private by turning sharing on or off. Click the "Save" button to create the collection. Once saved, you'll need to add individual items to that collection. To do so, perform a search (if you haven't already) to find matching results, then hover over the relevant results, and select "Add to collection" (see Figure 6-65).

You'll be asked to choose from a list of your existing collections. Choose the appropriate one and click the "Save" button (see Figure 6-66). Figure 6-67

shows how I've added three locations to my BBQ in Lincoln collection.

From the collections editor you can choose several options under "Actions": "Show properties," "Map all," "Add to favorites," "Tour and make videos in 3D," "Add MapCruncher layer," "Send to…," "Export," and "Delete" (see Figure 6-68).

- **Show properties:**
  This option allows you to edit the title, notes, tags, and sharing options for this collection.
- **Map all:**
  This option changes the zoom level and centering of the map to include all locations in the collection.
- **Add to favorites:**
  Within the larger universe of Windows Live, you can mark individual searches, maps, and other resources as favorites so you can return to them easily. This is similar to bookmarks in your browser, but instead of being kept offline they're stored within your Windows Live Account. Choose this

Figure 6-63   The "print" view

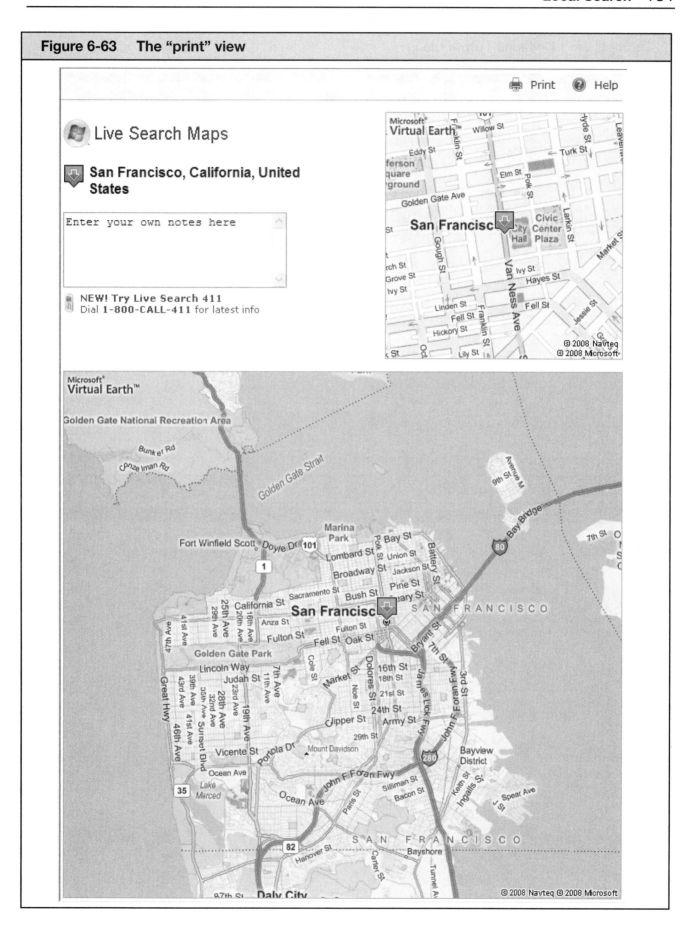

Figure 6-64   Collection properties

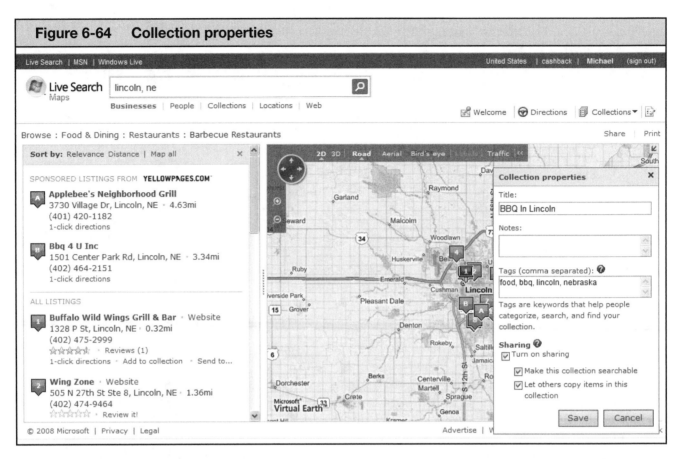

Figure 6-65   Add to a collection

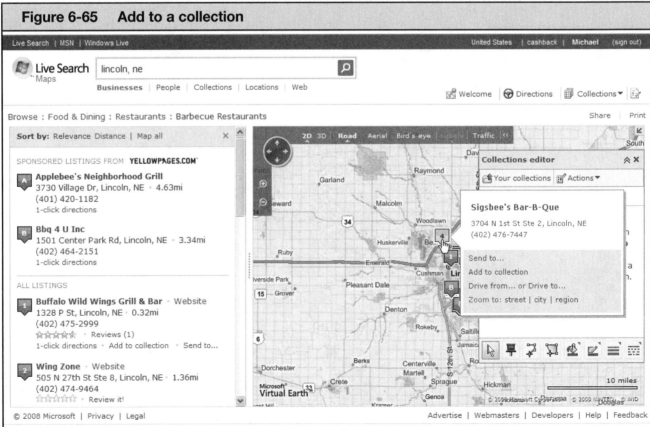

Figure 6-66   Save to a collection

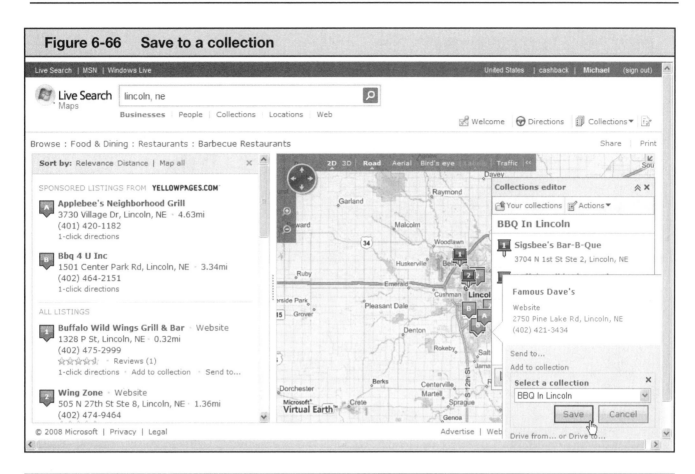

Figure 6-67   My "BBQ in Lincoln" collection

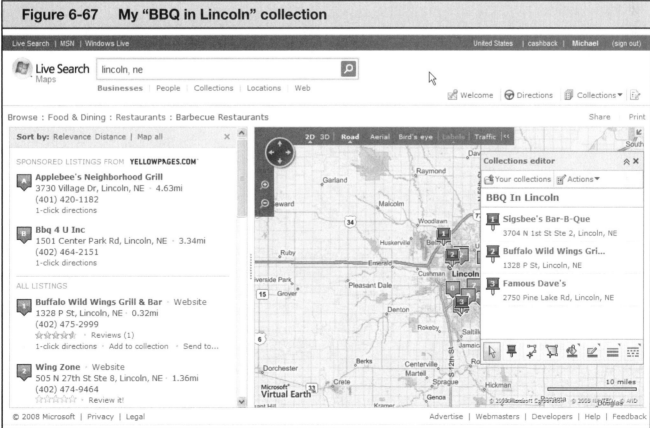

Figure 6-68 "Collections editor" actions

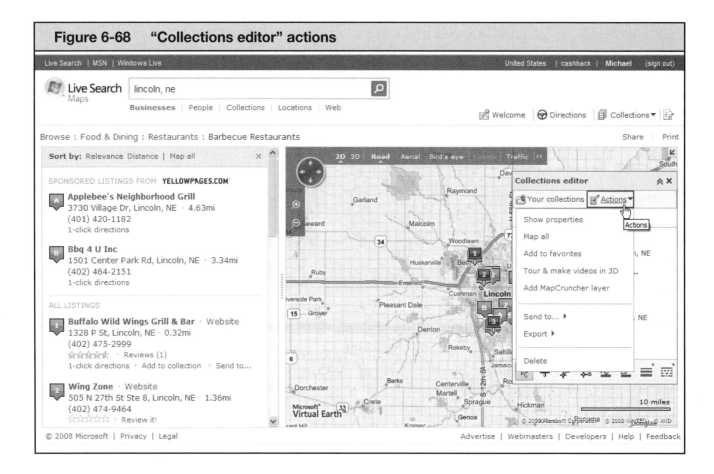

option to add this collection to your Windows Live favorites.

- **Tour and make videos in 3D:**
  With this option you can make a 3-D video tour of the locations in a collection. This service requires the installation of Virtual Earth 3D, which I discuss in the next section.
- **Add MapCruncher layer:**
  Using this option you can add additional information to your map, including "more information" and photos that can be stored in an external file (see Figure 6-69).
- **Send to . . . :**
  Choose this option to send this file either to a GPS device or to someone else as an e-mail.
- **Export:**
  Using this option you can export the data contained in this collection via one of the following three formats: KML (keyhole markup language), GPX (GPS exchange format), and GeoRSS (geographically encoded objects for RSS).

- **Delete:**
  This option will delete the collection.

To get to a list of your collections, just click on either the "Your Collections" link in the collections editor, if open, or click the "Collections" link above the map and select "Open Your Collections." Figure 6-70 shows my list of collections, including some that I've not yet saved. Unsaved collections will disappear when you log out of your Windows Live Account.

The last thing I'd like to point out in the collections editor are the drawing tools at the bottom of the editor (see Figure 6-71). Using these buttons you can manually add pushpins, draw lines, draw an area, set the fill color, set the line color, set line width, and set dash style, respectively. So, if you wish to customize your map, these buttons make that possible.

Working in Three Dimensions

You can use the 3-D environment, known as Microsoft Virtual Earth, as your interface for Windows Live

Figure 6-69   Add MapCruncher layer

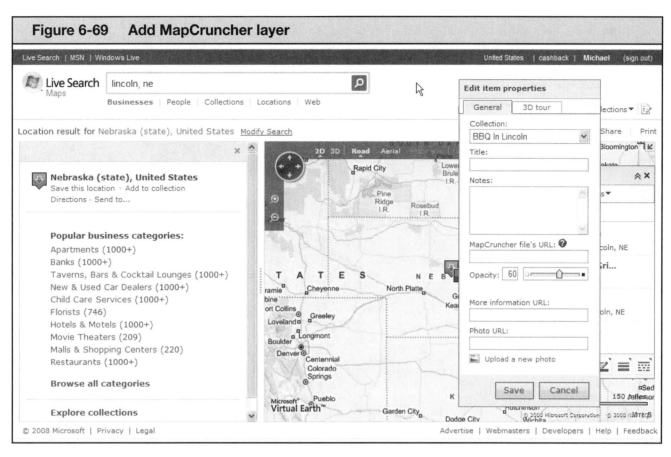

Figure 6-70   Your collections

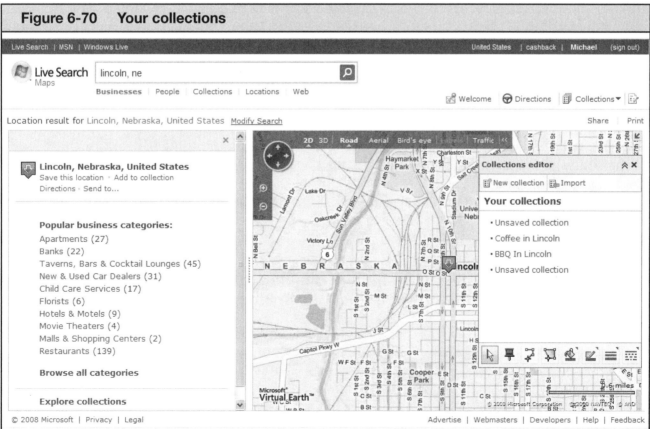

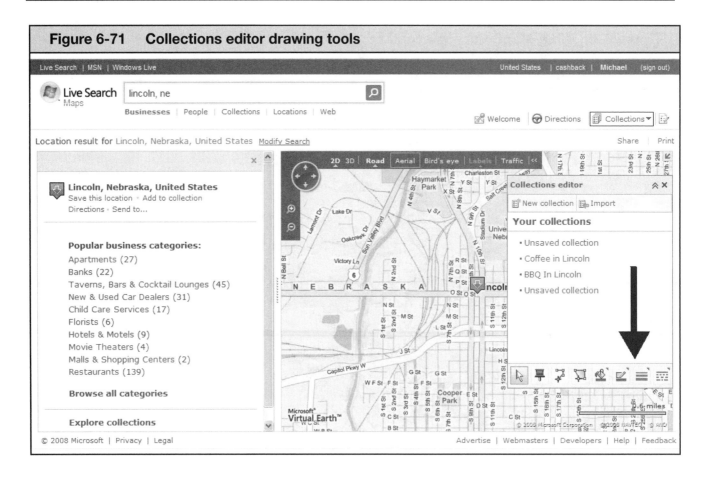

Figure 6-71   Collections editor drawing tools

Local. To take advantage of this, you will need to select "3D" from the toolbar in the upper left corner of your map. The first time you do this, you will be asked to download and install the Virtual Earth 3D software (see Figure 6-72). Just follow the onscreen download and installation instructions and you'll be all set in just a few minutes.

You'll be asked to choose the quality of your view. Your choices are "Best performance," "Balanced," and "Best quality" (see Figure 6-73). Your default choice will be determined by the software, and I suggest you take that recommendation. I've chosen "best quality" as this is what was recommended and best shows off the technology. You can always change your choice later.

Once installed, you will still have all of the tools and options discussed previously in this chapter but with a very slick 3-D view of your maps and directions. Figures 6-74 through 6-76 are just a few examples of what you'll see. Browsing your map will take a little more getting used to in this environment, as you now have controls for tilt and rotate, but with a little practice you'll get the hang of it.

CONCLUSION

Over the years I've found that questions involving directions or "Where can I find service X in town?" are some of the most commonly asked. In the past, the yellow pages and maps have been the reference librarian's tools for answering these questions. Unfortunately, and in most cases, the patron isn't allowed to take these resources with him or her. Now with services like Google Maps and Live Search Maps nearly any local resource can be found quickly. Directions from the patron's location to the resource can be quickly created and a simple printout or e-mail can be sent with a minimal amount of effort. The next chapter moves us away from the world of maps and directions into a world that's near and dear to many a librarian's heart: the world of books.

Figure 6-72   Install Virtual Earth 3D

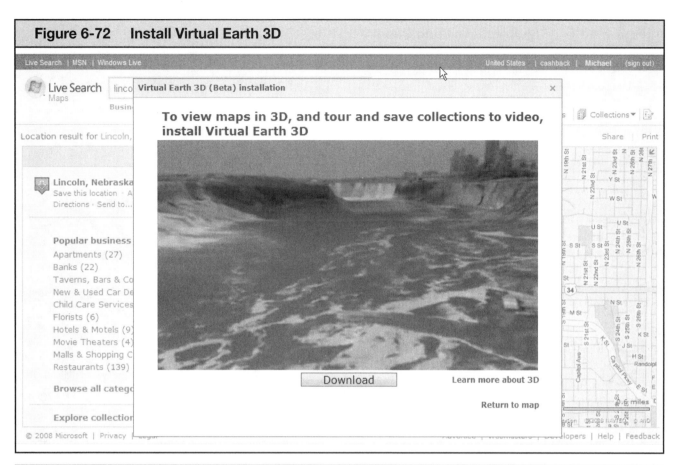

Figure 6-73   Virtual Earth quality settings

Figure 6-74   The Nebraska State Capitol

Figure 6-75   The Starbucks in North Platte, Nebraska

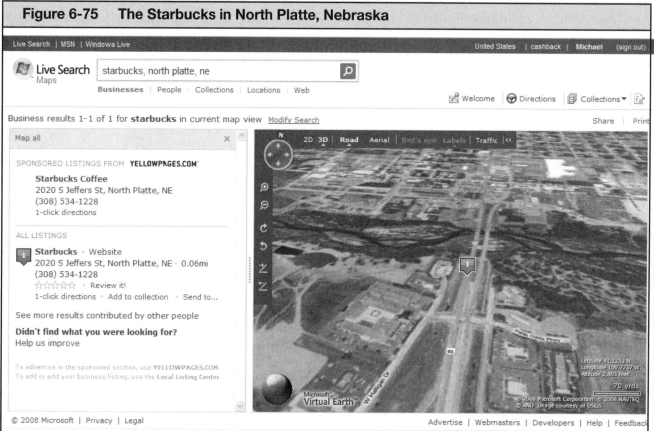

Figure 6-76   3-D directions from Lincoln, Nebraska, to Watertown, South Dakota

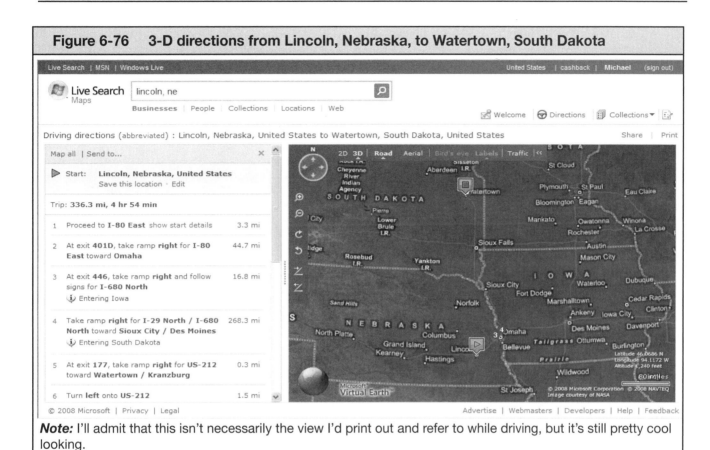

Note: I'll admit that this isn't necessarily the view I'd print out and refer to while driving, but it's still pretty cool looking.

EXERCISES

Use both Google Maps and Live Search Maps to answer the following questions. Compare the answers and what steps you needed to take to get the needed information.

1. Where can I find a coffee shop in town?
2. What is the quickest route from here to Lincoln, Nebraska?
3. How about from here to Lincoln, Nebraska, but by the scenic route?
4. Is there any road construction in town that I should know about?

NOTES

1. Here in Nebraska I've noticed that the shortest distance tends to be the slower route while the faster route tends to be longer from a distance perspective. Either way, I tend to get to where I need to be in the same amount of time. (There's something just not right about this.)

Chapter 7

Print Search

INTRODUCTION

Using Web-based tools to search for print materials is now considered commonplace. However, when it comes to searching for content *within* print material, we're still not all that comfortable. Granted, librarians constantly use online databases that contain digital versions of existing print content, but this isn't exactly what I mean.

What I'm talking about is the ability to do full-text searches of traditionally print-only books, to find particular words or phrases within a book, so that once you've confirmed that the book has what you're looking for, you can find the physical book in your collection. Think of it as an online full-text index that goes well beyond the one found in the back of the book itself. This chapter discusses the two most significant tools for searching this form of content: Google Book Search and Amazon.com's Search Inside the Book.[1]

GOOGLE BOOK SEARCH

Google is currently indexing books that are both in the public domain and copyrighted works. In-copyright works are sourced both from publishers from whom Google has permission (Google's "Partner Program")[2] and from the collections of nearly 20 libraries around the world (Google's "Library Project").[3] Books may be searched for from within the standard simple Google search interface. You can also browse for books via subjects and genres via the Google Book Search homepage at http://books.google.com (see Figure 7-1). In this chapter, I focus on searching as opposed to browsing.

Basic Search

As with most Google search services, there are two searching interfaces: the basic search and the advanced search. The basic book search is located on the Google Book Search homepage, as shown in Figure 7-1. In this case, just type in the keyword(s) you're searching for (title, author, subject, etc.) and click the "Search Books" button. This interface supports Boolean operators, +/– operators, and quotation marks for phrase searching.

Advanced Search

Clicking on the "Advanced Book Search" link to the right of the "Search Books" button will take you to the advanced book search interface (see Figure 7-2). Here you will be presented with 13 options for searching: find results (with four suboptions), search, language, title, author, publisher, subject, publication date, and ISBN.

- **Find results:**
  The "Find results" area allows you to build a Boolean-based query without knowing the specifics of Boolean operators.
  o *With **all** the words:*
    Any keywords entered into this field will be present in the search results (Boolean AND).
  o *With the **exact phrase:***
    Multiple words entered into this field will be treated as a phrase (as if enclosed in quotation marks).
  o *With **at least one** of the words:*
    At least one of the words entered into this field

Figure 7-1   The Google Book Search homepage

Figure 7-2   The Google advanced book search

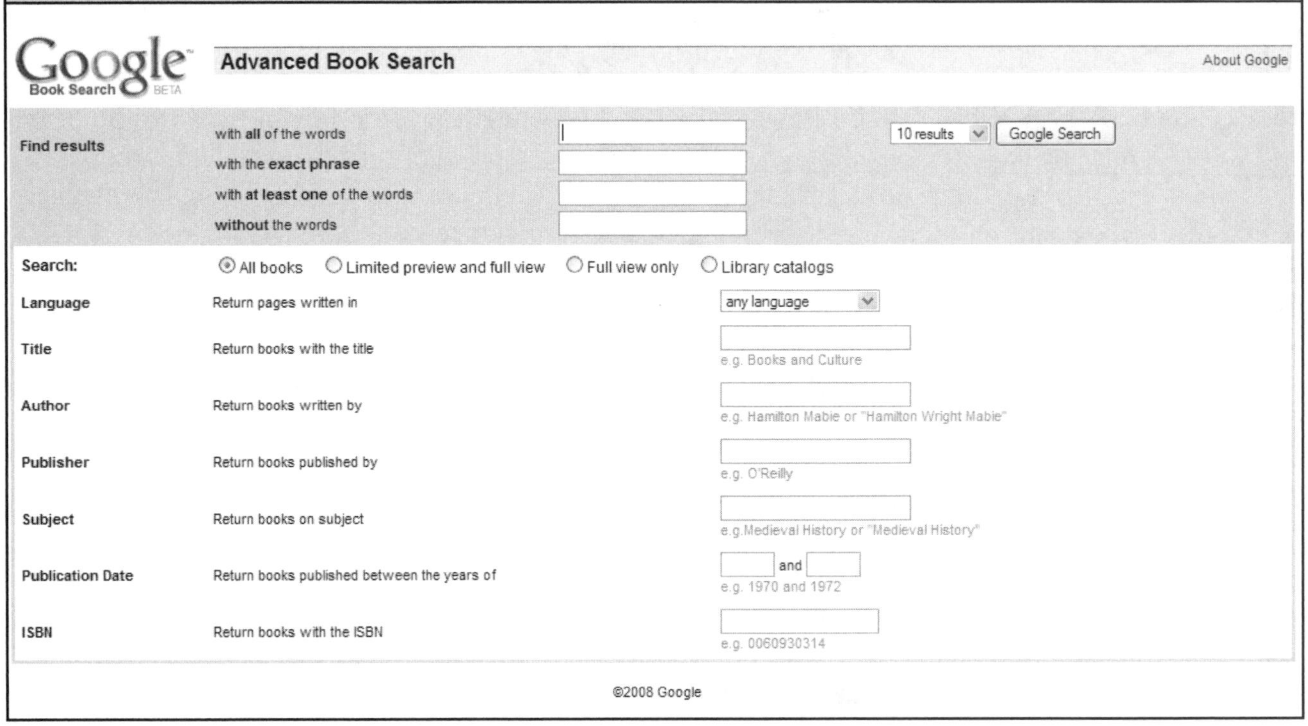

must be present in the search results (Boolean OR).

o **Without** *the words:*
Results will not include any of the words entered into this field (Boolean NOT). Additionally, you can specify 10, 20, 30, 50, or 100 results per page in this area.

- **Search:**
Here you can specify whether you wish to search "all books" in the collection, only books with a "limited preview" or "full view" results display (covered in the results section), or "Library Catalogs," which actually performs a Worldcat.org search instead of the standard book search. I generally recommend that you keep your searches to all books to retrieve the most results. The other three limiting options are most useful to those searchers who are not directly able to take advantage of other library resources, such as interlibrary loan, and wish to ensure that they can get exactly what they want online at the time of their search.

- **Language:**
Here you can limit your results to one of more than 40 different languages, ranging from Arabic to Vietnamese. Of course, the number of results will vary, and be sure to search for keywords in the appropriate language. Chances are, searching for English keywords within Arabic texts will not retrieve many results regardless of the size of the Arabic collection.

- **Title:**
Here keywords will appear within the title of the search results.

- **Author:**
Here keywords will appear in the author name of the search results. Single names (*koontz*), first/last (*dean koontz*), last/first (*koontz, dean*) and phrases (*"dean koontz"*) are all accepted but may yield different results. For example, a search for *koontz* will retrieve the authors Dean Koontz, Linda D. Koontz, and Louis Knott Koontz. Searches for *"dean koontz"* and *koontz, dean* will retrieve only "Dean Koontz," while searches for *dean koontz* will retrieve Dean Koontz, Dean R. Koontz, and Dean Ray Koontz (who are all the same person), which will retrieve the most results due to the different listings of his name over his publishing career.

- **Publisher:**
You can limit the search results by entering the name of a publisher in this field. I recommend using quotation marks on multiword publisher names (*"cemetery dance"* vs. *cemetery dance*) for a higher degree of accuracy.[4]

- **Subject:**
This field searches the subject headings associated with each book. The source of these subjects is unspecified within the Google system, so I suggest you keep this type of search limited until you become more familiar with the results. This field can also be considered a genre search when searching for fiction.

- **Publication date:**
Here there are two fields. The first is a starting year, the second an ending year. Filling in both allows you to limit your results to books published within that date range *inclusive*. In other words, "Return books published between the years of 2005 and 2007" will return results published in 2005, 2006, and 2007. It is also important to note that this is the publication date, not the copyright date. In other words, if a book was first published in 1969 but was reprinted in 2006, the previously described search will return it as a result.

- **ISBN:**
If you've got an ISBN and want to see if the book is in the system, just enter it here. Since ISBNs uniquely identify a particular edition of a title, you should receive only a single result. Once you've filled in the appropriate fields, click the "Google Search" button to perform your search and retrieve the results.

Book Search Results

Let's say I'm looking for some information about Alexander Hamilton. (We'll worry about specifically what I'm looking for a little later.) I'm going to perform a simple search for *alexander hamilton* to see what results I find (see Figure 7-3).

As with most Google search results pages, links to other types of searches are presented at the top of the page. The search box, with your search terms included, remains at the top, along with links to the advanced search and help pages. Just below this is a blue bar that shows you've performed a books search,

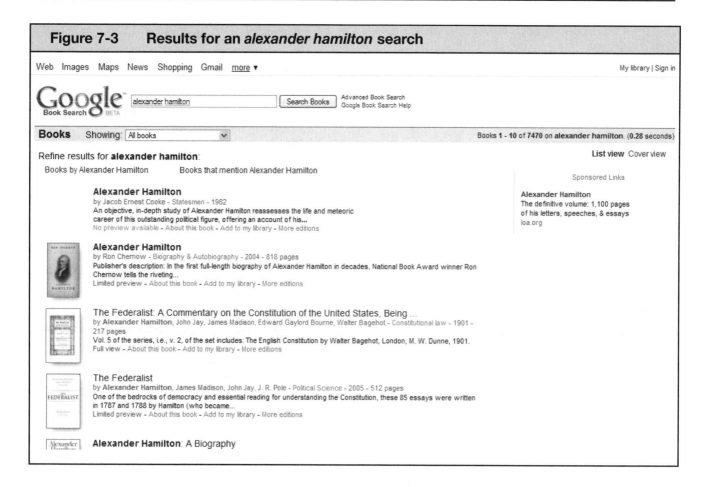

Figure 7-3   Results for an *alexander hamilton* search

with the number of results and the length of time it took Google to perform the search. The other common element is the sponsored links off to the right. At the bottom of the page are the standard next/previous page of results links and a re-presentation of your search terms in another search box.

However, the majority of the page is somewhat different from the typical Google search results page. Let's take a look at what this results screen has to offer. The blue bar above your results contains a drop-down menu with three important items: "All books," "Limited preview and full view," and "full view only." By choosing any of these three ("All books" is the default, assuming you didn't change this via an advanced search), you change which results are displayed for you. Selecting "All books" will display all results, selecting "Limited preview and full view" will display just the books with available limited previews and full view (see Figure 7-4), and selecting "Full view only" will display just the books with their full text available online (see Figure 7-5).

More details on these options are given later in this chapter.

Next you can change the presentation of the results by choosing either "List view" or "Cover view" via the links located to the right under the search time report. List view shows the book covers (when available) and book details (see Figure 7-6). Cover view shows just book covers, inserting generic covers when the originals are not available (see Figure 7-7).

Next we come to the individual search results themselves. I will focus on the "List view" since the information presented in the "Cover view" is extremely limited. In most cases, either the cover or first page of the book will be displayed to the left of the record. The text portion of the record will start with the title of the book. Clicking on either the image or the title will take you to either the preview of the book (if available) or the "About this book" page.

The next line contains the name of the author (unfortunately not hyperlinked for an author search),

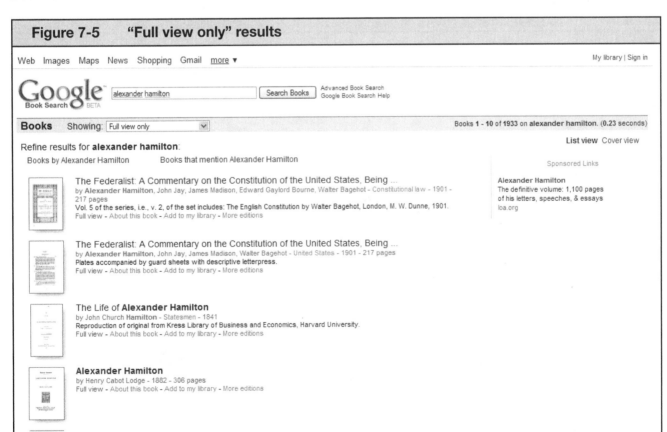

Figure 7-4   "Limited preview and full view" results

Web   Images   Maps   News   Shopping   Gmail   more ▼   My library | Sign in

Google
Book Search BETA

alexander hamilton   [Search Books]   Advanced Book Search
                                               Google Book Search Help

Books   Showing: [Limited preview and full view ▼]   Books **1 - 10** of **2224** on alexander hamilton. (0.22 seconds)

                                                                              List view Cover view

Refine results for **alexander hamilton**:

Books by Alexander Hamilton   Books that mention Alexander Hamilton   Sponsored Links

Alexander Hamilton   Alexander Hamilton
by Ron Chernow - Biography & Autobiography - 2004 - 818 pages   The definitive volume: 1,100 pages
Publisher's description: In the first full-length biography of Alexander Hamilton in decades, National Book Award winner Ron   of his letters, speeches, & essays
Chernow tells the riveting...   loa.org
Limited preview - About this book - Add to my library - More editions

The Federalist: A Commentary on the Constitution of the United States, Being ...
by Alexander Hamilton, John Jay, James Madison, Edward Gaylord Bourne, Walter Bagehot - Constitutional law - 1901 -
217 pages
Vol. 5 of the series, i.e., v. 2, of the set includes: The English Constitution by Walter Bagehot, London, M. W. Dunne, 1901.
Full view - About this book - Add to my library - More editions

The Federalist
by Alexander Hamilton, James Madison, John Jay, J. R. Pole - Political Science - 2005 - 512 pages
One of the bedrocks of democracy and essential reading for understanding the Constitution, these 85 essays were written
in 1787 and 1788 by Hamilton (who became...
Limited preview - About this book - Add to my library - More editions

Alexander Hamilton: A Biography
by Forrest McDonald - Biography & Autobiography - 1979 - 464 pages
This book re-examines Hamilton's policies as a secretary of the treasury.
Limited preview - About this book - Add to my library - More editions

Figure 7-5   "Full view only" results

Web   Images   Maps   News   Shopping   Gmail   more ▼   My library | Sign in

Google
Book Search BETA

alexander hamilton   [Search Books]   Advanced Book Search
                                               Google Book Search Help

Books   Showing: [Full view only ▼]   Books **1 - 10** of **1933** on alexander hamilton. (0.23 seconds)

                                                                              List view Cover view

Refine results for **alexander hamilton**:

Books by Alexander Hamilton   Books that mention Alexander Hamilton   Sponsored Links

The Federalist: A Commentary on the Constitution of the United States, Being ...   Alexander Hamilton
by Alexander Hamilton, John Jay, James Madison, Edward Gaylord Bourne, Walter Bagehot - Constitutional law - 1901 -   The definitive volume: 1,100 pages
217 pages   of his letters, speeches, & essays
Vol. 5 of the series, i.e., v. 2, of the set includes: The English Constitution by Walter Bagehot, London, M. W. Dunne, 1901.   loa.org
Full view - About this book - Add to my library - More editions

The Federalist: A Commentary on the Constitution of the United States, Being ...
by Alexander Hamilton, John Jay, James Madison, Walter Bagehot - United States - 1901 - 217 pages
Plates accompanied by guard sheets with descriptive letterpress.
Full view - About this book - Add to my library - More editions

The Life of **Alexander Hamilton**
by John Church **Hamilton** - Statesmen - 1841
Reproduction of original from Kress Library of Business and Economics, Harvard University.
Full view - About this book - Add to my library - More editions

Alexander Hamilton
by Henry Cabot Lodge - 1882 - 306 pages
Full view - About this book - Add to my library - More editions

Figure 7-6   List view

Web   Images   Maps   News   Shopping   Gmail   more ▾   My library | Sign in

 Book Search BETA   [alexander hamilton]   [Search Books]   Advanced Book Search
Google Book Search Help

Books   Showing: [All books   ▾]   Books 1 - 10 of 7470 on alexander hamilton. (0.27 seconds)

Refine results for **alexander hamilton**:   List view Cover view

Books by Alexander Hamilton   Books that mention Alexander Hamilton   Sponsored Links

Alexander Hamilton   Alexander Hamilton
by Jacob Ernest Cooke - Statesmen - 1982   The definitive volume: 1,100 pages
An objective, in-depth study of Alexander Hamilton reassesses the life and meteoric   of his letters, speeches, & essays
career of this outstanding political figure, offering an account of his...   loa.org
No preview available - About this book - Add to my library - More editions

 Alexander Hamilton
by Ron Chernow - Biography & Autobiography - 2004 - 818 pages
Publisher's description: In the first full-length biography of Alexander Hamilton in decades, National Book Award winner Ron
Chernow tells the riveting...
Limited preview - About this book - Add to my library - More editions

 The Federalist: A Commentary on the Constitution of the United States, Being ...
by Alexander Hamilton, John Jay, James Madison, Edward Gaylord Bourne, Walter Bagehot - Constitutional law - 1901 -
217 pages
Vol. 5 of the series, i.e., v. 2, of the set includes: The English Constitution by Walter Bagehot, London, M. W. Dunne, 1901.
Full view - About this book - Add to my library - More editions

The Federalist
by Alexander Hamilton, James Madison, John Jay, J. R. Pole - Political Science - 2005 - 512 pages
One of the bedrocks of democracy and essential reading for understanding the Constitution, these 85 essays were written
in 1787 and 1788 by Hamilton (who became...
Limited preview - About this book - Add to my library - More editions

---

Figure 7-7   Cover view

Web   Images   Maps   News   Shopping   Gmail   more ▾   My library | Sign in

 Book Search BETA   [alexander hamilton]   [Search Books]   Advanced Book Search
Google Book Search Help

Books   Showing: [All books   ▾]   Books 1 - 30 of 7470 on alexander hamilton. (0.26 seconds)

Refine results for **alexander hamilton**:   List view **Cover view**

Books by Alexander Hamilton   Books that mention Alexander Hamilton

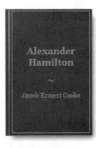   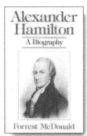 

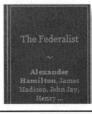  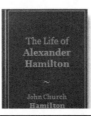 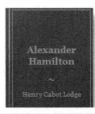 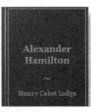

the book's subject (hyperlinked), the publication year, and number of pages. This will then be followed by a brief one- to two-line description or excerpt from the book. With newer books, this is typically taken from the dust jacket copy. Please note that not all of this information will be available for all records. The final line of a result tells what type of content is available from within the book itself: full view, limited preview, snippet view, or no preview available. Next are links for "About this book," "Add to my library," and "More editions."

The "More editions" link will take you to a page that presents you with other editions of the same title. For example, you might receive listings for hardcover and paperback editions of the same title. More historical items might provide you with listings for editions from many different publishers, containing not only the same basic text but also additional writings by the same author and/or forewords or afterwords by other authors.

Book Content

Selecting a particular book will take you to the book's "About this book" or "Preview this book" page. This mostly depends on whether any of the book's content is available. Whichever page you end up on, you can easily switch to the other via the tabs in the upper left corner of the page. I present them in the order in which those tabs appear.

About This Book

The information available for any particular book may vary widely depending on the book's copyright status and source (publisher, library, public domain). I'm using a more recent and popular title that has been included via the Partner Program as my illustration (see Figure 7-8) so that I can show a fuller record. For other books, not as much information may be presented to you.

A lot of information is presented here, and with the Web's hyperlinking technology, what you find here is just a starting point to much more. "About this book" can contain as many as 13 different sections: general information, selected pages, search in this book, contents, popular passages, reviews, references from Web pages, references from books, other edi-

tions, references from scholarly works, related books, key terms, and places mentioned in the book.

- **General information:**
  Here you will find an image of the book's cover or first page, along with the title, author, publication year, publisher (search hyperlinked), subject (search hyperlinked), page count, ISBN, and descriptive text. There are also additional links to "Add to my library," "Write a review," "Buy this book," and "Find this book in a library," which performs a WorldCat.org search for the book. If the book has content available for review, a button to "Preview this book" will appear beneath the book's image (see Figure 7-9).

- **Selected pages:**
  Here Google presents a few pages that represent the book's content with the hopes it will encourage you to examine the content more deeply. In the example shown in Figure 7-10, I'm presented with three pages of illustrations from the book.

- **Search in this book:**
  At first this section of the page contains just a search box allowing you to search the contents of the book itself (see Figure 7-11). I'll cover content searching in depth in the next section, but it is worth mentioning here solely for how it presents the results. Say I'm interested in mentions of the navy in this book. I can type in *navy* and click "Search," and, instead of being presented with a separate page of results, abbreviated results will appear in this section of this page, making for a potentially more useful printout for your patron. Each result will include a brief passage surrounding your keyword, along with links to the page containing that text if available (see Figure 7-12).

- **Contents:**
  Here you will find a basic table of contents for the book with links to each of those chapters within the book when available (see Figure 7-13).

- **Popular passages:**
  "Popular passages" is content from one book that is used across multiple books. In Figure 7-14, all of the passages are quotes from Hamilton himself that would tend to be reused in different histories and biographies.

(continued on p. 203)

Figure 7-8   About this book: *Alexander Hamilton* **by Ron Chernow**

Google Book Search [ ] [Search Books]

| About this book | Preview this book | **Alexander Hamilton** By Ron Chernow |

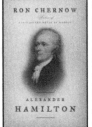

By Ron Chernow

Published 2004
Penguin

Statesmen/ United States / Biography

818 pages

ISBN:1594200092

Add to my library

Write review

[Preview this book]

Publisher's description: In the first full-length biography of Alexander Hamilton in decades, National Book Award winner Ron Chernow tells the riveting story of a man who overcame all odds to shape, inspire, and scandalize the newborn America. According to historian Joseph Ellis, Alexander Hamilton is "a robust full-length portrait, in my view the best ever written, of the most brilliant, charismatic and dangerous founder of them all." Few figures in American history have been more hotly debated or more grossly misunderstood than Alexander Hamilton. Chernow's biography gives Hamilton his due and sets the record straight, deftly illustrating that the political and economic greatness of today's America is the result of Hamilton's countless sacrifices to champion ideas that were often wildly disputed during his time. "To repudiate his legacy," Chernow writes, "is, in many ways, to repudiate the modern world." Chernow here recounts Hamilton's turbulent life: an illegitimate, largely self-taught orphan from the Caribbean, he came out of nowhere to take America by storm, rising to become George Washington's aide-de-camp in the Continental Army, coauthoring The Federalist Papers, founding the Bank of New York, leading the Federalist Party, and becoming the first Treasury Secretary of the United States. Historians have long told the story of America's birth as the triumph of Jefferson's democratic ideals over the aristocratic intentions of Hamilton. Chernow presents an entirely different man, whose legendary ambitions were motivated not merely by self-interest but by passionate patriotism and a stubborn will to build the foundations of American prosperity and power. His is a Hamilton far more human than we've encountered before-from his shame about his birth to his fiery aspirations, from his intimate relationships with childhood friends to his titanic feuds with Jefferson, Madison, Adams, Monroe, and Burr, and from his highly public affair with Maria Reynolds to his loving marriage to his loyal wife Eliza. And never before has there been a more vivid account of Hamilton's famous and mysterious death in a duel with Aaron Burr in July of 1804. Chernow's biography is not just a portrait of Hamilton, but the story of America's birth seen through its most central figure. At a critical time to look back to our roots, Alexander Hamilton will remind readers of the purpose of our institutions and our heritage as Americans.

Buy this book

Penguin.com

Amazon.com

Barnes&Noble.com - $35.00

Books-A-Million

BookSense.com

Google Product Search

Borrow this book

Find this book in a library

Contents

The Castaways	7
Christiansted, Alexander Hamilton, West Indies	
The Collegian	41
Myles Cooper, Elizabethtown, William Livingston	
The pen and the Sword	62
Continental Army, Myles Cooper, Horatio Gates	
A Frenzy of Valor	107
John Laurens, Continental Army, Hamilton	
The Lovesick Colonel	126
philip Schuyler, Tench Tilghman, James McHenry	
Raging Billows	167
Maria Reynolds, philip Schuyler, William Duer	

more »

Selected pages

Page 417   Page 408   Page 416

more »

Search in this book

[ ] [Search]

Popular passages

For why declare that things shall not be done which there is no power to do? Why, for instance, should it be said that the liberty of the press shall not be restrained when no power is given by which restrictions may be imposed? - Page 260
Appears in 312 books from 1838-2007

Is it not time to awake from the deceitful dream of a golden age and to adopt as a practical maxim for the direction of our political conduct that we, as well as the other inhabitants of the globe, are yet remote from the happy empire of perfect wisdom and perfect virtue? - Page 253
Appears in 118 books from 1811-2007

Humanity and good policy conspire to dictate that the benign prerogative for pardoning should be as little as possible fettered or embarrassed. The criminal code of every country partakes so much of necessary severity that without an easy access to exceptions in favor of unfortunate guilt, justice would wear a countenance too sanguinary and cruel. - Page 259
Appears in 90 books from 1833-2006

more »

Reviews

a balance...
every one should read...

make your own decisions.. but read this ....
User Review [Flag as inappropriate] View duffdog's library

A splendid life of an enlightened ...
... reactionary and forgotten Founding Father."In all probability," writes financial historian/biographer Chernow (Titan, 1998, etc.), "Alexander Hamilton is the foremost political figure in American ... more »
Kirkus Reviews Copyright (c) VNU Business Media, Inc.

After hulking works on J.P. Morgan, the ...
... Warburgs and John D. Rockefeller, what other grandee of American finance was left for Chernow's overflowing pen than the one who puts the others in the shade? Alexander Hamilton (1755-1804 ... more »
Reed Business Information (c) 2004

The empirepage.com - Book Reviews
In his new book, Ron Chernow attempts to set the achievement record straight on one of our lesser-known founding fathers, **Alexander Hamilton**. ...
empirepage.com

Lawyers, Guns and Money: Book Review: Alexander Hamilton
Recently finished reading Ron Chernow's **Alexander Hamilton**. I unreservedly recommend it to just about anyone interested in the Founding Fathers and the ...
blogspot.com

more »

Figure 7-8   About this book: *Alexander Hamilton* by Ron Chernow *(Continued)*

References from web pages

Alexander Hamilton on the Web
Guide to Alexander Hamilton. Over 150 annotated links.
www.isidore-of-seville.com/hamilton/

Repaying Alexander Hamilton - New York Times
New Jersey members of Congress are trying to persuade the federal government to
designate Paterson's historic manufacturing district as a national park
www.nytimes.com/2007/04/22/opinion/nyregionopinions/NJpaterson.html

Alexander Hamilton
In conjunction with the upcoming exhibition Alexander Hamilton: The Man Who ... the
new book Alexander Hamilton (The Penguin Press, 2004). Chernow won the ...
www.nyhistory.org/web/PDF/4-23-04_GilderLehrmanInstitute.pdf

Recovering a founder.(Museums)(Alexander Hamilton: The
THE year of Alexander Hamilton, which saw the publication of Ron Chernow's imposing
biography and the bicentennial of Hamilton's duel, comes to a co.
www.encyclopedia.com/doc/1G1-131003399.html

Founding Fathers At-A-Glance: Alexander Hamilton - The Liberty ...
Founding Fathers At-A-Glance Alexander Hamilton Alexander Hamilton was born on the
island of Nevis in the West Indies on January 11, in either 1755 (as.
www.libertylounge.net/forums/1007-founding-fathers-glance-alexander-hamilton.html

more »

References from books

Young Patriots: The Remarkable Story of Two Men, Their
Impossible Plan, and ...
by Charles A. Cerami - Political Science - 2005 - 354 pages
From "New York Times" bestselling author Cerami comes the great
underdog story of AlexanderHamilton and James Madison, who
envisioned a plan that no one else thought...
Limited preview - About this book - Add to my library

The Hypomanic Edge: The Link Between (a Little) Craziness
and (a Lot Of ...
by John D. Gartner - Business & Economics - 2005 - 368 pages
These are the real stories you never learned in school about some of
those men who made America:Columbus, who discovered the
continent, thought he was the messiah.
Limited preview - About this book - Add to my library

Aristotle And Hamilton on Commerce And Statesmanship
by Michael D. Chan - Political Science - 2006 - 236 pages
By reflecting on Hamilton in the context of Aristotle's own reflections on
commerce, Chan casts himin a new light that cuts across the ongoing
debate about liberal versus...
Limited preview - About this book - Add to my library

show more »

Other editions

Alexander Hamilton
by Ron Chernow - Biography & Autobiography - 2005 - 818 pages
Drawing upon extensive, unparalleled research including nearly fifty
previously undiscovered essayshighlighting Hamiltons fiery journalism
as well as his revealing missives to...
No preview available - About this book - Add to my library

Alexander Hamilton
by Ron Chernow - Biography & Autobiography - 2005
The renowned author of "Titan," whom the "New York Times" has called
"aselegant an architect of monumental histories as we've seen in
decades,"...
No preview available - About this book - Add to my library

Alexander Hamilton
by Ron Chernow - Biography & Autobiography - 2007 - 832 pages
Drawing upon extensive, unparalleled research--including nearly fifty
previously undiscovered essayshighlighting Hamilton's fiery journalism
as well as his revealing missives...
No preview available - About this book - Add to my library

show more »

References from scholarly works

Why Developing Countries Need Tariffs? How WTO NAMA Negotiations ...
Ha-Joon Chang

America's Deficit, the World's Problem
Maurice Obstfeld

Warlike Democracies
John Ferejohn, Frances McCall Rosenbluth

Warlike Democracies John Ferejohn and Frances Rosenbluth?
John Ferejohn, Frances Rosenbluth

The Statutory Foundations of Corporate Capitalism, 1865-1900 ...
Richard Bensel, Catherine Boone

show more »

Related books

Alexander Hamilton: A Life
by Willard Sterne Randall - Biography & Autobiography - 2003 - 512 pages
In this meticulously researched, illuminating, and lively account, Willard Sterne Randall mines thelatest
scholarship to provide a new perspective on Alexander Hamilton, his...
Limited preview - About this book - Add to my library

Alexander Hamilton: A Biography
by Forrest McDonald - Biography & Autobiography - 1979 - 464 pages
This book re-examines Hamilton's policies as a secretary of the treasury.
Limited preview - About this book - Add to my library

Alexander Hamilton and the Growth of the New Nation
by John Chester Miller - Biography & Autobiography - 2003 - 659 pages
Here is the premier biography of Alexander Hamilton, written by one of the foremost scholars of earlyAmerican
history.
Limited preview - About this book - Add to my library

show more »

Figure 7-8   About this book: *Alexander Hamilton* **by Ron Chernow** *(Continued)*

Key terms

Alexander Hamilton, Aaron Burr, Maria Reynolds, Robert Troup, John Adams, philip Schuyler, George Clinton, James McHenry, Rufus King, John Laurens, Republican, Oliver Wolcott, William Duer, Jay Treaty, Gouverneur Morris, Continental Army, Timothy pickering, Nathaniel pendleton, James Madison, George Washington

Places mentioned in this book

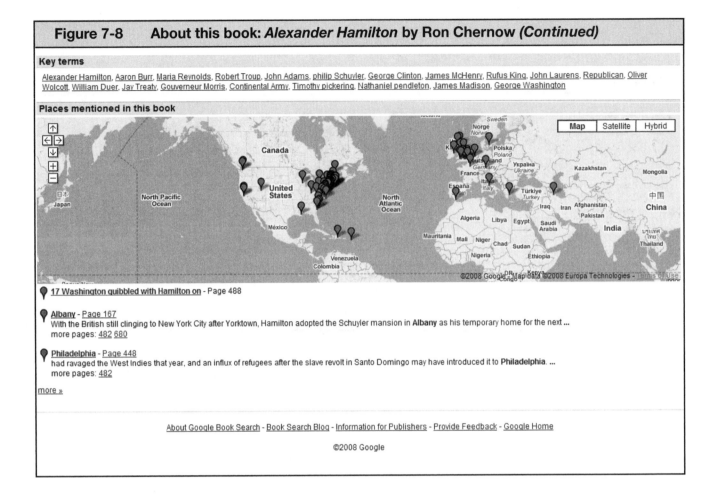

🔵 17 Washington quibbled with Hamilton on - Page 488

🔵 Albany - Page 167
   With the British still clinging to New York City after Yorktown, Hamilton adopted the Schuyler mansion in **Albany** as his temporary home for the next ...
   more pages: 482 680

🔵 Philadelphia - Page 448
   had ravaged the West Indies that year, and an influx of refugees after the slave revolt in Santo Domingo may have introduced it to **Philadelphia**. ...
   more pages: 482

more »

About Google Book Search - Book Search Blog - Information for Publishers - Provide Feedback - Google Home

©2008 Google

Figure 7-9   About this book: General information

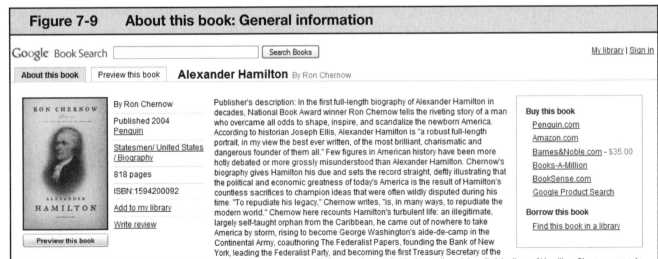

Figure 7-10 About this book: Selected pages

Selected pages

Page 417   Page 408   Page 416

more »

Figure 7-11 About this book: Search this book (before)

Search in this book

navy   [Search]

Figure 7-12 About this book: Search this book (after)

Search in this book

navy   [Search]

Page 67
Everyone knew that Manhattan, encircled by water, was vulnerable to the royal armada and would not be defensible for long without a **navy**. ...

Page 80
"So terrible and so incessant a roar of guns few even in the army and **navy** had ever heard before," said Lord Howe's ...

Page 139
Instead of bickering congressional boards, he wanted strong executives and endorsed single ministers for war, foreign affairs, finance, and the **navy**: "There ...

Page 162
Day and night, the cannonade exploded with such unrelenting fury that one lieutenant in the Royal **Navy** said, "It seemed as though the heavens should split. ...

Page 175
Madison favored a standing army, a permanent **navy**, and other positions later associated with the Hamiltonians. If anything, Madison was even more militant ...

more »

Figure 7-13   About this book: Contents

Contents

The Castaways   7
   Christiansted, Alexander Hamilton, West Indies

The Collegian   41
   Myles Cooper, Elizabethtown, William Livingston

The pen and the Sword   62
   Continental Army, Myles Cooper, Horatio Gates

A Frenzy of Valor   107
   John Laurens, Continental Army, Hamilton

The Lovesick Colonel   126
   philip Schuyler, Tench Tilghman, James McHenry

Raging Billows   167
   Maria Reynolds, philip Schuyler, William Duer

more »

Figure 7-14   About this book: Popular passages

Popular passages

For why declare that things shall not be done which there is no power to do? Why, for instance, should it be said that the liberty of the press shall not be restrained when no power is given by which restrictions may be imposed? - Page 260
  Appears in 312 books from 1838-2007

Is it not time to awake from the deceitful dream of a golden age and to adopt as a practical maxim for the direction of our political conduct that we, as well as the other inhabitants of the globe, are yet remote from the happy empire of perfect wisdom and perfect virtue? - Page 253
  Appears in 118 books from 1811-2007

Humanity and good policy conspire to dictate that the benign prerogative for pardoning should be as little as possible fettered or embarrassed. The criminal code of every country partakes so much of necessary severity that without an easy access to exceptions in favor of unfortunate guilt, justice would wear a countenance too sanguinary and cruel. - Page 259
  Appears in 90 books from 1833-2006

more »

- **Reviews:**

  This section presents titles, brief excerpts, sources, and links to online reviews of this book. Reviews from professional literature and major newspapers are weighted heavily here, but others are available with a little digging (see Figure 7-15).

- **References from Web pages:**

  This section is the result of an equivalent standard Google Web search for this particular book. Titles, links to, brief excerpt, and URL of each result are provided (see Figure 7-16).

- **References from books:**

  This is basically your online citation service. Here you'll find links to other books in Google that cite the book you're currently viewing (see Figure 7-17).

- **Other editions:**

  This area lists the other editions of this book available via Google Book Search (see Figure 7-18).

- **References from scholarly works:**

  Taking citation searching one step further, the items listed here are those that reference this book found via Google Scholar (see Figure 7-19).

- **Related books:**

  Here you'll find other books related to the topic of the book you're viewing. In Figure 7-20, the list includes other biographies of Alexander Hamilton.

- **Key terms:**

  This section lists hyperlinks of terms commonly used within the text. Think of this as if the book's index had a "most popular" category. Selecting any of these terms will perform a search for that term

Figure 7-15   About this book: Reviews

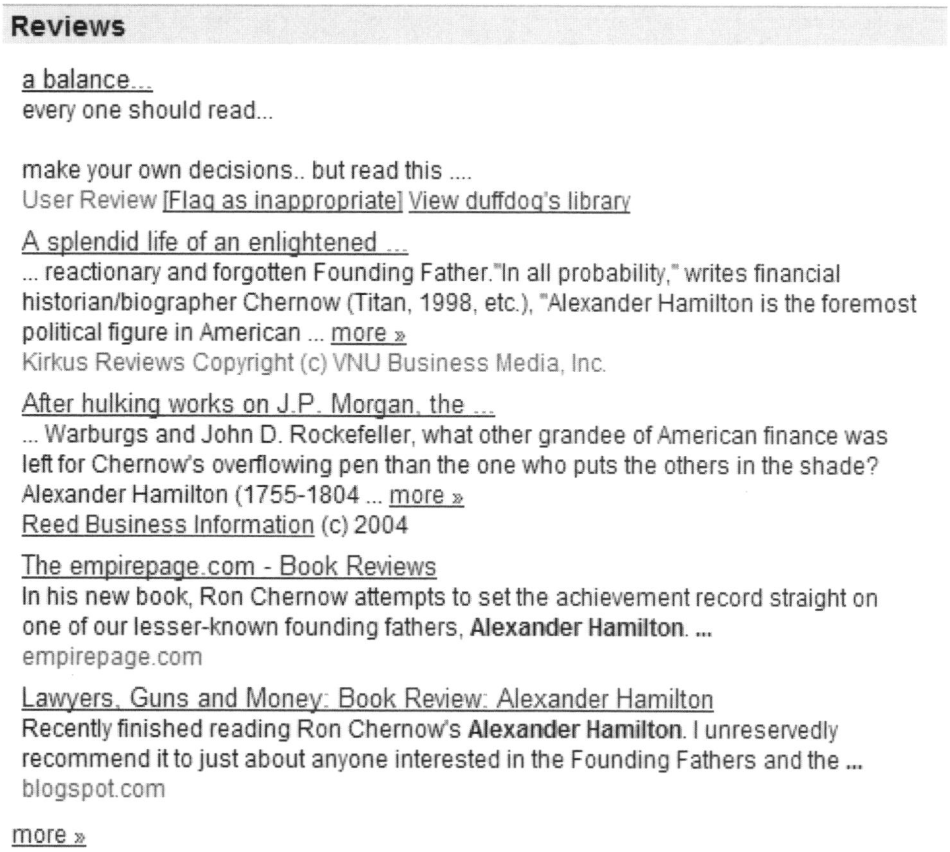

Reviews

a balance...
every one should read...

make your own decisions.. but read this ....
User Review [Flag as inappropriate] View duffdog's library

A splendid life of an enlightened ...
... reactionary and forgotten Founding Father."In all probability," writes financial historian/biographer Chernow (Titan, 1998, etc.), "Alexander Hamilton is the foremost political figure in American ... more »
Kirkus Reviews Copyright (c) VNU Business Media, Inc.

After hulking works on J.P. Morgan, the ...
... Warburgs and John D. Rockefeller, what other grandee of American finance was left for Chernow's overflowing pen than the one who puts the others in the shade? Alexander Hamilton (1755-1804 ... more »
Reed Business Information (c) 2004

The empirepage.com - Book Reviews
In his new book, Ron Chernow attempts to set the achievement record straight on one of our lesser-known founding fathers, **Alexander Hamilton**. ...
empirepage.com

Lawyers, Guns and Money: Book Review: Alexander Hamilton
Recently finished reading Ron Chernow's **Alexander Hamilton**. I unreservedly recommend it to just about anyone interested in the Founding Fathers and the ...
blogspot.com

more »

Figure 7-16   About this book: References from Web pages

References from web pages

Alexander Hamilton on the Web
Guide to Alexander Hamilton. Over 150 annotated links.
www.isidore-of-seville.com/hamilton/

Repaying Alexander Hamilton - New York Times
New Jersey members of Congress are trying to persuade the federal government to
designate Paterson's historic manufacturing district as a national park
www.nytimes.com/2007/04/22/opinion/nyregionopinions/NJpaterson.html

Alexander Hamilton
In conjunction with the upcoming exhibition Alexander Hamilton: The Man Who ... the
new book Alexander Hamilton (The Penguin Press, 2004). Chernow won the ...
www.nyhistory.org/web/PDF/4-23-04_GilderLehrmanInstitute.pdf

Recovering a founder.(Museums)(Alexander Hamilton: The
THE year of Alexander Hamilton, which saw the publication of Ron Chernow's imposing
biography and the bicentennial of Hamilton's duel, comes to a co.
www.encyclopedia.com/doc/1G1-131003399.html

Founding Fathers At-A-Glance: Alexander Hamilton - The Liberty ...
Founding Fathers At-A-Glance Alexander Hamilton Alexander Hamilton was born on the
island of Nevis in the West Indies on January 11, in either 1755 (as.
www.libertylounge.net/forums/1007-founding-fathers-glance-alexander-hamilton.html

more »

Figure 7-17   About this book: References from books

References from books

 Young Patriots: The Remarkable Story of Two Men, Their Impossible Plan, and ...
by Charles A. Cerami - Political Science - 2005 - 354 pages
From "New York Times" bestselling author Cerami comes the great
underdog story of AlexanderHamilton and James Madison, who
envisioned a plan that no one else thought...
Limited preview - About this book - Add to my library

 The Hypomanic Edge: The Link Between (a Little) Craziness and (a Lot Of ...
by John D. Gartner - Business & Economics - 2005 - 368 pages
These are the real stories you never learned in school about some of
those men who made America:Columbus, who discovered the
continent, thought he was the messiah.
Limited preview - About this book - Add to my library

 Aristotle And Hamilton on Commerce And Statesmanship
by Michael D. Chan - Political Science - 2006 - 236 pages
By reflecting on Hamilton in the context of Aristotle's own reflections on
commerce, Chan casts himin a new light that cuts across the ongoing
debate about liberal versus...
Limited preview - About this book - Add to my library

show more »

Figure 7-18   About this book: Other editions

Other editions

Alexander Hamilton
by Ron Chernow - Biography & Autobiography - 2005 - 818 pages
Drawing upon extensive, unparalleled research including nearly fifty
previously undiscovered essayshighlighting Hamiltons fiery journalism
as well as his revealing missives to...
No preview available - About this book - Add to my library

Alexander Hamilton
by Ron Chernow - Biography & Autobiography - 2005
The renowned author of "Titan," whom the "New York Times" has called
"aselegant an architect of monumental histories as we've seen in
decades,"...
No preview available - About this book - Add to my library

Alexander Hamilton
by Ron Chernow - Biography & Autobiography - 2007 - 832 pages
Drawing upon extensive, unparalleled research--including nearly fifty
previously undiscovered essayshighlighting Hamilton's fiery journalism
as well as his revealing missives...
No preview available - About this book - Add to my library

show more »

Figure 7-19   About this book: References from scholarly works

References from scholarly works

Why Developing Countries Need Tariffs? How WTO NAMA Negotiations ...
Ha-Joon Chang

America's Deficit, the World's Problem
Maurice Obstfeld

Warlike Democracies
John Ferejohn, Frances McCall Rosenbluth

Warlike Democracies John Ferejohn and Frances Rosenbluth?
John Ferejohn, Frances Rosenbluth

The Statutory Foundations of Corporate Capitalism, 1865-1900 ...
Richard Bensel, Catherine Boone

show more »

Figure 7-20   About this book: Related books

Related books

Alexander Hamilton: A Life
by Willard Sterne Randall - Biography & Autobiography - 2003 - 512 pages
In this meticulously researched, illuminating, and lively account, Willard Sterne Randall mines thelatest scholarship to provide a new perspective on Alexander Hamilton, his...
Limited preview - About this book - Add to my library

Alexander Hamilton: A Biography
by Forrest McDonald - Biography & Autobiography - 1979 - 464 pages
This book re-examines Hamilton's policies as a secretary of the treasury.
Limited preview - About this book - Add to my library

Alexander Hamilton and the Growth of the New Nation
by John Chester Miller - Biography & Autobiography - 2003 - 659 pages
Here is the premier biography of Alexander Hamilton, written by one of the foremost scholars of earlyAmerican history.
Limited preview - About this book - Add to my library

show more »

Figure 7-21   About this book: Key terms

Key terms

Alexander Hamilton, Aaron Burr, Maria Reynolds, Robert Troup, John Adams, philip Schuyler, George Clinton, James McHenry, Rufus King, John Laurens, Republican, Oliver Wolcott, William Duer, Jay Treaty, Gouverneur Morris, Continental Army, Timothy pickering, Nathaniel pendleton, James Madison, George Washington

---

in the text and present the results in the previously mentioned "Search in this book" section of this page. See Figure 7-21.

- **Places mentioned in this book:**
  Here you'll see a Google map with markers for significant locations as featured within the book (see Figure 7-22).

In most cases, at the bottom of each of these sections there is a "more »" or "show more »" link giving you the ability to expand the information from that section without leaving the page. As with content searching on this page, this potentially increases the value of a resulting printout.

Preview This Book

As with the previous section, not all of the items described here will be available with all books. Before I proceed, I want to explain the three different versions of availability that Google offers: full view, limited preview, and snippet view. The preview homepage can be seen in Figure 7-23.

FULL VIEW

Full view means that the complete contents of the book are available for reading within Google Book Search (see Figure 7-24). This option is generally available only on books that are clearly out of copyright.

Figure 7-22   About this book: Places mentioned in this book

Places mentioned in this book

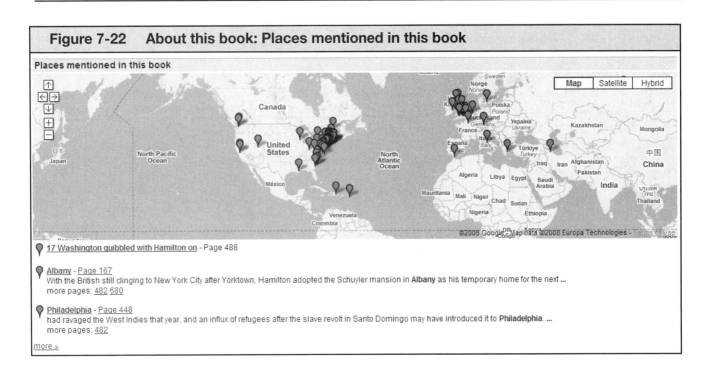

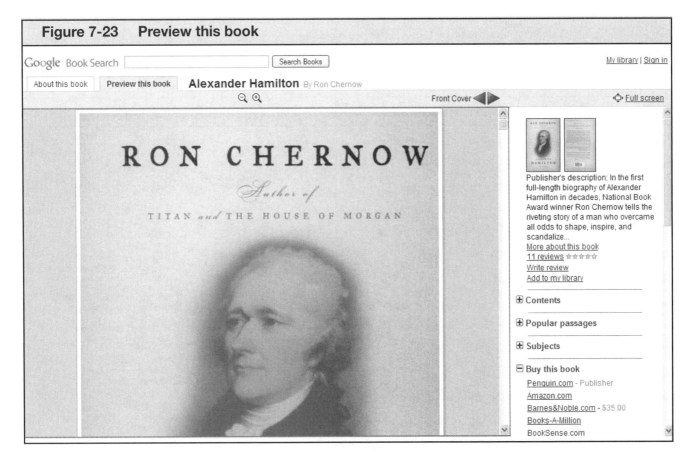

17 Washington quibbled with Hamilton on - Page 488

Albany - Page 167
With the British still clinging to New York City after Yorktown, Hamilton adopted the Schuyler mansion in **Albany** as his temporary home for the next ...
more pages: 482 680

Philadelphia - Page 448
had ravaged the West Indies that year, and an influx of refugees after the slave revolt in Santo Domingo may have introduced it to **Philadelphia**. ...
more pages: 482

more »

Figure 7-23   Preview this book

Google Book Search [   ] [Search Books]   My library | Sign in

| About this book | Preview this book | **Alexander Hamilton** By Ron Chernow |

Q Q   Front Cover ◀▶   ⊕ Full screen

RON CHERNOW

Author of

TITAN *and* THE HOUSE OF MORGAN

Publisher's description: In the first full-length biography of Alexander Hamilton in decades, National Book Award winner Ron Chernow tells the riveting story of a man who overcame all odds to shape, inspire, and scandalize...
More about this book
11 reviews ☆☆☆☆☆
Write review
Add to my library

⊞ Contents

⊞ Popular passages

⊞ Subjects

⊟ Buy this book
Penguin.com - Publisher
Amazon.com
Barnes&Noble.com - $35.00
Books-A-Million
BookSense.com

| Figure 7-24 | Full view example |

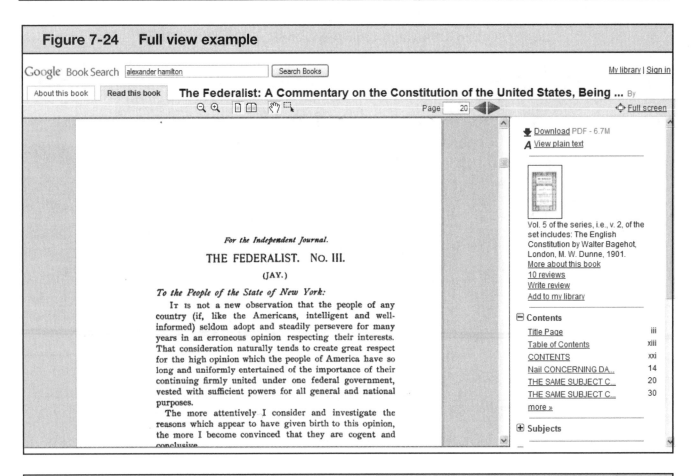

| Figure 7-25 | Limited preview example |

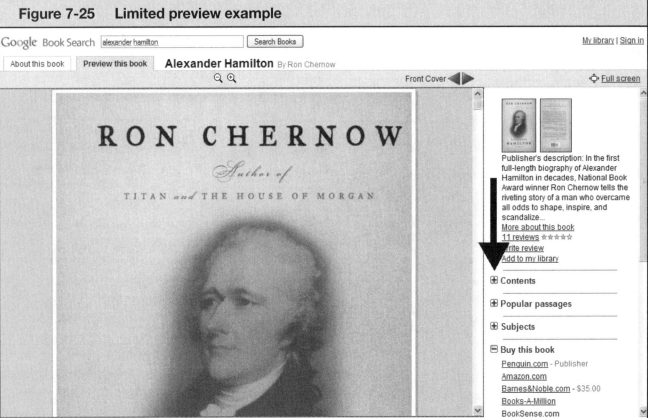

LIMITED PREVIEW

Limited preview is generally available for books that have been contributed to Google Book Search through its publisher Partner Program. In this case, you're able to see a limited number of complete pages from the book. In some cases, these are specific pages or a certain number of pages of your choosing. The method and number are not determined by Google and therefore vary from book to book and publisher to publisher, so more specific information is unavailable. A limited preview page can be seen in Figure 7-25.

SNIPPET VIEW

The snippet view is generally reserved for books that are in-copyright but have been added to the collection via the Library Project and without the explicit permission of the copyright holder.[5] The snippet view shows only small sections of a page of text surrounding the particular terms that have been searched for (see Figure 7-26). Additionally,

the number of viewable snippets is limited, but that number is not explicitly stated by Google.

Depending on the amount available, the page will be labeled "Preview this book," when incomplete content is available, or "Read this book," when full content is available. I'll be using "Preview this book" for the rest of this section since my example book is not completely available. In all of these views, any of your search keywords will be highlighted in yellow.

Book Info

Despite the amount of actual content available, this page will still generally show a good bit of detail about the book itself. Listed down the right side of the screen, these items include: general info, contents, popular passages, subjects, buy this book, search in this book, publisher info, and other edition. At first most of these sections will be collapsed so that you can only see the section heading (see Figure 7-27). To expose the information in each section, just

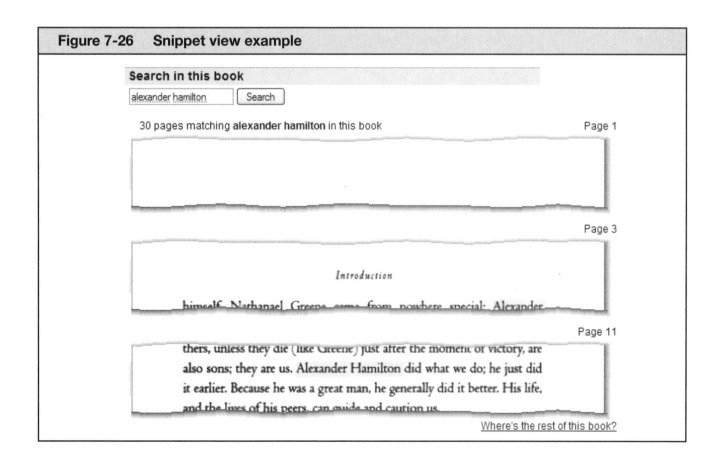

Figure 7-26   Snippet view example

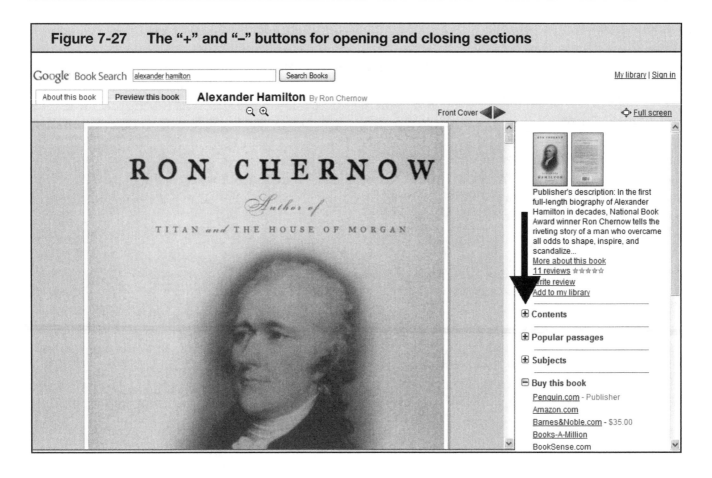

Figure 7-27   The "+" and "–" buttons for opening and closing sections

click the "+" to the left of the section's name. Once opened, the "+" will change to a "–" which can be used to collapse that section again.

- **General info:**
  Here you'll find thumbnail images from the book, typically front and back cover, along with a brief description and links to "more about this book" (which will take you back to the "About this book page"), "Write review," and "Add to my library" (see Figure 7-28).

- **Contents:**
  This will list the major contents of the book with page numbers and links to those pages in the book. This is not necessarily a complete reproduction of the book's table of contents, as you can see in Figure 7-29.

- **Popular passages:**
  As with the equivalent section on the "About this book" page, here you'll find brief content from within the book that Google considers popular.

Typically only two or three passages will be listed here with a "more »" link available to expand the content (see Figure 7-30).

- **Subjects:**
  This is a listing of Google subject headings assigned to the book. Each is presented as a link to a Google Book Search on that subject (see Figure 7-31).

- **Buy this book:**
  Here there are links to various online purchasing options, including the publisher, new and used bookstores, and even a link to a WorldCat.org search as "Find this book in a library" (see Figure 7-32).

- **Search in this book:**
  Here is another search box that will allow you to perform a content search of the book (see Figure 7-33). As with the search on the "About this book" page, results will be presented to you here instead of on a new page.

Figure 7-28   Preview this book: General info

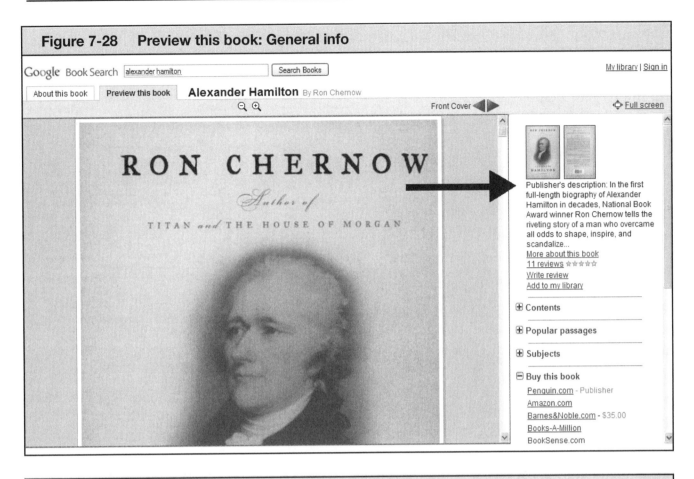

Figure 7-29   Preview this book: Contents

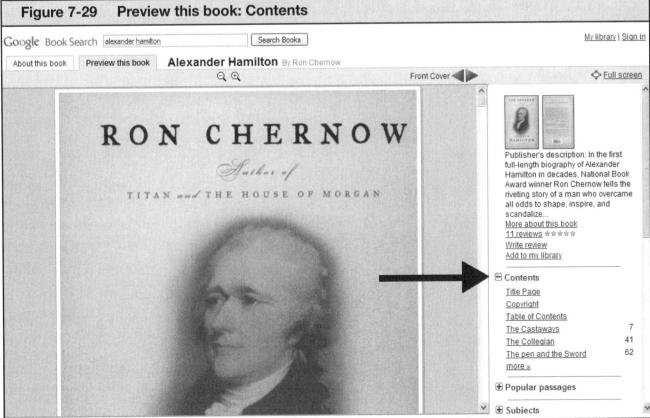

Figure 7-30   Preview this book: Popular passages

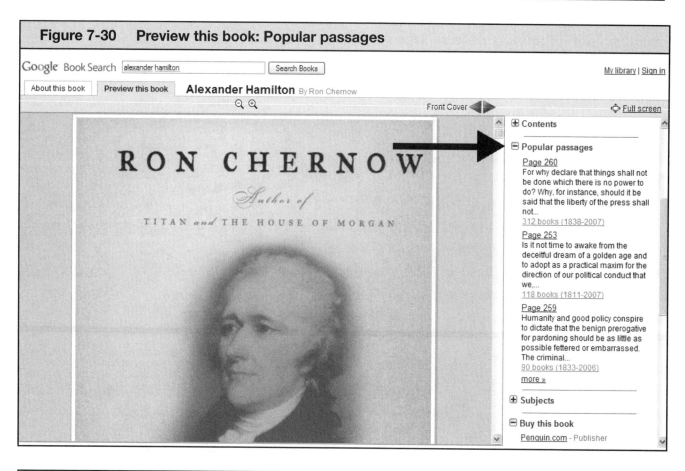

Figure 7-31   Preview this book: Subjects

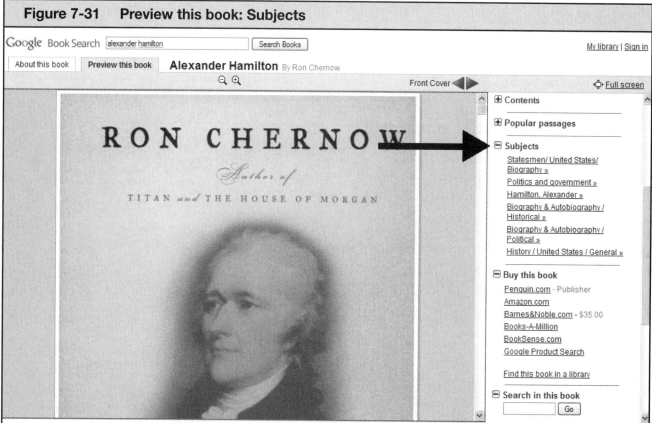

Figure 7-32   Preview this book: Buy this book

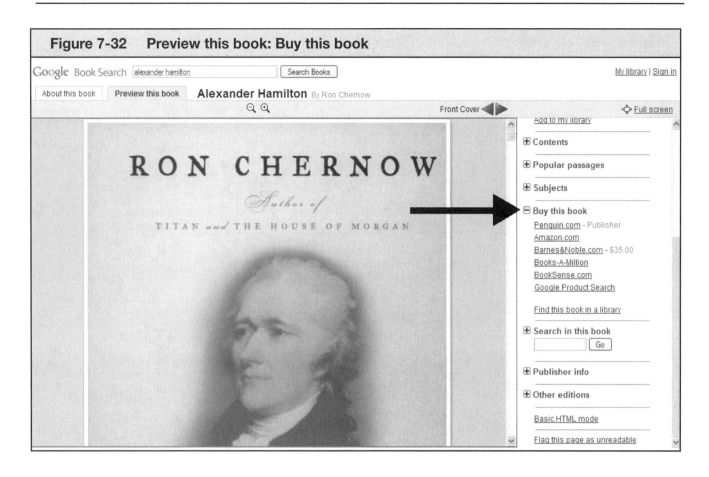

Figure 7-33   Preview this book: Search in this book

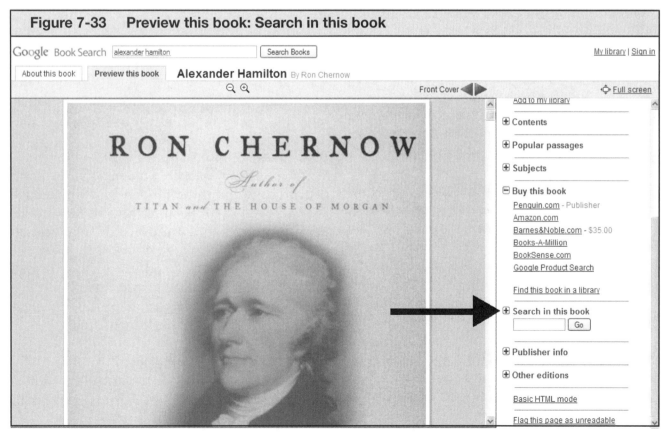

Figure 7-34   Preview this book: Publisher info

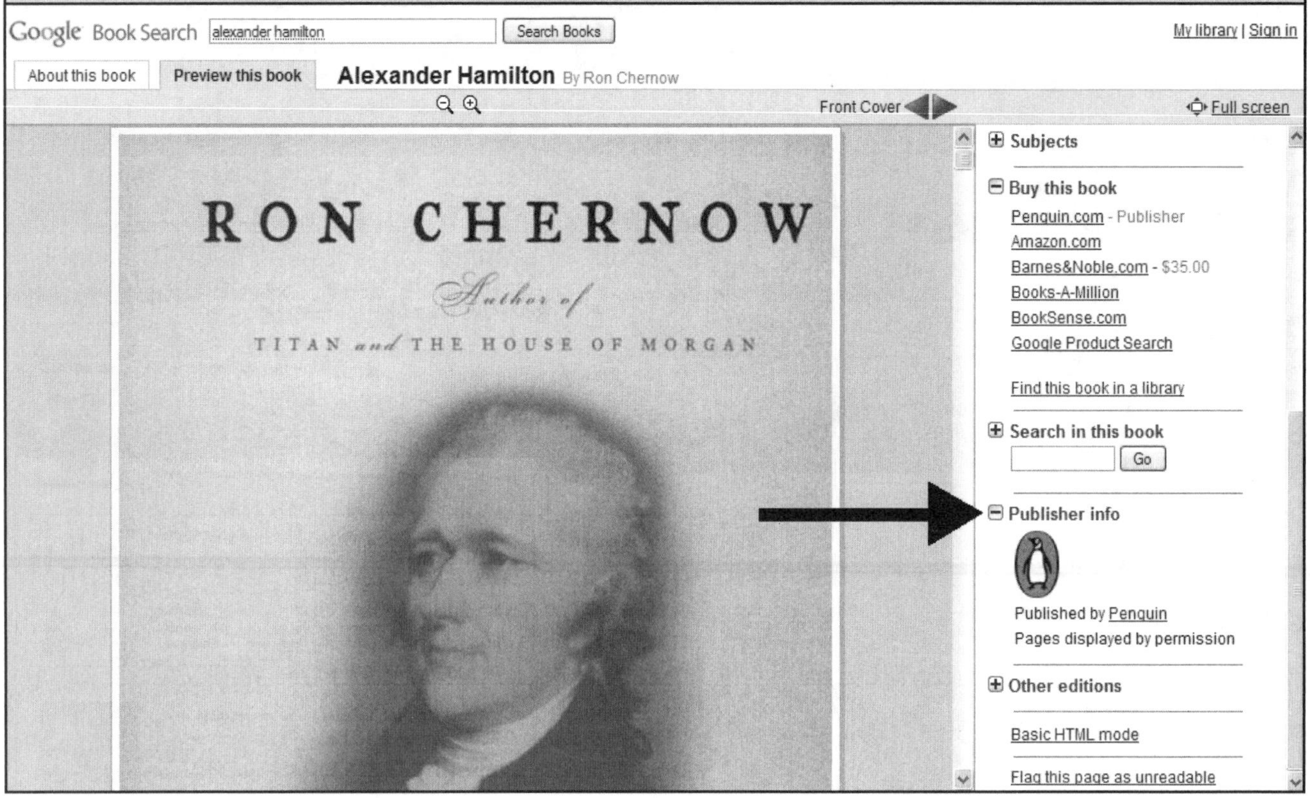

- **Publisher info:**
  Typically this section will show the publisher's logo, the publisher's name along with a link to the publisher's Web site, and relevant permission information. In Figure 7-34, it states "Pages displayed by permission," indicating that this book has been included under the Google Partner Program.

- **Other editions:**
  This includes information on the publisher and publication date of other editions of this title. The title-based links will take you to the "About this book" page of those editions. If more than two additional editions are available, click on the "show more »" link to see them (see Figure 7-35). Unlike searching on this page, clicking this link will display the results on another page.

Last, there is a "Basic HTML mode" link at the bottom of this frame. Clicking on this link will both take the page out of a frames-based display and remove the +/– system of navigation. This is of use to

those using older browsers or slower connections. My suggestion is to use this only if you're having trouble with the standard interface. You can also "Flag this page as unreadable" should you feel that the scanning job was subpar and needs to be redone.

BOOK CONTENT NAVIGATION

Keeping in mind that the actual amount of a particular book will vary, let me now take you through the basic options of book navigation. Most of the navigation options are available in the light blue bar near the top of the window, just above the book (see Figure 7-36). Here you'll find buttons for zooming, previous/next page, and full screen. Additionally, you can navigate via scrolling and dragging. Let's take a look at each of these in a little more detail.

- **Scrolling and dragging:**
  Located between the book images and the information on the right of the screen is a scrollbar. By using this scrollbar, you can quickly scroll through

Figure 7-35   Preview this book: Other editions

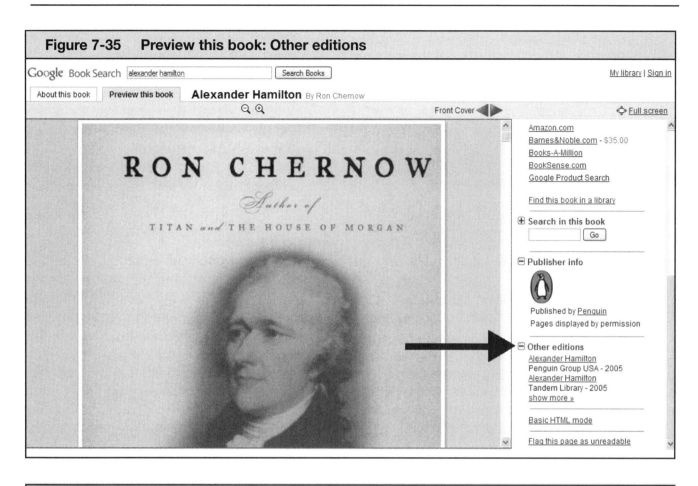

Figure 7-36   The navigation bar

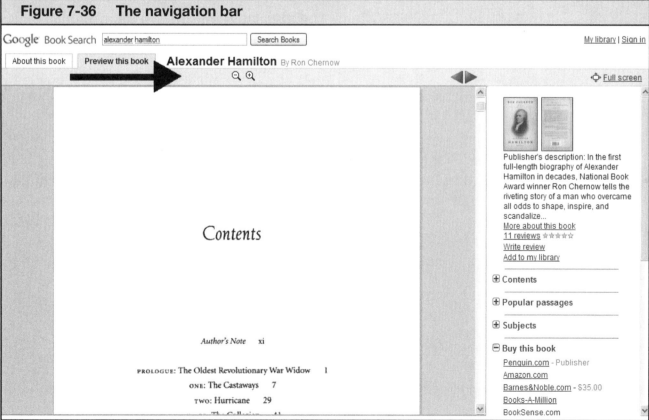

the available contents of the book. Additionally, you can move your mouse pointer over the image to change it into a hand. Clicking and holding your left mouse button will "grab" the page and allow you to move the image up, down, left, or right with your mouse. This is especially handy when zoomed in on a page.

- **Zoom:**
  The zoom buttons are located in the navigation bar, centered over the book image. Clicking on the minus magnifying glass icon will zoom out, while the plus magnifying glass icon will zoom in (see Figure 7-37). There are a total of five zoom levels.

- **Previous/Next page:**
  The previous and next page icons are also located in the navigation bar and can be found above and to the left of the book's scrollbar. These icons are in the shape of left- and right-pointing triangles similar to the back and forward buttons in Web browsers. Click the left-pointing triangle to go to the previous page and click the right-pointing triangle to go to

the next page. The current page number will be displayed to the left of these icons.

- **Full screen:**
  If you prefer to remove all of the book information and other Google information from the screen and just focus on the book's images, click on the "Full screen" link located on the navigation bar. To return to the standard screen layout, click on the link again, which will read "Exit full screen." See Figure 7-38 for an example of a full-screen view.

Searching Book Content

Searching for keywords within the text of a book is simple and can be done from either of the "Search in this book" fields. For simplicity's sake, I'm going to use the one from the "About this book" page, but everything I do will also work on the "Preview this book" page.

Say I'm interested in knowing what Alexander Hamilton thought about the navy. So I'm going to search in this book for *navy*. I'm presented with five results in page order, as shown in Figure 7-39. The

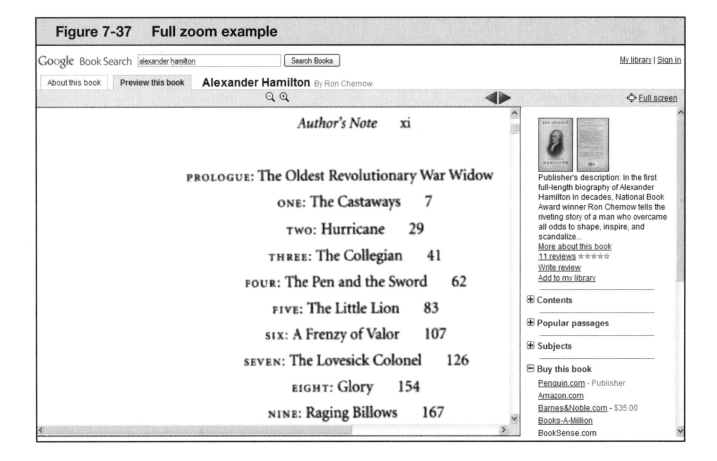

Figure 7-37   Full zoom example

Figure 7-38 Full-screen mode

Exit full screen
Contents
Author's Note xi
PROLOGUE: The Oldest Revolutionary War Widow 1
ONE: The Castaways 7
TWO: Hurricane 29
THREE: The Collegian 41
FOUR: The Pen and the Sword 62
FIVE: The Little Lion 83

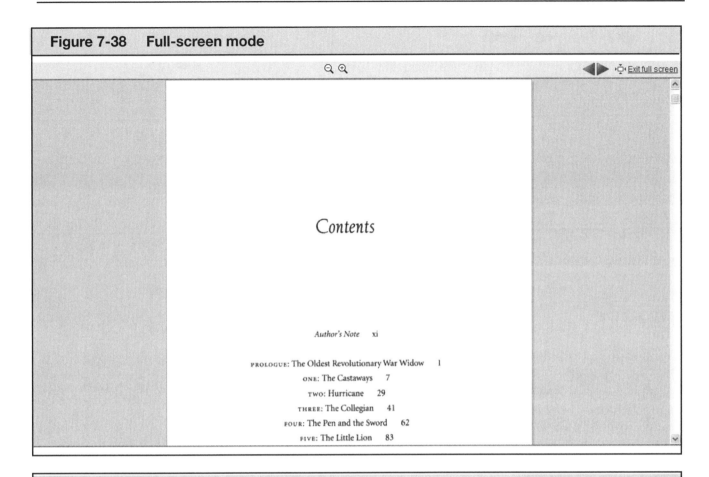

Figure 7-39 The first five results

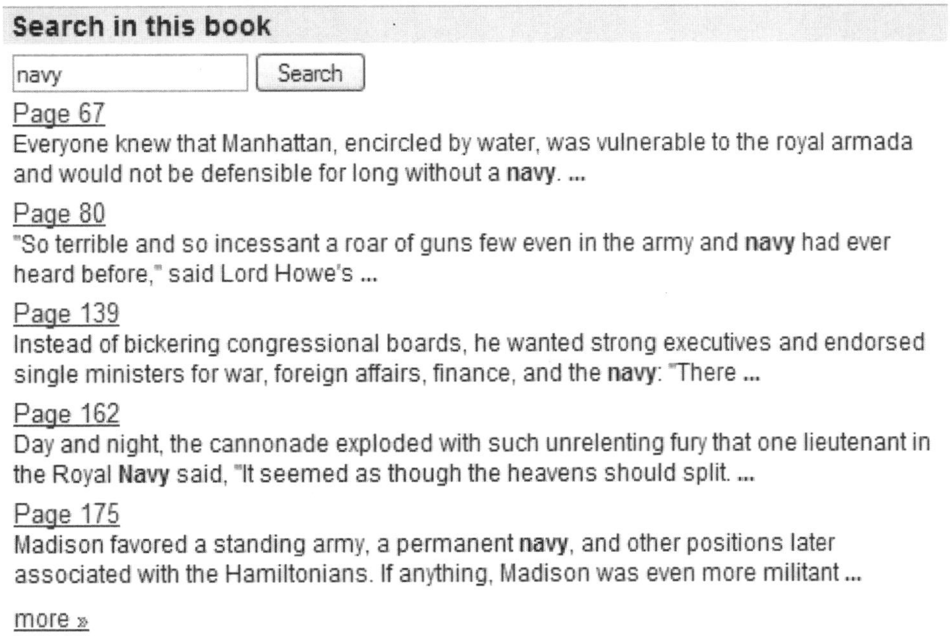

Search in this book
navy
Search
Page 67
Everyone knew that Manhattan, encircled by water, was vulnerable to the royal armada and would not be defensible for long without a navy. ...
Page 80
"So terrible and so incessant a roar of guns few even in the army and navy had ever heard before," said Lord Howe's ...
Page 139
Instead of bickering congressional boards, he wanted strong executives and endorsed single ministers for war, foreign affairs, finance, and the navy: "There ...
Page 162
Day and night, the cannonade exploded with such unrelenting fury that one lieutenant in the Royal Navy said, "It seemed as though the heavens should split. ...
Page 175
Madison favored a standing army, a permanent navy, and other positions later associated with the Hamiltonians. If anything, Madison was even more militant ...
more »

Figure 7-40   More results

Search in this book

[navy] [Search]

Page 67
Everyone knew that Manhattan, encircled by water, was vulnerable to the royal armada and would not be defensible for long without a **navy**. ...

Page 80
"So terrible and so incessant a roar of guns few even in the army and **navy** had ever heard before," said Lord Howe's ...

Page 139
Instead of bickering congressional boards, he wanted strong executives and endorsed single ministers for war, foreign affairs, finance, and the **navy**: "There ...

Page 162
Day and night, the cannonade exploded with such unrelenting fury that one lieutenant in the Royal **Navy** said, "It seemed as though the heavens should split. ...

Page 175
Madison favored a standing army, a permanent **navy**, and other positions later associated with the Hamiltonians. If anything, Madison was even more militant ...

Page 220
... Excellency George Clinton, Esquire, the Governor-General and Commander-in-Chief of all the militia, and Admiral of the **Navy** of the State of New-York. ...

Page 254
4- With a powerful union, America would strike better commercial bargains and create a respectable **navy**. ...

Page 255
4* Economic and military strength went hand in hand: "If we mean to be a commercial people ... we must endeavour as soon as possible to have a **navy**. ...

Page 290
... of the states under a strong federal government, timely payment of its debts, creation of an army and a **navy**, and harmony among its people. ...

Page 293
... and sold lumber to the British **Navy**. Because he had befriended Myles Cooper in England, Duer came to know Hamilton while he was still studying at King's ...

Page 295
Far from weakening the country, it had produced manifold benefits. Public credit had enabled England to build up the Royal **Navy**, to prosecute wars around ...

Page 370
As much as the Bank of England, the British Exchequer, and the Royal **Navy**, these industrial breakthroughs had catapulted Britain to a leading position in ...

Page 435
The United States did not even possess a regular **navy**. At such a moment, Hamilton said, war would be "the most unequal and calamitous in which it is ...

Page 460
Sorry, this page's content is restricted.

Page 462
Sorry, this page's content is restricted.

Page 485
Nor did he obtain satisfaction for American sailors abducted by the British **Navy**. Americans had expected him to uphold the traditional prerogatives of a ...

Figure 7-40   More results (Continued)

Page 527
Sorry, this page's content is restricted.

Page 548
... ships and chiding them for having "inflicted a wound in the American breast"11 He also announced plans to expand the **navy** and bolster the militias. ...

Page 550
16 Congress rushed through a program for fortifying eastern seaports and augmenting the army and **navy**. The Republicans contrived ways to rationalize what ...

Page 553
18 Unlike many Federalists, John Adams thought a **navy** and militia would suffice to guard the country and feared a large standing army as a "many bellied ...

Page 556
Sorry, this page's content is restricted.

Page 565
Sorry, this page's content is restricted.

Page 597
Sorry, this page's content is restricted.

Page 602
With his hyperactive mind, he drafted a bill for a military academy encompassing the **navy** as well as the army and another for an army corps of engineers. ...

Page 628
Sorry, this page's content is restricted.

Page 636
... provided "assurances on certain points: the maintenance of the present system, especially on the cardinal articles of public credit, a **navy**, neutrality. ...

Page 638
... Bayard set forth some Federalist prerequisites for supporting Jefferson: he would have to preserve Hamilton's financial system, maintain the **navy**, ...

Page 646
Jefferson intended to cut taxes and public debt, contract the **navy**, and shrink the central government — a swollen bureaucracy of 150 employees! ...

Page 809
570 **Navy**, US, 290, 460, 462, 527, 546. 656, 658, 646 Adams's plans for, 548, 550 **Navy** Department, US, 555 Necker, Jacques, 287, 295 neutrality, ...

Page 813
... 55-54, 56-59, 208 reports on American Revolution in, 68-69, 72, 74, 75,79-80 Royal Gazette, 70, 185 Royal **Navy**, British, 67, 70, 76-77, 78, 79, 98, 162, ...

« less

order of the results is important to note. They are not sorted by relevance but in the order the result is found within the book. To see more results, just click on the "more »" link. Doing so will display the rest of the results (see Figure 7-40).

Each result presents a page number and a brief contextual preview of that page's content. As you can see in Figure 7-40, I'm being told "Sorry, this page's content is restricted" in some cases since this book is available only under limited preview. To view a result in context, click on the page number link. In Figure 7-41, you can see that I've opened page 602, which talks about Hamilton's drafting of "a bill for a military academy encompassing the navy as well as the army."

Moving to the next or previous result is not nearly as straightforward as most would like. The simplest way to do so is to scroll down to the "Search in this book" section of the book information area on the right. Here you'll find your list of results, though only the first five. To see the rest, click on the "more »" link. Once you see the result you're looking for, click on its page number link to retrieve that page.[6]

My Library

If you have a Google account (who doesn't these days?) and you sign in to Google at any time during your use of Google Book Search, you will have access to "My Library," the link you can find in the upper right corner of the page, along with "My Ac-

Figure 7-41   Page 602

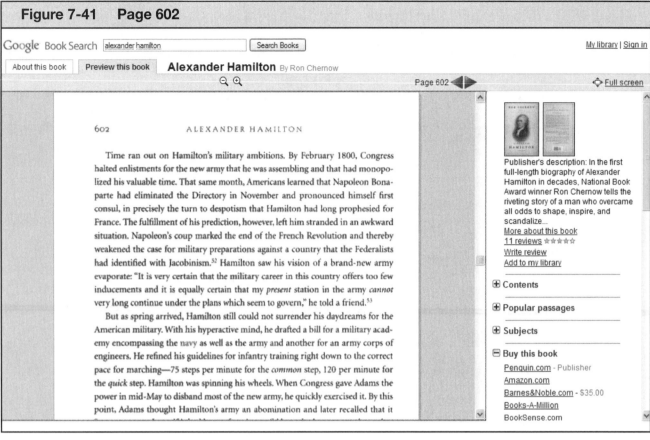

Figure 7-42   Michael's library

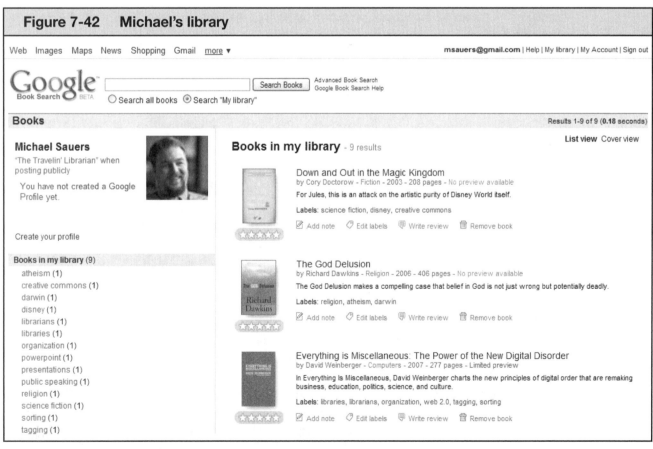

count" and "Sign in/out." If you select "My Library" and aren't logged in to Google, you'll be asked to first log in or create an account if you don't already have one. Just what is "My Library"? Think of it as a bookmarking system or virtual holds list for Google Books. Figure 7-42 shows the current contents of my "My Library."

Adding a book to your library can be done by clicking any of the multiple "Add to my library" links that you'll find while perusing Google Book Search. Once a book has been added to your library, the text will change to "In my library [Remove]," with "Remove" as the link to remove that book from your library.

At its basic level, "My Library" is a simple way to keep track of books in Google Book Search that you may want to return to in the future. In other ways it attempts to be something more social, akin to LibraryThing.[7] Let's take a look at its features. For each book in your library, you'll see a thumbnail of

the book's cover (when available), the title and author, its subject, publication date, and page count. The titles are hyperlinked to the book's "Preview/Read this book" page. Author names are not hyperlinked.[8]

You'll also have links to "Add labels" and "Write review." The last line of information will include information about the level of content available, a link to "about this book," its in-library status with a link to "Remove" it from your library, and a link to "More editions" when other editions are available. You can also use the "Cover view" link in the upper right corner of the screen to switch to a cover-only view of your library just as you could for search results (see Figure 7-43).

As useful as this basic remembering-for-easy-future-access functionality may be, "My Library" does have some additional features with distinct possibilities: tagging, searching "My Library," importing and exporting, and RSS (really simple syndication).

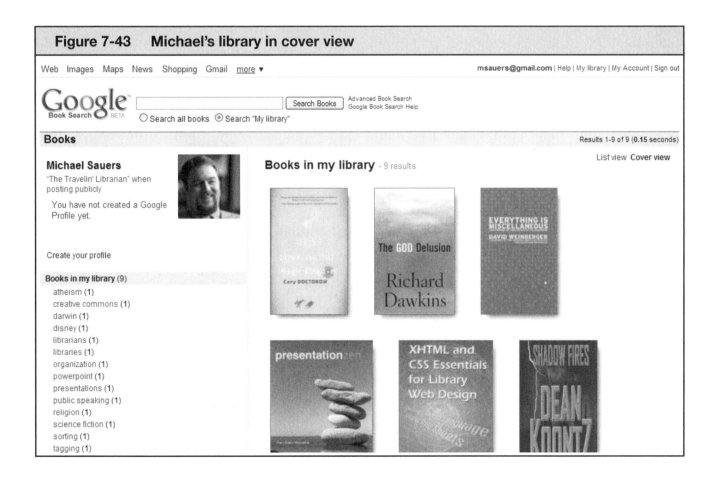

Figure 7-43   Michael's library in cover view

Figure 7-44   Adding label

Figure 7-45   Labels in "my library"

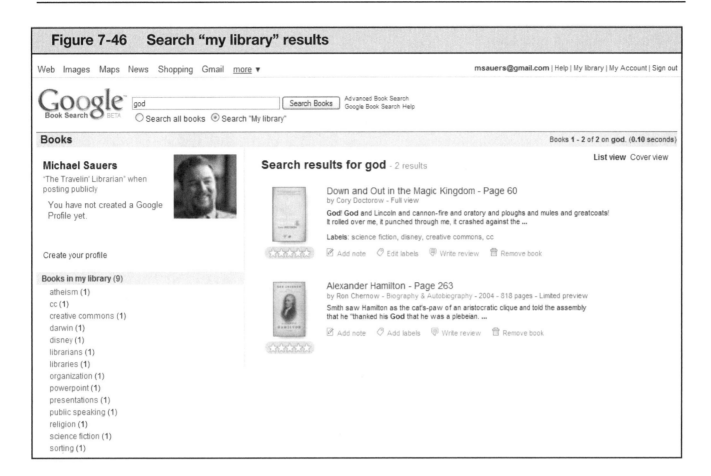

Figure 7-46   Search "my library" results

Web Images Maps News Shopping Gmail more ▼

msauers@gmail.com | Help | My library | My Account | Sign out

Google Book Search BETA [god] [Search Books]

Advanced Book Search
Google Book Search Help

○ Search all books ◉ Search "My library"

Books   Books 1 - 2 of 2 on god. (0.10 seconds)

                                                          List view Cover view

Michael Sauers
'The Travelin' Librarian' when
posting publicly

You have not created a Google
Profile yet.

Create your profile

Books in my library (9)
atheism (1)
cc (1)
creative commons (1)
darwin (1)
disney (1)
librarians (1)
libraries (1)
organization (1)
powerpoint (1)
presentations (1)
public speaking (1)
religion (1)
science fiction (1)
sorting (1)

Search results for god - 2 results

Down and Out in the Magic Kingdom - Page 60
by Cory Doctorow - Full view
God! God and Lincoln and cannon-fire and oratory and ploughs and mules and greatcoats!
It rolled over me, it punched through me, it crashed against the ...

Labels: science fiction, disney, creative commons, cc

☑ Add note   ◌ Edit labels   ▤ Write review   🗑 Remove book

Alexander Hamilton - Page 263
by Ron Chernow - Biography & Autobiography - 2004 - 818 pages - Limited preview
Smith saw Hamilton as the cat's-paw of an aristocratic clique and told the assembly
that he "thanked his **God** that he was a plebeian. ...

☑ Add note   ◌ Add labels   ▤ Write review   🗑 Remove book

- **Add labels (tagging):**
  Click on the "Add labels" link or the "Write review" link, as both will send you to the same page. This page allows you to rate the book (on a scale of one to five stars), write a review of the book, and/or add "labels." In Google-speak, labels are just tags, as I described in Chapter 1. Figure 7-44 shows that I've added the labels "science fiction," "Disney," and "creative commons" to the book *Down and Out in the Magic Kingdom* by Cory Doctorow. In Google's system, multiple tags may be added by creating a comma-delimited list. I note that those labels have been added to the book's record, and I'm presented with the option to change them in the future with an "edit labels" link. Also, a list of my labels has been added to the column on the left side of the screen (see Figure 7-45). Clicking on any of these labels will display only those books in my library with that particular label.[9]

- **Search "My Library"**
  Let's say you're doing research on a particular topic and you've collected an extensive Google library of books that you believe are relevant. With "Search My Library," you can now perform a keyword search across all of the books in your library. Figure 7-46 shows the results of a search for *god* across all of the books in my library.

- **Import books:**
  If you have a list of books you're interested in searching using Google Book Search and you don't want to look them up one at a time, you're in luck. Just click on the "Import books" link and provide a list of ISBNs. Be sure to enter them one per line, as shown in Figure 7-47. Once you've clicked the "Import" button, give Google a little bit of time and your books will start appearing in your library (see Figure 7-48).

- **Export my library:**
  Clicking "Export my library" will produce an XML file of your library's content (see Figure 7-49). The file will include the URL of your library along with the title, author, identifier (typically the ISBN), labels, Google ID, and Google URL of every book in your library. Although this file may seem unwieldy to

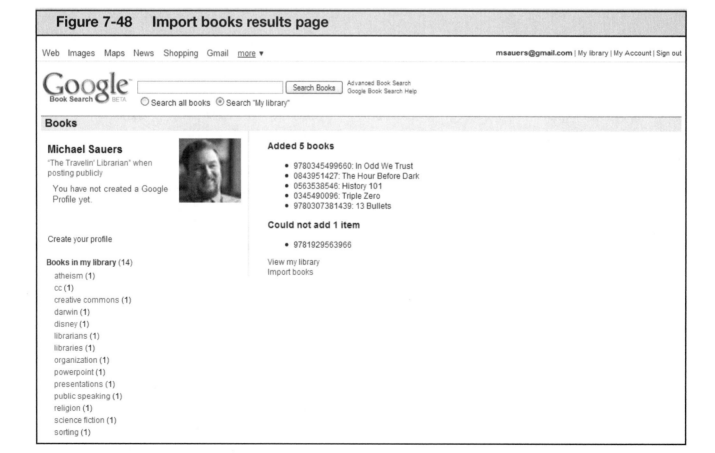

Figure 7-47   Import books

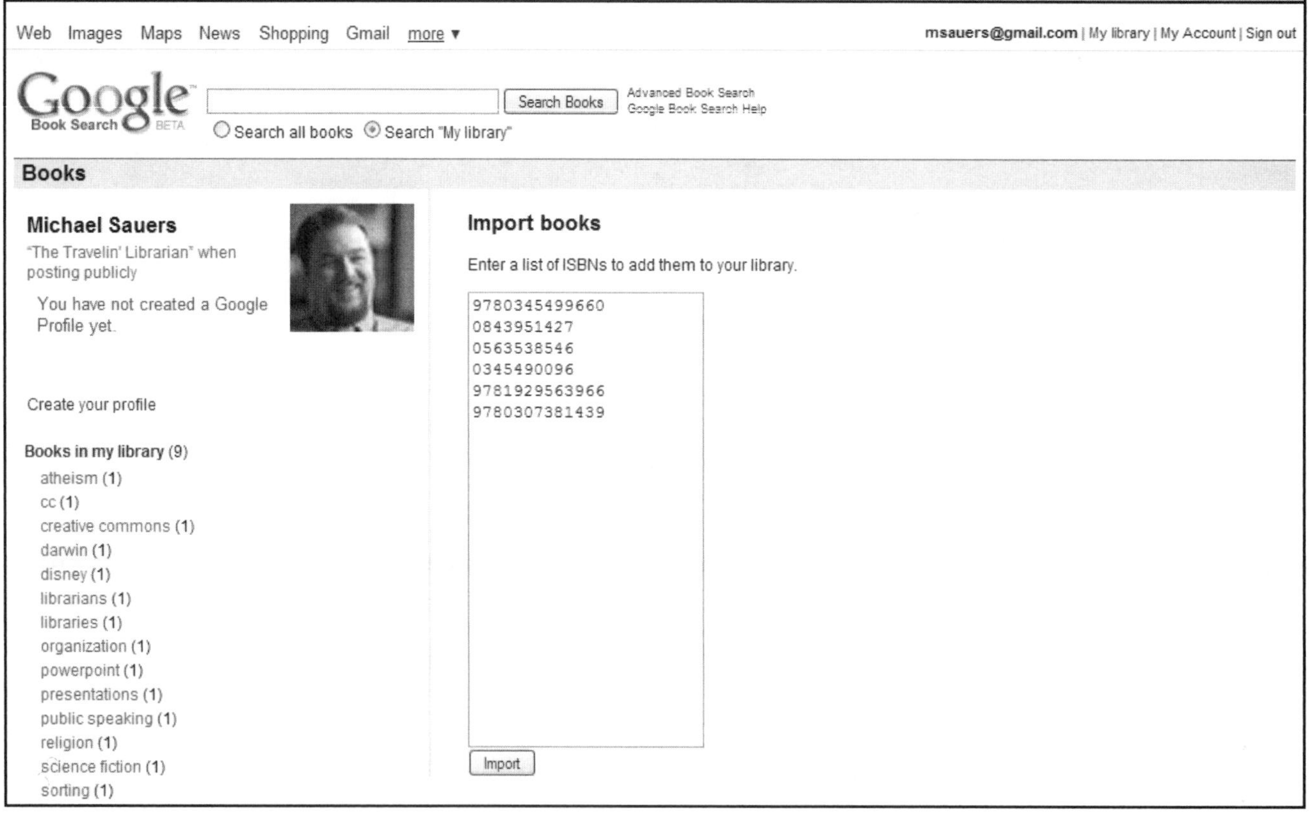

Figure 7-48   Import books results page

Figure 7-49   Exported XML file

```xml
<?xml version="1.0" encoding="UTF-8" ?>
<library>
  <url>http://www.google.com/books?uid=14093248889147761860</url>
  <books>
    <book>
      <id>u7F6AAAACAAJ</id>
      <url>http://www.google.com/books?id=u7F6AAAACAAJ</url>
      <title>13 Bullets: A Vampire Tale</title>
      <contributor>David Wellington</contributor>
      <identifier>
        <type>ISBN</type>
        <value>0307381439</value>
      </identifier>
    </book>
    <book>
      <id>UHJ9AAAACAAJ</id>
      <url>http://www.google.com/books?id=UHJ9AAAACAAJ</url>
      <title>Triple Zero</title>
      <contributor>Karen Traviss</contributor>
      <identifier>
        <type>ISBN</type>
        <value>0345490096</value>
      </identifier>
    </book>
    <book>
      <id>BZQEAAAACAAJ</id>
```

Editor | Preview | Output | Split View

beginning users, try opening it in Excel. It may take some massaging to get it to do what you need, but it does work fairly well (see Figure 7-50).[10]

- **RSS:**
  The last item in the left column is an RSS link. Behind this link is the URL of the feed for your library, allowing you to receive notifications of any new books added to your library. Naturally, subscribing to your own library would be unnecessary, but providing a link to the feed on your blog or other Web site would allow others to subscribe to your library and keep up to date on what you're adding. Figure 7-51 shows what the feed for my library looks like in Bloglines.

Well, that's it for Google Book Search. Now let's take a look at a similar service, Amazon.com's Search Inside the Book.

AMAZON.COM'S SEARCH INSIDE THE BOOK

Unlike Google Book Search, where you can go to a particular URL to start searching, Search Inside the Book is much more integrated into the whole Amazon.com user experience. Basic information on how it works can be found at www.amazon.com/Search-Inside-Book-Books/B?ie=UTF8&node=10197021. You start by searching for a particular book and then discover whether Search Inside the Book is available on a case-by-case basis.

Let's again use *Alexander Hamilton* by Ron Chernow as our example. Go to the Amazon.com homepage, specify Books for your search, and type in *alexander hamilton*. Figure 7-52 shows that the book I'm seeking is the first result, and superimposed over the top of the book is the "Search Inside" logo. In fact, most of the books on this first page of results feature this option.

After selecting the appropriate title, I'm sent to the book's page and again see the "Search Inside" logo on the book. Before we get to the "Search Inside" interface itself, take a moment to hover your mouse pointer over the dust jacket image. Since "Search

FIGURE 7-50   THE XML FILE OPENED IN MICROSOFT EXCEL

	A	B	C	
1	url	id	url2	title
2	http://www.google.com/books?uid=14093248889147761860	u7F6AAAACAAJ	http://www.google.com/books?id=u7F6AAAACAAJ	13 Bullets: A Vampire
3	http://www.google.com/books?uid=14093248889147761860	UHJ9AAAACAAJ	http://www.google.com/books?id=UHJ9AAAACAAJ	Triple Zero
4	http://www.google.com/books?uid=14093248889147761860	BZQEAAAACAAJ	http://www.google.com/books?id=BZQEAAAACAAJ	History 101
5	http://www.google.com/books?uid=14093248889147761860	LckHAAAACAAJ	http://www.google.com/books?id=LckHAAAACAAJ	The Hour Before Dark
6	http://www.google.com/books?uid=14093248889147761860	msMXHwAACAAJ	http://www.google.com/books?id=msMXHwAACAAJ	In Odd We Trust
7	http://www.google.com/books?uid=14093248889147761860	dgMuJifleIMC	http://www.google.com/books?id=dgMuJifleIMC	Down and Out in the N
8	http://www.google.com/books?uid=14093248889147761860	dgMuJifleIMC	http://www.google.com/books?id=dgMuJifleIMC	Down and Out in the N
9	http://www.google.com/books?uid=14093248889147761860	dgMuJifleIMC	http://www.google.com/books?id=dgMuJifleIMC	Down and Out in the N
10	http://www.google.com/books?uid=14093248889147761860	dgMuJifleIMC	http://www.google.com/books?id=dgMuJifleIMC	Down and Out in the N
11	http://www.google.com/books?uid=14093248889147761860	CYc4HgAACAAJ	http://www.google.com/books?id=CYc4HgAACAAJ	The God Delusion
12	http://www.google.com/books?uid=14093248889147761860	CYc4HgAACAAJ	http://www.google.com/books?id=CYc4HgAACAAJ	The God Delusion
13	http://www.google.com/books?uid=14093248889147761860	CYc4HgAACAAJ	http://www.google.com/books?id=CYc4HgAACAAJ	The God Delusion
14	http://www.google.com/books?uid=14093248889147761860	tG9zVRNTb4sC	http://www.google.com/books?id=tG9zVRNTb4sC	Everything is Miscellar
15	http://www.google.com/books?uid=14093248889147761860	tG9zVRNTb4sC	http://www.google.com/books?id=tG9zVRNTb4sC	Everything is Miscellar
16	http://www.google.com/books?uid=14093248889147761860	tG9zVRNTb4sC	http://www.google.com/books?id=tG9zVRNTb4sC	Everything is Miscellar
17	http://www.google.com/books?uid=14093248889147761860	tG9zVRNTb4sC	http://www.google.com/books?id=tG9zVRNTb4sC	Everything is Miscellar
18	http://www.google.com/books?uid=14093248889147761860	tG9zVRNTb4sC	http://www.google.com/books?id=tG9zVRNTb4sC	Everything is Miscellar
19	http://www.google.com/books?uid=14093248889147761860	tG9zVRNTb4sC	http://www.google.com/books?id=tG9zVRNTb4sC	Everything is Miscellar
20	http://www.google.com/books?uid=14093248889147761860	Rft9GQAACAAJ	http://www.google.com/books?id=Rft9GQAACAAJ	Presentation Zen: sim
21	http://www.google.com/books?uid=14093248889147761860	Rft9GQAACAAJ	http://www.google.com/books?id=Rft9GQAACAAJ	Presentation Zen: sim
22	http://www.google.com/books?uid=14093248889147761860	Rft9GQAACAAJ	http://www.google.com/books?id=Rft9GQAACAAJ	Presentation Zen: sim
23	http://www.google.com/books?uid=14093248889147761860	te5iAAAACAAJ	http://www.google.com/books?id=te5iAAAACAAJ	XHTML and CSS Essent
24	http://www.google.com/books?uid=14093248889147761860	VN9AAAAACAAJ	http://www.google.com/books?id=VN9AAAAACAAJ	Shadowfires
25	http://www.google.com/books?uid=14093248889147761860	2DhZAAAACAAJ	http://www.google.com/books?id=2DhZAAAACAAJ	The History of the Hob
26	http://www.google.com/books?uid=14093248889147761860	XMOXAAAACAAJ	http://www.google.com/books?id=XMOXAAAACAAJ	The History of the Hob

Sheet1 / Sheet2 / Sheet3

Figure 7-51   **My library feed in Bloglines**

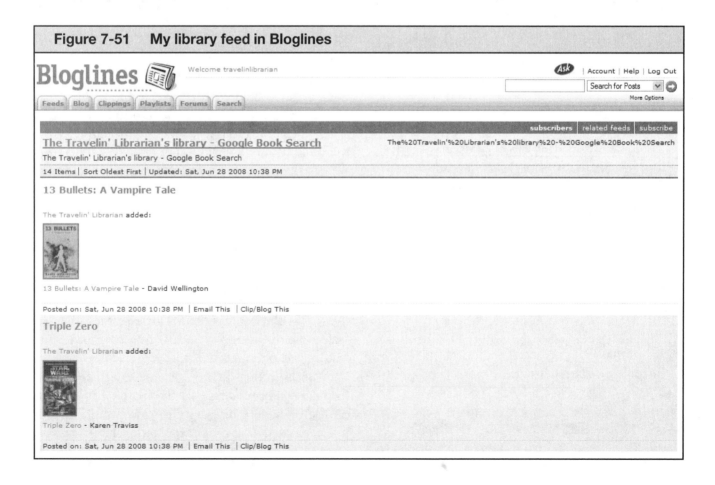

Figure 7-52   The search results showing titles with "search inside" available

Inside" is available for this title, we'll be presented with a window containing related options, as shown in Figure 7-53.

In this particular case, since we're not viewing the page of the available edition of this title, the options are labeled "Inside Another Edition of this Book." Don't worry; in our case, this is close enough. Another example would be if the hardcover is searchable but you're on the page for the mass-market paperback. If you're on the page for the exact edition, this window will be labeled "Inside This Book."

Clicking on any of these links will take you directly to that particular item for the book within the "Search Inside" interface. I cover each of these in turn within that interface next. Click on the book cover and you'll be taken to the "Search Inside" interface for this title, as shown in Figure 7-54.

First, let's close the notice that we're looking at the "Hardcover Edition (2004) from Penguin Press" instead of the bargain edition (which is exactly the same book). To do this, click the "x" in the upper right corner of the notice. This gets it out of our way for the rest of this chapter.

As with Google Book Search, the amount of text varies from work to work. Unlike Google Book Search, Amazon.com displays content only from books that are in the public domain or for which the publisher has granted permission. Additionally, you can "upgrade" a book you've purchased from Amazon.com for "online reading." If you have done this, and providing this feature is available on a particular title, you will then have full access and full searchability of the content. Here I'll be working with a book whose content is partially available by permission of the publisher.

As you can see in Figure 7-54, the interface is divided into five basic sections: the Amazon Online Reader toolbar across the top, book information, search and navigation on the left, and images of the book's content, which takes up the majority of the

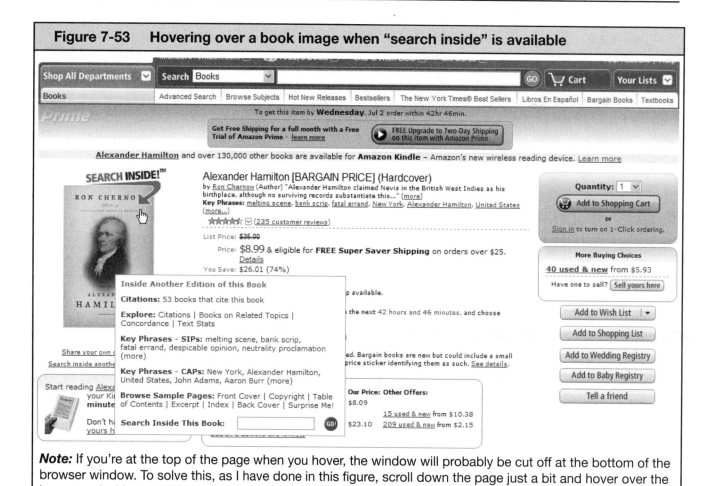

Figure 7-53   Hovering over a book image when "search inside" is available

Note: If you're at the top of the page when you hover, the window will probably be cut off at the bottom of the browser window. To solve this, as I have done in this figure, scroll down the page just a bit and hover over the image again. You should now see the whole window of options.

screen. I'll walk you through the features of each of these sections but in a more logical order than they're presented on the screen.

Book Information

The blue box at the top of the left column contains basic information about the book you're viewing. Here you'll find a thumbnail of the book's cover, the book's price, links for "Add to Cart" and one-click ordering (if you're signed in), as well as information about the availability and pricing of used copies (see Figure 7-55).

Navigation

Basic navigation within a book is very simple. When you're looking at the cover of the book, find the gray vertical bar with a right-pointing triangle along the right side of the page. Click this to go to the next page. As soon as you're on the next page, a similar

gray bar with a left-pointing triangle will appear along the left side of the page. This is what you click to go to the previous page. When you're on the last page of a book, typically the back cover, no next page bar will be available. Figure 7-56 shows a page with both navigation bars displayed.

You can also quickly navigate to preselected portions of the text via the links located in the "Sections" box in the left column (see Figure 7-57). The links available will vary, but typical links include "Front Cover," "Front Flap," "Table of Contents," "Copyright," "Excerpt," "Index," "Back Flap," and "Back Cover." There is also a "Surprise Me!" link that will take you to a random page in the book.

A few additional navigational options appear under the "View" drop-down menu located in the Amazon Online Reader toolbar across the top of the page. The options are single page or continuous, zoom in or out, annotations on page, and left

Figure 7-54   "Search inside this book" for *Alexander Hamilton* by Ron Chernow

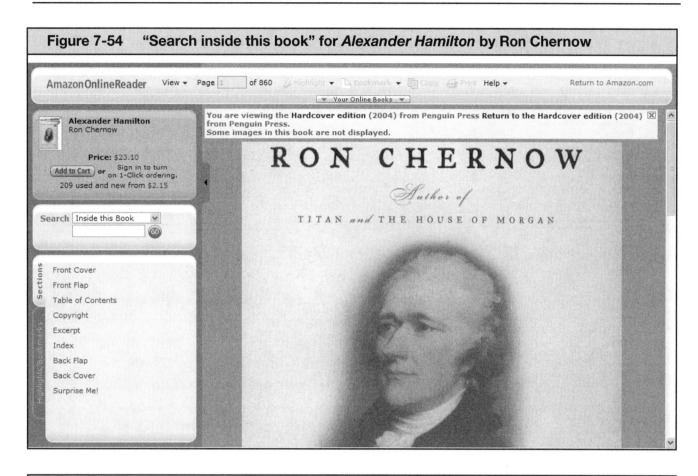

Figure 7-55   Book information

Figure 7-56   A book's page with both navigation bars displayed

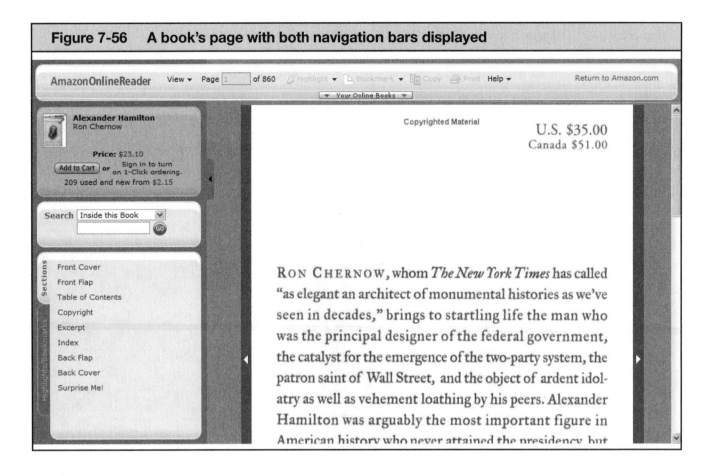

panels. To the right of the "View" menu is a "Page X of Y" option in which you can enter a specific page number you'd like to display.

- **Page X of Y:**
  This area shows you the page number of the current page along with the total number of pages in the book. Unless you've "upgraded" the book for online access, this area is nonfunctional. I'll cover its functionality later on.

- **Single page or continuous:**
  By default, images are displayed in a page-by-page interface. Selecting the "continuous" option here switches the page display to one similar to the one used in Google Book Search. Scrolling through the book is then done via dragging up or down the slider-bar now located to the right of the image, as shown in Figure 7-58.

- **Zoom in or out:**
  The zoom in or out function allows you to increase

or decrease the size of the displayed image. There are two levels of zoom, compared to Google Book Search's four. Figure 7-59 shows a page that has been zoomed in.

- **Annotations on page:**
  By default, this option is turned on and causes any highlighted text or annotations you've added to be displayed. You can turn this off only for books you've "upgraded," that is, paid to have online access. With paid access you can also add highlighted sections or bookmarks. I'll discuss this in more detail as well in a little bit.

- **Left panels:**
  Unchecking this option will hide the left column that includes the book information, search interface, and sections area. Doing so creates more room on the screen for the book images to be displayed (see Figure 7-60). The same result can also be accomplished by clicking the left-pointing triangle located to the right of the book information area.

Figure 7-57 "Sections" navigation

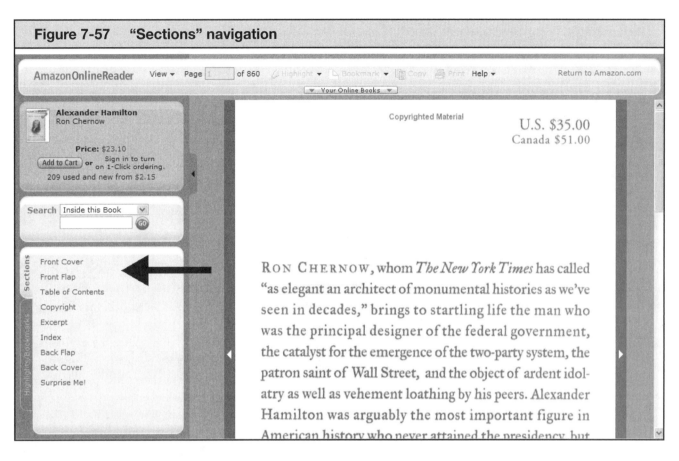

Figure 7-58 The slider bar in the "continuous" view

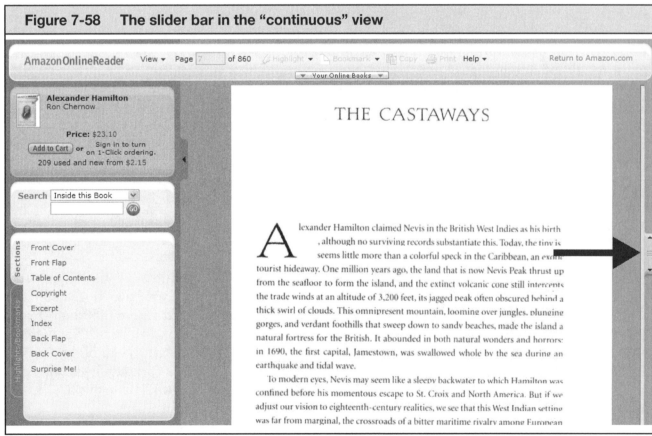

Figure 7-59   Zoomed view

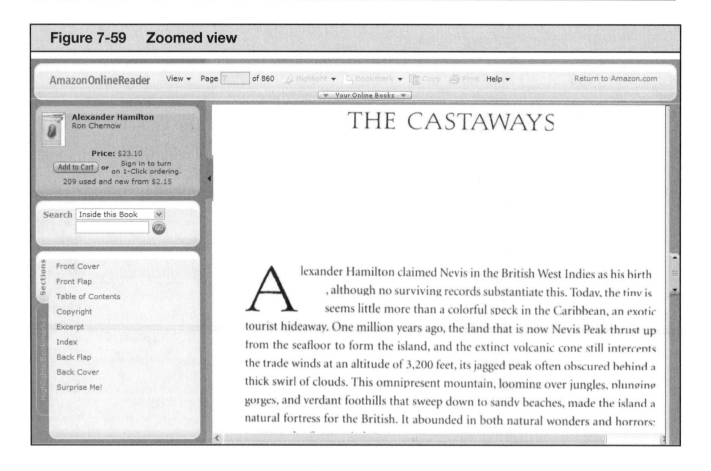

Searching

The search field located in the search area in the middle left of the screen (Figure 7-61) defaults to searching the content of the book you're currently viewing. Should you wish to do so, you can search Amazon.com's book selection, all of Amazon.com's products, or the Web via the A9 search engine. I'll be sticking to the default "Inside this Book" search.

For ease of comparison, I'm going to perform the same search I did for this book in Google Book Search by typing in *navy* and clicking the "go" button. The results will be displayed in the main portion of the screen, overwriting the book image, as shown in Figure 7-62.

Figure 7-62 shows 31 results, of which the first 10 are displayed. As with Google Book Search, results are displayed in the order in which they are found within the book. Each result has with it the page number, hyperlinked to that page's image. Following the page number is a two-line excerpt of the text containing my search keyword(s) in bold. At the top and bottom of the results page is a "Return to

the book" link, with links to the rest of your search results also at the bottom. Clicking on the link to a result page will display that page, but unfortunately without highlighting my keyword, requiring me to read the page to find my keyword instead of being able to easily spot the reference.

To return to your list of results, click the "Back to search results" link that now appears in the search area on the left (see Figure 7-63). Be careful here—clicking your browser's back button will take you back to the book's Amazon.com selling page.

Tools

"Search Inside" has a few useful tools. Unfortunately, they are available only if you have "upgraded" your book for online access. To see if you have any books that fall into this category, click on the "Your Online Books" button at the bottom center of the Amazon Online Reader toolbar. I currently have one book available for online access.[11] I'll use this book as my example for the rest of this chapter.

Once you've selected an upgraded book, you'll

Figure 7-60   Left panels display turned off

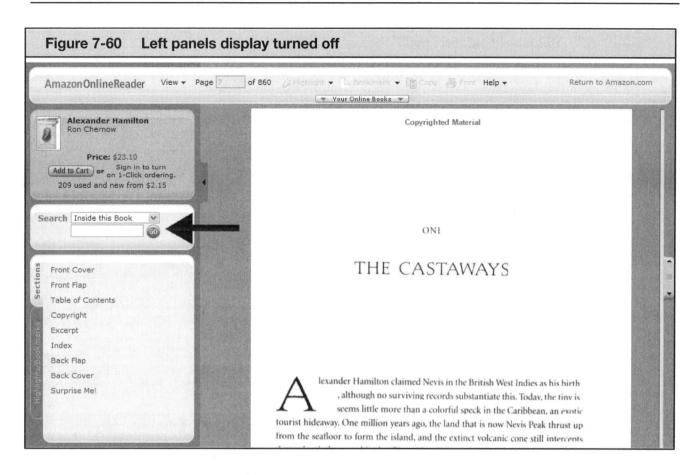

Figure 7-61   The search interface

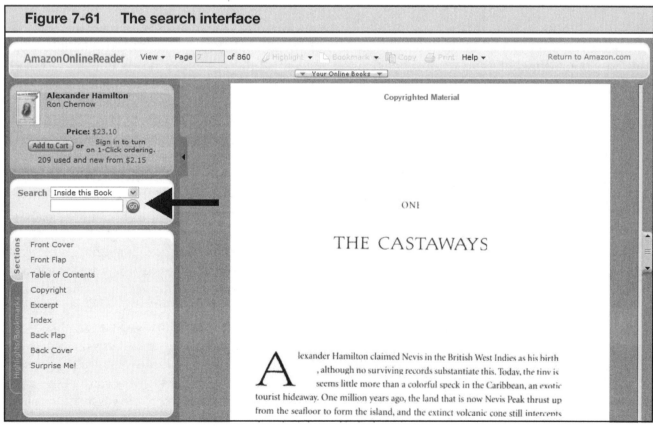

Figure 7-62   Search results for *navy*

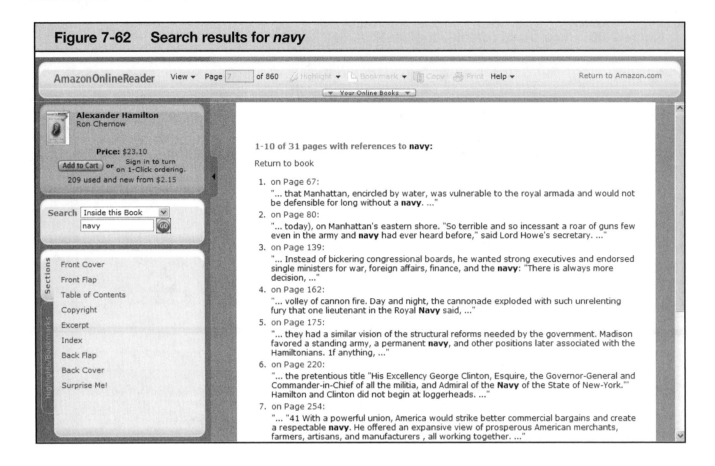

have access to several or all of the following tools: page jumping, highlighting and tagging, bookmarking, copying, and printing. Here are the details of each of these features:

- **Page jumping:**
  Now that you have full access to the book online, you can navigate to a specific page of the text by entering it into the "Page X of Y" field in the toolbar at the top of the window. In Figure 7-64, you can see that I've jumped to page 100 of this 184-page book. Some pages are not exactly "numbered" in this interface. For example, Figure 7-65 shows the page number for this book's copyright page as "Copy of 184."

- **Annotations: Highlighting and tagging:**
  To highlight an important passage, click on the "Highlight" button in the top toolbar. Next, move your cursor to before the first word you wish to highlight, press and hold the left mouse button, and drag your mouse cursor to the end of the last word

in the passage. Once you let up on the mouse button your highlight will appear along with a balloon window into which you can type notes about and assign tags to this passage, as shown in Figure 7-66. You can also reposition the balloon by dragging the top, right, or bottom edges and resize it by dragging the right edge with your mouse. Once you're done adding notes and tags, click the "x" in the balloon's upper right corner to close it. To make the balloon reappear, double-click or right-click on the highlighted passage. Additionally, you can remove highlighted text or make it public, along with associated notes and tags, via the appropriate selected options located under the "Highlight" menu (see Figure 7-67). Last, selecting "Settings" from the "Highlight" menu will give you the ability to change the defaults for the reading mode as well as the left pane. You will be presented with options to change the colors for your annotations, toggle show/hide annotations, and whether annotations should be private or public (see Figure 7-68).

Figure 7-63   The "back to the search results" link

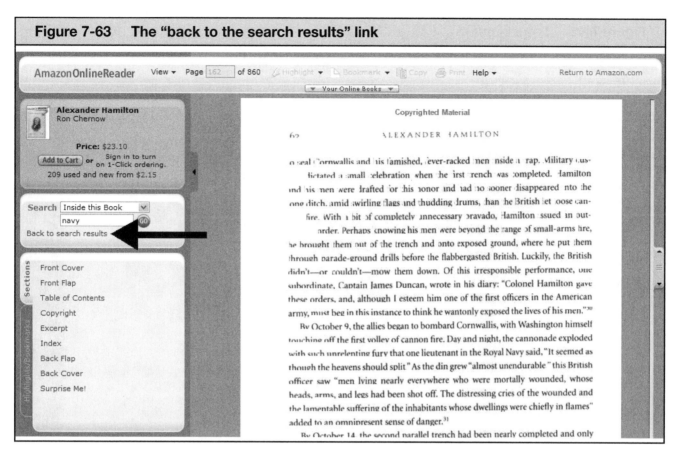

Figure 7-64   Page 100 of 184

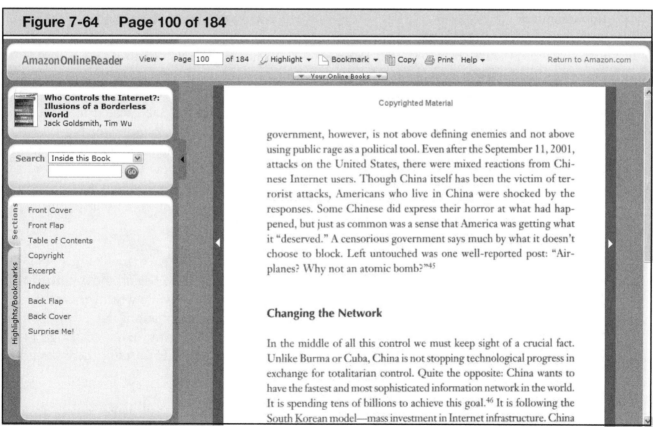

Figure 7-65   Page copy

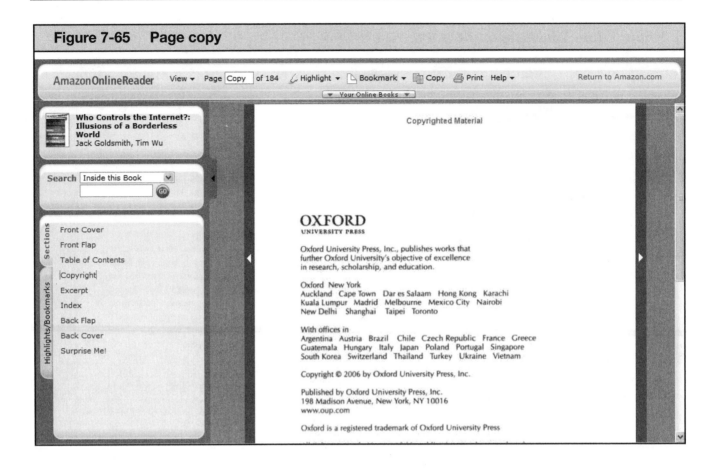

- **Bookmarking:**

  Clicking on the "Bookmark" button adds a bookmark to the page you're currently viewing. When this happens, the upper right corner of the page will "fold" and you'll be presented with a balloon into which you can add notes and tags related to this bookmark (see Figure 7-69). This balloon can be closed and accessed in the same way as the ones associated with annotations. Bookmarks can be removed by choosing "Remove Bookmark" from the Bookmark drop-down menu. Clicking on "Settings" on the Bookmark menu will access the same settings screen as the "Settings" choice on the Highlight menu.

- **Copying:**

  To copy text, select it with your mouse as you would in any regular document and click the "Copy" button. The selected text will be placed into your operating system's clipboard for pasting into another program. Not all books allow copying.

- **Printing:**

  Click the "Print" button to initiate a print job for the book. Using your browser's print button will not work to print the book. Instead you'll receive a printout indicating that you should use this print button instead. Not all books allow printing.[12]

One additional area you'll have access to is the "Highlights/Bookmarks" tab located alongside the "Sections" tab in the left column (see Figure 7-70). Once you've added highlights and/or bookmarks to a book, this area will allow you to see a list of the marks you've left. Also, it will grant you access to any highlights or bookmarks that others have contributed and made public.

PROS AND CONS

In using both Google Book Search and Amazon.com's Search Inside the Book while writing this chapter, I made a few specific observations that I think should be mentioned before we move on. Although I find that both can be extremely useful, there are a few key differences:

- Amazon.com has vastly more content available for searching due to the release of their eBook

Figure 7-66   Adding highlight notes and tags

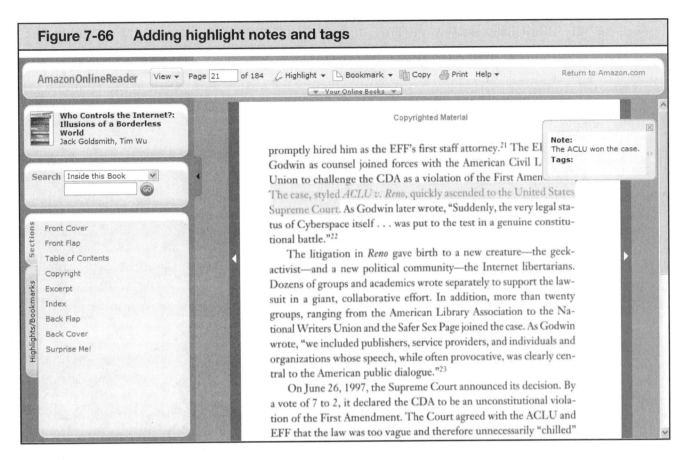

Figure 7-67   The highlight menu

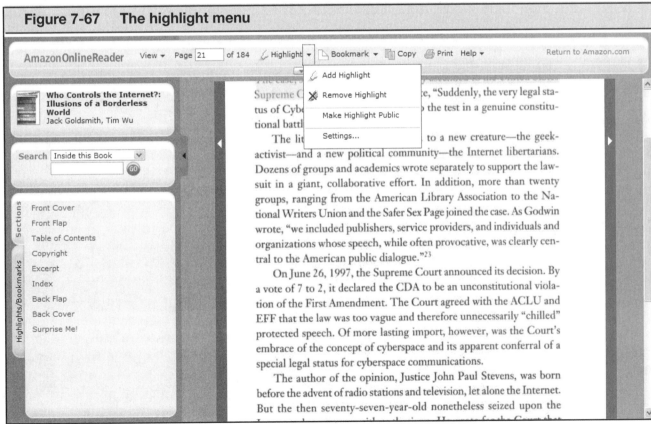

Figure 7-68   Annotations settings

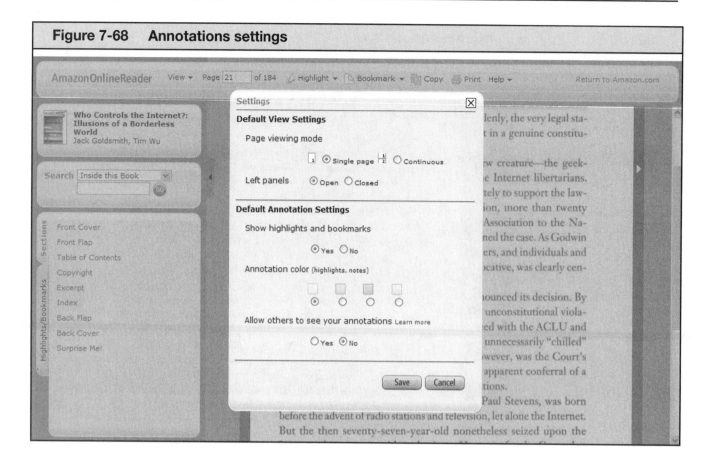

Figure 7-69   Bookmark with associated notes and tags

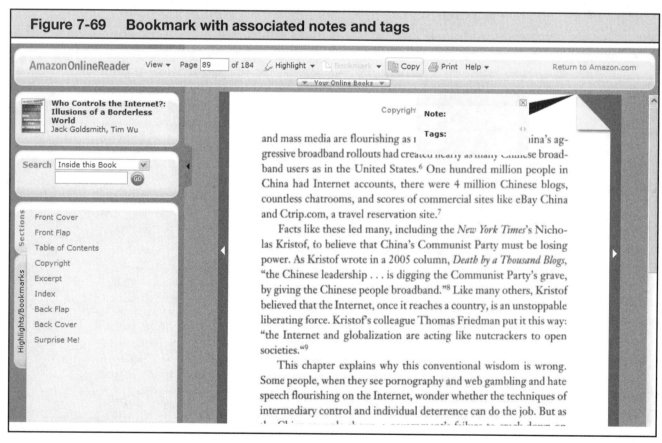

Figure 7-70   Highlights/bookmarks showing "your notes"

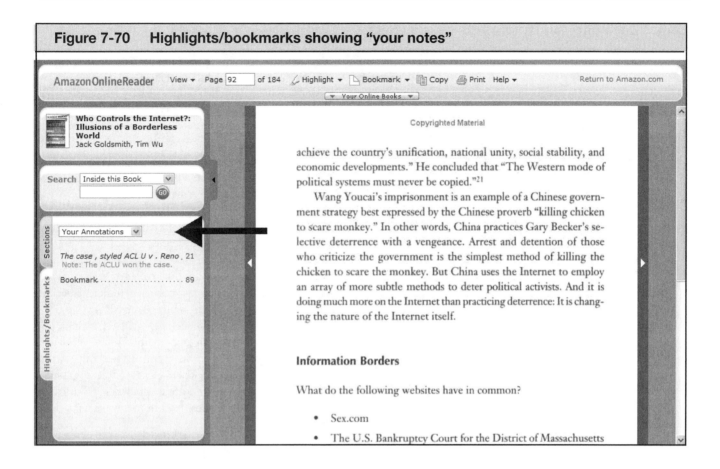

reader, The Kindle, at the end of 2007. As far as I can tell, if a book is available in the Kindle format, the "Search Inside" feature should also be available. However, I did notice that the quality of the images in Amazon was sometimes visibly poorer than for the same ones in Google.

- Google, despite having less full content available, is more user-friendly, in my opinion, due to the user interface: most of the options are displayed on the screen and not hidden under menus and tabs.
- Many of Amazon.com's tools are available only with purchase of the book.
- Google's "My Library" feature is a useful feature that is lacking in Amazon.com. Amazon.com's "Your Online Books" is similar to Google's "My Library" feature but requires paid access, and I recommend avoiding things that cost real dollars.
- Ultimately, as the library program continues, I think that Google will contain more obscure material

while Amazon will continue to focus more on current content.

CONCLUSION

The world of searching for complete content within printed materials is still new. In fact, during the editing process of this book, Microsoft's book searching project called Live Search Books was discontinued.[13] Also, the controversial issue of search versus copyright is ongoing and actively being litigated. The results of lawsuits may determine how this technology evolves. My suggestion is to take advantage of it while we can and hope that such tools continue to be available in the future. In the next chapter, we turn to how to find materials that are considered "no longer online."

EXERCISES

Find a book on a topic that you're interested in and know something about that is available in Google

Book Search and can be searched via Amazon's Search Inside the Book and answer the following questions:

1. Is this book currently in-copyright or in the public domain?
2. How much of the content of the book is available in each? Does one service have more content than the other? Does Amazon require you to purchase online access to the book to see the full content?
3. Perform a keyword search in both systems. Are the results the same or different?
4. Browse through the book using both services. Which interface do you prefer?

Now search for an author you're familiar with in both systems and answer these questions:

1. Is the same number of titles available in both? Is one service missing any significant titles?
2. Are there significant differences in the amount of content available?

NOTES

1. It is not my intention in this chapter to cover any of the controversies over these services. The issues of copyright and fair use have been hotly debated for several years with no end in sight. My purpose is to cover how you can use these tools in your library to assist in your reference duties. Any larger issues should be dealt with in another forum.
2. Google, "Google Book Search: Free Sales and Marketing for Your Titles," https://Books.google.com/partner/.
3. Google, "Library Partners," http://Books.google.com/googlebooks/partners.html.
4. As a collector of small-press books, I've always wondered why no OPAC I've ever encountered as a library patron has allowed me to search based on publisher. I'm sure it's hardly a popular search, but the records have the data, so why can't they be searched?
5. This is the source of the aforementioned controversy. Some authors and publishers claim that this violates copyright while Google claims their snippet view is fair use.
6. What I'd prefer is a set of previous/next result icons in the navigation bar. Maybe Google will add this feature in the future.
7. I use LibraryThing extensively and love it. My library is not serious competition in any way other than the access to the book's full text when available.
8. It baffles me that authors are not hyperlinked within Google Book Search. At a minimum, inking them to a search on that name wouldn't be so difficult.
9. Here's another case where Google could do a little better. Why not allow labels to be tracked across accounts? I'd like to be able to click on my creative commons label and see a list of books that others have similarly labeled.
10. The resulting Excel worksheet will typically contain one row for each title for each label the title has. If a title has three labels, it will appear in the worksheet three times, each on its own row. The key to cleaning this up (assuming the labels aren't the important data you need) is to use Excel's "Remove Duplicates" feature and instruct it to look for duplicates in the "title" column.
11. The ability to "upgrade" books varies from publisher to publisher and book to book. If you have no books available, the "Your Online Books" area will give you a link to see which of your previous purchases are available for upgrading. Of course, you will need to pay for this upgrade, and the cost varies widely. Due to the cost involved, I hesitate to cover this in detail, but you may decide that $3.19 (what I paid for upgrading the one book I have available) might just be worth it to get access to these features.
12. You can still take a screenshot of your screen and print the resulting image, but this is hardly an efficient way of printing a whole book, though it could be useful for printing brief passages.
13. Live Search, "Book Search Winding Down," May 23, 2008, http://Blogs.msdn.com/livesearch/Archive/2008/05/23/Book-search-winding-down.aspx.

Chapter 8

Google Cache, the Wayback Machine, and Wikipedia: Searching the Past

INTRODUCTION

There comes a time in every searcher's life when the current version of a page, assuming the page you're looking for exists at all, is not going to answer your question. For example, you have a link to an online newspaper article that a colleague sent you a month ago and you've recently rediscovered it buried in your inbox. When you click on the link, the newspaper's Web site informs you that the article you've requested "no longer exists" or has been moved into the "subscriber area" and you are asked for your credit card number. Another example would be a case in which a patron is interested in the initial reactions to an event that happened weeks or even months ago—not a piece that looks back, but a source from the day the event occurred.

To handle both of these types of questions, let's take a look at two easily missed resources, Google Cache and the Wayback Machine, and one often overlooked tool, Wikipedia's history function.

GOOGLE CACHE

What many Internet users don't realize is that every time Google indexes a document it keeps a copy of that document, preserving that document's look and

---

Google Cache Quick Steps

Step one: Perform a Google search.
Step two: Click the "Cached" link (at the bottom of the result) to view the version of the page Google most recently indexed.

---

content in virtual perpetuity. Some question what Google will do with all of this preserved content in the long run and the potential copyright and privacy implications of keeping all of these copies, but for our purposes, we're glad they're doing what they're doing.

The unfortunate part is that Google is allowing us to access only the most recent copy, not the complete archive. (I believe this is how they're avoiding the potential copyright issues.) The copy that they're allowing us to access is known as the "cached" copy. Most of you will be familiar with the concept of a cache as it relates to your browser: a copy of a page stored on your hard drive that can be retrieved faster than a live copy from the Internet. In this case, the concept is very similar.

The issue with a search engine such as Google is that when a user performs a search against the database of content, what the user is actually searching against is what that content was *when the content was indexed*, not what the content is, necessarily, on the live Web site at the moment. In other words, when you search Google or any other search engine, you're searching a moment of time that does not necessarily reflect reality at the time you perform the search.

What causes this problem is the constantly changing content of the Internet. The rise of Web 2.0 and the participatory Web only increases this problem. For example, how many times have you done a search only to find that, despite Google providing a particular Web page as a good match, the live page doesn't have the content you're seeking? This can happen for several reasons, but the one that's important here is that the page's author may have changed the content since Google last indexed it.

Let's try looking at it this way:

January 1	A Web page is created. The content of the page contains the word "Iraq."
January 15	Google indexes the page's content, including the word "Iraq."
February 1	The page's author edits the page's content removing the word "Iraq."
February 2	A user searches Google for the word "Iraq" and finds a match pointing to the Web page in question. The user clicks on the link and retrieves the page. The user reads the whole page but finds the word "Iraq" nowhere on the page.

This situation can be solved by Google Cache. Let's take a look at a simple example of Google Cache in action. Figure 8-1 shows the results of a simple Google search for *cnn*.

If I click on the CNN.com link at the beginning of the first result, I will get the *current* version of the CNN homepage, as shown in Figure 8-2. As you can see, it was last updated at 12:48 p.m. EST, Saturday, March 1, 2008.

However, if I go back to the list of Google results and click on the "Cached" link in the results listing, then I get the page in Figure 8-3. In this case, I'm looking at a CNN homepage from 8:54 a.m. EST, Thursday, February 28, 2008, as shown in the CNN content, that was indexed by Google on February 28, 2008, at 10:41 a.m. EST, as shown in the large notification by Google at the top of the page.

The purpose of the large box at the top of the cached page is to make it perfectly clear to the user that this is not the live version of the page and that any or all of the information might be incorrect. However, this is the version of the page that you're actually searching against when you search Google: content that is days old. I'm not saying that Google is worthless once you understand that it, and every other search engine, is not allowing you to search the current live content—the ability to search the Internet as it exists at any particular moment is

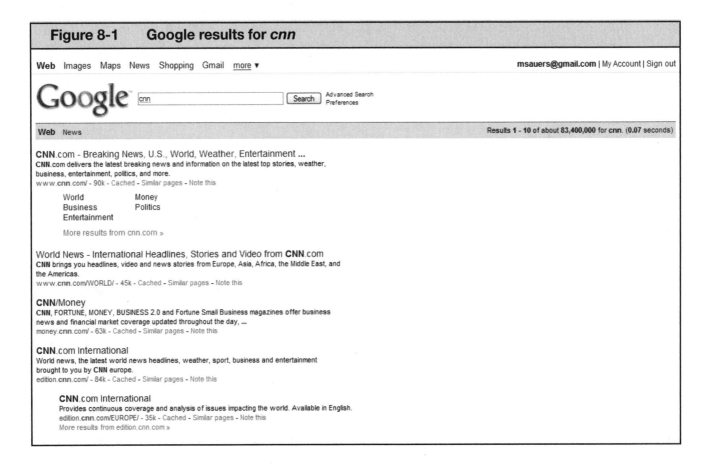

Figure 8-1   Google results for *cnn*

Web Images Maps News Shopping Gmail more ▼   msauers@gmail.com | My Account | Sign out

Google [cnn   ] [Search] Advanced Search
                                    Preferences

Web News   Results 1 - 10 of about 83,400,000 for cnn. (0.07 seconds)

CNN.com - Breaking News, U.S., World, Weather, Entertainment ...
CNN.com delivers the latest breaking news and information on the latest top stories, weather, business, entertainment, politics, and more.
www.**cnn**.com/ - 90k - Cached - Similar pages - Note this

    World   Money
    Business   Politics
    Entertainment

    More results from cnn.com »

World News - International Headlines, Stories and Video from **CNN**.com
CNN brings you headlines, video and news stories from Europe, Asia, Africa, the Middle East, and the Americas.
www.**cnn**.com/WORLD/ - 45k - Cached - Similar pages - Note this

CNN/Money
CNN, FORTUNE, MONEY, BUSINESS 2.0 and Fortune Small Business magazines offer business news and financial market coverage updated throughout the day, ...
money.**cnn**.com/ - 63k - Cached - Similar pages - Note this

CNN.com International
World news, the latest world news headlines, weather, sport, business and entertainment brought to you by **CNN** europe.
edition.**cnn**.com/ - 84k - Cached - Similar pages - Note this

    CNN.com International
    Provides continuous coverage and analysis of issues impacting the world. Available in English.
    edition.**cnn**.com/EUROPE/ - 35k - Cached - Similar pages - Note this
    More results from edition.cnn.com »

Figure 8-2   The live CNN homepage

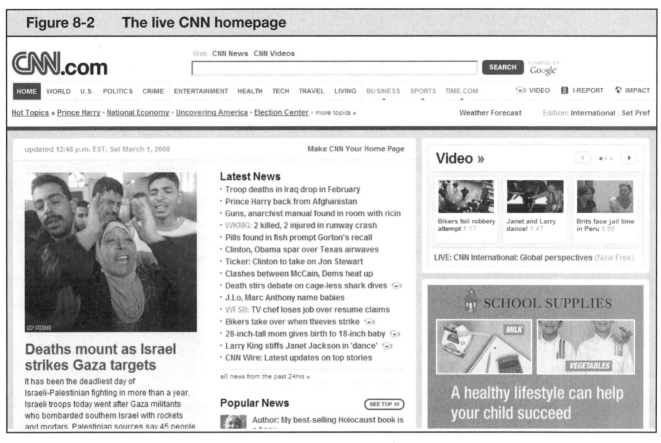

Figure 8-3   The cached copy of the CNN homepage

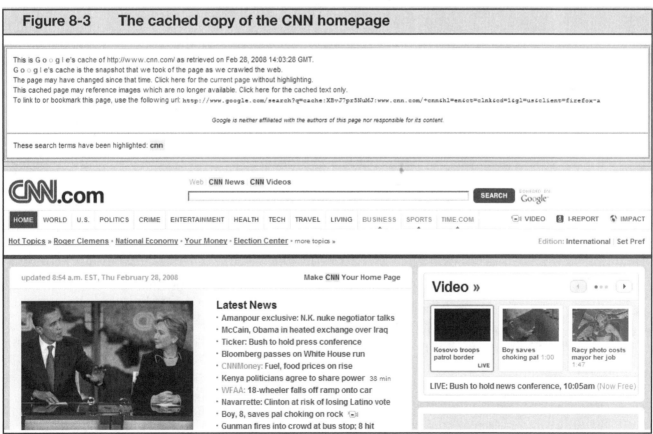

technically impossible. What I am showing you is that, with Google Cache, you do have the ability to peer back into the past just a little bit.

You may also be asking yourself, Why not just go to CNN.com in the first place and search its archives? Good question, but that assumes one of two things: either (1) you are familiar with CNN as a site and know that it has a searchable archive, or (2) your intention all along was to search the content of CNN.com. Remember, I'm using CNN as an example, but the point of Google Cache applies to other sites too.

With assumption 1 you might be searching a site with which you're not as familiar. Do you know that *somenewssite.com* has an easily searchable archive? Maybe, maybe not. As for assumption 2, you may just be searching Google for a particular topic and CNN is one of the retrieved results and you'd like to take a peek at what Google's offering before going into the site and searching its archive. In the end, you have to keep in mind that Google Cache is only going to show you the most recently indexed version of a page that Google has in its archive. If you need to go further back in time, such as months or even years, then the Wayback Machine is the tool you need.

THE WAYBACK MACHINE

Consider two more scenarios in which the ability to look back into the Web's past would be very useful: With the advent of blogs, Web pages more often contain links to articles from other Web sites of interest to the blogger. Since blogs are plentiful, they are being indexed by the big search engines, and many times the results of your search will include blog posts on your topic. As reliable or unreliable as you may view blog posts on a topic, if that post contains a link to

---

Wayback Machine Quick Steps

Step one: Find the URL of the page for which you wish to see the history.

Step two: Enter that URL into the Wayback Machine's search box.

Step three: Click "Take Me Back."

Step four: Choose the date you wish to view from the results.

---

a "more reliable" resource (an article from the *New York Times*, for example), you can count the result as a success. Problems arise when that link points to a Web page that no longer exists. Now what do you do? Or, how about the traditional school project on what happened on the day you were born? There's always been the traditional route of reading the newspaper and the more recent ability to look at "this day in history" Web sites, but how could a child look to see what the headlines were on MSNBC or CNN on that particular day? How could you possibly search for content that existed years ago? In either case, you could take the URL of the page you're trying to find and head off to the Wayback Machine (www.archive. org/web/web.php), whose homepage is shown in Figure 8-4.

The Wayback Machine, named after the time travel device used by the cartoon characters Mr. Peabody and his boy Sherman on the *Rocky & Bullwinkle Show*, is a service of the Internet Archive (http://www. archive.org). The Internet Archive's mission is to create a searchable representative archive of Internet content, and it has been building this archive since 1996. The Wayback Machine is the name of the search engine that allows you to access the content of this archive.

To use the Wayback Machine, just enter the URL of the page you wish to find and click the "Take Me Back" button. Assuming the page you're looking for is in the archive (the more popular and well-known the site, the more likely it is to be included), you'll be presented with a list of dates on which an archived copy of the page was made. Figure 8-5 shows the results of the *Lincoln Journal Star*'s homepage as searched for on March 1, 2008.

As you can see, the results are sorted by date, and results that are duplicates of previously archived copies have been removed. In other words, by default, only the changed versions are shown. In some cases, to see every archived version, you'll be presented with a "See all" link near the upper left corner of the screen. Major news sites will have an increased number of results available starting shortly after September 11, 2001, in an attempt to archive the vast amounts of reporting related to those events.

To see the page as it appeared on a particular day, just click on the link for the desired date. If the exact

Figure 8-4   The Wayback Machine homepage

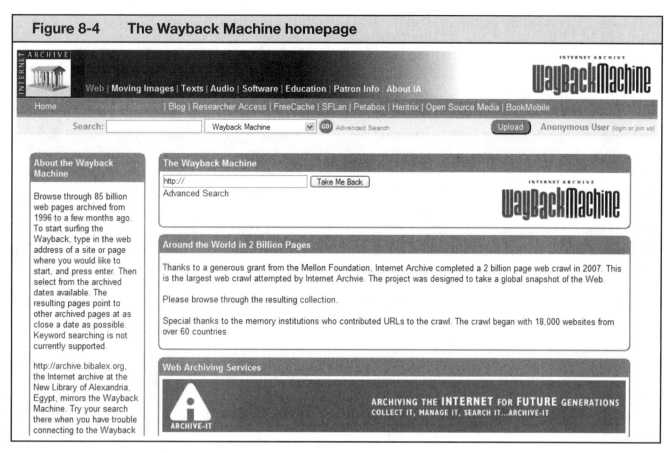

Figure 8-5   Wayback Machine results for *http://www.journalstar.com/*

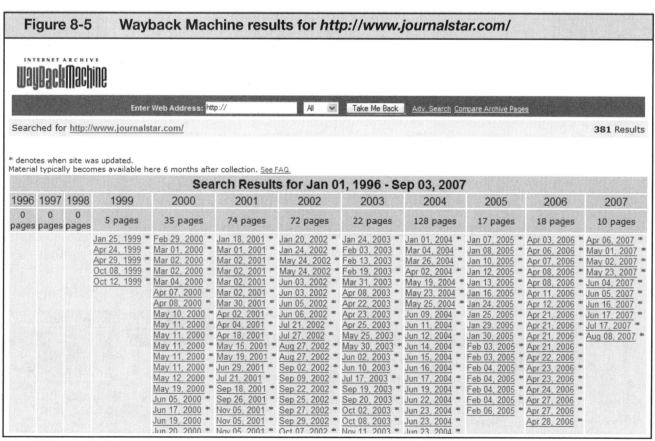

date doesn't appear, click on the date most closely preceding yours. This will be the closest match and, in cases with more heavily indexed pages (such as in Figure 8-5), will most likely match the content of the page you're seeking. Figure 8-6 shows the *Lincoln Journal Star*'s homepage on July 6, 2000. In most cases, the links on this page will work but will take you to the version of the closest page hosted by the Wayback Machine. For example, clicking on the "Opinion" link on this older page will take you to the July 3, 2000, version of the paper's Opinion page. In many cases, you can navigate for at least several pages, but be aware that you will eventually run into broken links, and be sure to note the date of any page you view.

One word of warning: unlike pages from Google Cache, which clearly indicate at the top of the page that you're viewing an archived version, pages displayed via the Wayback Machine can be identified only by looking at the URL of the page. Each will start with "http://web.archive.org/." Also, not all of the images from the original versions of the pages (most usually advertisements) will always appear on

archived versions. If you look again at Figure 8-6, you'll see the lack of images in the boxes on the page. Generally, since the advertisements are what is missing, this shouldn't cause your patrons to complain.

WIKIPEDIA PAGE HISTORIES

In Chapter 4 I briefly mentioned that wikis keep every version of their pages and allow users to not only see all of those versions but also compare dif-

---

Wikipedia Histories Quick Steps

Step one: Find the article you're interested in.

Step two: Click the "History" tab at the top of the page.

Step three: Choose the previous version you wish to view by clicking the date/time of that version.

Step four: Step through the page's history via the "← Older version" and "Newer version →" links.

Step five: Use the radio buttons on the history page to select two versions to compare to view the differences between those two versions.

Figure 8-6   The *Lincoln Journal Star* homepage on July 6, 2000

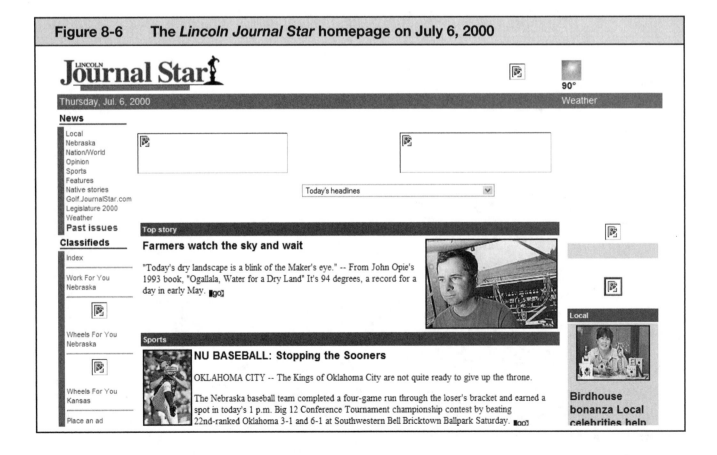

ferent versions to see what changes have been made. Here is where I cover this in more detail using the Wikipedia article for the London Bombings of July 7, 2005.

Figure 8-7 shows the page as it appeared at the time of this writing.[1] The link for accessing the history of a Wikipedia article can be found at the top of the page. Figure 8-8 shows the first history page for this article, containing information on the latest 50 edits to the article.

Each edit will contain the following information:

- The date and time that the edit was made.
- The username or IP address of the person who made the edit.
- The name of the section of the page that was edited. If nothing is listed, this means that the editor made changes to the whole article instead of editing a subsection of the article.
- A brief description of the changes that were made. This is optional and set by the editor, so sometimes

there will be little to no explanation of what was changed.

On the history page you have many options for how to proceed. Here are the options that you'll use the most often:

- To see the article as it appeared on a particular date at a particular time, click on the time/date link from the list (e.g., "23:51, 4 June 2006").
- To change the number of edits listed per screen choose from the (20 | 50 | 100 | 250 | 500) list.
- Click on "previous 50" or "next 50" as appropriate to move back or forward through the list of edits. If you've changed the number of listed edits shown, the numbers in these links will change appropriately.
- Use the "Latest" and "Earliest" links to move to the top or bottom of the list.

Stepping through History

Figure 8-9 shows the very first version of the example

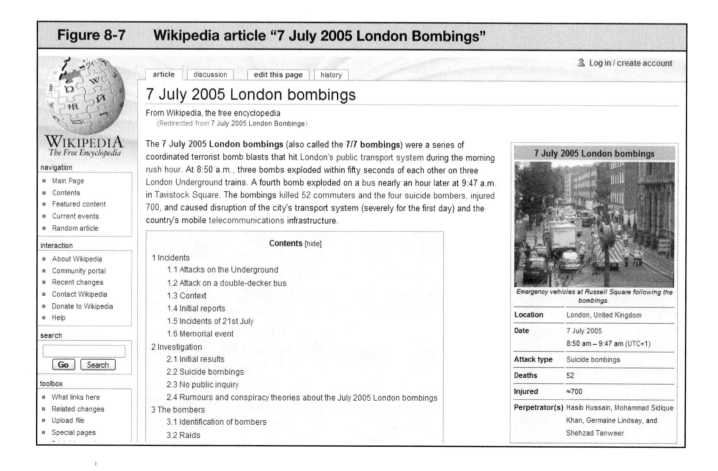

Figure 8-7   Wikipedia article "7 July 2005 London Bombings"

| Figure 8-8 | The first history page for the "7 July 2005 London Bombings" article |

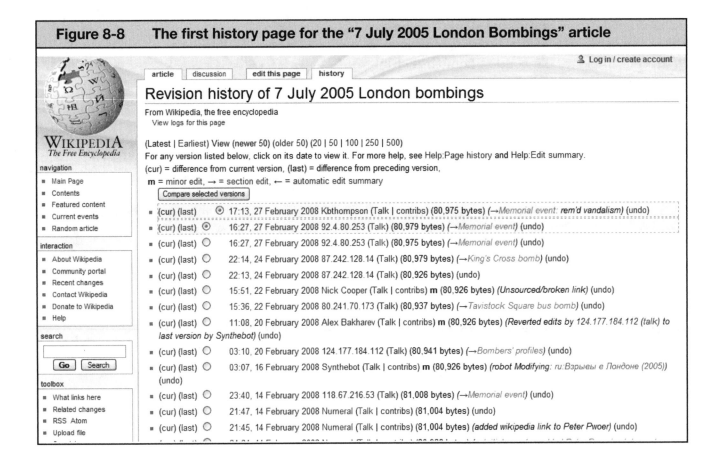

article. I found this by going to the article's history page, clicking on the "Earliest" link, scrolling to the bottom of the page, and clicking on the "09:18, 7 July 2005" link.

In Figure 8-9, I've circled an area of links in the upper left corner of the page. The "view current version" link will always take you back to the current live version of the article. What's more important here are the "← Older version" and "Newer version →" links. Clicking on these links allows you to move, step by step, through the versions of the article. This is a great way to see how an article develops. Using an example such as this, a current event for which the information changed every few minutes, can be an amazing way to show people the power of a resource such as Wikipedia.

Comparing Two Specific Versions

What stepping through an article, as interesting as that is, will not show you is exactly what changes were made between two different versions. Granted, in the early versions of any article, it will be easy

to spot these changes. However, as the article gets longer, the edits can be hidden within a multiscreen document, and the edits themselves may become more subtle. This is where a wiki's ability to compare two versions of an article comes into play.

As a simple example, I looked at the history of this article and noticed that on February 24, 2008, a user from IP address 87.242.128-14 made an edit to the article section on the Kings Cross bomb but did not leave a description of that edit. So, as shown in Figure 8-10, I've selected the "22:13, 24 February 2008" version of the article and the "22:14, 24 February 2008" version. To compare these two versions, I then clicked on the "Compare selected versions" button. Figure 8-11 shows the results of this comparison.

What you can see here is that the later version of the article is displayed but with a new section at the top of the page highlighting the change that was made. This is done mostly through color, so it is not as obvious here in the book. In this example the content:

Figure 8-9 The first version of the "7 July 2005 London Bombings" article highlighting the step-through links

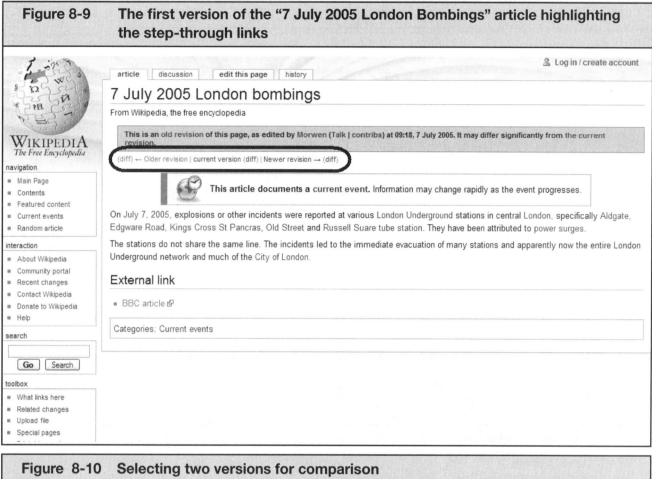

Figure 8-10 Selecting two versions for comparison

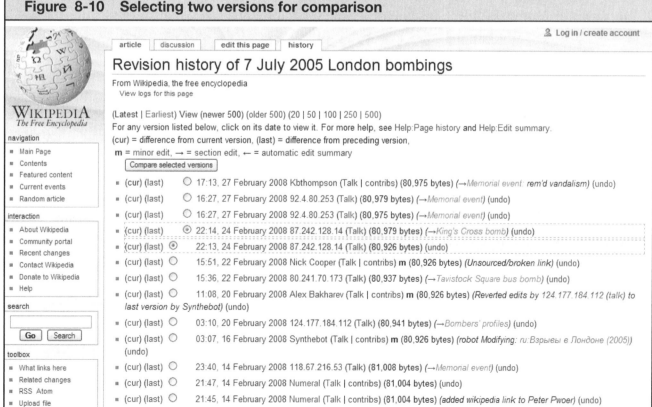

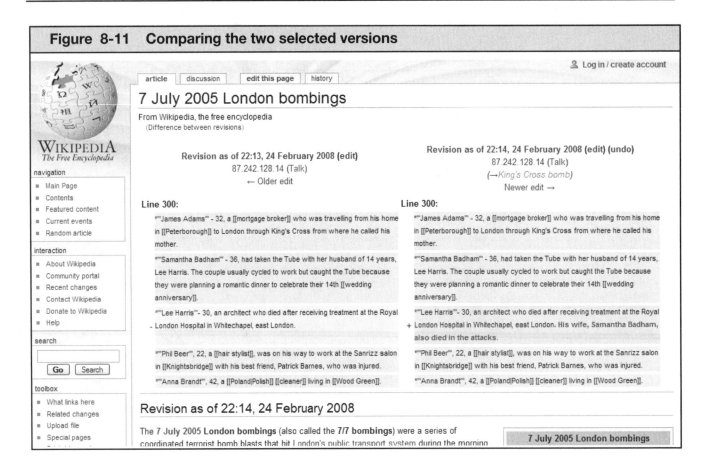

Figure 8-11   Comparing the two selected versions

*"'Lee Harris'"–30, an architect who died after receiving treatment at the Royal London Hospital in Whitechapel, east London.

was changed to:

*"'Lee Harris'"– 30, an architect who died after receiving treatment at the Royal London Hospital in Whitechapel, east London. *His wife, Samantha Badham, also died in the attacks.*

The change is the addition of the information about Samantha Badham.

Additionally, you can continue to step through the changes in this format (with changes highlighted) by using the "← Older edit" and "Newer edit →" links found at the top of the two columns. As with all pages in Wikipedia, errors can exist, and most likely errors have been introduced, whether intentional or not, within the page's history. Whenever you decide to cite a Wikipedia page, it would behoove you to take a look back (or forward) through the page's history to see if the current information is considered

"correct." In some cases, the most immediate or next version may be the "better" version.

CONCLUSION

This chapter examined three tools that you can use to look into the Web's past. With Google Cache, we are able to look at the recent past, most specifically to see the version of a page on which Google is actually basing its search results. With the Wayback Machine, we are able to look at snapshots of pages that have changed over the past several years to retrieve information that may no longer exist on the site itself. Last, with Wikipedia's history feature, we are able to take a step-by-step approach to seeing how articles have changed and developed over time and to see what was considered accurate information in a previous time.

As the number of people contributing content online continues to grow, the ever-changing nature of that content will only pick up pace. With tools such as the ones presented in this chapter, you can increase your chances of finding the information you're looking for, even if you missed it the first time around. In the next chapter, we take a look at search from a different angle. How can you make it easier to search other sites without having to go to those sites first?

EXERCISES

1. Search Google for a major and/or local news source. Compare the current version of the site's homepage with Google's cached version. How much time has passed between Google's indexing of the page and now? How much has changed? How would this amount of time and/or change affect a current event search?

2. Search the Wayback Machine for your local newspaper's or television station's homepage. How far back is it indexed? How often is an archived copy made? Compare this to a search for another local news source. How might the Wayback Machine help with student questions regarding the events of their birthday or other specific date?

3. Search Wikipedia for your city/town and view the article's history. How long ago was the article created? How many changes have been made since? Do any particular users stick out as regular editors of the article? Do you see a significant number of edits to undo vandalism? Try stepping through some of the early edits of the article to see how it developed.

NOTE

1. *Wikipedia, the Free Encyclopedia*, s.v. "7 July 2005 London Bombings," February 27, 2008, http://en.wikipedia.org/w/index.php?title=7_July_2005_London_bombings&oldid=194447339 (accessed March 1, 2008).

Chapter 9

Searching There without Being There: OpenSearch

INTRODUCTION

As most any user of today's browsers will notice, there is a search box in the upper right corner of the browser. Typically this search box has a Google logo next to it (see Figure 9-1). In Internet Explorer, instead of a logo, the name of the search engine is displayed inside the box, as shown in Figure 9-2. The assumption is that if you were to type keywords into this box and press "Enter" or click on the magnifying glass icon, a Google search would be performed, displaying the results in the browser. I've found that the vast majority of first-time Google searches are performed in this manner. It just makes sense. Why bother going to the Google homepage first when you can just skip that step altogether by using the search box built into the browser?

What many people don't notice is the small triangle (▼) to the right of the Google logo or magnifying glass. Clicking on this icon will open a drop-down list of other available search engines. The default list of available search engines will vary from browser to browser, but typical choices include Yahoo!, Wikipedia, and Amazon.com (see Figure 9-3). To perform a search in one of these other search engines, just open the list, select the appropriate search engine, enter your keywords, and press "Enter."

All of this is extremely handy, but there's more to it. The technology underlying this is known as Open-Search,[1] and it is supported by all of today's browsers. OpenSearch allows you not only to add additional search engines to your browser but also, with just a bit of code, to create your own OpenSearch plug-ins that others can add to their browsers. For example,

how would you like to give your patrons the ability to search your OPAC directly from their browsers? Sounds like a great idea to me. First, we'll take a look at how to find and install additional OpenSearch plug-ins (the user's point of view) and then switch gears to examine the steps required to create your own OpenSearch files for distribution to others.

FINDING AND INSTALLING OPENSEARCH FILES

There are two ways to find OpenSearch files to add to your browser. The first is to search online for directories of OpenSearch plug-ins, browse through them, and then select those that meet your search criteria. If you go to searchplugins.net you will find an extensive list (www.searchplugins.net/pluginlist.aspx), as shown in Figure 9-4. There you will find a searchable list of over 11,000 search engines that you can add to your browser.

To install a plug-in from the list, click on the "I" link to the left of the entry. (The "S" link will show you the plug-in's source code, while the "R" link is for

---

Installing an OpenSearch Plug-in

1. Find a page that offers a plug-in, indicated by a glowing icon for the current search plug-in.
2. Click the ▼ to the right of the current icon to see the list of currently installed plug-ins.
3. Select the install choice found near the bottom of the list.
4. Confirm your wish to install the new plug-in and choose to use it immediately, as appropriate.

Figure 9-1   The Google search box in Firefox 2.0

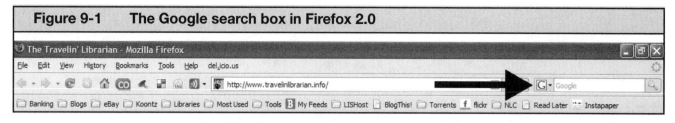

Figure 9-2   The Google search box in Internet Explorer 7

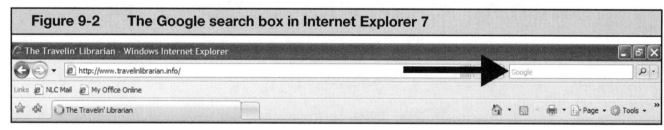

Figure 9-3   A list of available search engines in my browser (your results will vary)

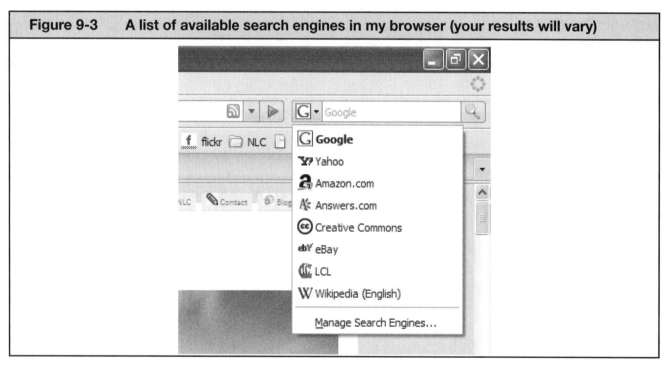

reporting nonworking plug-ins.) Firefox will ask you to confirm that you wish this plug-in to be installed and if you would like to set it as your current search engine (see Figure 9-5). Choose to use it immediately if you wish, and click the "Add" button. In Internet Explorer, you'll need to select the down arrow to the right of the magnifying glass icon by the browser's search box (see Figure 9-6) and select it from the list. Once done, your new search engine will be available from the drop-down list.

The other way you can find and install Open-Search plug-ins is to keep an eye on the OpenSearch icon in your browser and watch for the "glow." Here's

the scenario: I recently heard that there was a video on the Net of a *60 Minutes* report on video piracy from the late 1970s. I do a quick Google search for *60 minutes piracy video* and quickly discover that the video I'm looking for can be found on YouTube. I click on the link in Google's results list and find myself viewing the video on YouTube's site. As I'm watching the video, I happen to glance up at the OpenSearch box and notice that the Google icon is glowing. Figure 9-7 shows my full screen. Since the icon in question is rather small, Figure 9-8 shows the relevant portion of the screen at double size. Also, since it may be difficult to see the "glow" in a

Figure 9-4   List of OpenSearch plug-ins at www.searchplugins.net

Figure 9-5   Adding a new OpenSearch plug-in to Firefox

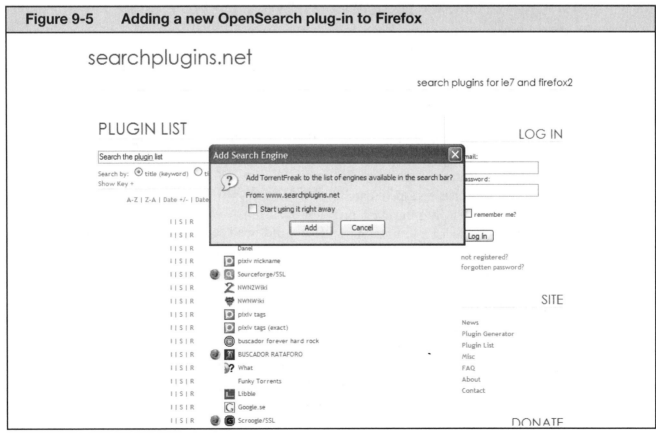

Figure 9-6   Adding a new OpenSerch plug-in to Internet Explorer

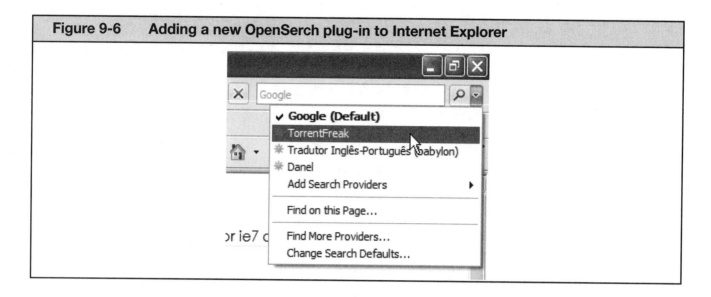

Creating an OpenSearch Plug-in

1. Perform a test search.
2. Evaluate and deconstruct the URL of the search results.
3. Edit the XML (extensive markup language) code or fill in the plug-in generation form based on the information retrieved in step 2.
4. Give your plug-in a title, tags, adult content rating, and icon, as appropriate.
5. Upload the plug-in to your Web server.
6. Insert the markup code into your Web page to connect to the plug-in.
7. Install the plug-in yourself.
8. Test the plug-in and make adjustments as needed for proper functionality.

grayscale image, Figure 9-9 shows the same enlarged section of the screen without the glow effect.

The glow indicates that the site I'm currently viewing (YouTube, not Google) has an OpenSearch plug-in available. To install this plug-in, click on the OpenSearch icon to open the list and find "Add 'YouTube Video Search'" at the bottom of the list, as shown in Figure 9-10. Selecting this option will automatically add the new plug-in and set it to the default search (see Figure 9-11). In limited cases, you may be provided with multiple choices of plug-ins to add. Just select and add whichever are appropriate for you.

Unfortunately, not all Web sites with OpenSearch plug-ins have added the necessary code for this to work. (I'll show you how to do this in the next sec-

tion of this chapter.) This is why it's still good to look through the directories every so often.

CREATING YOUR OWN OPENSEARCH PLUG-INS

For those of you who are unfamiliar with XML code, there's no need to skip this section of the chapter. Creating OpenSearch plug-ins is typically very easy to do using any number of available online tools. However, for the code geeks in the audience, here's what the code looks like and what it does:

The Code

The following is an example of the code for an OpenSearch plug-in for the Lincoln City Libraries, along with a description of what each line of code does:

1. `<?xml version="1.0" encoding="UTF-8"?>`	• Line one is the XML declaration. It states that this file is written in an XML–based language and is using the UTF–8 (unicode transformation format) character encoding.
2. `<OpenSearchDescription>`	• Line two starts the OpenSearch code.
3. `<ShortName>LCL</ShortName>`	• Line three is the name of the search plug-in. This is what will be displayed in the browser's OpenSearch list, so choose wisely.
4. `<Description>Search the Lincoln City Libraries online catalog</Description>`	• Line four is a brief description of the plug-in. The browser won't do anything with this information, but you should still write a good one in case this changes in the future.
5. `<Tags>library nebraska lincoln</Tags>`	• Line five contains a space-delimited list of tags for this plug-in.
6. `<Image height="16" width="16" type="image/x-icon">http://www.searchplugins.net/images/favicon.ico</Image>`	• Line six specifies the dimensions and URL of the icon to be used for this plug-in. I'll discuss this more later on.
7. `<Url type="text/html" method="GET" template="http://webpac.lincoln libraries.org/ipac20/ipac.jsp?index=.GW&term={searchTerms}"/>`	• Line seven is the important one. This code instructs OpenSearch on how to build the query that is sent to the search engine. The URL from plug-in to plug-in will differ, but somewhere in there you must include {searchTerms}. Again, I'll cover this in more detail shortly.
8. `<InputEncoding>UTF-8</InputEncoding>`	• Line eight specifies the character set that the input keywords will be using. Leave this at UTF–8 unless you're building a plug-in for a search engine in Russian, Japanese, Chinese, Hebrew, or another language that doesn't use the Latin character set.
9. `<AdultContent>false</AdultContent>`	• Line nine specifies whether the search engine being referenced should allow adult content, where "true" would allow adult content and "false" would not allow adult content. This is a judgment call on your part, but I believe that all library catalogs can easily claim false in this case.
10. `</OpenSearchDescription>`	• Line ten ends the code.

Figure 9-7   My YouTube video page with a glowing OpenSearch icon

Figure 9-8   Enlarged version of a glowing OpenSearch icon

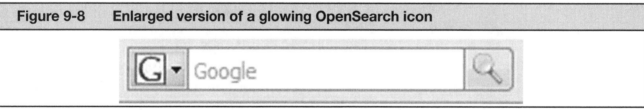

Figure 9-9   Enlarged version of a non-glowing OpenSearch icon

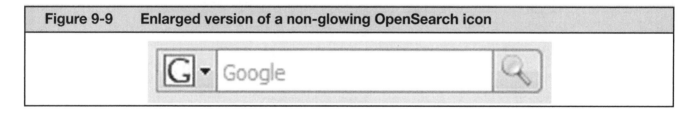

Figure 9-10   Adding an OpenSearch plug-in from the list

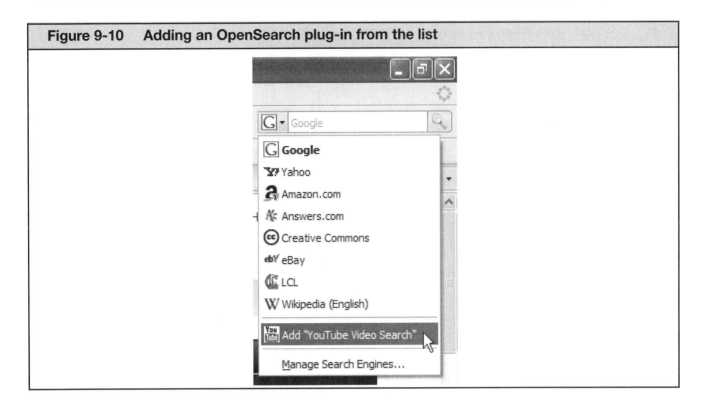

Figure 9-11   The results of adding the YouTube OpenSearch plug-in

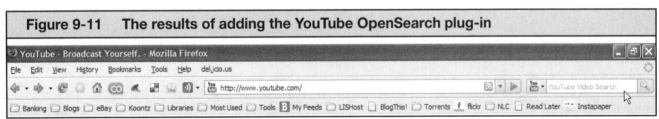

Really, when you compare this code to XHTML (extensible hyptertext markup language) or CSS (Cascading Style Sheets), or even MARC (machine-readable cataloging) for that matter, it isn't all that complicated.

The Plug-in

Now let's build our own OpenSearch plug-in. I'm going to use the OPAC from Lincoln City Libraries, the library where I'm a patron, to build my search. And, instead of writing all of the code from scratch, I'm going to use the "Generate Plugins" tool from search-plugins.net (www.searchplugins.net/generate.aspx) to automatically generate my code. Before attempting this with your own OPAC, I suggest reading through this section and the next. You may need to overcome some hurdles before all of this will work.

Figure 9-12 shows the "Generate Plugins" tool.

In it are seven fields that you will need to fill in or choose from a list. They are: "Search URL," "Search plugin title," "Search Method," "Search Results Format," "Input Encoding," "Adult Content," and "Icon." Before we fill these in, you first need to make a decision, and then you will need to perform a test search.

The decision, in the case of OPACs, is what search you want this plug-in to perform. Take a look at the main search screen for Lincoln City Libraries' OPAC, as shown in Figure 9-13. Here I can perform any one of many different searches depending on which of the seven different fields I fill in. In the case of an OpenSearch plug-in, you want to keep your searches simple (i.e., using only a single field) and ones that your users are most likely to use. So, in this case, let's build a plug-in that does a general keyword search.

Figure 9-12   searchplugins.net's "generate plugins" tool

Having decided on which search field to use, I enter the keyword TEST (yes, it needs to be in all caps) into the "General Keyword" field (see Figure 9-14) and press "Enter" to perform my search. My results are shown in Figure 9-15.

Next, you need to look for some specific information in the URL of the results page. Here's the URL I have to work with:

http://webpac.lincolnlibraries.org/ipac20/ipac.jsp?**session=119143R19F468.57235**&menu=search&aspect=subtab13&npp=10&ipp=20&spp=20&profile=external&ri=&term=&index=ALLTITL&x=0&y=0&aspect=subtab13&term=&index=PAUTHOR&term=&index=PSUBJ&term=&index=.TW&term=&index=.NW&term=&index=.SW&term=**TEST**&index=.GW

The first thing to look for in the URL is the word TEST. (I've bolded it in the example URL.) If TEST appears, you're all set. If it doesn't, check the next section for a possible solution before continuing.

The other thing to look for in the URL is any session IDs that may appear. (I've also bolded this in my example.) If you find one of these, skip to the next section for a possible solution to this problem. In short, remove it and see if you still get the same results. If you do, you can proceed:

http://webpac.lincolnlibraries.org/ipac20/ipac.jsp?menu=search&aspect=subtab13&npp=10&ipp=20&spp=20&profile=external&ri=&term=&index=ALLTITL&x=0&y=0&aspect=subtab13&term=&index=PAUTHOR&term=&index=PSUBJ&term=&index=.TW&term=&index=.NW&term=&index=.SW&term=TEST&index=.GW

Copy this URL to your clipboard and head back to the "Generate Plugin" tool. Here's what you need to do for each field:

- **Search URL:**
  Paste the URL of your search results page into this field. From this information, the tool will create a correctly formatted line of code that the plug-in needs to pass on the searcher's keywords to your OPAC.

Figure 9-13 Lincoln City Libraries' OPAC search page

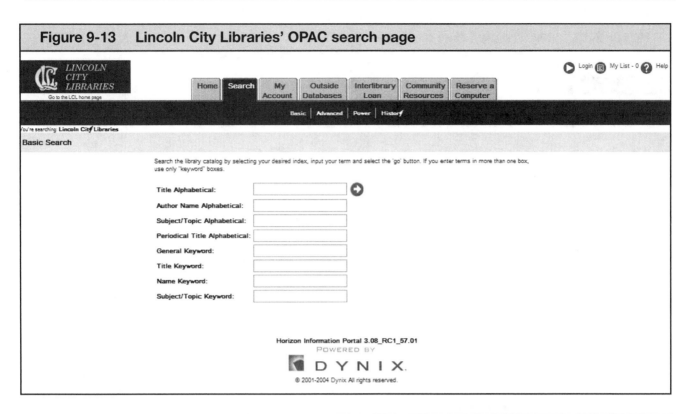

Figure 9-14 Entering my test search keyword

Figure 9-15   The results of my test search

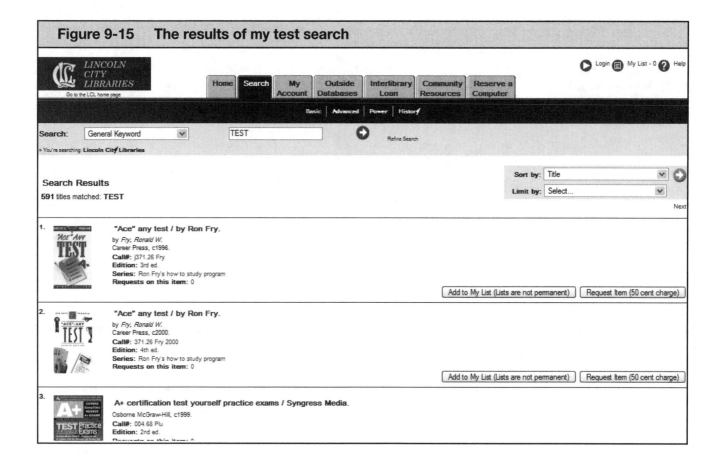

- **Search plug-in title:**
  What words do you want the plug-in users to see when then view their plug-in list? Keep in mind that this should be descriptive but not too long, as there's only so much space on the screen. Abbreviations are okay, provided that your users know their meaning. For example, "OPAC" may not be the best choice. "Catalog" may be better.

- **Tags:**
  What tags would you like associated with your plug-in? Feel free to enter multiple tags; just separate them with spaces.

- **Search method:**
  Here you have the option of choosing GET or POST. This relates to the way your search form sends data to the script that actually runs the script. Please notice that choosing "post" will work only in Firefox 2.0, so I don't advise that you use it. This also relates to whether your TEST keyword appeared in the URL of your search results page. See the next section, on potential problems, for more details.

- **Search results format:**
  OpenSearch also has the ability to output results in RSS and Atom formats for later processing and/or syndication. Since these output types are beyond the scope of this book, just leave this field as HTML.

- **Input encoding:**
  Assuming that you're working in English, German, French, Italian, or Spanish, UTF–8 is the appropriate (and default) option for this field. Those interested in accepting keywords in other character sets, such as Cyrillic, Kanji, or Chinese, need to fill in the appropriate alternate value.[2]

- **Adult content:**
  Choose "True" if the results of a search in your plug-in could contain adult material. Since I'm searching an OPAC, I'll leave this as "False."

- **Icon:**
  Here you have four choices: "No Icon," "Website Favicon (auto detect)," "Website Favicon (manual)," and "Upload Icon." No icon leaves the box empty looking. The auto detect of the Web site's favicon

should work if you have one associated with your Web site. If not, a generic search icon will be used. You can choose the manual favicon application if you have a favicon and auto detect didn't work. If you've created an icon specifically for the purpose of attaching it to your search plug-in and the file is currently on your hard drive, choose the upload icon option. The next section, on potential problems, has some pointers for making this work if your site does not already have a favicon.[3]

Figure 9-16 shows my completed form. Now click the "Create Plugin" button for your results (see Figure 9-17). Next, click Install to integrate your newly generated plug-in into your browser. I highly suggest you do this and then perform a few test searches in a new window/tab before proceeding. Just because the tool wrote your code doesn't mean the code works. If it doesn't work, check all of your

work and review the section on possible problems to see if you're able to fix what's wrong.[4]

Once everything's working, return to the tool to see what the code looks like. (Unfortunately, this is a little tricky.) To do this, right-click on the install link and select "copy link." Then paste the link into your browser's address bar. Before pressing Enter, remove all of the content from your address bar that isn't a URL. In my case, I started with *javascript: addProvider('http://www.searchplugins.net/createos. aspx?number=18723&temp=true');void(0)* and then reduced it to *http://www.searchplugins.net/createos. aspx?number=18723&temp=true*. Once you've done this, press the "Enter" key. A new page will open showing you the XML code for your plug-in. A few additional lines of code at the top indicate that you used the "Generate Plugins" tool. This won't affect your plug-in and will let people know where they can get help creating their own should they look at

Figure 9-16   My completed "generate plugins" form

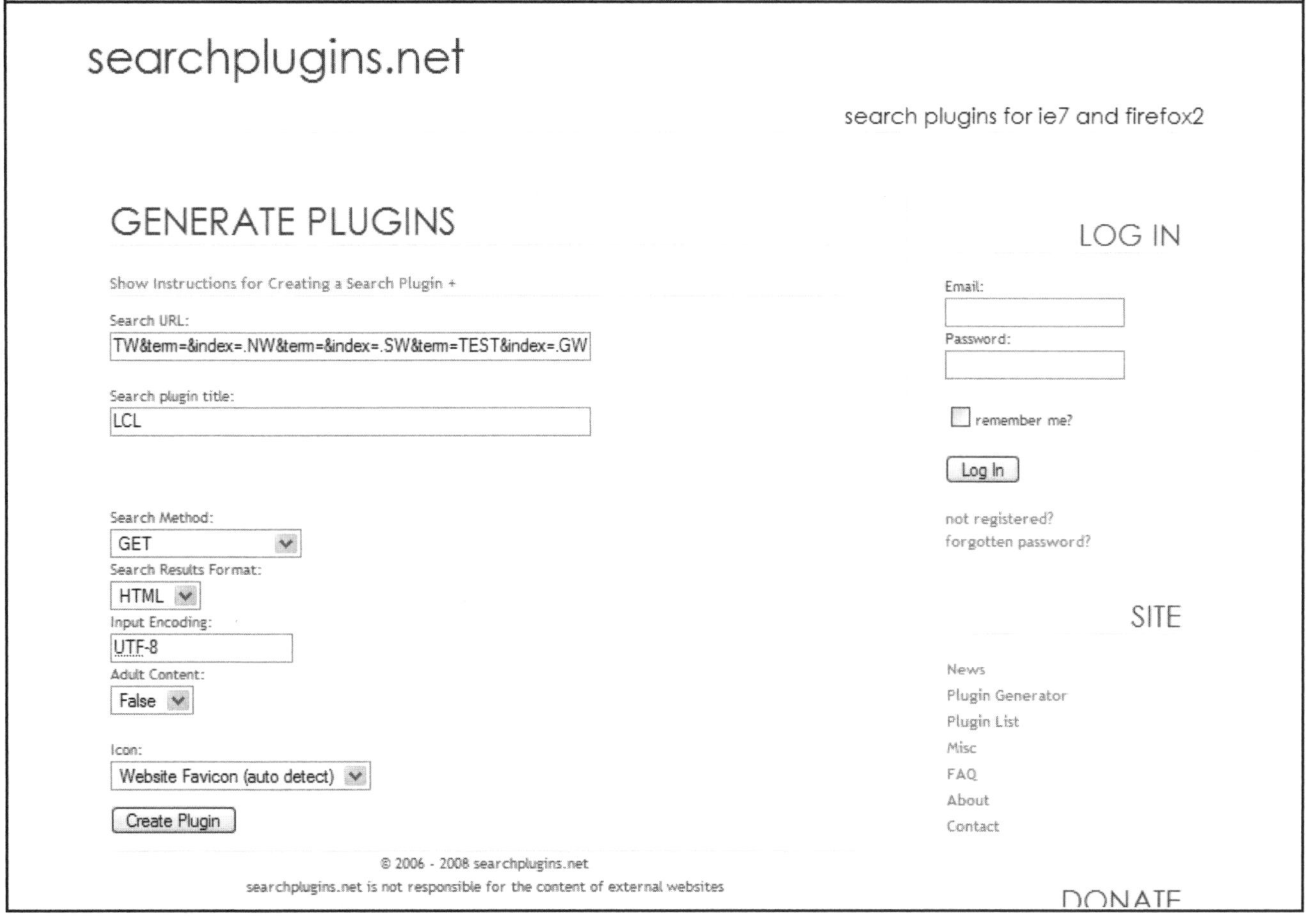

Figure 9-17 My results page

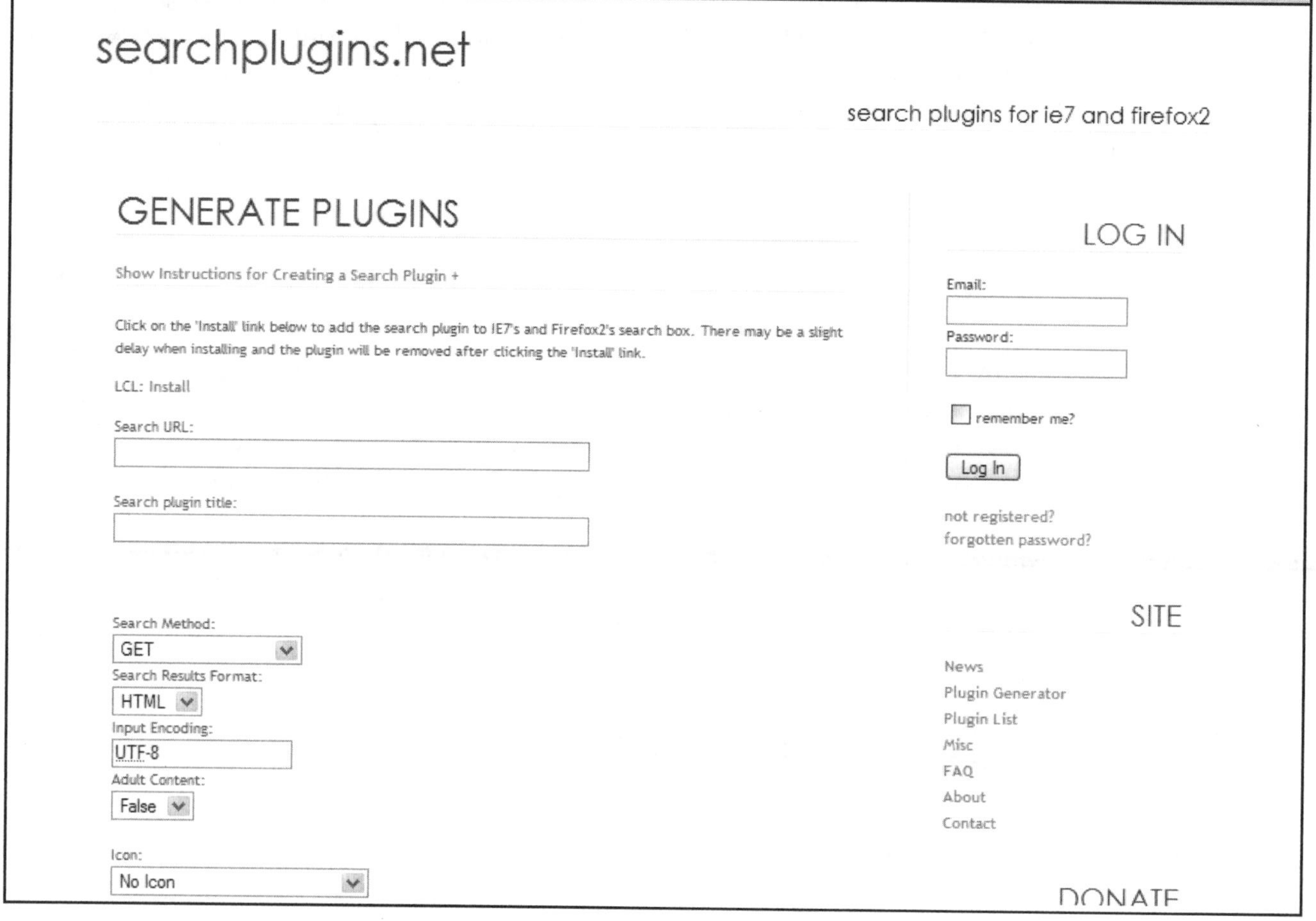

searchplugins.net

search plugins for ie7 and firefox2

GENERATE PLUGINS

Show Instructions for Creating a Search Plugin +

Click on the 'Install' link below to add the search plugin to IE7's and Firefox2's search box. There may be a slight delay when installing and the plugin will be removed after clicking the 'Install' link.

LCL: Install

Search URL:

Search plugin title:

Search Method:
GET

Search Results Format:
HTML

Input Encoding:
UTF-8

Adult Content:
False

Icon:
No Icon

LOG IN

Email:

Password:

☐ remember me?

Log In

not registered?
forgotten password?

SITE

News
Plugin Generator
Plugin List
Misc
FAQ
About
Contact

DONATE

your code. Figure 9-18 shows my resulting code. Due to the length of your search URL, you may need to scroll horizontally to see all of the code, as I do in my example.

From your browser's file menu, choose "Save Page As" ("Save As" on the "Page" menu in Internet Explorer), pick a location on your hard drive, and give it a filename of *search.xml*. Feel free to replace *search* with something a little more specific. In my case I'll call my file *lcl.xml*. Now that you have the necessary XML code saved, you need take only a few more steps to make it available to your users. But first, let me deal with some of the problems you may have encountered.

Dealing with Problems That May Arise

If you're lucky, everything I just walked you through worked exactly as planned. Unfortunately, sometimes it just doesn't go smoothly. Here are some of the problems that may develop and possible solutions:

- **My search term doesn't appear in the URL of my search results page:**

As mentioned previously, a form can send its content to the search engine in two ways, GET and POST. For an OpenSearch plug-in to work, your search engine needs to use the GET method. The simplest way to tell which one your search engine is using (without looking at the source code) is to look for your search term in the URL of the results page. If it's there, you're using GET. If not, you're using POST. If you find you're in a POST situation, all is not lost, at least not yet. There is a solution that will work in many situations. First, go find the frmget bookmarklet (www.squarefree.com/bookmarklets/forms.html) and install it into your browser. (Drag the link onto your bookmarks toolbar or right-click on it and select "Add to bookmarks/favorites.") Next, reopen your search page and click on the frmget bookmark. You'll receive a notice that your form has been changed to the GET method (see

Figure 9-18   My plug-in code

This XML file does not appear to have any style information associated with it. The document tree is shown below.

```
<!--
   Generated by searchplugins.net search plugin generator
-->
<!-- http://www.searchplugins.net/generate.aspx -->
<!--
   Plugin list available at http://www.searchplugins.net/pluginlist.aspx
-->
<OpenSearchDescription>
   <ShortName>LCL</ShortName>
   <Description>Search LCL</Description>
   <Tags>schadenfreude</Tags>
   <Url type="text/html" method="GET"
   template="http://webpac.lincolnlibraries.org/ipac20/ipac.jsp?menu=search&aspect=subtab13&npp=10&ipp=20&spp=20&profile=external&ri=&term=&index=ALLTITL&x=0
   <InputEncoding>UTF-8</InputEncoding>
   <AdultContent>false</AdultContent>
</OpenSearchDescription>
```

Figure 9-19). Now, try your search again and you should see your keyword in the URL of the results page. Use that URL in the "Generate Plugins" tool, and the process should now work. If it still doesn't work, sorry, but you're out of luck because the search engine you're trying to search against just will not support an OpenSearch plug-in.[5]

- **My OPAC requires a unique session ID for each search:**

  Unlike most search engines on the Net, a certain number of OPACs have been set up so that every time new users start a new search session, a unique identifier is embedded into the URL of every page they look at while in the OPAC. Once the users log out, or after a certain predetermined period of inactivity, the session ID is tossed out, never to be used again. This does have certain benefits in searching but plays havoc with OpenSearch plug-ins. If your search results page has one of these IDs, you may not be able to get an OpenSearch plug-in to work. Here's an example URL from a search result from the OPAC at Pittsburgh State University:

  http://ipac.pittstate.edu/ipac20/ipac.jsp?**sessi on=11K14VI490953.2355**&menu=search&a spect=basic_search&npp=10&ipp=20&spp=20 &profile=axe&ri=&index=AA&term=sauers%2C +michael&x=0&y=0&aspect=basic_search.

  The section in bold is the session ID, and the

problem I need to solve. To attempt to get this to work, I need to delete the bold part (and the "&" just after it) from the URL and press Enter to try the search again without the session ID. My new URL is:

  http://ipac.pittstate.edu/ipac20/ipac.jsp?men u=search&aspect=basic_search&npp=10&ipp =20&spp=20&profile=axe&ri=&index=AA&ter m=sauers%2C+michael&x=0&y=0&aspect=b asic_search.

  If you receive the same results as before, use this new URL in the "Generate Plugins" tool and everything should work out fine. If you receive anything else, typically some sort of cryptic server error message, then sorry again, you've hit the brick wall that nothing will fix.

- **My site doesn't have a custom icon:**

  This one is a little more difficult to handle, as I don't want to get into how to edit graphics, but I can offer a few pointers. If your site doesn't already have a custom icon, also known as a "favicon," you'll first need to create one. These files need to be 16 ×16 pixels and saved in the ".ico" format. The filename then should be "favicon.ico" and placed into your Web site's root directory. Once you've done this, you can rerun the "Generate Plugins" tool or just edit the XML file to point to your newly placed icon via its URL.

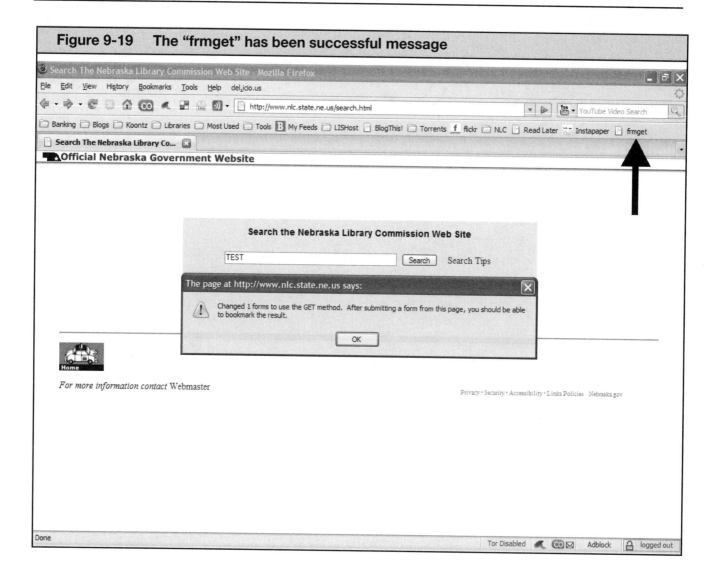

Figure 9-19   The "frmget" has been successful message

- **I've noticed that the "Generate Plugins" tool didn't put an XML declaration into my file:**

  Although this line of code technically isn't required for the OpenSearch plug-in to work, good practice says it should be there. To add it, just edit the XML file, add the new first line of code, and resave the file.

Making Your Plug-in Available

The first thing you need to do is get the XML file onto your Web server. Place your search.xml file into your Web site's root directory by whichever means you usually use to get Web pages onto your server—FTP, mapped network drive, sent to the Webmaster, etc. Next, you'll want to create one or

both of the following types of links to the plug-in. I highly recommend both.

The first type is to get the "glowing" OpenSearch icon. For any page in your site on which you would like this to occur, place the following line in the Web pages head:

```
<link rel="search" type="application/open
searchdescription+xml" href="/search.xml"
title="name of search plugin" />
```

Be sure to change the href value and the title value to match your plug-in. I've changed mine to read:

```
<link rel="search" type="application/
opensearchdescription+xml" href="/lcl.xml"
title="LCL OPAC" />
```

At a minimum, you should add this line of code to your homepage and the main page of your OPAC. If you have the ability through templates, adding it to every page on your site isn't a bad idea.

The other method is to promote your new plug-in a little more directly by offering a link for your users to click to install it (via the searchplugins.net directory). To do this, find an appropriate location on your site to place the link. You could keep it simple and offer it on the OPAC's homepage or create a new page describing how to install and use your OpenSearch plug-in. Or, better yet, both. Either way, the code for the link will need to look like this:

```
<a href="javascript:addProvider('/
search.xml','false')" title="plugin
name">install</a>
```

You'll need to edit this code to include your plug-in's filename, your plug-in's title, and whatever you'd like the link text to read. For example, mine would be:

```
<a href="javascript:addProvider('/lcl.
xml','false')" title="LCL OPAC">Install the
LCL OPAC OpenSearch Plugin</a>
```

Be sure to test all of this out on a computer or two before telling everyone else that it's available. One typo anywhere in all of that code and it won't work.

CONCLUSION

OpenSearch plug-ins are one of the most overlooked features of browsers today. Once a user becomes accustomed to using them, I've found that they tend to search directly for the information they're seeking more often than browsing through a site. Besides, being able to pick a site to search from a drop-down list is easier than having to remember the address of the site or find the bookmark, wait for the site to load, and then find the search box (usually another click or two off of the homepage).

Offering an OpenSearch plug-in for your library's Web site and/or OPAC, besides making your life easier, will also make it easier for your patrons to search your information. Take the time. It will be worth it in the long run.

Well, that's it for searching "out there." In the next chapter, we'll take a look inward and learn how to search for information in that vast collection of data known as "My Computer."

EXERCISES

Really, the only possible exercise for this chapter is to create an OpenSearch plug-in for your library's OPAC. Refer to the second sidebar in this chapter, Creating an OpenSearch Plug-in, for a short list of steps you'll need to follow. If one already exists or ends up failing for one of the reasons discussed in this chapter, find another site that you search regularly and create one for that site instead.

NOTES

1. "OpenSearch was created by A9.com, an Amazon.com company, and the OpenSearch format is now in use by hundreds of search engines and search applications around the Internet. The OpenSearch specification is made available according to the terms of a Creative Commons license so that everyone can participate" (OpenSearch.org, "Introduction," http://www.opensearch.org/Home). The Firefox browser moved to the OpenSearch format with the release of version 2.0, replacing their proprietary Firefox search plug-ins format. Internet Explorer implemented OpenSearch with the release of version 7.

2. A list of possible values can be found at The Internet TESL Journal, "Character Sets," http://A4esl.org/c/charset.html.

3. Even more detail on just what favicons are and how you can create them can be found at *Wikipedia, the Free Encyclopedia,* s.v. "Favicon," October 7, 2008, http://en.wikipedia.org/wiki/Favicon.

4. If you do need to go back and fix something, you must uninstall the plug-in before you reinstall it. In Firefox "open the plug-ins" list, select "manage search engines . . . ," select the plug-in you wish to remove, and click the "remove" button. Click "OK" to return to your browser. To remove a plug-in from Internet Explorer, open the plug-ins list, choose "change search defaults . . .," select the plug-in you wish to remove, and click the "remove" button. Click "OK" to return to your browser.

5. This is the reason that I didn't use the search engine for the Nebraska Library Commission Web site as the example for this chapter.

Chapter 10

Desktop Search

INTRODUCTION

Desktop search, the ability to find files not on the Internet but on your own computer, has always intrigued me. First, I tend to be rather organized, so I rarely have trouble finding what I'm looking for (I am a librarian so I'm sure that has something to do with it). Then again, my home desktop computer currently has more than 1 TB (terabyte) worth of storage across five hard drives—two internal and three external. Plus my old Windows NT desktop, which I use for backups, and my laptop, which I have hooked up to my HDTV for watching videos, all of which are connected to a home network. So even I sometimes can't remember where I put a particular file. The amount of information in my situation requires searchability.

On the other hand, with more and more information being stored online, not on my desktop—bookmarks in Delicious, photos in Flickr, and documents in Google Docs and Spreadsheets, for example—I'm keeping less of my content on my local computer. Wouldn't this lead to less need for desktop-based searching? Well, yes and no.

Eventually we'll be able to put a search term into a search box and search across everything that's on our computer, no matter where it's located. We're getting close, assuming all of our "stuff" is stored within a common system (all with Google-owned services, for example). But for now, we're going to need some tools to help us find the files we seek.[1]

This chapter covers two downloadable desktop search applications: Google Desktop and Windows Search.[2] Also discussed are the many advances made by Microsoft in regard to desktop search in Windows Vista. One word of warning: installing multiple desktop search applications can cause problems and seriously degrade system performance. It is highly recommended that you either install Google Desktop *or* Windows Desktop Search, but not both. If you're already a Windows Vista user, you don't need to install either of them.

GOOGLE DESKTOP

Google Desktop is software available from Google that when installed will allow you to perform the following four functions: "Search your computer as easily as you search the web with Google," "Find and launch applications and files with just a few keystrokes," "Get news, weather and more anywhere on your desktop," and "Add Google Gadgets to customize your desktop and iGoogle" (see Figure 10-1). Since only the first feature of Google Desktop is relevant to this book, that's the only one I'll cover.[3]

To install Google Desktop, go to http://desktop.google.com and click on the "Install Google Desktop" button. You will then download and run the Google Desktop installation file by following the on-screen installation instructions (see Figure 10-2). Linux and Mac versions are also available. Links to them can be found below the install button. During the installation process, you'll be asked to choose from a few options:

- **Find files by name and launch applications:** This option is for the basic indexing of your files and applications. Without this, the program will not function.

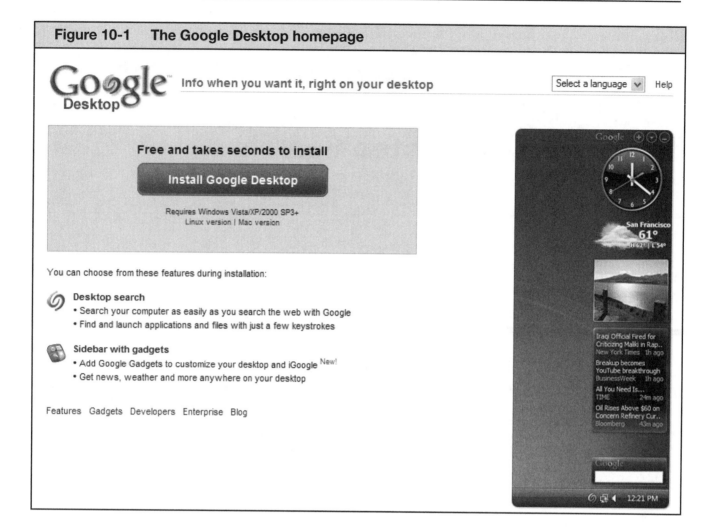

Figure 10-1　The Google Desktop homepage

- **Also search the content of files, e-mail, Web history, and more:**
  By default, Google Desktop will index only file-names. Checking this option will also allow Google Desktop to index the actual content of many of your files. This will increase the size of the index but allow you to find more items on your computer.
- **Display news, e-mail, weather, and many more gadgets right on your desktop:**
  Checking this option installs the Google Sidebar. As previously mentioned, I do not cover this feature.
- **Set Google as your homepage and default browser search:**
  Uncheck this option if you wish not to have your browser's homepage changed to Google.
- **Improve Google Desktop by sending crash reports and anonymous usage data:**
  Checking this option does exactly what it says and

helps improve service. Whether you choose this option or not is completely up to you.

As previously stated, all of these options can be changed later. At this time, your settings for these options will not affect the material in the rest of the chapter. When the installation process has finished, you should see a Google Desktop icon in your system tray and a Google search box in the Windows taskbar, as shown in Figure 10-3.[4]

Indexing

Once installed, Google Desktop will attempt to immediately start indexing the content of your computer. However, to save system resources and prevent slowing down your computer, indexing will occur only while your computer is idle. I generally recommend that shortly after you install Google Desktop

Figure 10-2   Google Desktop installation options

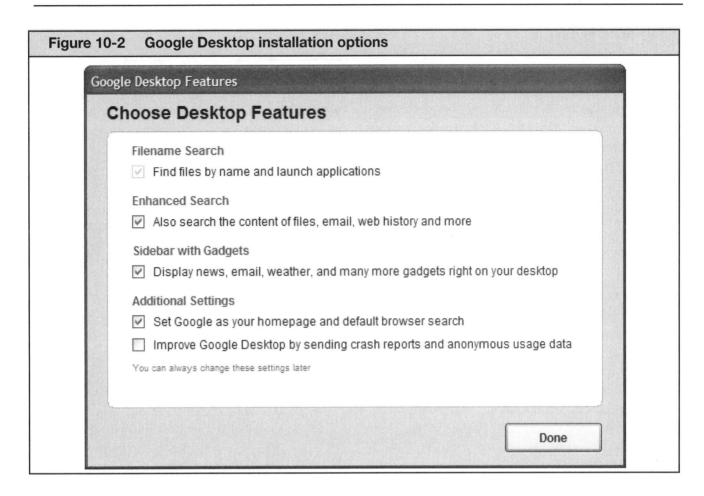

Figure 10-3   The Google Desktop icon in the Windows system tray

you leave your computer alone for a while so it can do its work. (Just before you leave for your lunch or dinner break would be a great time, as it will probably be done by the time you get back. In the case of a computer with a very large amount of storage, you may even want to let this run overnight.)

You also have the ability to control when and how the indexing is done. To access these options, right-click on the Google Desktop icon in the system tray and select indexing. Here you will have three options: pause/resume indexing, re-index, and index status.

- **Pause/resume indexing:**
  If you believe that the indexing process is slowing down your computer more than you're willing to accept, you can select this option. Once selected, indexing will be stopped completely for one hour. This option changes to "Resume Indexing" in the event you want to resume the process before that hour is up.

- **Re-index:**
  At first Google Desktop will index the complete contents of your computer. From that point forward it will index only files that have changed after the initial indexing process. Choosing re-index will clear any existing entries regarding the content of your computer and start the process all over again from scratch. I recommend this option only in cases in which you seem to be receiving erroneous results from the program.

- **Index status:**
Choosing this option will open your browser and display the status of any indexing that is currently being done to your computer. Figure 10-4 shows the indexing status of my computer approximately 15 minutes after installing the program. (It's been working pretty quickly despite the fact that I've been continuing to write this chapter the whole time.)

Before we do some actual searches, let's take a look at the other options and preferences that are available.

Indexing Options

To access the indexing options, right-click on the Google Desktop icon in the system tray and select "Options." This will load the Google Desktop preference page in your browser. On this page are four sections: desktop search, Google account features, display, and other. Each section has a variety of options you can modify to control how Google Desktop works. I'll focus just on those parts relevant to Desktop Search.

Desktop Search

The Desktop Search screen contains the majority of the options relevant to indexing your computer's contents (see Figure 10-5). These are: "Enable Con-tent Indexing," "Search Types," "Indexing Plug-ins," "Search Locations," "Google Integration," "Encrypt Index," and "Remove Deleted Items." After you change any of these settings, be sure to click the "Save Preferences" button before moving on to another screen. Failure to do so will result in your changes being discarded.

- **Enable content indexing:**
This option controls the program's ability to in-dex the actual content of many file types. When checked it will index the content within your files, and when unchecked it will index filenames only.
- **Search types:**
By default, Google Desktop will index the follow-ing file types: e-mail, Web history, media files, text and other files, Word, Excel, PowerPoint, PDF, contacts, calendar, tasks, notes, journal, and zip files. Not only will it index the files by filename but also the content of those files. Additionally, you can have it index chats, password-protected Office documents (Word and Excel), and secure pages (HTTPS) in Web history. To change the setting for a particular file type, just check or uncheck its box as appropriate.
- **Indexing plug-ins:**
Google Desktop can index other file types not listed previously with the addition of plug-ins—additional software that adds features to another program.

Figure 10-4   Google Desktop indexing status

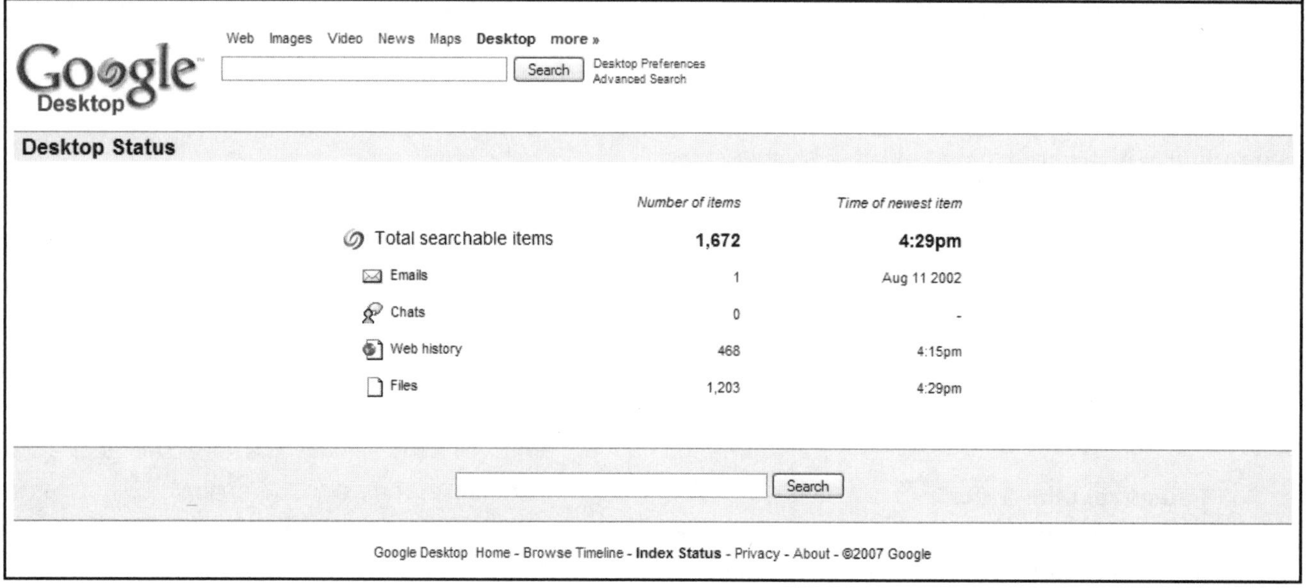

Web   Images   Video   News   Maps   **Desktop**   more »

Google Desktop

[Search]   Desktop Preferences
Advanced Search

Desktop Status

	Number of items	Time of newest item
Total searchable items	**1,672**	**4:29pm**
Emails	1	Aug 11 2002
Chats	0	-
Web history	468	4:15pm
Files	1,203	4:29pm

[Search]

Google Desktop Home - Browse Timeline - **Index Status** - Privacy - About - ©2007 Google

Figure 10-5 Local indexing preferences

Go🌀gle
Desktop

Preferences   Preferences Help

Save your preferences when finished. Changes apply to Google Desktop.

| Desktop Search | Google Account Features | Display | Other | Save Preferences |

Enable Content Indexing   ☐ Enable content indexing for new items. Without content indexing, The Quick Search Box and other Google search boxes can still be used to search filenames and launch applications.

Search Types   Index the following items so that you can search for them:

☑ Email   ☑ Word   ☑ Calendar
☐ Chats   ☑ Excel   ☑ Tasks
☑ Web history   ☑ PowerPoint   ☑ Notes
☑ Media files   ☑ PDF   ☑ Journal
☑ Text and other files   ☑ Contacts   ☑ Archives (ZIP)

☐ Password-protected Office documents (Word, Excel)
☐ Secure pages (HTTPS) in web history

Indexing Plug-ins   To install plug-ins to index other items, visit the Plug-ins Download page.

Search Locations   Index additional drives and networked folders. All fixed drives are indexed by default.
Add drive or folder to search

Do not search the following files, folders or web sites:
Add file or folder to exclude or [http://   ]   [Add URL]

Google Integration   ☑ Show Desktop Search results on Google Web Search result pages.
Your personal results are private from Google.

Encrypt Index   ☐ Encrypt Google Desktop index and data files
This will reduce the performance of Google Desktop. Learn more.

Remove Deleted Items   ☐ Remove deleted files from search results.

Save your preferences when finished. Changes apply to Google Desktop.   Save Preferences

Google Desktop Home – Browse Timeline – Index Status – Privacy – About

©2007 Google

To access the list of available indexing plug-ins, click on the link to the "Plug-ins Download" page. From there select the plug-in you wish to add and follow the on-screen download and installation instructions. A few examples of the indexing plug-ins include ones for DLL (dynamic link library) files, Java source files, Google Video, and Outlook Express e-mail.

- **Search locations:**
  By default, Google Desktop will index only the physical hard drives attached to your computer. If, however, you are on a network and have mapped network drives or have a USB hard drive that stays connected to your computer at all times, you can add them to the indexing list by clicking on the "Add drive or folder to search" link. Just browse for the appropriate drive or folder and click "OK." Google Desktop will proceed to add the contents of that location to your index.

- **Google integration:**
  If this option is checked, when you do a search on the Google Web site, you will receive results not only from the Google index but also from the indexed content of your computer (see Figure 10-6). This can be quite handy. For example, you might search for a particular document using Google and, through this feature via integrated results, find that you previously downloaded a copy and had forgotten about it.

- **Encrypt index:**
  Should you wish an additional level of privacy beyond just limiting access to your computer via a password, you can request that Google Desktop encrypt all of its data. As a result, your index will be unreadable should someone obtain a copy of it. As warned, this will reduce the performance of Google Desktop, but it will keep your data secure.

- **Remove deleted items:**
  Google Desktop offers the added safety net of indexing items that have been deleted from your computer via the Google Desktop cache. Google Desktop takes snapshots of your files and stores them for later retrieval. I cover this feature in more detail a little later in this chapter. If you prefer not to have deleted files indexed, just choose this item. Because I have heard stories of this program finding files people thought were gone forever, I'd suggest you leave this option alone. One more safety net never hurts.

Google Account Features

The two options on this page are "Gmail" and "Search Across Computers" (see Figure 10-7).

- **Gmail:**
  If you have a Gmail account, Google's free Web-based e-mail service, you can tell Google Desktop to index the content of that account. Remember my wish to search my online and offline content all

Figure 10-6   Google Web search results with integrated Desktop Search results

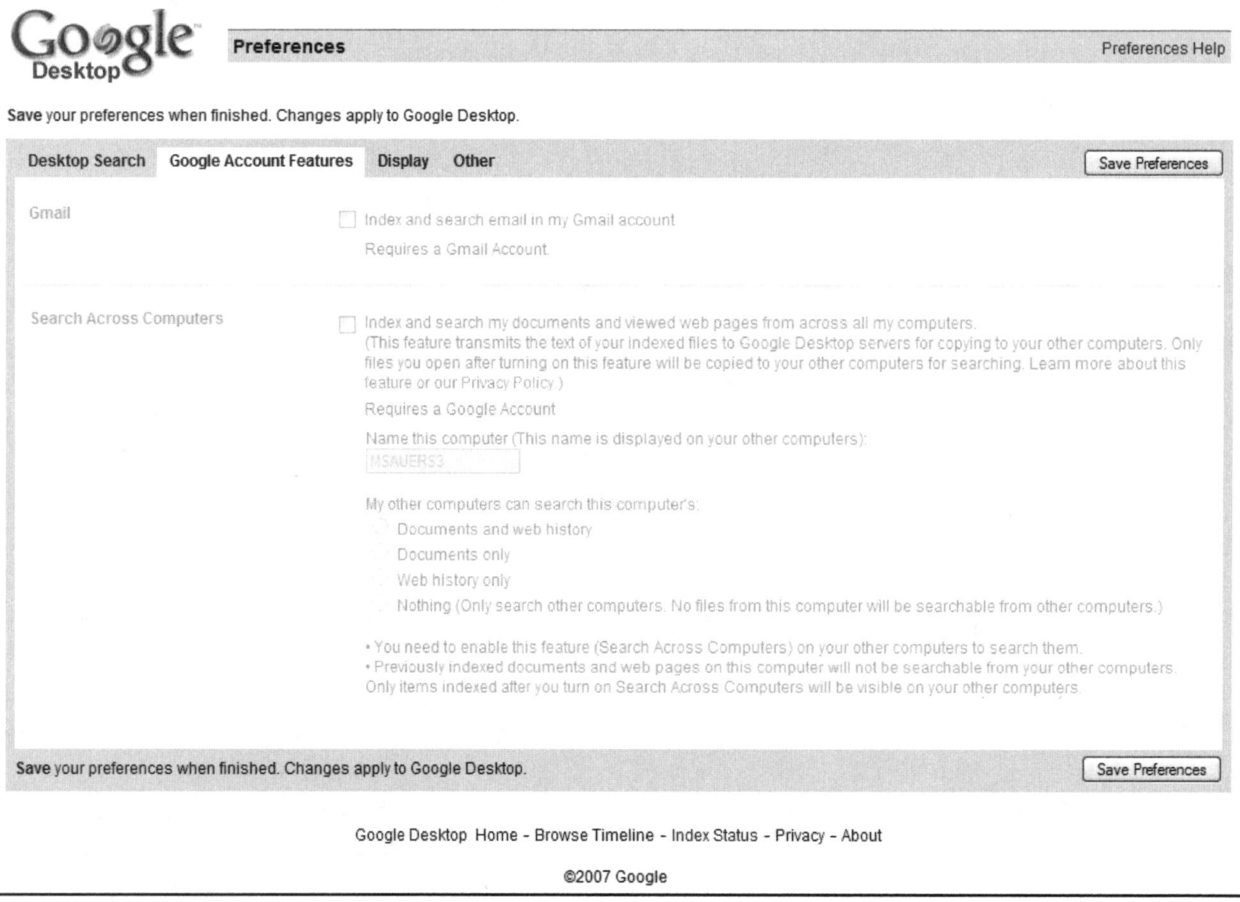

Figure 10-7   Google account features preferences

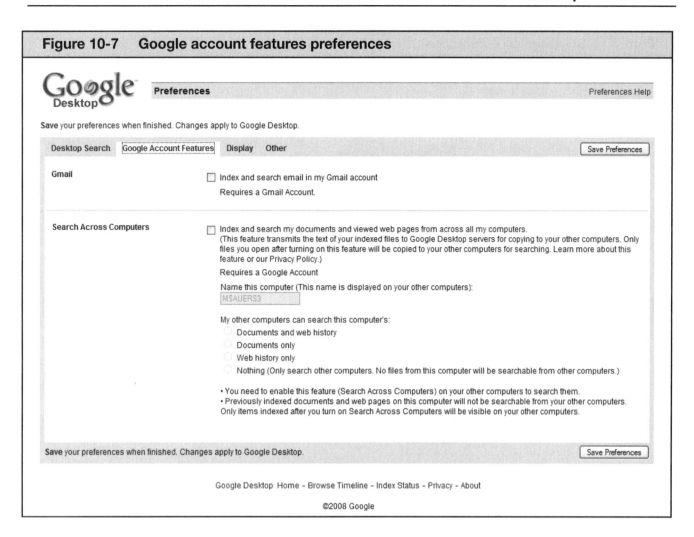

at once? To turn the feature on, just check this option, supply your Gmail username and password, and click "OK."

- **Search across computers:**
Google Desktop takes everything up a notch by now allowing you to index the contents of multiple computers. Since network and computer setups vary, I will not offer too much detail, but by installing Google Desktop on multiple computers and enabling this feature, you can create a single index of all of your files. So when you do a desktop search, you're *searching across multiple computers.* As amazing as this feature is, it can be scary to some people. Yes, you'll be able to search across computers, and, yes, you'll have access to those files on the different computers, but for this to work, you'll be uploading copies of all of your indexed files onto Google's servers, which is an outside computer. This fact alone makes some

people extremely nervous. Whether to enable this is yet another decision that I leave completely up to you. Just be sure to read the Google Privacy Policy before turning on this feature. There's a link on this page.

Display

Only three of the four options on this page are relevant to search: "Quick Search Box," "Quick Find," and "Display Mode" (see Figure 10-8).

- **Quick search box:**
The "Quick Search Box" is especially handy if you've chosen not to display the search box on the desktop or in the sidebar. By checking "Enable Quick Search Box with Hotkey," you now have the ability to double-tap the "Ctrl" key and bring up a Desktop Search box on your screen (see Figure 10-9).

Figure 10-8   Display preferences

- **Quick find:**

  "Quick Find" is Google Desktop's ability to show you results as you type in your search terms without your needing to tell it to perform a search. With "Quick Find" you will have access to four additional options. The first is the number of quick results you'd like displayed (the default is six and your options range from one to ten). The next option is whether you'd like the search box to perform a search or act as a launching platform. For example,

  if you type in *word* as a search, it will show you all indexed files containing the term "word." If you choose the launch option, typing in *word* and pressing enter will run Microsoft Word. The third option is whether you would like the quick results to include the contents of documents and e-mail messages (if so then check) or just filenames (if so then leave unchecked). The fourth option is whether you'd like spelling corrections to be displayed (e.g., when you type *futyre,* it will ask you,

"Did you mean: future?"). If you're a horrible typist, as I am, this is definitely a feature you'll want to leave on.

- **Display mode:**

  Here you can choose the location of the desktop search box. Your choices are (1) in the sidebar, which if chosen will turn on the sidebar even if you did not choose this option during installation; (2) deskbar, the default and what you already have; (3) a floating deskbar, similar to the deskbar but on the desktop instead of on the taskbar; or (4) none, which turns off the search box completely. These options can also be chosen by right-clicking on the icon in the system tray, as shown in Figure 10-10.

Other

Neither of the options on the "Other" preferences page is relevant to search, so I will not go into them. You can see the options in Figure 10-11.

Searching

Once Google Desktop has finished indexing your computer, you're ready to start searching.[5] You can access the search interface in two different ways: from the Google homepage or from the Google Desktop icon. There are six different ways to access Google Desktop Search:

1. Via a search box displayed in the sidebar, taskbar, or floating deskbar, as chosen in the display preferences

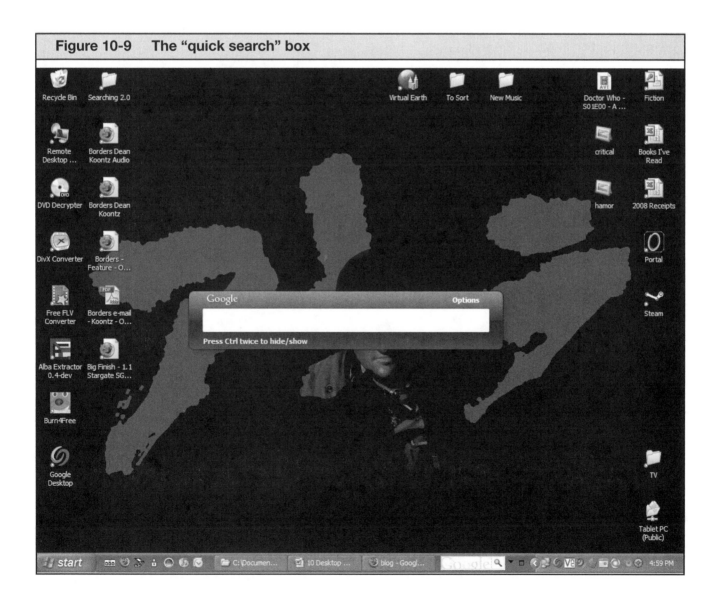

Figure 10-9   The "quick search" box

Figure 10-10 The "quick find" options from the system tray

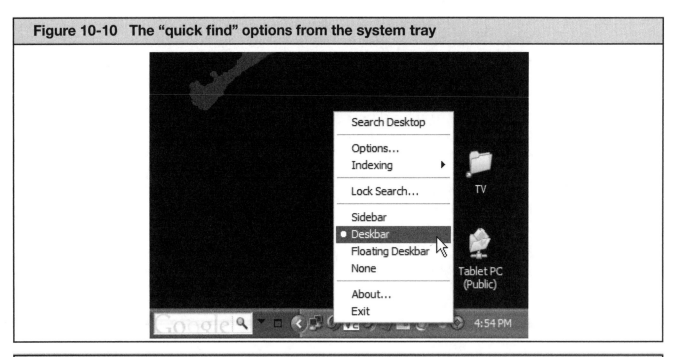

Figure 10-11 Other preferences

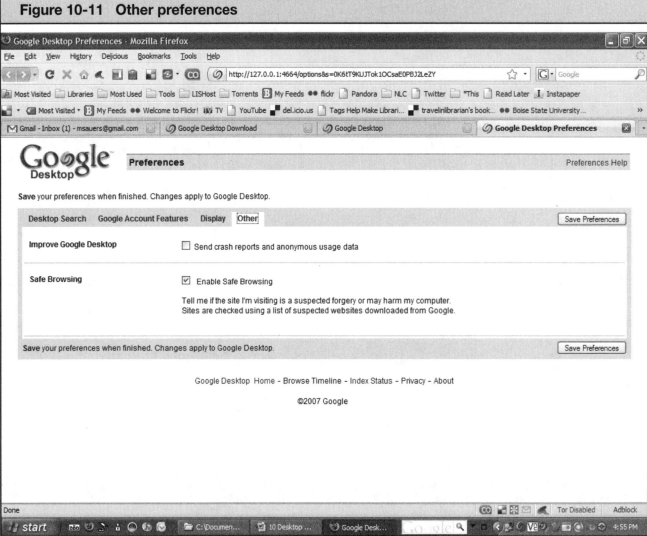

2. Via the quick search box
3. Via another Google search, provided Google Integration has been turned on in the display preferences
4. From the Google homepage by selecting the "more ▼" link in the upper left corner of the page and then choosing "Desktop"
5. By either double-clicking or right-clicking and selecting "Search Desktop" on the Google Desktop icon in the system tray
6. By opening the "Indexing Status" page and using the search box

Once you've opened a search box, just type in your keywords and click the associated search button. Pressing "Enter" usually works too. You're results will be sorted by date, unlike other Google search results. A "Sort by relevance" link in the upper right corner can change your results order. There are multiple differences with the display between Google Desktop search and regular Web-based search, as Figure 10-12 illustrates.

As shown in this example, I searched for *google* and received 218 results, of which 91 are e-mails, 107 are files, 3 from my Web history, zero from chat (as I don't have any chat logs to be indexed on this computer), and 17 other files. To limit results to one type, click on the appropriate link at the top of the page. Figure 10-13 shows just my file results. The numbers in Figure 10-12 differ from those in 10-13 because the indexing was performed live.

Once the search is performed and results returned, you can then use additional filters to zero in on desired results. In the case of file-based searches, I can further limit my search results to a particular type of file via the drop-down menu under "View." Figure 10-14 shows my results limited to just Word files (.doc/.docx).

The results themselves will contain an icon representative of that file type, the filename, up to two lines of content showing the keyword's context (text-based files) or descriptive information (images), a preview link (text-based files), the location of the file, links to open the containing folder, cached versions, and the time stamp of the file's most recent version. Image files will, instead of a preview link, show a thumbnail version to the right of the result.

For any result, clicking on the filename will open that file in its associated program. Clicking on an image's thumbnail will have the same result. Of these mentioned, I focus most specifically on the preview, cached, and timeline links.

Preview

Clicking on either the + icon or the "Preview" link for a result will open a small window on your screen, below the search result, that contains the content of that document. The document will not be formatted as in the original document and will not contain any embedded graphics. Figure 10-15 shows the preview of a Word document, while Figure 10-16 shows the preview of a PowerPoint slide show. The benefit of this preview is the ability to see the contents of a document without actually needing to load the document and the relevant program. To close a preview window, click on the "−" icon or the "Hide Preview" link.

Cached

"Google Desktop creates cached copies (snapshots) of your e-mail, files and other items each time you view them. These cached copies are stored on your computer's hard drive. As a result, you can often use Google Desktop to find items you have since deleted after installing Desktop."[6] When you do a search, Google Desktop will find the current version of the document but will also give you access to previous versions of the document via the cache (see Figure 10-17). Even more impressive, it will keep cached copies of files you've previously deleted (provided you didn't turn off this feature in the preferences, as discussed earlier).

Selecting one of the cached versions will open it up in your browser, as shown in Figure 10-18. This version, as with the preview, will not be formatted and will not contain any images from the file, but in a crunch it's a great way to prevent you from re-creating an accidentally deleted file from scratch.

Timeline

The Google Desktop timeline can be accessed via the time stamp listed for a particular item in the results list. When opened, you will receive a list of

(continued on p. 286)

Figure 10-12   Google Desktop search results

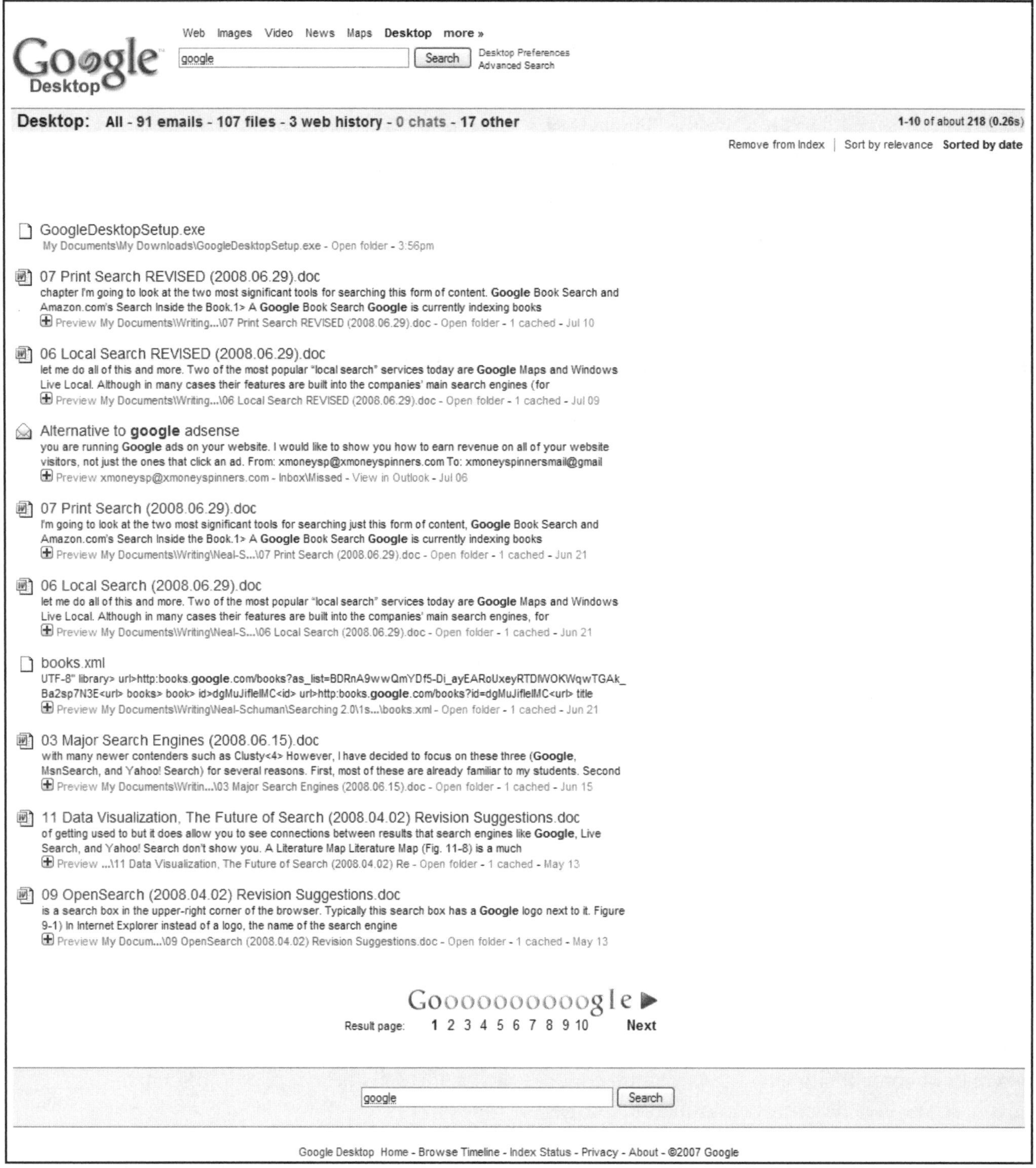

Web   Images   Video   News   Maps   **Desktop**   more »

Go*o*gle
Desktop

google | Search | Desktop Preferences
Advanced Search

Desktop: All - 91 emails - 107 files - 3 web history - 0 chats - 17 other

1-10 of about 218 (0.26s)

Remove from Index | Sort by relevance   **Sorted by date**

GoogleDesktopSetup.exe
My Documents\My Downloads\GoogleDesktopSetup.exe - Open folder - 3:56pm

07 Print Search REVISED (2008.06.29).doc
chapter I'm going to look at the two most significant tools for searching this form of content. **Google** Book Search and
Amazon.com's Search Inside the Book.1> A **Google** Book Search **Google** is currently indexing books
Preview My Documents\Writing...\07 Print Search REVISED (2008.06.29).doc - Open folder - 1 cached - Jul 10

06 Local Search REVISED (2008.06.29).doc
let me do all of this and more. Two of the most popular "local search" services today are **Google** Maps and Windows
Live Local. Although in many cases their features are built into the companies' main search engines (for
Preview My Documents\Writing...\06 Local Search REVISED (2008.06.29).doc - Open folder - 1 cached - Jul 09

Alternative to **google** adsense
you are running **Google** ads on your website. I would like to show you how to earn revenue on all of your website
visitors, not just the ones that click an ad. From: xmoneysp@xmoneyspinners.com To: xmoneyspinnersmail@gmail
Preview xmoneysp@xmoneyspinners.com - Inbox\Missed - View in Outlook - Jul 06

07 Print Search (2008.06.29).doc
I'm going to look at the two most significant tools for searching just this form of content, **Google** Book Search and
Amazon.com's Search Inside the Book.1> A **Google** Book Search **Google** is currently indexing books
Preview My Documents\Writing\Neal-S...\07 Print Search (2008.06.29).doc - Open folder - 1 cached - Jun 21

06 Local Search (2008.06.29).doc
let me do all of this and more. Two of the most popular "local search" services today are **Google** Maps and Windows
Live Local. Although in many cases their features are built into the companies' main search engines, for
Preview My Documents\Writing\Neal-S...\06 Local Search (2008.06.29).doc - Open folder - 1 cached - Jun 21

books.xml
UTF-8" library> url>http:books.**google**.com/books?as_list=BDRnA9wwQmYDf5-Di_ayEARoUxeyRTDlWOKWqwTGAk_
Ba2sp7N3E<url> books> book> id>dgMuJiflelMC<id> url>http:books.**google**.com/books?id=dgMuJiflelMC<url> title
Preview My Documents\Writing\Neal-Schuman\Searching 2.0\1s...\books.xml - Open folder - 1 cached - Jun 21

03 Major Search Engines (2008.06.15).doc
with many newer contenders such as Clusty<4> However, I have decided to focus on these three (**Google**,
MsnSearch, and Yahoo! Search) for several reasons. First, most of these are already familiar to my students. Second
Preview My Documents\Writin...\03 Major Search Engines (2008.06.15).doc - Open folder - 1 cached - Jun 15

11 Data Visualization, The Future of Search (2008.04.02) Revision Suggestions.doc
of getting used to but it does allow you to see connections between results that search engines like **Google**, Live
Search, and Yahoo! Search don't show you. A Literature Map Literature Map (Fig. 11-8) is a much
Preview ...\11 Data Visualization, The Future of Search (2008.04.02) Re - Open folder - 1 cached - May 13

09 OpenSearch (2008.04.02) Revision Suggestions.doc
is a search box in the upper-right corner of the browser. Typically this search box has a **Google** logo next to it. Figure
9-1) In Internet Explorer instead of a logo, the name of the search engine
Preview My Docum...\09 OpenSearch (2008.04.02) Revision Suggestions.doc - Open folder - 1 cached - May 13

Goooooooooogle ▶

Result page: **1** 2 3 4 5 6 7 8 9 10   **Next**

google | Search |

Figure 10-13   Search results limited to a particular type

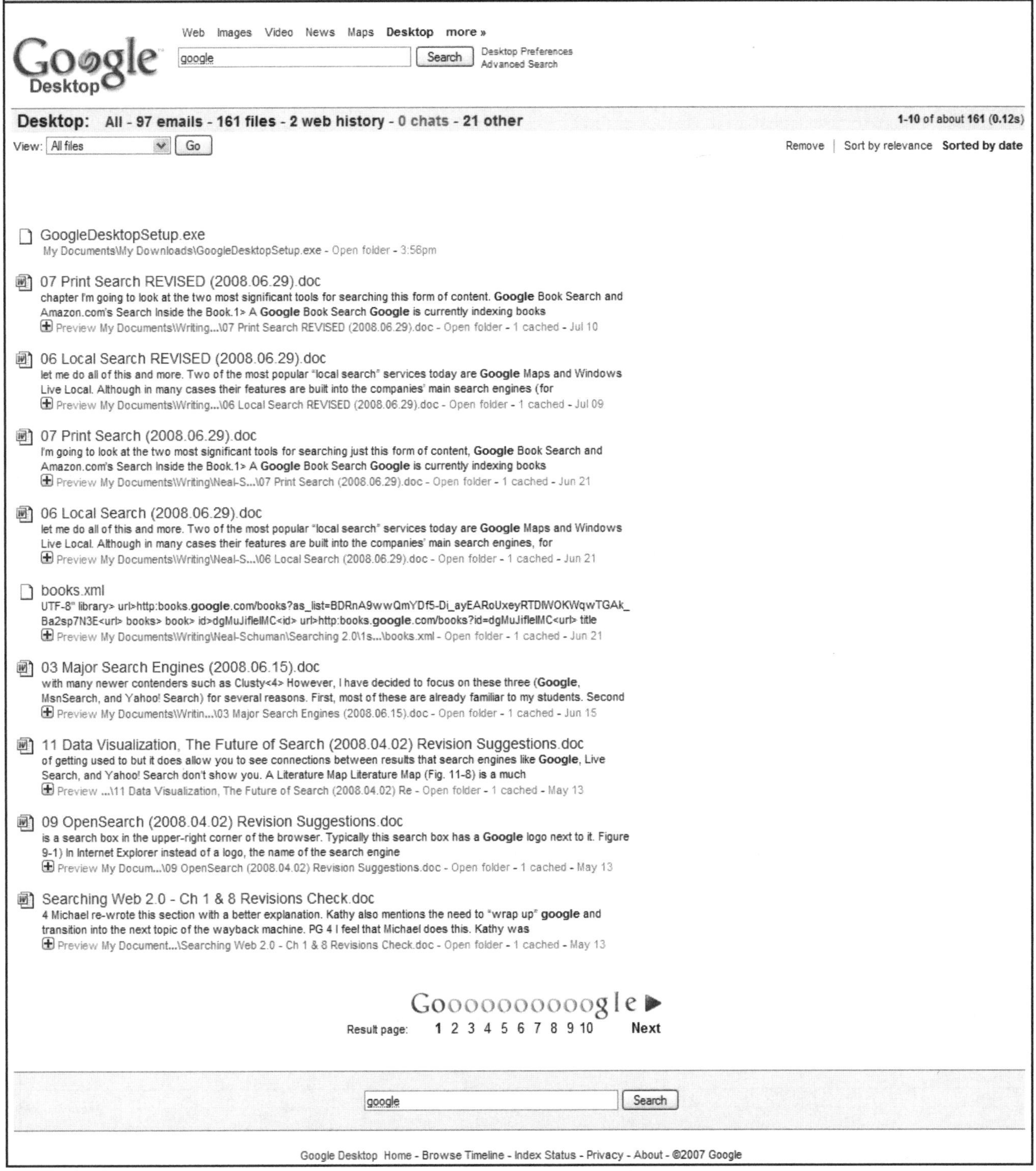

Google Desktop

Web   Images   Video   News   Maps   **Desktop**   more »

google   [Search]   Desktop Preferences
Advanced Search

Desktop: All - 97 emails - 161 files - 2 web history - 0 chats - 21 other

1-10 of about 161 (0.12s)

View: [All files ▼] [Go]

Remove | Sort by relevance **Sorted by date**

GoogleDesktopSetup.exe
My Documents\My Downloads\GoogleDesktopSetup.exe - Open folder - 3:56pm

07 Print Search REVISED (2008.06.29).doc
chapter I'm going to look at the two most significant tools for searching this form of content. **Google** Book Search and
Amazon.com's Search Inside the Book.1> A **Google** Book Search **Google** is currently indexing books
⊞ Preview My Documents\Writing...\07 Print Search REVISED (2008.06.29).doc - Open folder - 1 cached - Jul 10

06 Local Search REVISED (2008.06.29).doc
let me do all of this and more. Two of the most popular "local search" services today are **Google** Maps and Windows
Live Local. Although in many cases their features are built into the companies' main search engines (for
⊞ Preview My Documents\Writing...\06 Local Search REVISED (2008.06.29).doc - Open folder - 1 cached - Jul 09

07 Print Search (2008.06.29).doc
I'm going to look at the two most significant tools for searching just this form of content, **Google** Book Search and
Amazon.com's Search Inside the Book.1> A **Google** Book Search **Google** is currently indexing books
⊞ Preview My Documents\Writing\Neal-S...\07 Print Search (2008.06.29).doc - Open folder - 1 cached - Jun 21

06 Local Search (2008.06.29).doc
let me do all of this and more. Two of the most popular "local search" services today are **Google** Maps and Windows
Live Local. Although in many cases their features are built into the companies' main search engines, for
⊞ Preview My Documents\Writing\Neal-S...\06 Local Search (2008.06.29).doc - Open folder - 1 cached - Jun 21

books.xml
UTF-8" library> url>http:books.**google**.com/books?as_list=BDRnA9wwQmYDf5-Di_ayEARoUxeyRTDIWOKWqwTGAk_
Ba2sp7N3E<url> books> book> id>dgMuJiflelMC<id> url>http:books.**google**.com/books?id=dgMuJiflelMC<url> title
⊞ Preview My Documents\Writing\Neal-Schuman\Searching 2.0\1s...\books.xml - Open folder - 1 cached - Jun 21

03 Major Search Engines (2008.06.15).doc
with many newer contenders such as Clusty<4> However, I have decided to focus on these three (**Google**,
MsnSearch, and Yahoo! Search) for several reasons. First, most of these are already familiar to my students. Second
⊞ Preview My Documents\Writin...\03 Major Search Engines (2008.06.15).doc - Open folder - 1 cached - Jun 15

11 Data Visualization, The Future of Search (2008.04.02) Revision Suggestions.doc
of getting used to but it does allow you to see connections between results that search engines like **Google**, Live
Search, and Yahoo! Search don't show you. A Literature Map Literature Map (Fig. 11-8) is a much
⊞ Preview ...\11 Data Visualization, The Future of Search (2008.04.02) Re - Open folder - 1 cached - May 13

09 OpenSearch (2008.04.02) Revision Suggestions.doc
is a search box in the upper-right corner of the browser. Typically this search box has a **Google** logo next to it. Figure
9-1) In Internet Explorer instead of a logo, the name of the search engine
⊞ Preview My Docum...\09 OpenSearch (2008.04.02) Revision Suggestions.doc - Open folder - 1 cached - May 13

Searching Web 2.0 - Ch 1 & 8 Revisions Check.doc
4 Michael re-wrote this section with a better explanation. Kathy also mentions the need to "wrap up" **google** and
transition into the next topic of the wayback machine. PG 4 I feel that Michael does this. Kathy was
⊞ Preview My Document...\Searching Web 2.0 - Ch 1 & 8 Revisions Check.doc - Open folder - 1 cached - May 13

Goooooooooogle ▶

Result page: **1** 2 3 4 5 6 7 8 9 10   **Next**

google   [Search]

Google Desktop Home - Browse Timeline - Index Status - Privacy - About - ©2007 Google

Figure 10-14   Search results further limited to Word files

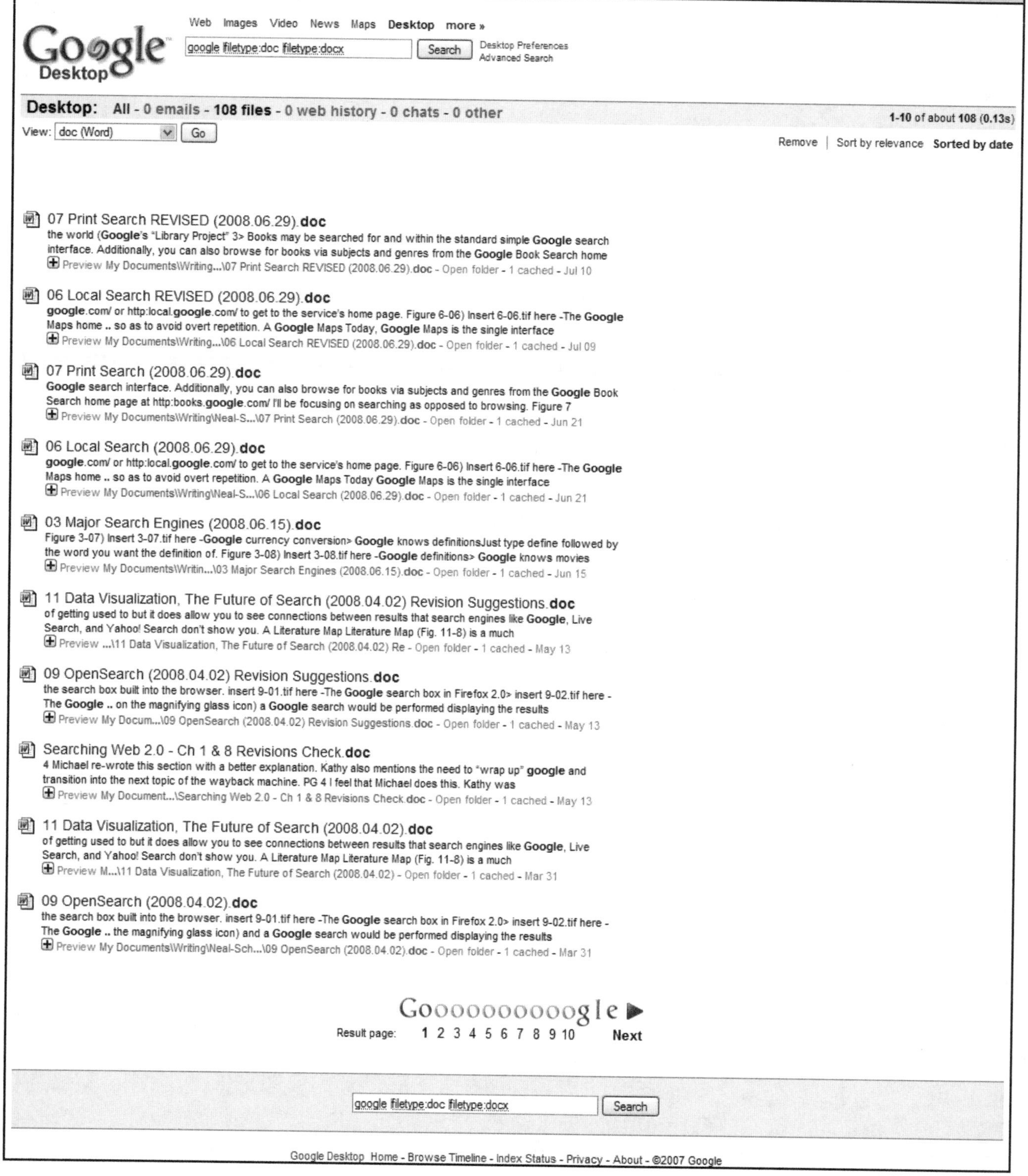

Web   Images   Video   News   Maps   **Desktop**   more »

Google Desktop

google filetype:doc filetype:docx   [Search]   Desktop Preferences
Advanced Search

Desktop: All - **0 emails** - **108 files** - 0 web history - 0 chats - 0 other

1-10 of about **108** (0.13s)

View: [doc (Word)] [Go]   Remove | Sort by relevance **Sorted by date**

07 Print Search REVISED (2008.06.29)**.doc**
the world (**Google**'s "Library Project" 3> Books may be searched for and within the standard simple **Google** search
interface. Additionally, you can also browse for books via subjects and genres from the **Google** Book Search home
⊞ Preview My Documents\Writing...\07 Print Search REVISED (2008.06.29)**.doc** - Open folder - 1 cached - Jul 10

06 Local Search REVISED (2008.06.29)**.doc**
google.com/ or http:local.**google**.com/ to get to the service's home page. Figure 6-06) Insert 6-06.tif here -The **Google**
Maps home .. so as to avoid overt repetition. A **Google** Maps Today, **Google** Maps is the single interface
⊞ Preview My Documents\Writing...\06 Local Search REVISED (2008.06.29)**.doc** - Open folder - 1 cached - Jul 09

07 Print Search (2008.06.29)**.doc**
Google search interface. Additionally, you can also browse for books via subjects and genres from the **Google** Book
Search home page at http:books.**google**.com/ I'll be focusing on searching as opposed to browsing. Figure 7
⊞ Preview My Documents\Writing\Neal-S...\07 Print Search (2008.06.29)**.doc** - Open folder - 1 cached - Jun 21

06 Local Search (2008.06.29)**.doc**
google.com/ or http:local.**google**.com/ to get to the service's home page. Figure 6-06) Insert 6-06.tif here -The **Google**
Maps home .. so as to avoid overt repetition. A **Google** Maps Today **Google** Maps is the single interface
⊞ Preview My Documents\Writing\Neal-S...\06 Local Search (2008.06.29)**.doc** - Open folder - 1 cached - Jun 21

03 Major Search Engines (2008.06.15)**.doc**
Figure 3-07) Insert 3-07.tif here -**Google** currency conversion> **Google** knows definitionsJust type define followed by
the word you want the definition of. Figure 3-08) Insert 3-08.tif here -**Google** definitions> **Google** knows movies
⊞ Preview My Documents\Writin...\03 Major Search Engines (2008.06.15)**.doc** - Open folder - 1 cached - Jun 15

11 Data Visualization, The Future of Search (2008.04.02) Revision Suggestions**.doc**
of getting used to but it does allow you to see connections between results that search engines like **Google**, Live
Search, and Yahoo! Search don't show you. A Literature Map Literature Map (Fig. 11-8) is a much
⊞ Preview ...\11 Data Visualization, The Future of Search (2008.04.02) Re - Open folder - 1 cached - May 13

09 OpenSearch (2008.04.02) Revision Suggestions**.doc**
the search box built into the browser. insert 9-01.tif here -The **Google** search box in Firefox 2.0> insert 9-02.tif here -
The **Google** .. on the magnifying glass icon) a **Google** search would be performed displaying the results
⊞ Preview My Docum...\09 OpenSearch (2008.04.02) Revision Suggestions.**doc** - Open folder - 1 cached - May 13

Searching Web 2.0 - Ch 1 & 8 Revisions Check**.doc**
4 Michael re-wrote this section with a better explanation. Kathy also mentions the need to "wrap up" **google** and
transition into the next topic of the wayback machine. PG 4 I feel that Michael does this. Kathy was
⊞ Preview My Document...\Searching Web 2.0 - Ch 1 & 8 Revisions Check.**doc** - Open folder - 1 cached - May 13

11 Data Visualization, The Future of Search (2008.04.02)**.doc**
of getting used to but it does allow you to see connections between results that search engines like **Google**, Live
Search, and Yahoo! Search don't show you. A Literature Map Literature Map (Fig. 11-8) is a much
⊞ Preview M...\11 Data Visualization, The Future of Search (2008.04.02) - Open folder - 1 cached - Mar 31

09 OpenSearch (2008.04.02)**.doc**
the search box built into the browser. insert 9-01.tif here -The **Google** search box in Firefox 2.0> insert 9-02.tif here -
The **Google** .. the magnifying glass icon) and a **Google** search would be performed displaying the results
⊞ Preview My Documents\Writing\Neal-Sch...\09 OpenSearch (2008.04.02)**.doc** - Open folder - 1 cached - Mar 31

Goooooooooogle ▶

Result page: **1** 2 3 4 5 6 7 8 9 10   **Next**

google filetype:doc filetype:docx   [Search]

Figure 10-15 A Word document preview from the search results

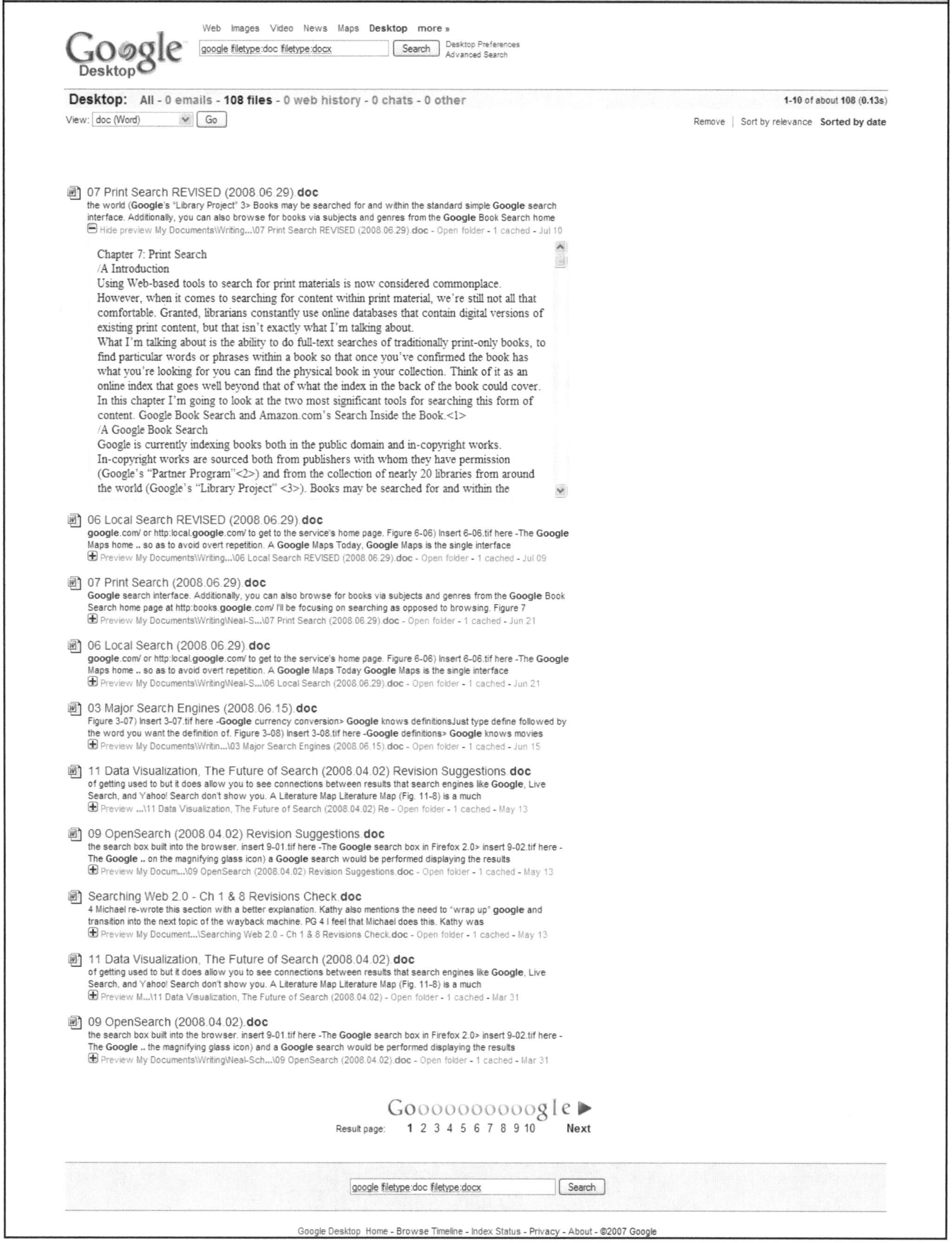

Web   Images   Video   News   Maps   **Desktop**   more »

Google Desktop

google filetype:doc filetype:docx   [Search]   Desktop Preferences
Advanced Search

Desktop: All - 0 emails - **108 files** - 0 web history - 0 chats - 0 other   1-10 of about 108 (0.13s)

View: doc (Word) [v] [Go]   Remove | Sort by relevance **Sorted by date**

07 Print Search REVISED (2008.06.29).**doc**
the world (**Google**'s "Library Project" 3> Books may be searched for and within the standard simple **Google** search
interface. Additionally, you can also browse for books via subjects and genres from the **Google** Book Search home
⊟ Hide preview My Documents\Writing...\07 Print Search REVISED (2008.06.29).**doc** - Open folder - 1 cached - Jul 10

> Chapter 7: Print Search
> /A Introduction
> Using Web-based tools to search for print materials is now considered commonplace.
> However, when it comes to searching for content within print material, we're still not all that
> comfortable. Granted, librarians constantly use online databases that contain digital versions of
> existing print content, but that isn't exactly what I'm talking about.
> What I'm talking about is the ability to do full-text searches of traditionally print-only books, to
> find particular words or phrases within a book so that once you've confirmed the book has
> what you're looking for you can find the physical book in your collection. Think of it as an
> online index that goes well beyond that of what the index in the back of the book could cover.
> In this chapter I'm going to look at the two most significant tools for searching this form of
> content. Google Book Search and Amazon.com's Search Inside the Book.<1>
> /A Google Book Search
> Google is currently indexing books both in the public domain and in-copyright works.
> In-copyright works are sourced both from publishers with whom they have permission
> (Google's "Partner Program"<2>) and from the collection of nearly 20 libraries from around
> the world (Google's "Library Project" <3>). Books may be searched for and within the

06 Local Search REVISED (2008.06.29).**doc**
google.com/ or http:local.**google**.com/ to get to the service's home page. Figure 6-06) Insert 6-06.tif here -The **Google**
Maps home .. so as to avoid overt repetition. A **Google** Maps Today, **Google** Maps is the single interface
⊞ Preview My Documents\Writing...\06 Local Search REVISED (2008.06.29).**doc** - Open folder - 1 cached - Jul 09

07 Print Search (2008.06.29).**doc**
Google search interface. Additionally, you can also browse for books via subjects and genres from the **Google** Book
Search home page at http:books.**google**.com/ I'll be focusing on searching as opposed to browsing. Figure 7
⊞ Preview My Documents\Writing\Neal-S...\07 Print Search (2008.06.29).**doc** - Open folder - 1 cached - Jun 21

06 Local Search (2008.06.29).**doc**
google.com/ or http:local.**google**.com/ to get to the service's home page. Figure 6-06) Insert 6-06.tif here -The **Google**
Maps home .. so as to avoid overt repetition. A **Google** Maps Today **Google** Maps is the single interface
⊞ Preview My Documents\Writing\Neal-S...\06 Local Search (2008.06.29).**doc** - Open folder - 1 cached - Jun 21

03 Major Search Engines (2008.06.15).**doc**
Figure 3-07) Insert 3-07.tif here -**Google** currency conversion> **Google** knows definitionsJust type define followed by
the word you want the definition of. Figure 3-08) Insert 3-08.tif here -**Google** definitions> **Google** knows movies
⊞ Preview My Documents\Writin...\03 Major Search Engines (2008.06.15).**doc** - Open folder - 1 cached - Jun 15

11 Data Visualization, The Future of Search (2008.04.02) Revision Suggestions.**doc**
of getting used to but it does allow you to see connections between results that search engines like **Google**, Live
Search, and Yahoo! Search don't show you. A Literature Map Literature Map (Fig. 11-8) is a much
⊞ Preview ...\11 Data Visualization, The Future of Search (2008.04.02) Re - Open folder - 1 cached - May 13

09 OpenSearch (2008.04.02) Revision Suggestions **doc**
the search box built into the browser. insert 9-01.tif here -The **Google** search box in Firefox 2.0> insert 9-02.tif here -
The **Google** .. on the magnifying glass icon) a **Google** search would be performed displaying the results
⊞ Preview My Docum...\09 OpenSearch (2008.04.02) Revision Suggestions.**doc** - Open folder - 1 cached - May 13

Searching Web 2.0 - Ch 1 & 8 Revisions Check.**doc**
4 Michael re-wrote this section with a better explanation. Kathy also mentions the need to "wrap up" **google** and
transition into the next topic of the wayback machine. PG 4 I feel that Michael does this. Kathy was
⊞ Preview My Document...\Searching Web 2.0 - Ch 1 & 8 Revisions Check.**doc** - Open folder - 1 cached - May 13

11 Data Visualization, The Future of Search (2008.04.02).**doc**
of getting used to but it does allow you to see connections between results that search engines like **Google**, Live
Search, and Yahoo! Search don't show you. A Literature Map Literature Map (Fig. 11-8) is a much
⊞ Preview M...\11 Data Visualization, The Future of Search (2008.04.02) - Open folder - 1 cached - Mar 31

09 OpenSearch (2008.04.02).**doc**
the search box built into the browser. insert 9-01.tif here -The **Google** search box in Firefox 2.0> insert 9-02.tif here -
The **Google** .. the magnifying glass icon) and a **Google** search would be performed displaying the results
⊞ Preview My Documents\Writing\Neal-Sch...\09 OpenSearch (2008.04.02).**doc** - Open folder - 1 cached - Mar 31

Result page: **1** 2 3 4 5 6 7 8 9 10   **Next**

google filetype:doc filetype:docx   [Search]

Figure 10-16   A PowerPoint slide show preview from the search results

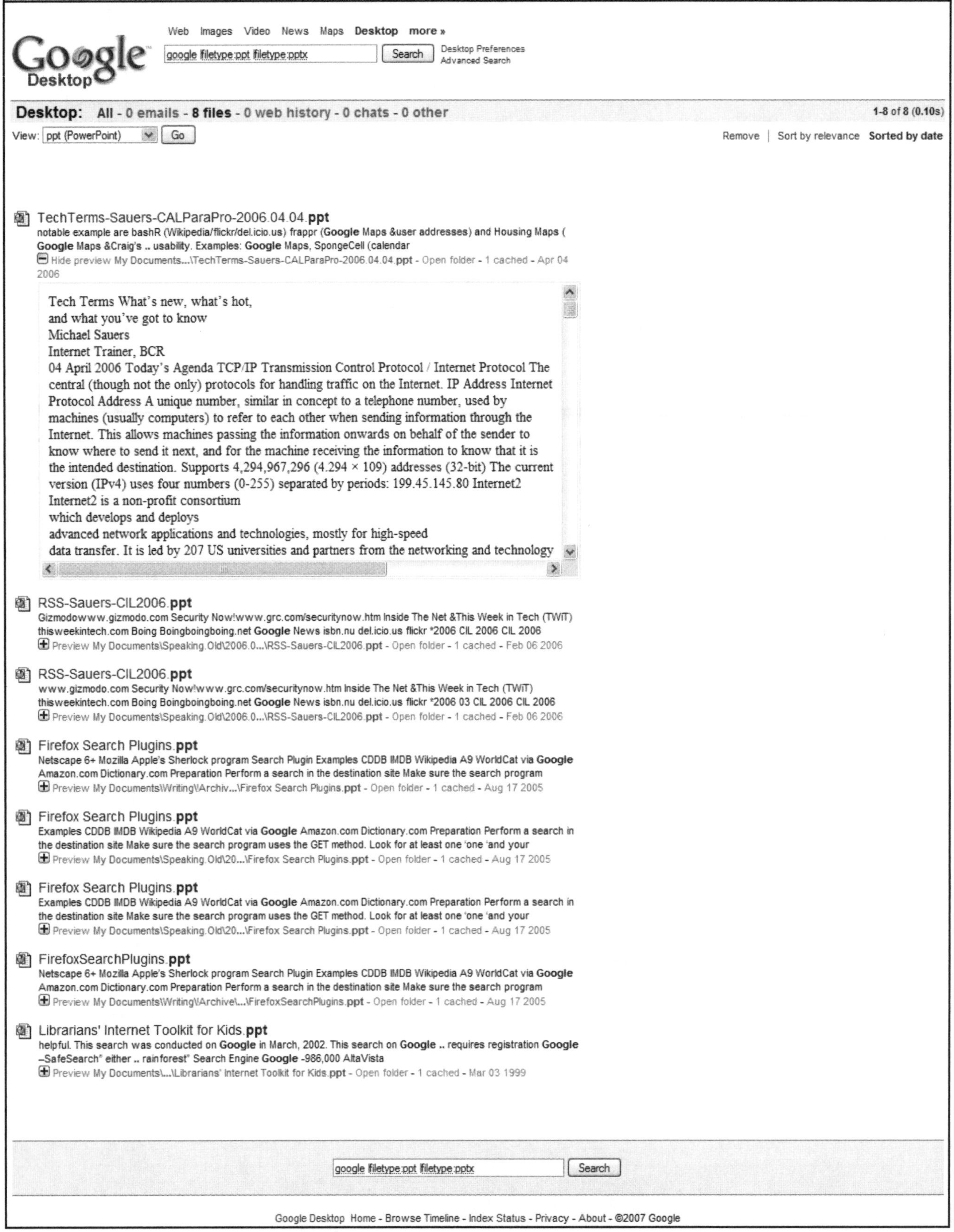

Web   Images   Video   News   Maps   **Desktop**   more »

Google Desktop

google filetype:ppt filetype:pptx   [Search]   Desktop Preferences
                                                     Advanced Search

Desktop: All - 0 emails - **8 files** - 0 web history - 0 chats - 0 other   1-8 of 8 (0.10s)

View: [ppt (PowerPoint) ▾] [Go]   Remove | Sort by relevance **Sorted by date**

▣ TechTerms-Sauers-CALParaPro-2006.04.04.**ppt**
notable example are bashR (Wikipedia/flickr/del.icio.us) frappr (**Google** Maps &user addresses) and Housing Maps (
Google Maps &Craig's .. usability. Examples: **Google** Maps, SpongeCell (calendar
⊟ Hide preview My Documents...\TechTerms-Sauers-CALParaPro-2006.04.04.ppt - Open folder - 1 cached - Apr 04
2006

> Tech Terms What's new, what's hot,
> and what you've got to know
> Michael Sauers
> Internet Trainer, BCR
> 04 April 2006 Today's Agenda TCP/IP Transmission Control Protocol / Internet Protocol The
> central (though not the only) protocols for handling traffic on the Internet. IP Address Internet
> Protocol Address A unique number, similar in concept to a telephone number, used by
> machines (usually computers) to refer to each other when sending information through the
> Internet. This allows machines passing the information onwards on behalf of the sender to
> know where to send it next, and for the machine receiving the information to know that it is
> the intended destination. Supports 4,294,967,296 (4.294 × 109) addresses (32-bit) The current
> version (IPv4) uses four numbers (0-255) separated by periods: 199.45.145.80 Internet2
> Internet2 is a non-profit consortium
> which develops and deploys
> advanced network applications and technologies, mostly for high-speed
> data transfer. It is led by 207 US universities and partners from the networking and technology

▣ RSS-Sauers-CIL2006.**ppt**
Gizmodowww.gizmodo.com Security Now!www.grc.com/securitynow.htm Inside The Net &This Week in Tech (TWiT)
thisweekintech.com Boing Boingboingboing.net **Google** News isbn.nu del.icio.us flickr *2006 CIL 2006 CIL 2006
⊞ Preview My Documents\Speaking.Old\2006.0...\RSS-Sauers-CIL2006.ppt - Open folder - 1 cached - Feb 06 2006

▣ RSS-Sauers-CIL2006.**ppt**
www.gizmodo.com Security Now!www.grc.com/securitynow.htm Inside The Net &This Week in Tech (TWiT)
thisweekintech.com Boing Boingboingboing.net **Google** News isbn.nu del.icio.us flickr *2006 03 CIL 2006 CIL 2006
⊞ Preview My Documents\Speaking.Old\2006.0...\RSS-Sauers-CIL2006.ppt - Open folder - 1 cached - Feb 06 2006

▣ Firefox Search Plugins.**ppt**
Netscape 6+ Mozilla Apple's Sherlock program Search Plugin Examples CDDB IMDB Wikipedia A9 WorldCat via **Google**
Amazon.com Dictionary.com Preparation Perform a search in the destination site Make sure the search program
⊞ Preview My Documents\Writing\Archiv...\Firefox Search Plugins.ppt - Open folder - 1 cached - Aug 17 2005

▣ Firefox Search Plugins.**ppt**
Examples CDDB IMDB Wikipedia A9 WorldCat via **Google** Amazon.com Dictionary.com Preparation Perform a search in
the destination site Make sure the search program uses the GET method. Look for at least one 'one 'and your
⊞ Preview My Documents\Speaking.Old\20...\Firefox Search Plugins.ppt - Open folder - 1 cached - Aug 17 2005

▣ Firefox Search Plugins.**ppt**
Examples CDDB IMDB Wikipedia A9 WorldCat via **Google** Amazon.com Dictionary.com Preparation Perform a search in
the destination site Make sure the search program uses the GET method. Look for at least one 'one 'and your
⊞ Preview My Documents\Speaking.Old\20...\Firefox Search Plugins.ppt - Open folder - 1 cached - Aug 17 2005

▣ FirefoxSearchPlugins.**ppt**
Netscape 6+ Mozilla Apple's Sherlock program Search Plugin Examples CDDB IMDB Wikipedia A9 WorldCat via **Google**
Amazon.com Dictionary.com Preparation Perform a search in the destination site Make sure the search program
⊞ Preview My Documents\Writing\Archive\...\FirefoxSearchPlugins.ppt - Open folder - 1 cached - Aug 17 2005

▣ Librarians' Internet Toolkit for Kids.**ppt**
helpful. This search was conducted on **Google** in March, 2002. This search on **Google** .. requires registration **Google**
–SafeSearch° either .. rainforest" Search Engine **Google** -986,000 AltaVista
⊞ Preview My Documents\...\Librarians' Internet Toolkit for Kids.ppt - Open folder - 1 cached - Mar 03 1999

google filetype:ppt filetype:pptx   [Search]

Google Desktop Home - Browse Timeline - Index Status - Privacy - About - ©2007 Google

Figure 10-17   The link to cached versions

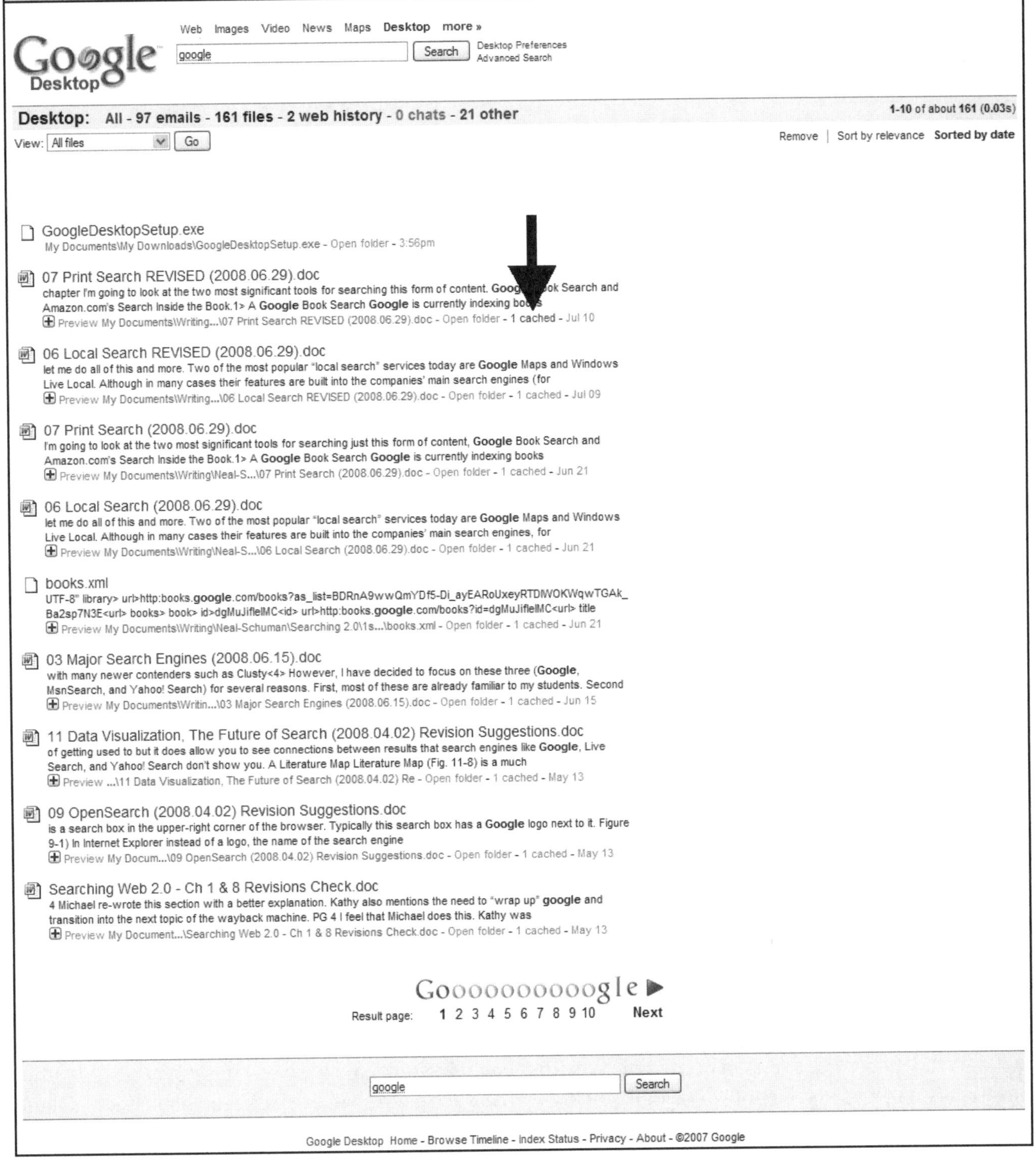

Web   Images   Video   News   Maps   **Desktop**   more »

Google Desktop

google   [Search]   Desktop Preferences
                                             Advanced Search

Desktop: All - 97 emails - 161 files - 2 web history - 0 chats - 21 other   1-10 of about **161** (0.03s)

View: [All files ▾]   [Go]   Remove | Sort by relevance **Sorted by date**

☐ GoogleDesktopSetup.exe
   My Documents\My Downloads\GoogleDesktopSetup.exe - Open folder - 3:56pm

📄 07 Print Search REVISED (2008.06.29).doc
   chapter I'm going to look at the two most significant tools for searching this form of content. Google Book Search and
   Amazon.com's Search Inside the Book.1> A **Google** Book Search **Google** is currently indexing books
   ⊞ Preview My Documents\Writing...\07 Print Search REVISED (2008.06.29).doc - Open folder - 1 cached - Jul 10

📄 06 Local Search REVISED (2008.06.29).doc
   let me do all of this and more. Two of the most popular "local search" services today are **Google** Maps and Windows
   Live Local. Although in many cases their features are built into the companies' main search engines (for
   ⊞ Preview My Documents\Writing...\06 Local Search REVISED (2008.06.29).doc - Open folder - 1 cached - Jul 09

📄 07 Print Search (2008.06.29).doc
   I'm going to look at the two most significant tools for searching just this form of content, **Google** Book Search and
   Amazon.com's Search Inside the Book.1> A **Google** Book Search **Google** is currently indexing books
   ⊞ Preview My Documents\Writing\Neal-S...\07 Print Search (2008.06.29).doc - Open folder - 1 cached - Jun 21

📄 06 Local Search (2008.06.29).doc
   let me do all of this and more. Two of the most popular "local search" services today are **Google** Maps and Windows
   Live Local. Although in many cases their features are built into the companies' main search engines, for
   ⊞ Preview My Documents\Writing\Neal-S...\06 Local Search (2008.06.29).doc - Open folder - 1 cached - Jun 21

☐ books.xml
   UTF-8" library> url>http:books.**google**.com/books?as_list=BDRnA9wwQmYDf5-Di_ayEARoUxeyRTDfWOKWqwTGAk_
   Ba2sp7N3E<url> books> book> id>dgMuJiflelMC<id> url>http:books.**google**.com/books?id=dgMuJiflelMC<url> title
   ⊞ Preview My Documents\Writing\Neal-Schuman\Searching 2.0\1s...\books.xml - Open folder - 1 cached - Jun 21

📄 03 Major Search Engines (2008.06.15).doc
   with many newer contenders such as Clusty<4> However, I have decided to focus on these three (**Google**,
   MsnSearch, and Yahoo! Search) for several reasons. First, most of these are already familiar to my students. Second
   ⊞ Preview My Documents\Writin...\03 Major Search Engines (2008.06.15).doc - Open folder - 1 cached - Jun 15

📄 11 Data Visualization, The Future of Search (2008.04.02) Revision Suggestions.doc
   of getting used to but it does allow you to see connections between results that search engines like **Google**, Live
   Search, and Yahoo! Search don't show you. A Literature Map Literature Map (Fig. 11-8) is a much
   ⊞ Preview ...\11 Data Visualization, The Future of Search (2008.04.02) Re - Open folder - 1 cached - May 13

📄 09 OpenSearch (2008.04.02) Revision Suggestions.doc
   is a search box in the upper-right corner of the browser. Typically this search box has a **Google** logo next to it. Figure
   9-1) In Internet Explorer instead of a logo, the name of the search engine
   ⊞ Preview My Docum...\09 OpenSearch (2008.04.02) Revision Suggestions.doc - Open folder - 1 cached - May 13

📄 Searching Web 2.0 - Ch 1 & 8 Revisions Check.doc
   4 Michael re-wrote this section with a better explanation. Kathy also mentions the need to "wrap up" **google** and
   transition into the next topic of the wayback machine. PG 4 I feel that Michael does this. Kathy was
   ⊞ Preview My Document...\Searching Web 2.0 - Ch 1 & 8 Revisions Check.doc - Open folder - 1 cached - May 13

Goooooooooogle ▶

Result page: **1** 2 3 4 5 6 7 8 9 10   **Next**

google   [Search]

Google Desktop Home - Browse Timeline - Index Status - Privacy - About - ©2007 Google

Figure 10-18   A cached version of Chapter 7

This is one version of C:\Documents and Settings\Michael Sauers\My Documents\Writing\Neal-Schuman\Searching 2.0\2nd Draft response\07 Print Search REVISED (2008.06.29).doc from your personal cache.
The file may have changed since that time. Click here for the current file.
Since this file is stored on your computer, publicly linking to it will not work.

Google may not be affiliated with the authors of this page nor responsible for its content. This page may be protected by copyright.

Chapter 7: Print Search
/A Introduction
Using Web-based tools to search for print materials is now considered commonplace. However, when it comes to searching for content within print material, we're still not all that comfortable. Granted, librarians constantly use online databases that contain digital versions of existing print content, but that isn't exactly what I'm talking about.
What I'm talking about is the ability to do full-text searches of traditionally print-only books, to find particular words or phrases within a book so that once you've confirmed the book has what you're looking for you can find the physical book in your collection. Think of it as an online index that goes well beyond that of what the index in the back of the book could cover.
In this chapter I'm going to look at the two most significant tools for searching this form of content. Google Book Search and Amazon.com's Search Inside the Book.<1>
/A Google Book Search
Google is currently indexing books both in the public domain and in-copyright works. In-copyright works are sourced both from publishers with whom they have permission (Google's "Partner Program"<2>) and from the collection of nearly 20 libraries from around the world (Google's "Library Project" <3>). Books may be searched for and within the standard simple Google search interface. Additionally, you can also browse for books via subjects and genres from the Google Book Search home page at http://books.google.com/. (I'll be focusing on searching as opposed to browsing). (Figure 7-01)
<Insert 7-01.tif here - The Google Book Search home page
/B Searching Interfaces
As with most Google search services, there are two searching interfaces: the basic search and the advanced search.
/C Basic Search
The basic book search is located on the Google Book Search home page as shown in figure 7.1. In this case, just type in the keyword(s) you're searching for (title, author, subject, etc.) and click the Search Books button. This interface supports Boolean operators, +/- operators, and quotation marks for phrase searching.
/C Advanced Search
Clicking on the "Advanced Book Search" link to the right of the Search Books button will take you to the Advanced Book Search Interface. (Figure 7-02) Here you will be presented with twelve options for searching: Find Results (with four sub options), Search, Language, Title, Author, Publisher, Subject, Publication Date, and ISBN.
<Insert 7-02.tif here - The Google Advanced Book Search>
Find Results

events, as recorded by Google Desktop, centered on the document that led you to the timeline page, as shown in Figure 10-19.

This page can show you what else you were working on around the same time as the searched-for file. This might not seem completely relevant at first, so let me give an example. Let's say that I'm working on a magazine article in which I need to reference a number of different Web sites. As I work on the article in Word, I also use Firefox to open several relevant Web sites. Technology being what it is, my computer crashes without my having recently saved my article or bookmarked those Web sites. Once I reboot my computer, I can bring up Google Desktop Search and look for my document. There, in the cache, is the most recent version of my article, with most of my changes that I'd not yet saved. Quickly I copy that text into Word and resave it. I then check the timeline relevant to the document and see the URLs of the Web sites I'd been viewing because they're in my browser's history. It also leads me to drafts of e-mails that I've written but did not send

out. Google Desktop has just saved me an hour or two of retyping my article and re-searching for those sites I was referencing. No complaints here.

You can move to earlier or later times in the timeline via the "< Older" and "Newer >" links at the top of the page. You can also limit the timeline to show only files of certain types—all, e-mails, files, Web history, and chats—via the links in the light blue bar near the top of the page.

Advanced Desktop Searching
Last, I'd like to mention the advanced searching features of Google Desktop. To access them, click on the "Advanced Search" link to the right of the search box. This can be found only on the Desktop Search pages in your Web browser. It is not accessible from the sidebar, taskbar, or quick search interfaces. Figure 10-20 shows the advanced search interface.

Here you'll be able to change the default set of results and find four options for modifying your search: "Show results," "Has the words," "Doesn't have," and "Date within."

Figure 10-19   The Google Desktop timeline

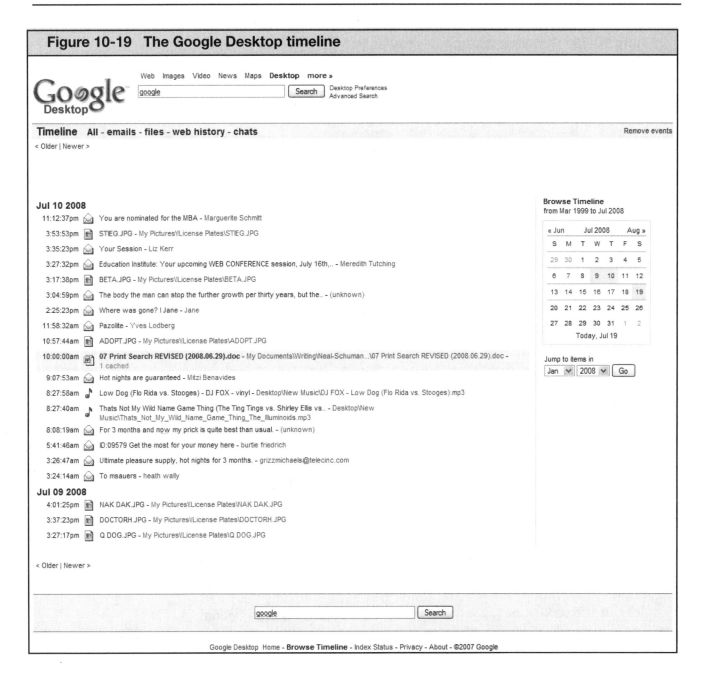

- **Show results:**

  The "Show results" option allows you to limit your results to a particular file type. The default is "all," but you may also limit your search results to e-mails, files, Web history, chat, or other. Keep in mind that if you do search for all, you can limit to each of those categories on the results page. I suggest you search everything and limit later if you need to. If you limit now, you might miss something.

- **Has the words:**

  This is your standard search box. Keywords you

  enter here must appear in the results. (Boolean operators and quotation marks are allowed.)

- **Doesn't have:**

  This is your Boolean NOT. Any keywords entered here must not appear in the results.

- **Date within:**

  If you find yourself asking, "What have I done involving [insert topic of choice here] in the past week?" use this search option. Here you can choose one of eight predefined timeframes: one day, three days, one week, two weeks, one month, two months, six months, or one year, all from a particular date.

Figure 10-20 Google Desktop's advanced search interface

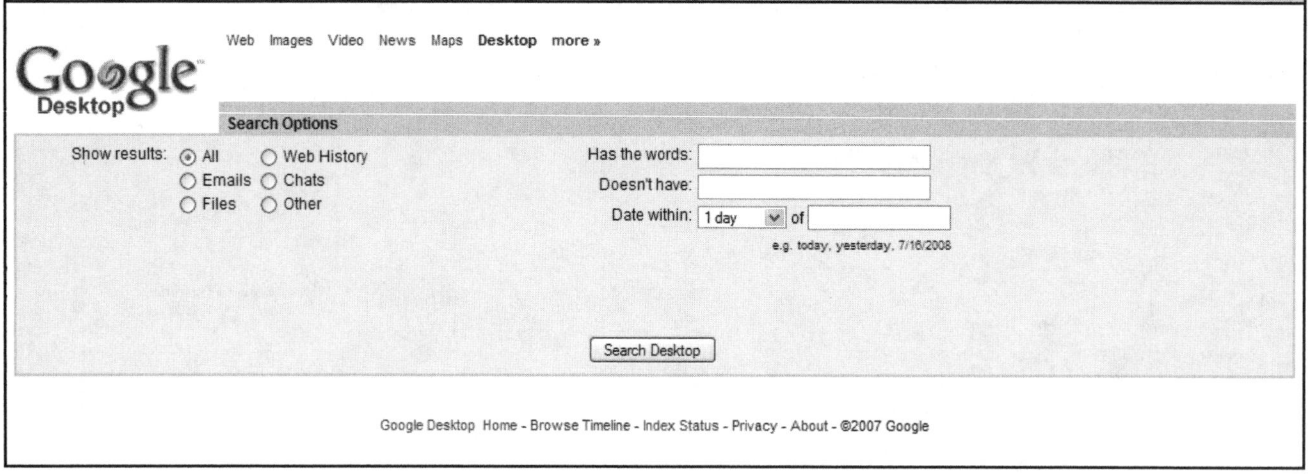

In the date field you can provide a day/month/year entry or type words such as "today" or "yesterday." I've tried other entries such as "last friday" and they seem to work, so feel free to experiment.

WINDOWS SEARCH

If you're running Windows XP, you may want to consider Microsoft's Windows Search instead of Google Desktop. I don't want to get into a big discussion over the benefits or lack thereof with Microsoft versus non-Microsoft products, but when it comes right down to it, programs by Microsoft do tend to run smoother and integrate better with the Windows Operating System. That being said, there are different features and other subtle differences between Google's and Microsoft's desktop search products, so you'll need to decide which is right for you.

Available for Windows XPsp2 and higher, Windows Search acts as a replacement for the built-in search that you can find on the Windows Start menu. To get it, go to the Windows Search page on the Microsoft Web site at www.microsoft.com/windows/products/winfamily/desktopsearch/default.mspx, as shown in Figure 10-21, choose the "Get it now" link, and follow the on-screen instructions for downloading and installing the software.

Once installed, you'll have two ways to access Windows Search. The first is via a search box now appearing in your taskbar (just as with Google Desktop Search). The second is the more full-featured interface accessible by opening the Start menu

and clicking "Search."[7] Figure 10-22 shows both of these options. Throughout the rest of the discussion of Windows Search, I'll focus on the Start/Search version.

As with Google Desktop, Windows Desktop Search will need some time to index your computer's contents. This is set to be done automatically and in the background so as to not degrade system performance. You may want to install it and leave your computer alone for a bit to get it completely indexed. Again, you can search before indexing is complete, but the results will be only as complete as the indexing. Let's cover the program's options before talking about search.

Desktop Search Options

To access the options for Desktop Search, click the "Views" icon—the second icon from the right in the top right of the window—and select "Desktop Search Options." Despite the simple window that opens (see Figure 10-23), there's actually a lot hiding in here.

What this window shows is a list of what's being indexed by your computer. By default, you should see "Documents and Settings" and Microsoft Outlook Express (unless you've uninstalled it). If you also have Microsoft Outlook on your computer, this too should be automatically listed. You may also see any additional drives that you have installed on your computer other than C. For example, Figure 10-23 shows that my drives F, G, H, and M are also being indexed. You then have three buttons to choose from:

Figure 10-21   The Windows Search homepage

Figure 10-22   Selecting "search" on the Windows start menu

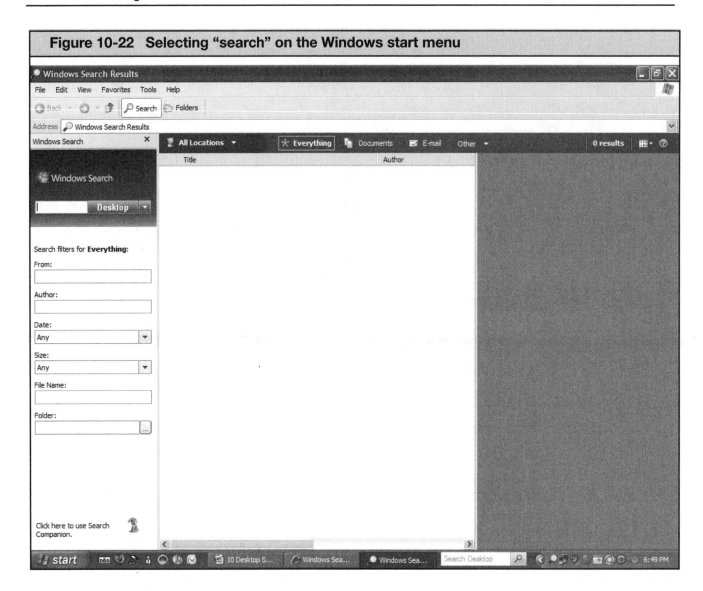

"Modify," "Advanced," and "Close." Click the "Close" button to exit from the options interface. The other two are a bit more complex.

Modify

If you wish to change what areas of your computer are being indexed, select the "Modify" button. This will open a new window, as shown in Figure 10-24. Here you can browse your computer and select or unselect on a folder-by-folder basis (what folders you do or do not want indexed). To index a folder, check the box to the left of that folder. To remove it from indexing, uncheck its box. Once you have made your changes, click "OK" to exit from this screen. Click "Cancel" to exit without accepting your changes.

Advanced

Selecting the Advanced button will open a new window with three tabs: "Index Settings," "File Types," and "Add UNC Location."

INDEX SETTINGS

This tab has three sections: file settings, troubleshooting, and index location, as shown in Figure 10-25.

- **File settings:**
  There are two options here. The first is "Index encrypted files." This option is available only if you've turned on Windows' hard drive encryption. If you've done so and you want those files to be indexed, check this option. The second option

Figure 10-23 Indexing options

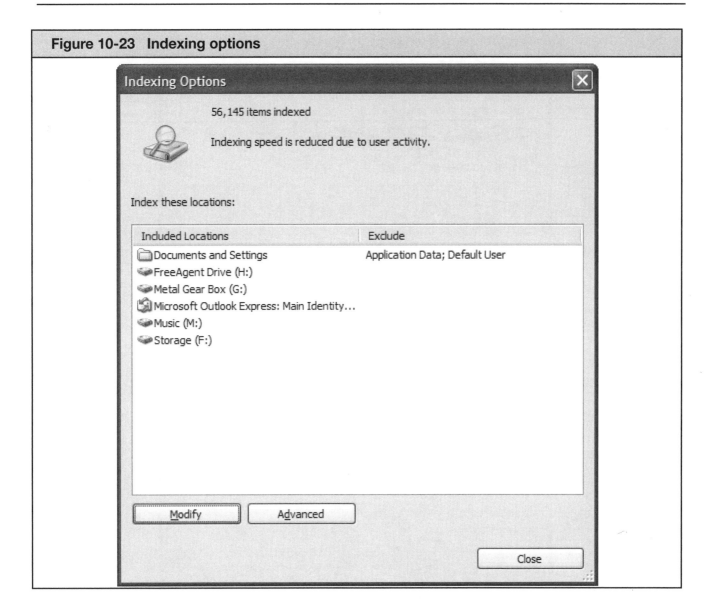

is "Treat similar words with diacritics as different words." By default the indexing engine in Windows Desktop Search considers *resume* and *résumé* to be the same words. Checking this option will cause your index to be re-created with these words being treated as different entries. You might want to use this if you are aware of documents that contain words in English and in other languages that have different meanings due to the appearance of the diacritics.

• **Troubleshooting:**
Here you have two options. The first is "Rebuild," which when clicked will erase your current index and rebuild a new one from scratch with your current settings. Do this only if you think you have a

corrupted index. The second is "Restore Defaults," which will undo any changes to your indexing settings you made since installing the program.

• **Index location:**
Here you are shown the location of the index file. Clicking the "Select New" button will allow you to browse for a new location in which to store your index. For example, you've recently added a new second hard drive and wish to store your data there instead of on the main drive. Select the new location, click "OK," then click "OK" again to exit this window. Your indexed file will be moved to the new location. Returning to this screen should now show the current location as the location you just chose.

Figure 10-24   Modifying indexed locations

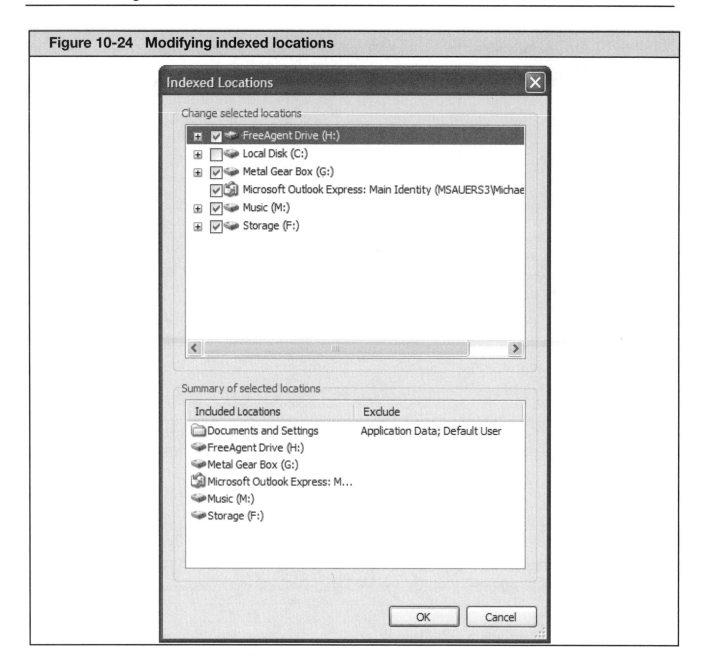

The file types tab gives you control over which types of files are to be indexed. Every registered file type on your computer will be listed here, and the vast majority of them will be preselected for you. To add or remove a file type from indexing, check or uncheck its box as appropriate.

On a file-by-file basis, you can also choose how the file type should be indexed (see Figure 10-26). Your choices are either "Index Properties Only" (these include filename, date, file type, and other properties) or "Index Properties and File Contents" (all of the

previous plus the actual content of the file). For example, MP3s default to properties only, as Microsoft has yet to figure out how to index the actual contents of audio files at this level, whereas Word Documents are set to index the properties and contents, as that's easy to do with text-based files.

ADD UNC LOCATION

If you wish to have your computer also index networked-based locations (that are not connected to your computer as mapped drives), this is the screen you need. Just enter the UNC (Universal Naming

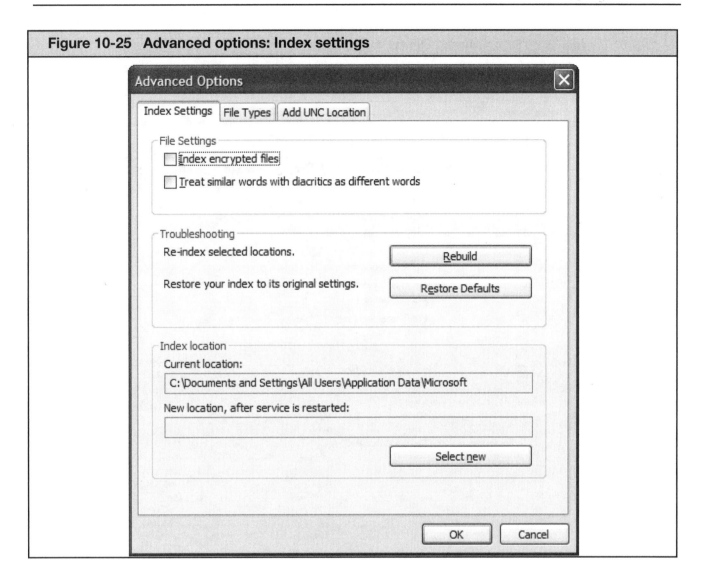

Figure 10-25 Advanced options: Index settings

Convention) path for the location you wish to index and click the "Add" button. You'll need to do this once for each network location you wish to add (see Figure 10-27).

Searching

Now that we've set our options and given the program enough time to index our computer's content, let's take a look at the Windows Desktop Search interface. As a reminder, here it is again in Figure 10-28.

As you can see, this is a Windows-based program, as opposed to the Web-based Google Desktop discussed earlier. Also, all of the searching options are readily displayed for you in a single interface instead of being separated into a default simple search and advanced search. To do a simple search, enter your keywords into the search box near the upper left of the window and click the "Desktop" button. You can also press your "Enter" key to activate your search. Notice the white triangle to the right of the desktop button. Clicking this gives you the ability to change from a desktop search to a Web search. Web searches will be run against Microsoft's Live Search, as covered in Chapter 3.

The results of your search will be shown in the middle pane of the three-pane interface. Here you'll see seven columns of information: relevance score (as one to three asterisks, with more asterisks indicating higher relevance), title, author, date, size, type, and folder. You'll most likely have to do some horizontal scrolling to see all of the information. By default, results are sorted in reverse chronological order, with newest results at the top. You can re-sort the results

Figure 10-26 Advanced options: File types

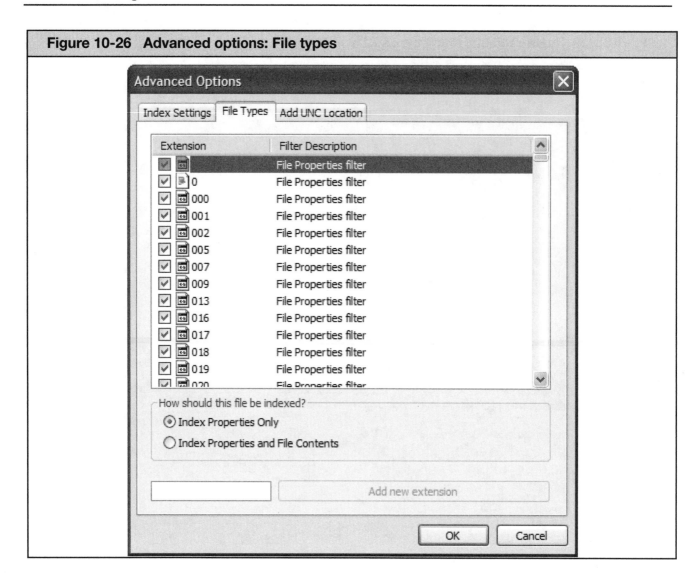

by clicking on any of the column headings. To reverse the sort order on a particular column, click on that column's heading again.

Once you have your list of results, selecting a result from the list will in most cases open a preview of that file in the preview pane to the right. Figures 10-29 through 10-31 show preview results for a Word document, an MP3 file, and an image, respectively.

You should be aware of several things about these previews. First, not all files will be previewable, such as those that are currently in the recycle bin. Second, many but not all previews will be fully formatted in the preview window, unlike with Google Desktop. Those that aren't fully formatted (as with Google Desktop) will say "Preview is not available for this document." This means that a fully formatted version

is not available.[8] Third, some file types, such as PDF files, will report "Previews of attachments with this file extension are disabled" and will show as unformatted previews. This is a security "feature" for which I have not discovered a means to disable.[9]

Right-clicking on any result gives the same options as right-clicking on the file while browsing it on your computer. You'll also receive a new option, "Open containing folder," which, when selected, will open the folder that contains that file so you can see other related files (see Figure 10-32).

Limiting Your Existing Results

If you find that you have too many results (as I did, when most of my test searches regularly returned more than 500 results), you can easily limit your

(continued on p. 300)

Figure 10-27   Advanced options: Add UNC location

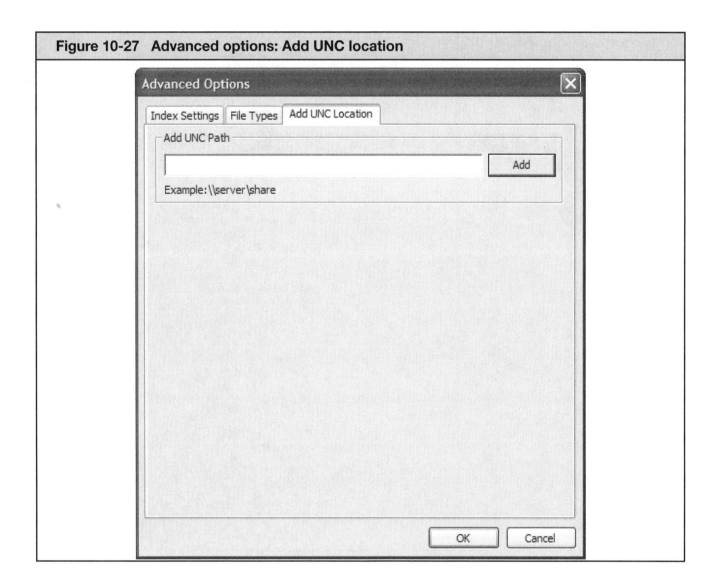

Figure 10-28   Windows desktop search

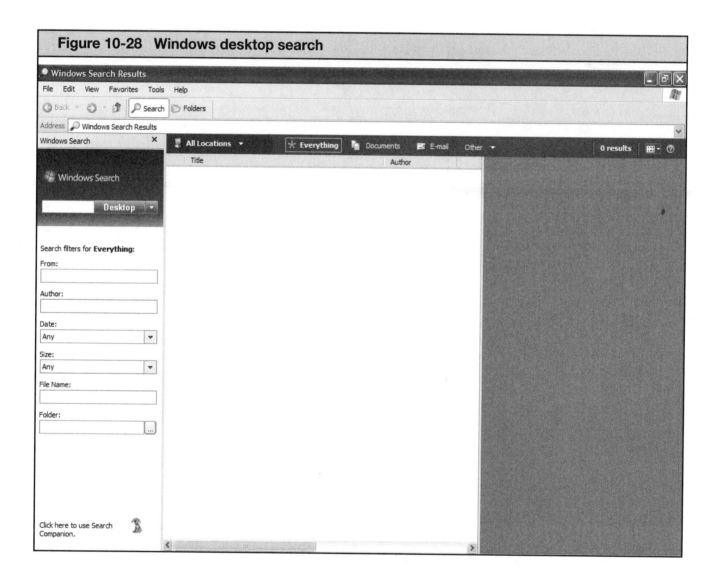

Figure 10-29   Preview of a Word document

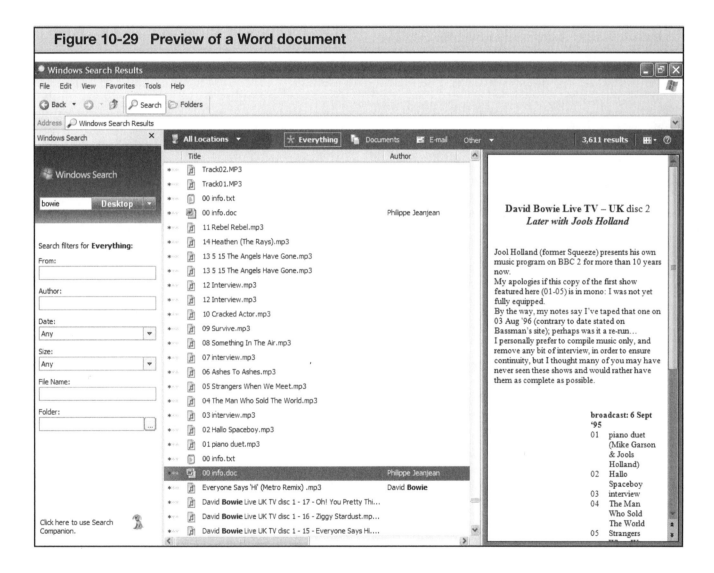

Figure 10-30   Preview of an MP3 file

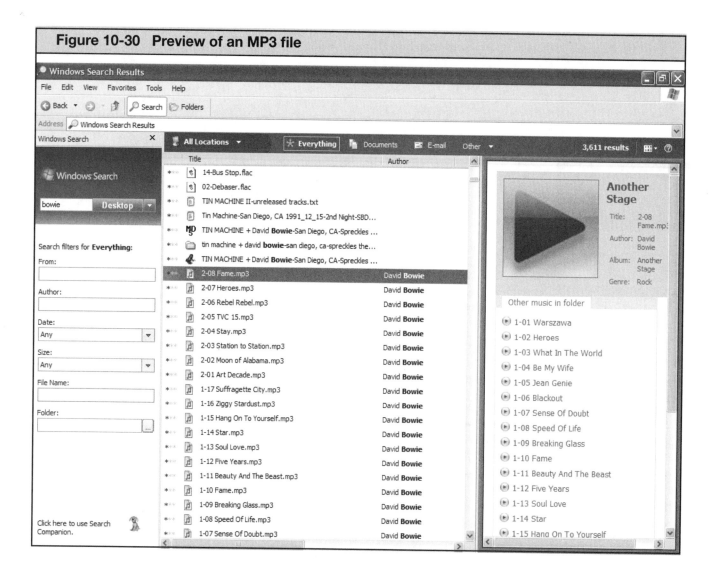

Figure 10-31 Preview of an image

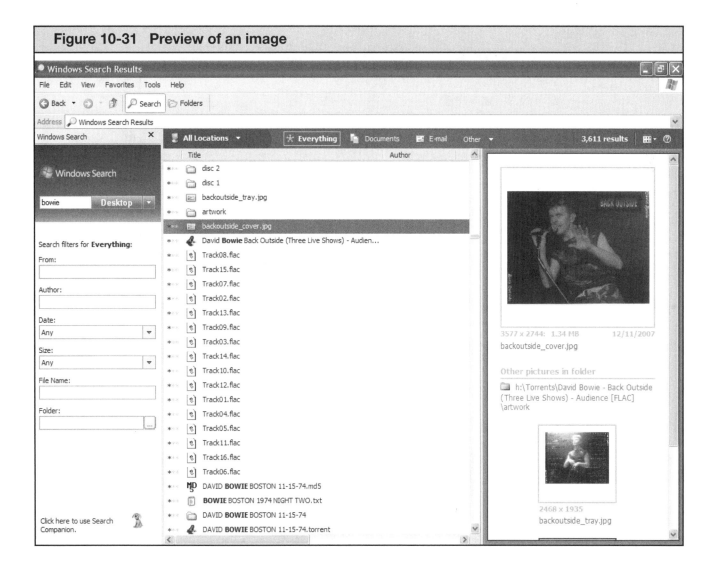

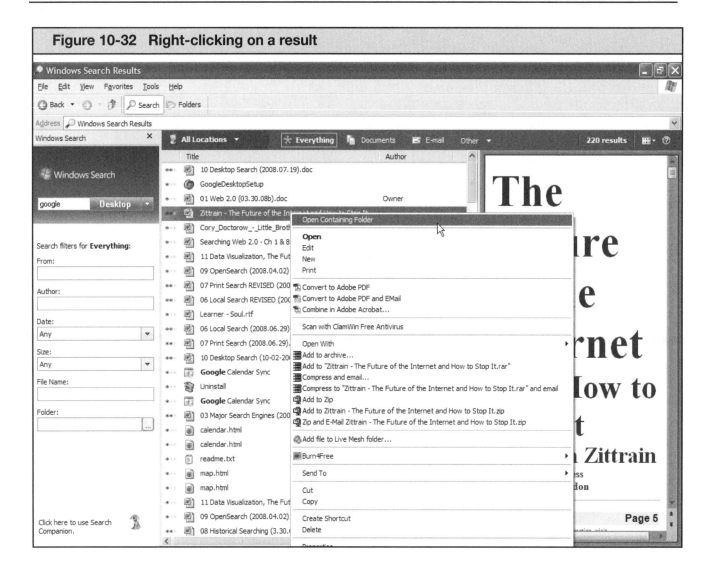

Figure 10-32   Right-clicking on a result

results to certain file types. The easiest way to do this is to use the links in the blue bar above your results and preview pane (see Figure 10-33).

The limiters that are available will vary based on your results, but you will typically see limiting factors such as documents and e-mail. To limit your results displayed to just one of these types, click on it. Figure 10-34 shows my results displaying just picture and video results. Additional options are always available by opening the "Other" drop-down list (see Figure 10-35).

You can also change the displayed results and the list of available limiters by clicking on the "All locations" drop-down list at top left on the results list (see Figure 10-36). When opened, you will receive other choices, such as "Files" and "Outlook," which

you can choose as limiters. Once selected, your list of other limiters will change accordingly to provide options related to the ones you've just chosen.

Search Filters

If a simple search isn't specific enough for you, you can use one of several search filters available in the left search pane. They are: from, author, date, size, file name, and folder. The use of these fields still requires that you search for a keyword first.

- **From:**

  The "From" field matches the "From" field in e-mails and related attachments. So, if you're looking for files or e-mails from a particular individual, just enter his or her name or part of his or her name in

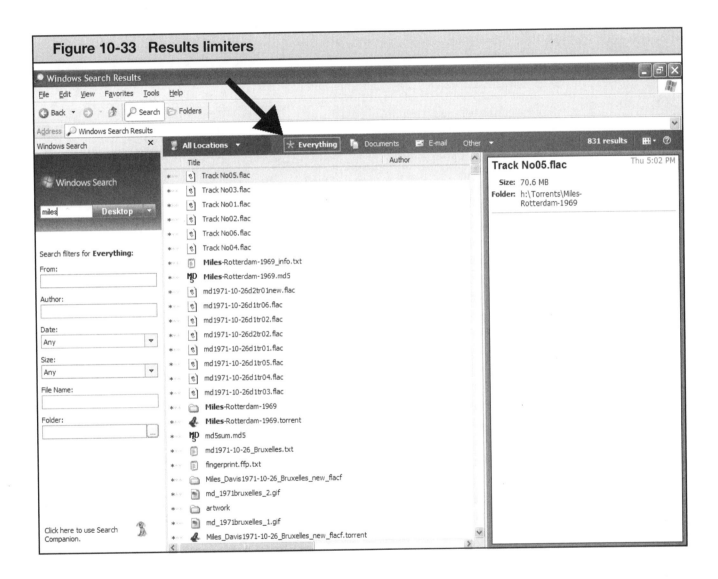

Figure 10-33 **Results limiters**

Figure 10-34   Limiting my results to just documents

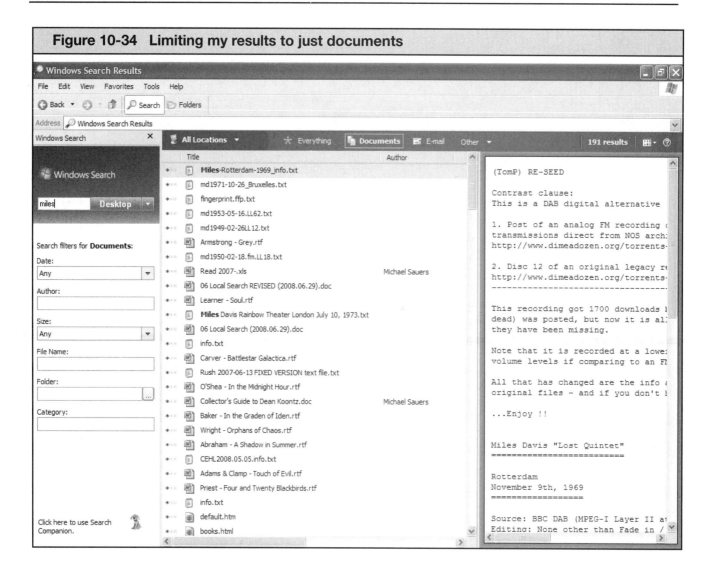

this field before performing your search (see Figure 10-37).

- **Author:**

  Filling in the "Author" filter matches the "Author" field in documents, again, such as e-mails (To:) and in Office documents. In many cases, this may return the same results as with the "From" filter, but not always. For example, Mary may send you an e-mail with an attached Word document written by Steve. Using the author filter to search for *steve* will return the Word document, but not the e-mail to which it was attached (see Figure 10-38).

- **Date:**

  Your five choices for the date filter are any (the default), today, yesterday, last week, and last month. Apparently, Microsoft considers these to be the most commonly used options, as there is

no method for entering a particular date or date range.

- **Size:**

  This is another filter that has only built-in options, though I don't mind as much with this as I do with the date filter. In this case, you can filter by file size. Your choices are small (less than 100 KB), medium (less than 1 MB), large (more than 1 MB), and huge (more than 5 MB).[10]

- **File name:**

  At first this may not seem useful, but if you're consistent in how you name your files, it could come in handy. For example, all of the files for the different chapters of my books are in the format "*book title* chapter # *chapter title.*" So, if I'm looking for all of the chapter files (originals, backups, forgotten versions) on my computer related to this book, then I

Figure 10-35   The "other" limiters

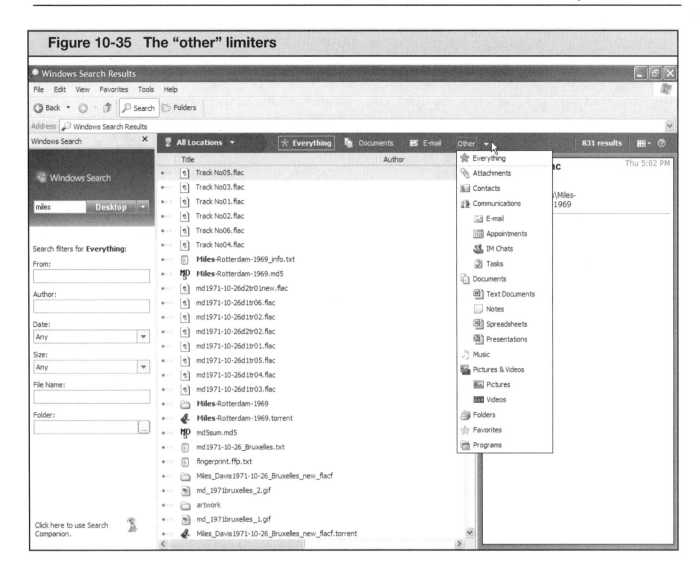

Figure 10-36   The "all locations" drop-down list

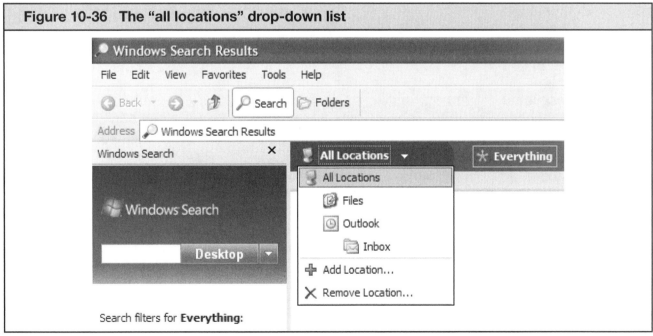

Figure 10-37   Results of a search using the "from" search filter

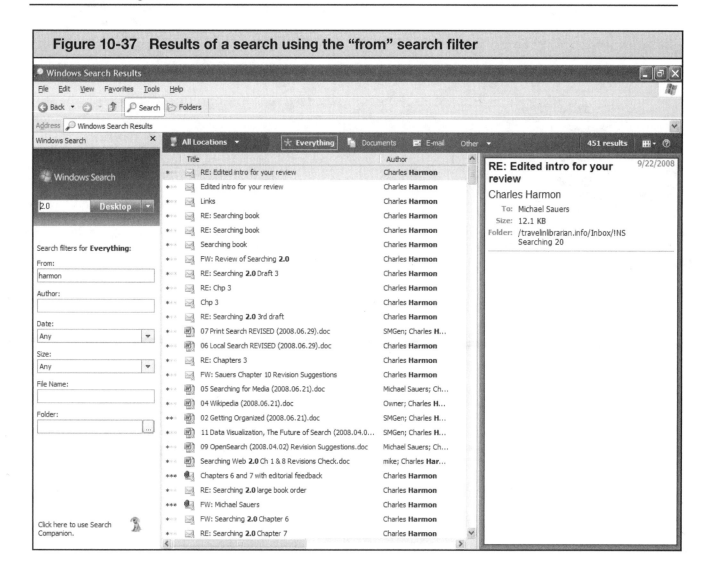

could search for *searching 2.0* and enter *chapter* in the filename filter.

- **Folder:**

    The folder filter allows you to limit your search to a particular section of your computer. For example, if I wanted to look for *blogging* but just for files in My Documents, I would use the "…" button to browse for that folder, select it, and then perform my search.

Now that we've examined two add-ons, let's move on to see what Microsoft has done with the release of Windows Vista.

WINDOWS VISTA

The basic thrust of desktop-based search in Windows Vista is that all of the features of the previously discussed Windows Desktop Search have been completely integrated into Vista itself.[11] The need for any add-ons, such as Windows or Google Desktop Search, has been virtually eliminated. Beyond this, the integration makes how you find your files on your computer a very different experience. Since many of you may have not yet made the switch to Vista, let me introduce to you some of the newer and more used features.

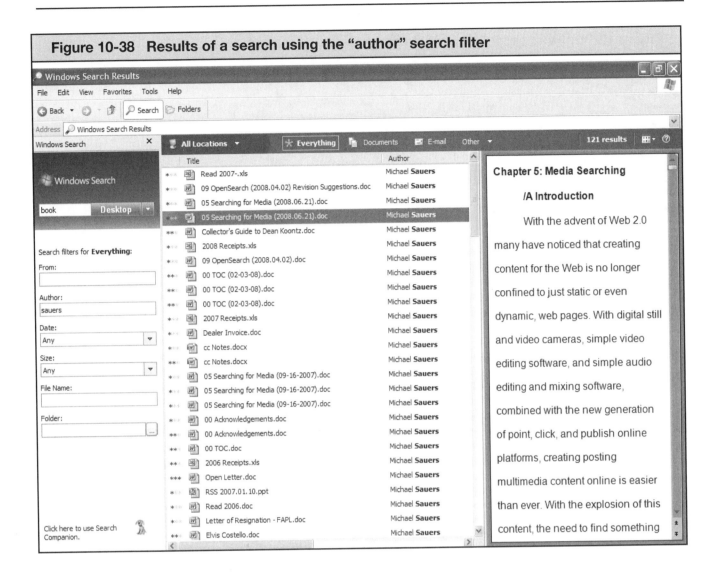

Figure 10-38 Results of a search using the "author" search filter

Search from the Start Menu

The first difference in searching with Vista that people mention to me is the ability to search directly from the Start menu. Despite the cosmetic differences between the Windows XP Start menu and the Vista Start menu, they both basically work the same. However, Vista has a search box at the bottom of the Start menu that automatically contains your cursor when you open the menu (see Figure 10-39).

This means that the moment the Start menu appears on the screen, whether by using your mouse and clicking on the Windows logo or tapping the Windows key on your keyboard, you can start searching your computer. The best part of this search is that you don't need to type in your keywords, press enter or click on a search button, or wait for the results. The moment you start typing in the search box,

your standard Start menu choices disappear and are replaced by your search results. So if I was looking for files that mention blogging, I would simply start typing the word. Figures 10-40 through 10-43 show the step-by-step results of typing *b* then *l* then *o* then *g*. I could continue with *g*, then *i*, then *n*, then *g*, but I think you get the point.

Your search results will be organized into appropriate categories that will typically include "Programs," "Files," and "Communications." Assuming the file you're looking for is in the results list, you have many options as to how to proceed. First, you can click on a filename to open it. You can right-click on the filename to see your standard list of options. You can also select one of the two links at the bottom of the list. The first, "See all results," will open a new window similar to the one used in Windows

Figure 10-39 **The search box on Vista's start menu**

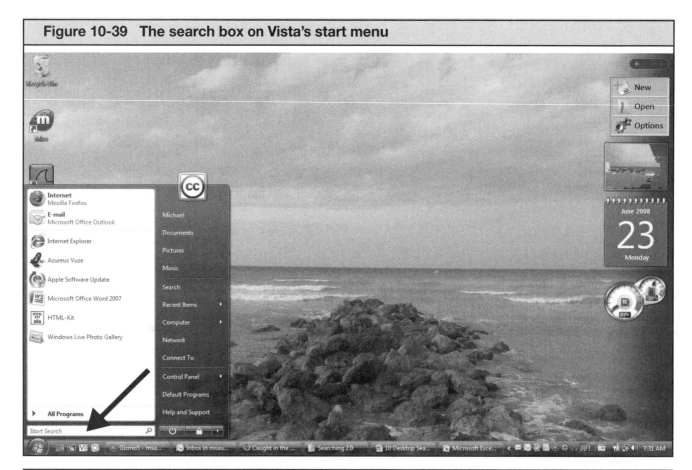

Figure 10-40 **The start menu after searching for "b"**

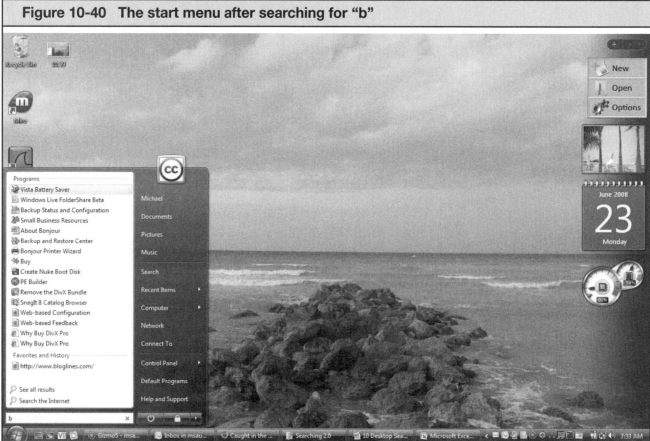

Figure 10-41 The start menu after searching for "bl"

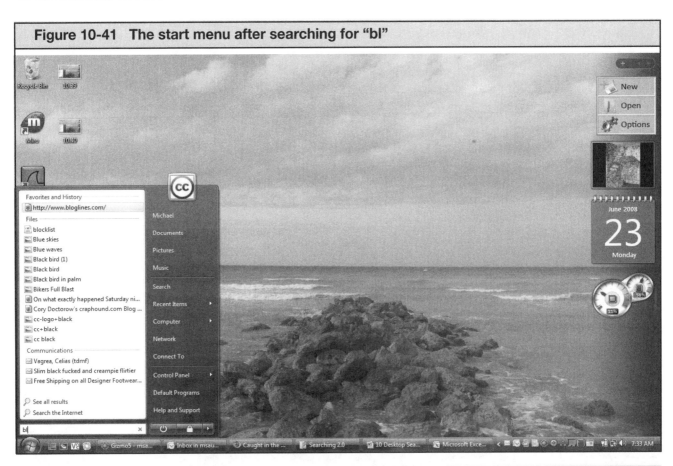

Figure 10-42 The start menu after searching for "blo"

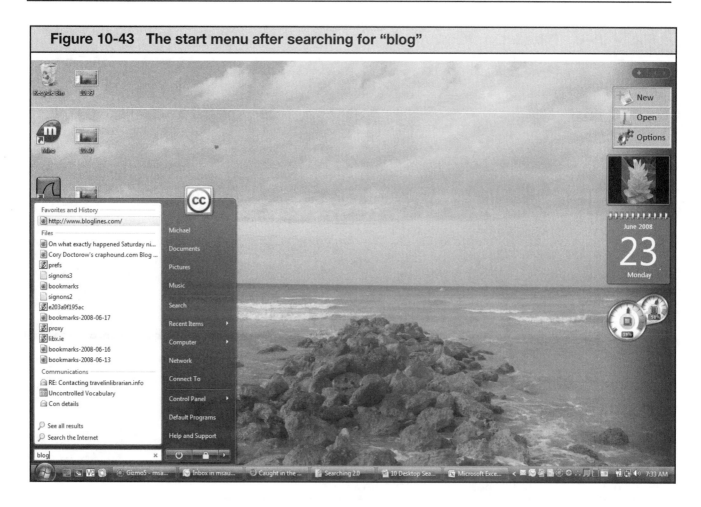

Figure 10-43   The start menu after searching for "blog"

Desktop Search (see Figure 10-44). The other is "Search the Internet," which will open your browser and submit your search term to your browser's default search engine.

Taking this one step further, if you do type in a search term and press enter, Vista will determine which file or program is the best match for what you've typed and load it for you. For example, I can press the Windows key, type *ou,* and press "Enter," and Outlook will be launched. All of the search results are based on (assuming you don't change the indexing options, as discussed in the Windows Desktop Search section) the filename, properties, and file contents, as appropriate. Even more impressive, Vista has added a new indexed property: tags!

Tagging

Vista has built-in support for tagging most file types.[12] For example, Figure 10-45 shows that I've selected a Word document. If you look to the bottom of the window, you'll see the file's properties, including

the filename, title, author, size, date modified, and, here it is, tags.

To add tags, just click on "Add a tag" (the title and author fields are also editable this way), enter your tag, and press "Enter" or click the "Save" button. Voilà! You've just added an indexable tag to your file. These tags will be displayed in the properties pane at the bottom of the window and in the tags column when you're in the details view, as shown in Figure 10-46.

If you're viewing image files in Windows Photo Gallery, you can view and add tags (and a caption) to images in the properties pane to the right. You can then display images containing certain tags by selecting them from the tags list to the left (see Figure 10-47).

Indexing Options

The indexing options in Vista are virtually the same as in Windows Desktop Search. The only noticeable difference is in how to get to them. Instead of being

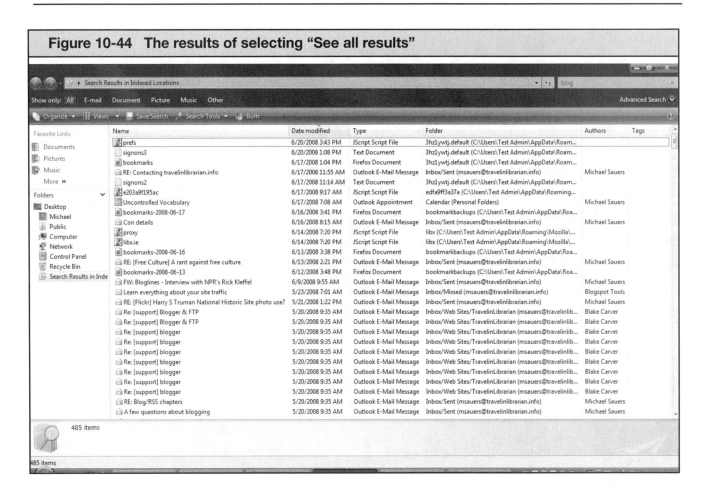

Figure 10-44 The results of selecting "See all results"

located within a program, they have been moved into the Control Panel. Just open it up and find the "Indexing Options" icon (see Figure 10-48).

As you look at the indexing options interface, as shown in Figure 10-49, you may notice that despite the slight redesign in Vista, the options available are exactly the same as those in Windows Search on Windows XP. Thus, I won't repeat the details of the options here.

There's also one additional hidden feature in Vista's desktop search that I'd like to mention: natural language searching. To find this option, open any folder, open the "Organize" menu and select "Folder and Search Options." Then select the "Search" tab, check "Use natural language search," and click "OK" to apply the change. Now, instead of using Microsoft's search syntax, you can just tell Vista what you're looking for. Here are a few examples:

- When searching for music, instead of using *kind: music artist:Pink Floyd,* type *music Pink Floyd*

or *music by Pink Floyd.* You can search also for albums, tracks, etc. (e.g., *album High Hopes).*
- When searching e-mail messages, use statements like these: *email from Joe received this month, mail to George about Windows Vista,* and *email from Ana sent yesterday.*
- When searching for documents, use **.doc created this year, document about Windows Vista,* etc.[13]

I've played around with this option and I do like it. It makes looking for files on my computer much more natural than trying to figure out which syntax to use or dropping myself into the advanced search options.

CONCLUSION

As hard drives get larger and the cost of storage lower, more and more data will be kept on individual computers. As the amount of data increases, it becomes essential that we be able to easily search for what we seek. Both Google Desktop and Windows *(continued on p. 314)*

Figure 10-45 File properties in Windows Explorer

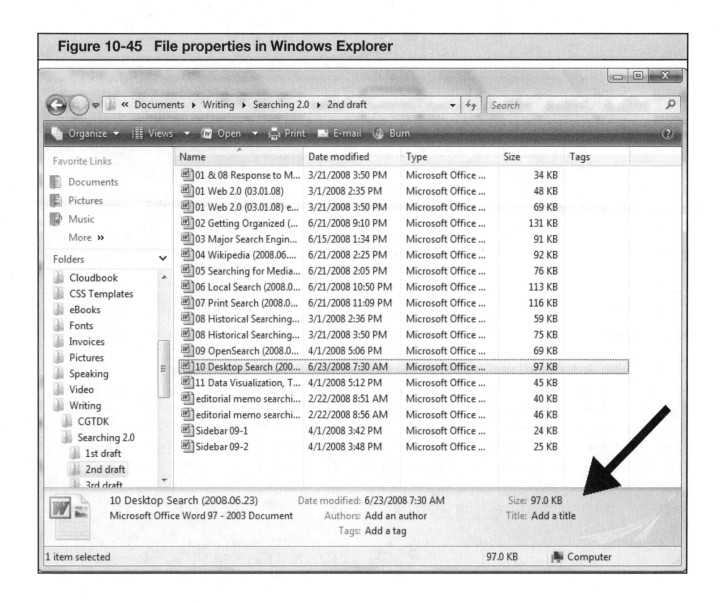

Figure 10-46   Tags on a file in Windows Explorer

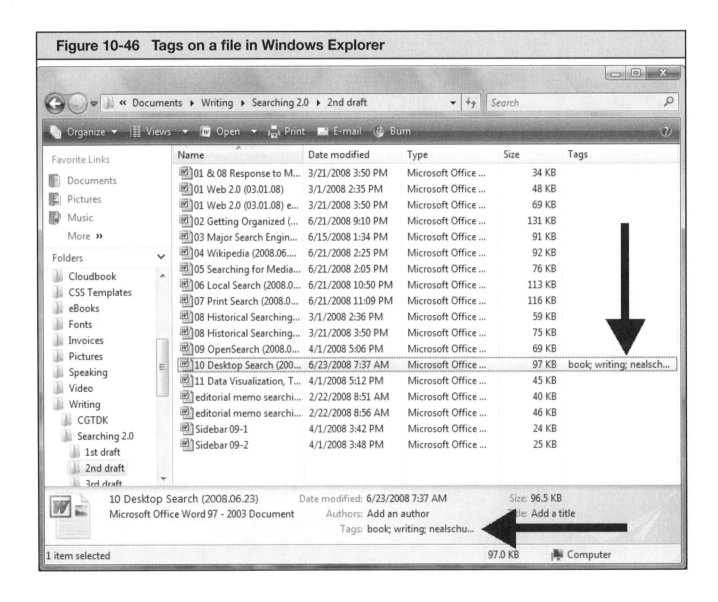

Figure 10-47 Tags in Windows Photo Gallery

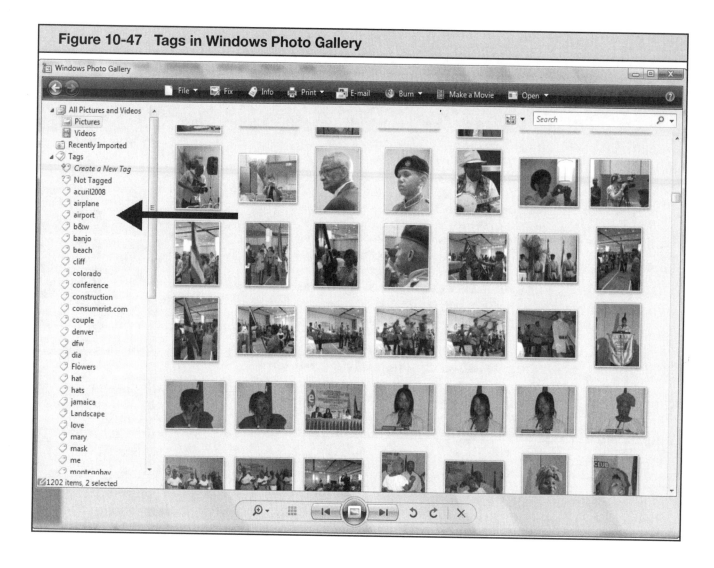

Figure 10-48   Indexing options in Vista's Control Panel (via the "Classic view")

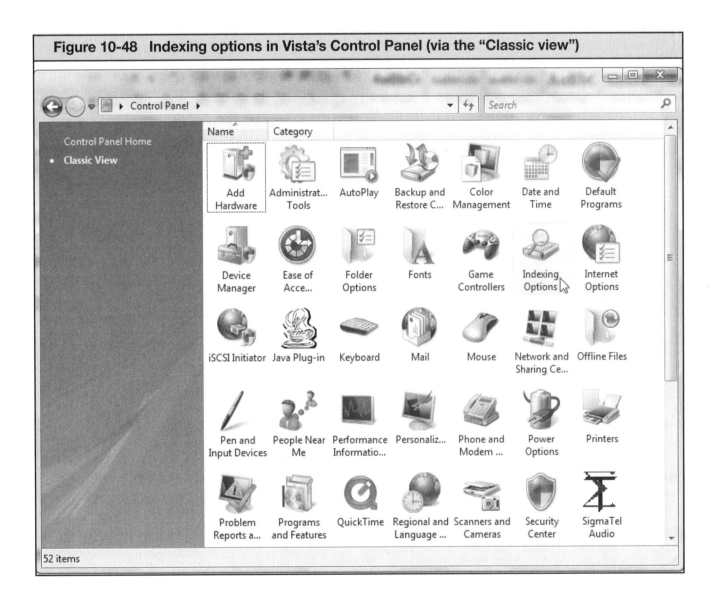

Figure 10-49   Vista's indexing options

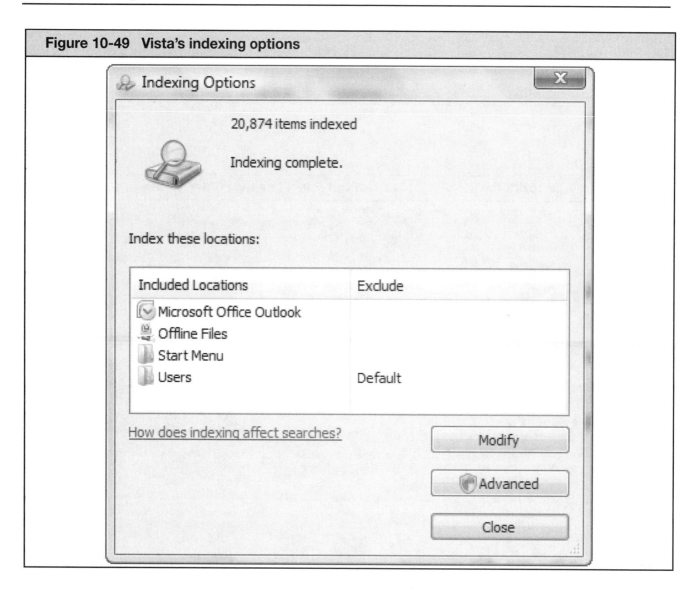

Search, when installed, allow for automatic indexing of not only filenames but the actual content of many of those files. As newer operating systems appear, Windows Vista for example, operating system manufacturers, realizing that this need is important, are beginning to build these indexing and searching capabilities right into the operating system itself.

Many times I've found the ability just to click, search, and go on my own computers much easier than browsing six levels down into my folder structure, no matter how "logical" that folder structure may be. I've also found files that I'd forgotten I had in the first place as a result of a search. I can say that I'm 100 percent positive that I never want to go without some sort of desktop search ever again. Now that we can find what we're looking for on our own computers, in the next and final chapter, we'll

take a look at what the future may hold for the world of search.

EXERCISES

Choose the desktop search option presented in this chapter that seems to fit your situation best. Then:

1. If you chose Google Desktop or Windows Search, download and install it. (Vista users can skip this step.)

2. Change any of the default settings as appropriate (to index file contents for example).

3. Give the indexing process a full 24 hours to index your data. (Vista users can skip this step unless you changed some of the indexing options.)

4. Perform a few sample searches to see what can be found. Try searching on some keywords you're

sure will produce certain results. Try again using some random keywords just to discover what files are found.

5. Perform a search that will receive a lot of results and try limiting your results to different file types.

6. If you're a Vista user, try turning on natural language searching and reperforming your searches.

NOTES

1. For more on new types of organization systems and on finding what you're looking for in your or another system, be sure to read David Weinberger, *Everything Is Miscellaneous* (New York: Times Books, 2006). The book covers many of the higher-level ideas that I've just touched on in this book, including much of what I discussed in Chapter 1. Besides, the book's dedication is "To the Librarians." If that isn't a reason to read it, nothing is.

2. I'll be demonstrating both of these applications in Windows XPsp3, as the release of Windows Vista has rendered both of these packages unnecessary.

3. There are two minor notes I'd like to add to this. First, Google has "Google Gadgets" that are related to search, such as the Wikipedia Search gadget (http://desktop. google.com/plugins/i/gd_WikipediaSearch.html?hl=en) and the 123-reg domain name search gadget (http:// desktop.google.com/plugins/i/123reg_hostingmarket. html?hl=en), but due to space requirements and what I'm going to tell you next, I do not cover Google Gadgets in this book. Second, Windows Vista has what's known as the "Sidebar," which allows for the installation of "Widgets." These are the same as Google Gadgets, just using a different technology.

4. If you installed the Sidebar, you'll also see this on your desktop off to the right. This is the tool that houses the Google Gadgets. Don't be afraid to play with it—it can be quite useful, especially if you have a widescreen monitor. To turn it off, right-click on the Google logo at the top and select "Close."

5. Actually, you can start searching almost immediately, but you will be able to find only items that have been indexed. It's best to wait for the first complete index to finish before you start doing any serious searching.

6. Google Desktop, "Finding Files: Deleted Files," http://desktop.google.com/support/Bin/Answer.py?answer=10081.

7. Once installed, clicking "search" on the start menu will open the Windows Desktop Search program. If you still wish to access the "classic" search interface, it is still available. Just use the "Click here to use the Search Companion" link in the bottom left corner of the screen.

8. This has happened in Figure 10-29, the preview of a Word document. This is due to a known bug between Windows Desktop Search and Office 2007.

9. None of the solutions I found online worked. Please let me know if you find one that does and I'll post it in the errata for this book.

10. I find their definitions of size interesting. I'm someone who regularly moves multi-gigabyte files, and I can hardly believe that a 5 MB file should be categorized as "huge."

11. Additional details from Microsoft on how search works in Vista can be found at Microsoft, "Windows Search 4.0," http://www.microsoft.com/windows/products/winfamily/desktopsearch/Choose/windowsvista/Business.mspx.

12. Audio and video files are the noticeable absences.

13. Ciprian Adrien Russen, "How to Enable Natural Search and How to Use It," August 26, 2008, http://www.vista4beginners. com/Enable-Natural-Search-and-learn-how-to-use-it.

Chapter 11

Data Visualization:
The Future of Search?

INTRODUCTION

Now that I've taken you through ten chapters covering the current state of reference resource management and search, let's briefly examine how search may look in the future. Simply put, data visualization is "to communicate information clearly and effectively through graphical means."[1] Anyone who's used a spreadsheet program to turn numbers into a graph or chart to illustrate a point has used a data visualization technique.

As more and more data become available, it is increasingly difficult to understand these data in their raw textual form. Therefore, the need for graphical representation of that data also increases. Additionally, in many cases, you can easily glean extra meaning from a graphical representation of data compared to a purely textual representation. Let's take a look at Figures 11-1 though 11-5. In each case, ask yourself what inferences can be drawn from the data just by looking at the image.

Just by glancing at these images, you can see where gas is most expensive, what Twitter users think of recent movies, that Jim Risch and CL Otter have many of the same contributors, that the United States and China won many more Olympic medals than most European countries, and that *The Dark Knight* made more money than most of the other currently running movies combined. So, what if we took this concept and applied it to search results?

Ever since electronic search started, results have been text-oriented—a list of words describing the results in some sort of order (by relevance, date, etc.). But as comfortable as we may be with results presented in this manner, it lacks something that could easily assist us in our research: the relationship of one result to the others. For example, often multiple pages within a single Web site will match our search. Some search engines will note the presence of multiple pages, but knowing which Web sites represented in our results have the most number of individual pages containing our search terms would be helpful as well. Also, what if several of our results contain other keywords we'd not previously considered? Wouldn't it be nice to see which of our results contain these other possibly useful keywords?

Showing relationships between items is difficult when working in a text-only environment, but when we move into graphical representations of results, meaningful relationships can easily be displayed. Let's take a look at two examples: Kartoo and Literature Map.

KARTOO

Kartoo (www.kartoo.net) has been around for several years, though, in my experience, does not have many users in the library world. Whenever I show it to a room full of librarians, most have typically one reaction or the other: "Wow, this is cool" or "I don't get it." Let's see if I can convince you to join the former camp rather than the latter.

Essentially, Kartoo is a meta-search engine drawing its results from the results of other search engines. However, where its true uniqueness lies is in how it presents results to the searcher.[2] Figure 11-6 shows the Kartoo homepage, into which I've entered *computers* as my search term. I've chosen to default to

Figure 11-1   United States national gas prices map
(www.gasbuddy.com/gb_gastemperaturemap.aspx)

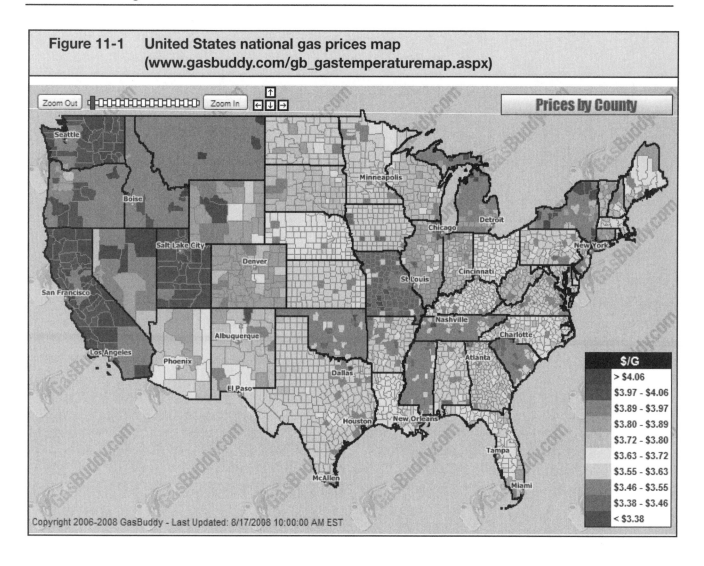

English-only pages for my results and then clicked the "OK" button. Figure 11-7 shows my results. As you can see, this is not your typical search results screen.[3]

Each result is represented by a thumbnail image of the linked page itself. Sites with multiple pages of results will have additional smaller page icons attached. Additionally, there are different colored borders and small icons, such as the green balls that indicate "sponsored content," for different types of pages. Figure 11-8 is the legend for these items. Obviously, this is better shown in full color and can be found online at www.kartoo.net/a/en/aide04.html.

As you hover your mouse pointer over the keywords shown on the results map, lines will appear drawing a connection to the sites which contain that word. Figure 11-9 shows the connections drawn when hovering over the word *laptop*. As with tag clouds in previously discussed sites, the more common the word, the larger it will appear on the screen. Selecting a word will reperform the original search with the addition of the selected keyword.

Hovering over a page icon will draw lines to show which of the additional listed keywords appear within that result. Figure 11-10 shows the keywords that appear in the result from www.dell.com.[4] Clicking on an icon will open that result. As you hover over icons, the upper left portion of the screen will change to show relevant content from that site. Additionally, an orange line will appear over each icon that you've "viewed" (i.e., hovered over) to give you a visual reference as to which sites you've already investigated.

The "Topics" area in the upper left corner of the screen (when not hovering over a site in the results map) shows you a text-based list of related concepts.

Figure 11-2   Twitter movie reviews (www.flixpulse.com)

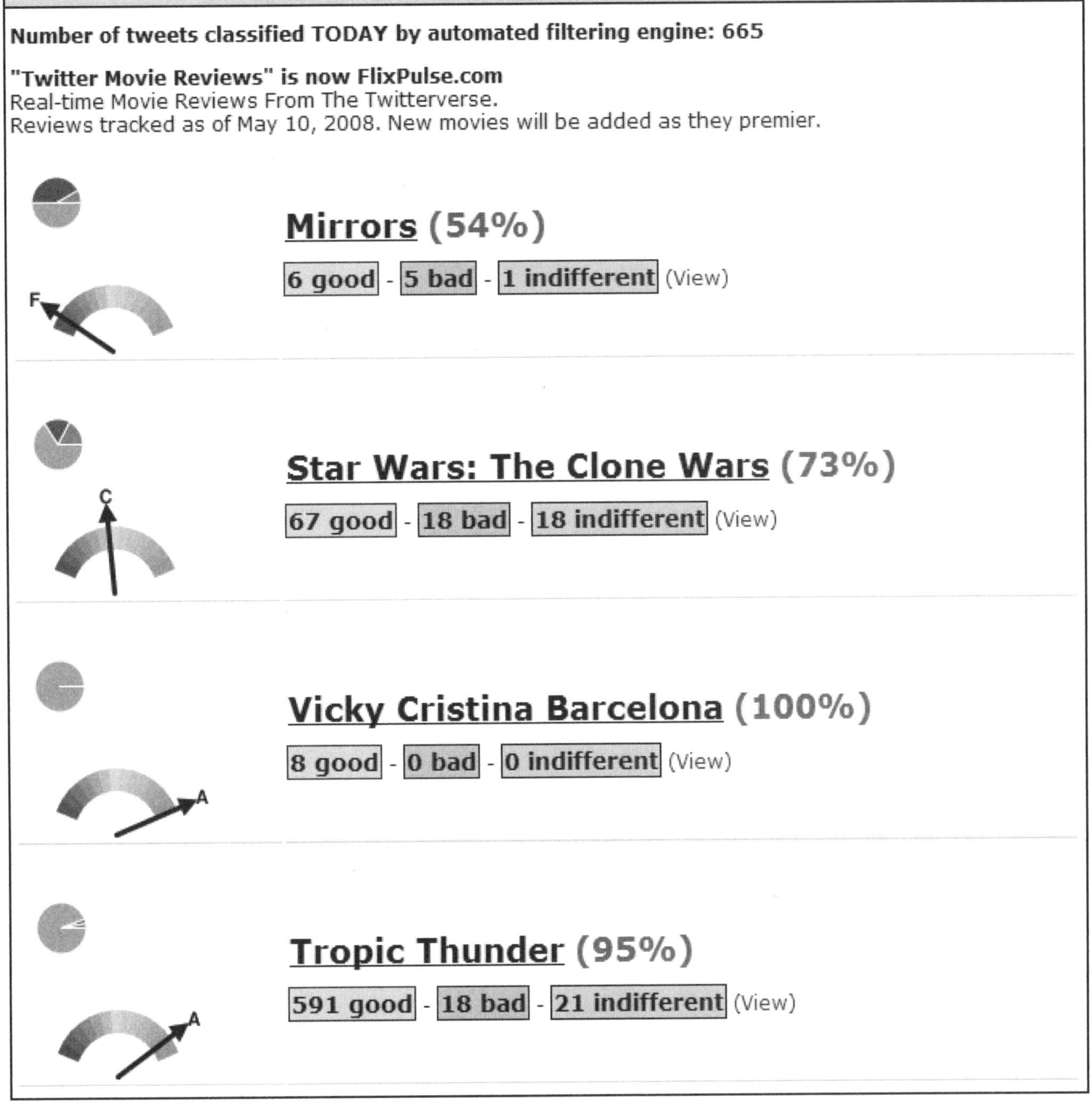

Number of tweets classified TODAY by automated filtering engine: 665

"Twitter Movie Reviews" is now FlixPulse.com
Real-time Movie Reviews From The Twitterverse.
Reviews tracked as of May 10, 2008. New movies will be added as they premier.

Mirrors (54%)

6 good - 5 bad - 1 indifferent (View)

Star Wars: The Clone Wars (73%)

67 good - 18 bad - 18 indifferent (View)

Vicky Cristina Barcelona (100%)

8 good - 0 bad - 0 indifferent (View)

Tropic Thunder (95%)

591 good - 18 bad - 21 indifferent (View)

Figure 11-3   Political contributions (http://www.weshowthemoney.com)

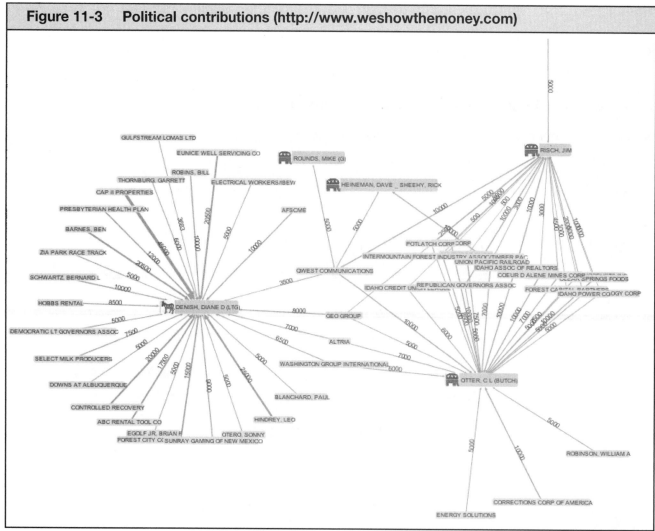

Figure 11-4   A map of olympic medals

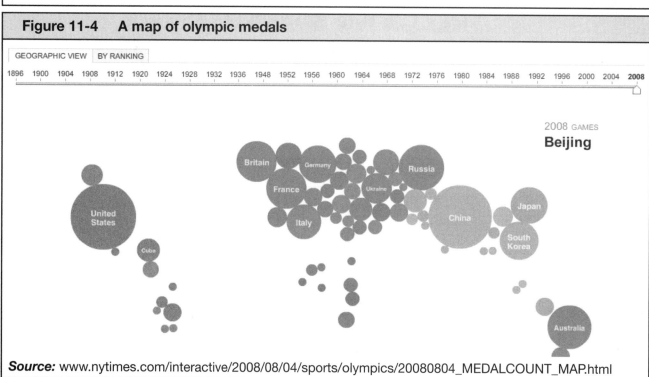

Source: www.nytimes.com/interactive/2008/08/04/sports/olympics/20080804_MEDALCOUNT_MAP.html

Figure 11-5   2008 U.S. movie box office (http://xach.com/moviecharts/2008.html)

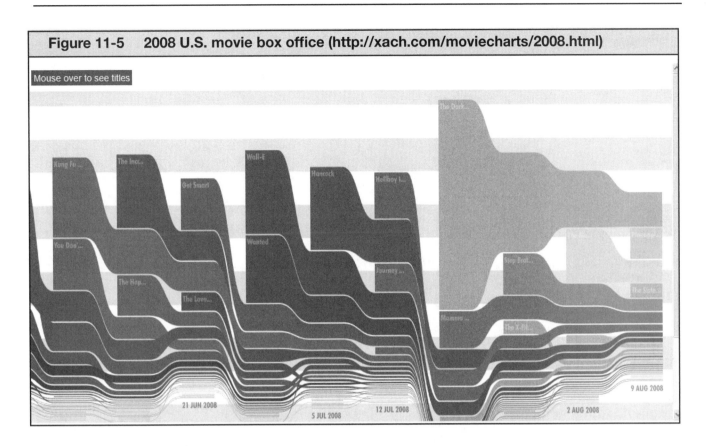

Figure 11-6   The Kartoo homepage

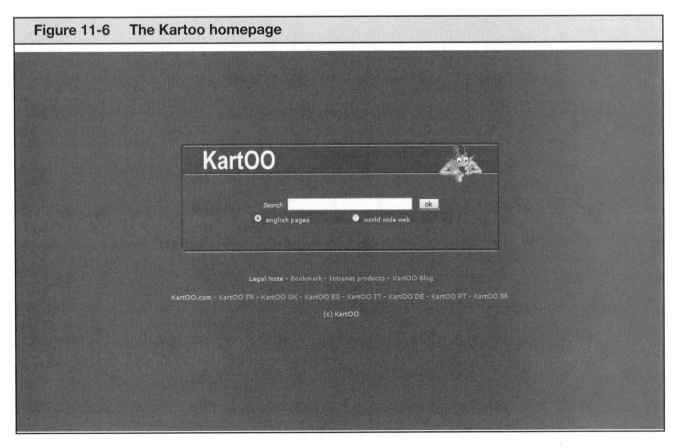

Figure 11-7   Kartoo results for search of *computers*

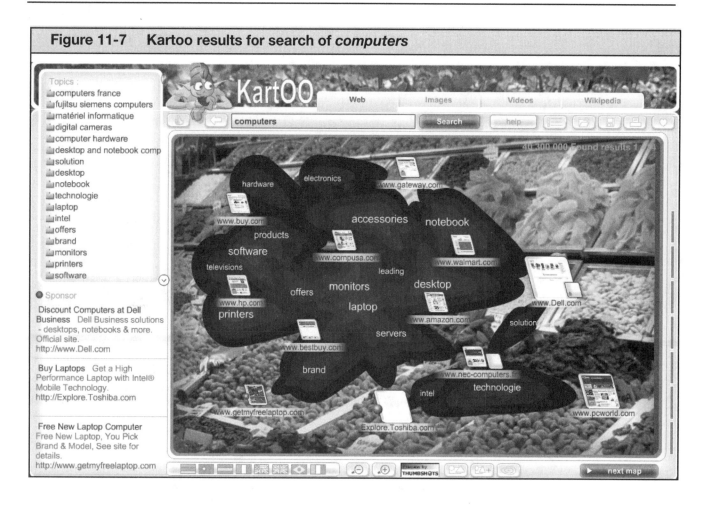

As you move your mouse over these topics, the results map will draw appropriate lines and highlight icons relevant to that topic. Figure 11-11 shows the results map as I hover over the *servers* topic.

The buttons along the top of the results map allow you to get help and change basic options, along with opening, saving, printing, and bookmarking results maps. Using the buttons beneath the results map, you can zoom in and out of the results map, change the color scheme, and even upload your own background, and you can get to the next and previous map of results (see Figure 11-12).

Using Kartoo can take some getting used to, but it does allow you to see connections between results that search engines like Google, Live Search, and Yahoo! Search don't show you.

LITERATURE MAP

Literature Map (see Figure 11-13) is a much simpler example of graphical-based search. In fact, it's less

search and more directory-based browsing, but directories (where information is organized hierarchically) still have their place when assisting patrons. If you're often called upon to perform reader's advisory duties, this might be a good site to add to your list of resources.

Located at www.literature-map.com, it bills itself as "the tourist map of literature." You start by simply typing in the name of an author you're interested in and click the "continue" button. After a few moments you'll be presented with a cloud of author names, all orbiting the name of your author located at the center of the cloud. Figure 11-14 shows the results cloud for author Neal Stephenson.

It may seem like a lot of movement at first, but give it some time. After 30 seconds or so, the names will start to settle down as they find their places and attempt not to overlap one another—well, not too much anyway. The closer another name is to your author's name, the more alike those two authors are.

Figure 11-8   The Kartoo results legend

Figure 11-9   Sites that contain the keyword *laptop*

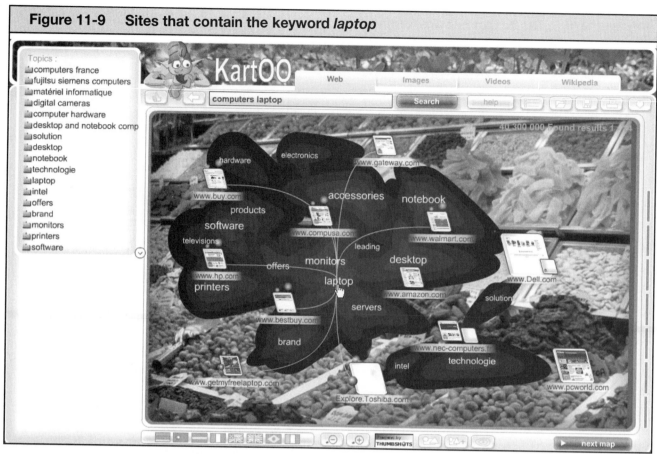

Figure 11-10   Keywords that appear in the search result for *www.Dell.com*

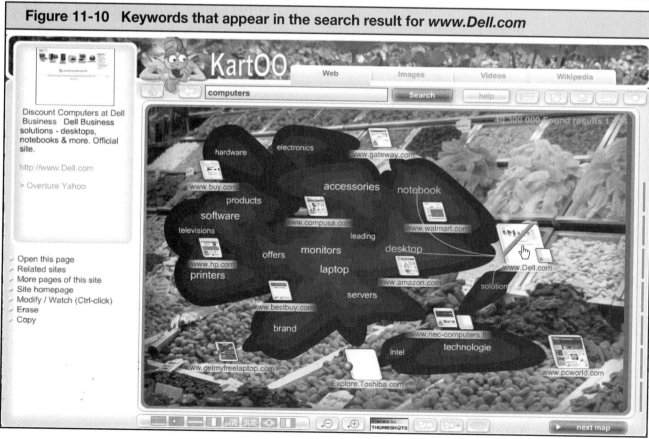

Figure 11-11   Sites that a relevant to the "servers" topic

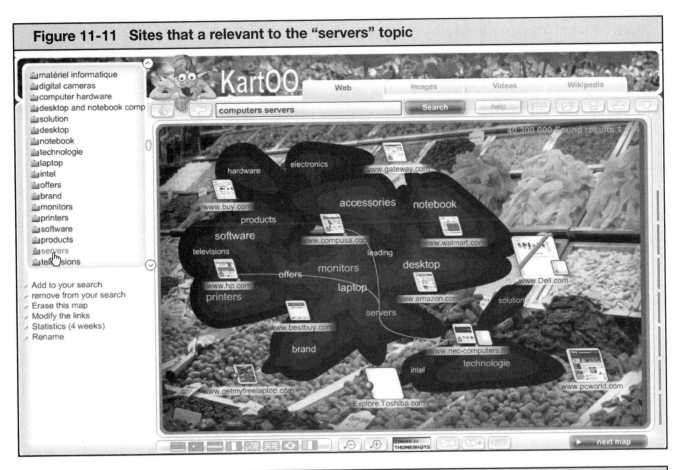

Figure 11-12   Kartoo's navigation buttons

Figure 11-13   The Literature Map homepage

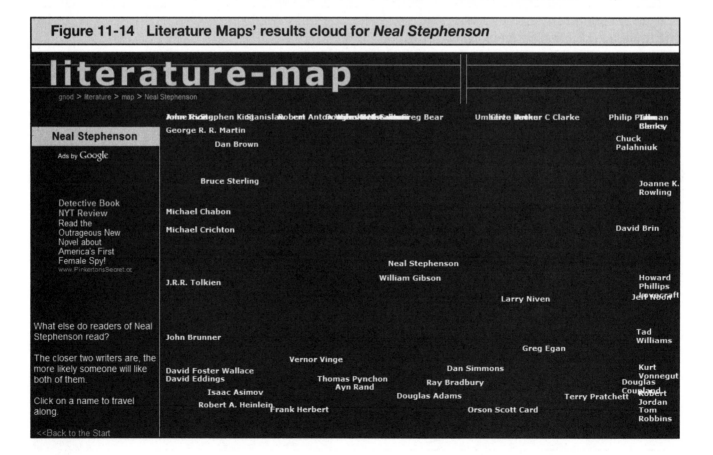

Figure 11-14   Literature Maps' results cloud for *Neal Stephenson*

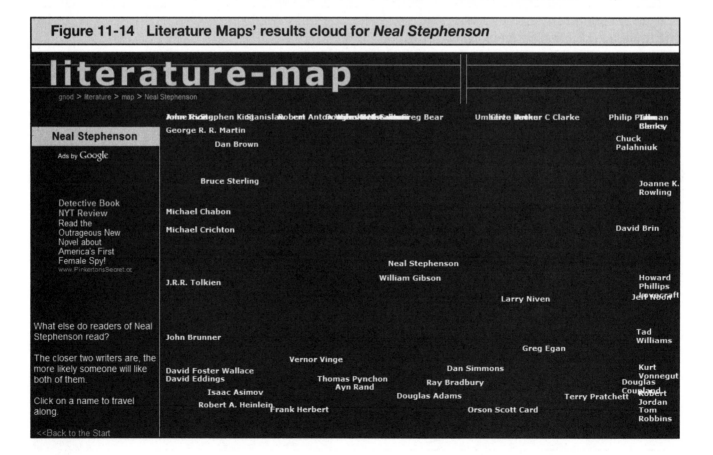

So, as you can see in this example, William Gibson is considered *very* similar to Neal Stephenson, while everyone else listed from Umberto Eco to Stephen King are considered relevant but not nearly as similar.

Clicking on any of the other names in the cloud will move the selected name to the center and redisplay the cloud with the newly relevant results. Figure 11-15 shows what I received when I selected Neil Gaiman. In this case, several names have close orbits (Terry Pratchett, Douglas Adams, and Neal Stephenson), along with others with medium and more distant orbits.

Although Literature Map doesn't give any results beyond the relationship between authors (no links to bibliographies, or reviews, or author homepages) as other search engines might, it may be a better place to start than any of the major search engines when attempting to answer the question, "I love to read Neal Gaiman. Who else should I read?" It can also be a good way to learn how cloud-based results work before moving on to other cloud-based systems in which related terms are presented via this method. Two of these are briefly described in the next section.

OTHER EXAMPLES

Many other graphically based search projects are out there today. The following are just some of them.

Ujiko

Ujiko is similar to Kartoo in its use of a graphical display to represent relationships between search results, but it does so more through the use of color instead of connecting lines. It can be found at www.ujiko.com. See Figure 11-16.

Aqua Browser

This OPAC interface displays standard text-based results in the main portion of the screen and a cloud of related search terms off to the side. It can be found at www.medialab.nl. The Queens Public Library currently makes this available to their patrons at http://aqua.queenslibrary.org/. See Figure 11-17.

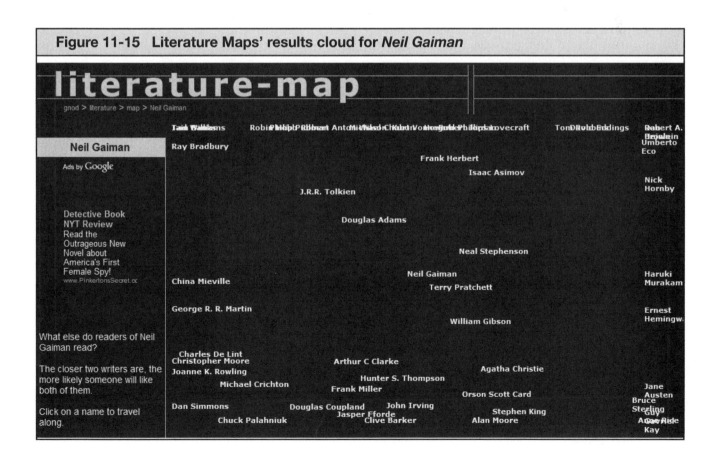

Figure 11-15 Literature Maps' results cloud for *Neil Gaiman*

Figure 11-16 Ujiko results for *nebraska*

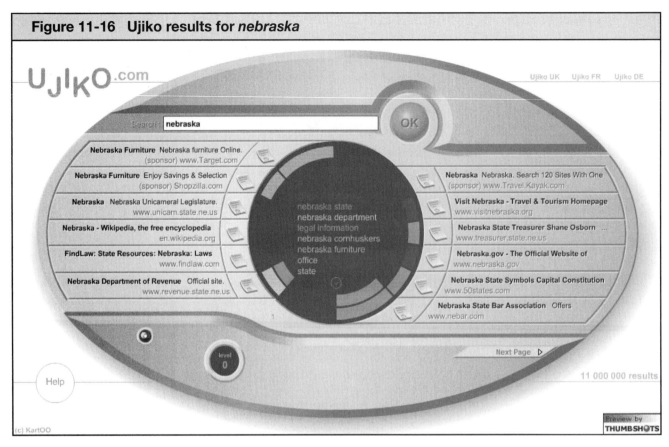

Figure 11-17 Aqua Browser results for *brian keene* from the Queens Public Library

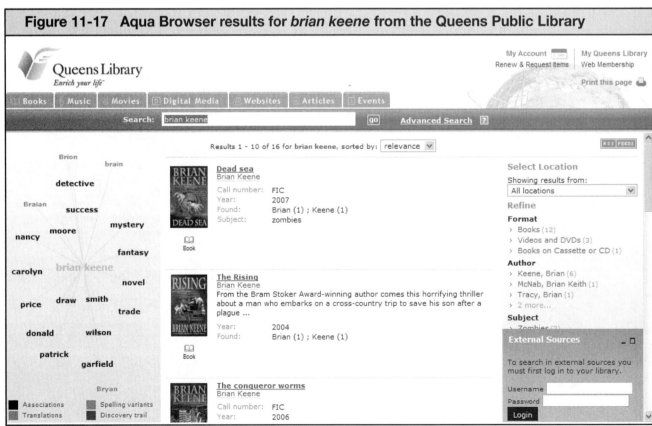

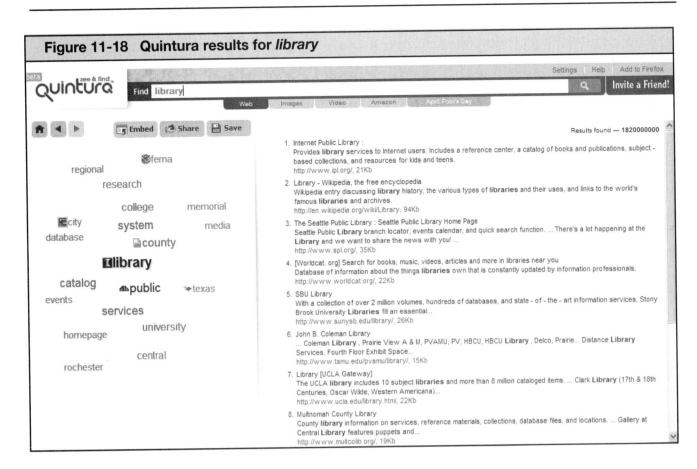

Figure 11-18 Quintura results for *library*

Quintura

Quintura is similar to Aqua Browser but for general Web searches. Search results are text-based on the right but a cloud of related terms appears on the left. It can be found at www.quintura.com. See Figure 11-18.

Flickr Graph

This graphically displays the relationships among Flickr users. It can be found at www.marumushi. com/apps/flickrgraph. See Figure 11-19.

6pli

This offers graphical representation of common tags across Delicious accounts. It's currently available only in a demo version. It can be found at www.6pli.com. See Figure 11-20.

CONCLUSION

Is this the way search will look in the future? Stay tuned. A lot has changed in the past nine years since my first book on search was published. Even if it doesn't look anything like these examples in another decade, one thing is certain: it will be different.

NOTES

1. *Wikipedia, the Free Encyclopedia,* s.v. "Data visualization," August 11, 2008, http://en.wikipedia.org/w/index. php?title=Data_visualization&oldid=231333969 (accessed August 17, 2008).

2. For the best experience, you should have the current version of the Flash player installed. If you don't, Kartoo will still work but will not be as interactive. All of the screenshots were done on a computer with Flash installed.

3. I do not cover many features of Kartoo in any detail here because the purpose of this chapter is to focus on the visualization features of Kartoo and not to cover how to use it in detail.

4. For my U.S. readers, be aware that Kartoo is located in France and thus tends to be more European centric than the other search engines I've discussed in this book.

Figure 11-19   Flickr Graph results for my account with several expanded relationships

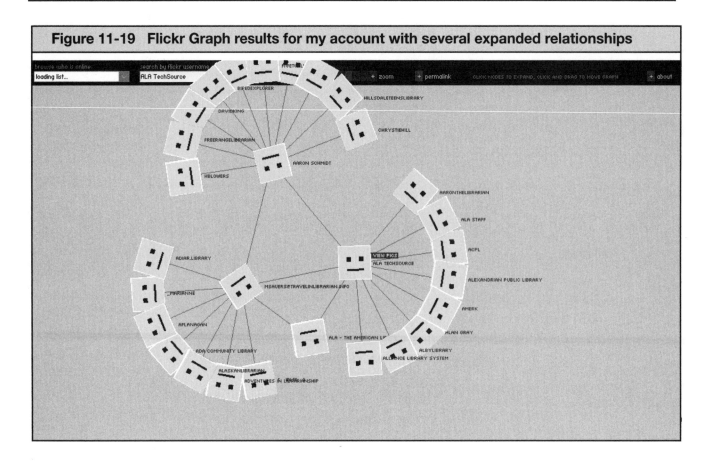

Figure 11-20   6pli example

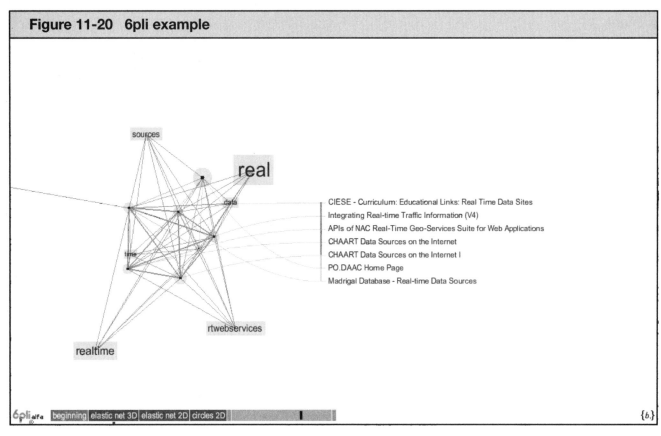

Index

About the Author

Michael P. Sauers is currently the Technology Innovation Librarian for the Nebraska Library Commission in Lincoln, Nebraska, and has been training librarians in technology for more than 13 years. He has also been a public library trustee, a bookstore manager for a library friends group, a reference librarian, serials cataloger, technology consultant, and bookseller. He earned his MLS in 1995 from the University at Albany's School of Information Science and Policy. *Searching 2.0* is Michael's ninth book, and he has also written dozens of articles for various journals and magazines. In his spare time, he blogs at travelinlibrarian.info, regularly contributes to the Uncontrolled Vocabulary podcast, runs Web sites for authors and historical societies, is vice-chair of the Nebraska Library Association's Information Technology and Access Round Table, takes many, many photos, and reads about 130 books per year.